Religions of New Zealanders

This project was assisted by grants from the *New Zealand 1990 Commission* (Lottery Board funds), the Adam Begg Fund, Presbyterian Church of New Zealand, and the Massey University Publications Committee.

Religions of New Zealanders

Edited by
Peter Donovan

© 1990 Peter Donovan
© 1990 The Dunmore Press Ltd

Published by the
Dunmore Press Ltd
P.O. Box 5115
Palmerston North

ISBN 0 86469 125 4

This text is set in Times Roman 10/12.5

Layout by Sherry Paranihi

Printed by Wright and Carman Ltd, Upper Hutt

Contents

GOVERNMENT HOUSE
WELLINGTON NEW ZEALAND

Foreword

During my time as Governor-General many guests have stayed with us at Government House. Those from Europe, once they have recovered from the surprise of finding the Head of State is also a Bishop, want to talk about God, the Church and themselves. For them the sacred and the secular, far from being opposed, exist in a slightly awkward but creative relationship.

Most New Zealanders would not know what you are talking about, but if pressed they would probably say the things of God and the things of the world have little in common. Yet one thing which this collection of essays shows is that religion and cultural expression go hand in hand. It is not simply a case of what you believe and do on the basis of that belief, but also how you do it. Manuka Henare asserts, for instance, that 'Religion is not an abstract concept for Maori. Rather it is a lived experience which is elaborated in the culture.'

So Hindu worship in New Zealand is home based and domestic in expression. Buddhism as I have experienced it in Sri Lanka or Thailand provides the cultural base for these countries. Not surprisingly, Ajahn Viradhammo compares a Buddhist temple to a marae. 'Like the marae the temple is a place of refuge where traditional values are honoured and where the community finds a common ground....'

The Christian churches exhibit the stress caused by rapid change. They seem almost overwhelmed by the issues of biculturalism, politics and liturgical change. There is great diversity in their midst. In my experience they do not shine much light on the majority which they have helped to shape.

But the diversity of religious expression and now the presence of the great world religions in New Zealand reflects an evolving society of many cultures which is revealing its face in our schools, and in suburbs such as Grey Lynn or Ponsonby.

Fear, hope, the search for security, are universal themes which all religions deal with. It will be interesting to see how these same religions relate to each other in New Zealand. Have they anything in common which their adherents would wish to explore? Some of them claim to be unique. What does that mean, and is it a barrier to an ecumenical dialogue?

24 September, 1990

The Most Reverend Sir Paul Reeves
Governor-General of New Zealand 1985-1990

Acknowledgements

Sincere thanks are owed to the Most Reverend Sir Paul Reeves for his kind interest in this project and his willingness to write a foreword; to John Bevan Ford, of Ngati Raukawa Ki Kapiti, for making available a drawing from his 'He Pihi' series for use on the cover, and Professor Mason Durie, of the Maori Studies Department at Massey University, for his guidance in various matters; to the team of authors for their readiness to take up the task, their careful scholarship and their great respect for the subject-matter they have dealt with; to Albert Moore in particular, and the others who have given assistance with the illustrations; to Wiebe Zwaga for help with chapter eighteen; to Sharon Cox and Richard Donovan for word-processing and proof-reading assistance respectively; and to Murray Gatenby and the Dunmore Press staff for their cheerful co-operation throughout.

Peter Donovan

Introduction

Religions are like ancient meandering rivers and tangled rain-forests. They fit uneasily, it seems, into a modern, rational landscape, obstructing progress, impeding development. Yet just as the world's waterways and jungles, now seen to be endangered, are beginning to be taken seriously, so there is a need for a greater appreciation of resources within the world's religions. Their contributions to our social and cultural ecology deserve to be better understood.

News-media bulletins bring us reminders almost every day that religion does continue to play a part in shaping the lives of people and nations. But the news is often bad. Violence and unrest are still fuelled by religious fervour. Followers of traditional faiths and creeds by no means always show reasonableness or concern for human life. So whether the good influence religions have outweighs this bad news, remains for many an open question.

This book is intended to help readers reach informed opinions about that question. New Zealanders in the 1990s are well placed to begin such an evaluation, with most of the main religions of the world now represented in significant numbers within Aotearoa itself.

No general conclusion will be reached here, however. The religions chosen for discussion, chapter by chapter, are described and explained, but not judged. Yet the overall message will be one of commendation. The authors themselves are all convinced that what they are writing about is intrinsically interesting, personally rewarding, and socially and culturally important. They hope to persuade readers to share at least some of those views.

The majority of contributors are academics connected with university departments of religious studies. In teaching about the many religions to be found here and world-wide, they adopt what is known as a *phenomenological* approach. They treat them as rich collections of inter-related phenomena: people, scriptures, objects, ideals, rituals, experiences, places, and so on, which are meaningful or sacred to the followers, believers, or devotees of the faiths or traditions in question.

Some of the contributors share the faiths they are writing about, to a greater or lesser degree. Others do not, but as competent scholars of religion have made it their business to get as close as they can to those faiths. They have cultivated an empathy with the 'insiders' point of view'. They try to be descriptive and objective (as they must if their work is to be scholarship, rather than mere opinion). Yet they appreciate also that religions generally have deep meaning for those committed to them, and that their essential insights and values may be largely missed by an outside observer.

Writing a book about religions, then, is far more than a purely academic exercise. Reading it effectively, too, will call for more than the simple desire for discovering facts. It will require imaginative, sympathetic participation in other people's lives; a sharing in points of view different from one's own; and a suspension of judgement about sometimes unfamiliar values and ideals. When it is one's fellow-citizens in Aotearoa/New Zealand that one is seeking to understand, the effort involved is clearly worth-while; still more is this so, when it means participating in what has been a *New Zealand 1990* project, with all that implies about partnership, sharing, and co-operation.

Aotearoa's
Spiritual Heritage

Te Pakaka Tawhai*

If you ask a Maori in a settlement such as Ruatoria (where Maoris constitute a majority of the population) what he understands by religion, expect him to scratch his head in thought, before at length replying 'Whose religion?' Religion and Christianity may be synonymous words for him, but what they mean will vary between 'a human recognition of a superhuman controlling power', on the one hand, and 'the preaching of one thing and too often the doing of something else', on the other. It was religion in the latter sense that the Christians who 'brought Jesus to civilise the natives' in earlier days seemed to follow, showing up their God in an adverse light in the eyes of the ancestors, whose traditional gods acted swiftly and usually harshly.

For all that, the ancestors were well able, soon after contact with Christianity, to distinguish the Message from the messengers. The Maori of Ruatoria will accept that Christianity is an integral part of his fellow Maori's life, but that each will also have his own brand of religion, for historic and other reasons; for instance Maori have the same religion as their forebears. While the Christian God provides Maoridom with its first Redeemer, he appears mostly to ignore needs at the temporal and profane level, leaving this domain to the ancestral gods who continue to cater for those needs. The tohunga, formally trained experts in various academic disciplines, say that in the 'long ago' the gods took an active interest in the affairs of humans, and interaction among them and the ancestors was the norm rather than the exception. Thus, in the long ago, marvellous events occurred, which would account, at least in part, for a past which today sounds more like fable than anything else.

Such issues as whether there was at some stage an entity that can be said to be the origin or architect of creation, and whether such an origin or architect had a single material form, if any, were and continue to be subjects of much speculation. Our typical Maori's tribal upbringing makes him familiar with the capacity of superhuman controlling powers to exist as they choose - in a single form, or transformed at will into numerous manifestations.

What immediately concerns him are such issues as the effectiveness of the relationship between a person and a superhuman controlling power in magnifying that person's capacity to

* First published as 'Maori Religion', in *The World's Religions*, edited by Stewart Sutherland, Leslie Houlden, Peter Clarke and Friedhelm Hardy, London: Routledge, 1988, this chapter is reprinted here by kind permission of the publishers and of Mrs Pamela Tawhai.

work his will; or the constraints and obligations upon that person in order to sustain the relationship. The ability to accommodate these issues rests a great deal upon knowledge based in turn upon korero tahito (ancient explanations). These may be called 'myths', if that word refers to material the main purpose of which is to express the beliefs and values of people.

That the korero tahito persist in influencing the Maori's mind is evident during hui (large social gatherings). Whether it is the occasion of a huritau (birthday), or tangi (a gathering to deal with a bereavement), each elder present uses the forum. Gazing around in assessment of those present, he rises in his turn to his feet and with measured dignity expounds in solemn rhetoric. To make his points he invokes the imagery of the tribal myths, with apt gesture, and with references to the symbolism, for example of the art and carving of the meeting-house.

The following passage is transcribed and translated from a speech by a tohunga Arnold Reedy, recorded in 1966. It conveys something of the way in which biblical ideas and korero tahito continue to interact, in the Maori way of thinking.

Should I happen to meet with [the Apostle] Paul I would probably say to him, 'By Gosh, Paul, those thoughts conflict greatly in my mind.'

The reason is that Adam is the ancestor of the Hebrews and of the Israelites. Whereas ours is this other: Io the Parent. That's ours. From Him/Her are Papa and Rangi and then the Tamariki. Such is the Maori whakapapa, right from Tikitiki-o-rangi.

There, then, is the difference between our God and the God of the Hebrews. The God of the Hebrews and Israelites they say has His residence in Heaven. Ours, and the God of our ancestors, resides there too. But they know that Tikitiki-o-rangi is the name of the residence of Io; it's there. Io has a house there, Matangireia by name. It has its own forecourt. All those sorts of things are there.

What, er... Paul is saying looks, to use an English term, very much confused, in my view.

Because, take Adam: Then said the God of the Hebrews, 'Let us create man after our image.' And so the god of the Hebrews created Adam. But when that Adam was born into this world, others resided there too, and he considered them: 'What an ineffectual state of affairs.' For sexual organs simply dangled there with nowhere to go, nowhere.

Let us observe the formalities in our discussion! [an elder's (female) voice].

People were born. What Paul is telling us here is that nobody was born. How did he manage it? He took hold of one of his ribs and yanked it out, and then said, 'This is Eve.' They had union and Cain and his younger brothers were born, the generations of whom Paul speaks; these are the Hebrews and the Israelites.

Look here, ours, not so; ours goes this other way. The tamariki of Papa and Rangi resided, but that God continued to reside above, the beginning and the ending. The visaged one, the faceless one. Io, Io the Parent, he is the beginning, he is the ending.

But the tamariki of this couple [Papa and Rangi] resided between then. Gradually, eventually, a stifled sense overwhelmed them; they of course being all male, there were no female ones. Some began to say, 'Let us kick our parents into separating, so that we may emerge into the ordinary world of light.' Others spoke. Tu Matauenga began to say, 'Let us slay our matua, slay them.' And others were saying, 'No, that is too shameful.' From that time hence, Tu Matauenga is god of war, of bloodshed.

Some began to say, 'How shall we proceed?' Tane lay down and raised his feet. Hmm! He began to kick, causing gradual separation, and hence was called by that name of his, Tane-toko-Rangi [Tane sunderer of the sky] - and so, there is separation, there is separation.

But at the separation of Papa, I of course do not agree with what Paul says; there is strong conflict in my mind, the matter is this other way. They were separated and the tamariki emerged.

Rongomaraeroa was guardian of fern; that's the Minister of Agriculture. Is it not so? Tu Matauenga, Minister of War - War Department. Er ..., Tane-nui-a-rangi: that was god of the forests. Minister of Forests ... Tangaroa, Tangaroa of the Marine Department. They now have these posts, they have. (Money had not been invented at that time.)

But here is the problem. These people were all male; there was no female. These people considered their situation: 'By golly, comrades, this is a distressing state! Just us, wherever you look it's the same.' Each one with his (male) sexual appendages. Gradually they became highly distressed by their own company. They began to ponder, 'What shall we do, what shall we do?'

'It is well!', Tane-nui-a-rangi informs them, 'it is well. I have the prescription for our disorder.' He, Tane-nui-a-rangi, proceeded to the beach at Kurawaka and arrived. He began to heap up sand, more sand. He pondered his appearance, and began to mould (the heap) into shape similar to his own. But he added length to the hair ... etc.

'O Ropi [the female elder, Mrs Ngaropi White], these are the words of Wi-o-te-rangi, O Ropi.'

The Maori on the street of Ruatoria, nowadays at least, is content with the knowledge that he has access to the expertise of tohunga like Arnold Reedy. To outsiders he is inclined to present a front of learning, as a defence against anything that might question the worth of his tribal culture; the treasures transmitted to him by his ancestors.

Before turning to the main task I will note something about myself. The aim is to indicate some of the traditional constraints under which I write, and also to provide some data concerning the reliability of individual sources.

I am of Ngati Uepohatu, a tribe whose unextinguished fires, lit by our explorer ancestor Maui, burn in the Waiapu valley near East Cape. The continuously burning fires refer to the state of being unconquered, and in turn refer to the tribe's unsullied prestige; that is the purity, inter alia, of its korero tahito. Maui is the legendary Maui Tikitiki a Taranga (Maui of the topknot of Taranga, his mother) who as our korero tahito explains discovered and settled Aotearoa (New Zealand). The name Aotearoa means 'long twilight', unlike the brief equatorial ones Maui and his crew were used to. Maui had voyaged out and Mount Hikurangi of Aotearoa had seemed to thrust up out of the sea as he sailed

Massey University

Te Pakaka Tawhai

toward shore. Noah on the other hand had waited patiently and it was the waters which subsided thereby exposing Mount Ararat. (I think this reflects something of the philosophies of the two peoples. The Maori view is that things come to those with the courage to get them. The Judaic view is that things come to those who can wait.)

My understanding is that each tribe has its own system of ancient explanations. The apparently permanent migration of some Maori into the tribal territories of other Maori has complicated the picture in some ways. And in relation to that and other matters, I recall an often quoted precept of the ancestors which goes: if you must speak, speak of your own. I speak of korero tahito and accordingly speak of Ngati Uepohatu ones. Our korero tahito have in the telling more or less depended in the past upon such factors as the appropriateness of the emotional climate in which it is told, the messages stated by the surroundings on the occasion, the body language of the narrator and the attributes that the human voice lends to words. Written presentation takes these things away. More than that, it tends to rigidify what has been and should remain pliant. Flexibility in our korero tahito enables them to accommodate the capacity of the narrator to render them more relevant to the issues of the day. It is therefore with misgivings and a sense of danger that I must explain that this telling is only for this time, and that tomorrow I would tell it another way.

Te Po

Te Kore evolved through aeons into Te Po. Te Po also evolved through generations countless to man to the stage of Te Ata (the Dawn). From Te Ata evolved Te Aoturoa (familiar daytime) out of which in turn evolved Te Aomarama (comprehended creation). The state of Whaitua emerges (the present tense is used to animate the narrative) with the recognition of space. There are several entities present. Among these are Rangi potiki and Papa who proceed to have offspring namely: Tane, Tu Matauenga (Tu for short), Rongomatane (Rongo for short) and Haumie tiketike (Haumie for short). The korero tahito ends.

In the Maori conception the creation is a great kin unit, and thus is thought of as having a genealogical structure. The genealogy begins with Te Kore. In the dialect of the Maori on the street of Ruatoria, the article 'te' has both negative and positive meaning, rendering Te Kore as an ambiguous name or title. Te Kore can mean either 'the Nothing' or 'not the Nothing', and in the Maori's thinking ambiguity is a trait of the superbeing and superior things. For reasons I have been unable to ascertain, Te Kore is hardly mentioned, and the common reference is instead to Te Po. The tohunga Arnold Reedy when asked what Te Po was, replied: 'The never-ending beginning.'

Te Po is not thought of as object, or as context. It is said that Te Po is oneness, meaning among other things that Te Po is both object and context.

The employment of the genealogical framework means that to reach Te Po would take a journey in mind, and a return in spirit to former times. During such former times the awareness of our pre-human ancestors operated at the intuitive level only. The situation is sometimes likened to that of a person who is in the grip of sleep, and in that unconsciousness nevertheless senses that although it is night now, dawn is at hand.

Reproduction occurs at the intuitive level. Te Po logically would be the forebear of the Maori on the street in Ruatoria. However the Maori has a strong impression that Te Po is not subject to logic, that Te Po is remote not only on account of the lapse of time but probably more importantly on account of magnitude. It is such as to appear to him to render it fanciful and perhaps even dangerous for him to contemplate Te Po as one of his pre-human ancestors. (The danger is not from Te Po whose magnitude and remoteness put in doubt an interest by Te Po in earthly activities and their performers. An assertion as to genealogical connection has the effect of boosting one spiritually, the boost being dependent on the spiritual level of the one being connected to genealogically. The danger is that at higher spiritual levels, different laws of nature operate and may not necessarily contribute to human survival.)

While Te Po is recognised as a superhuman controlling power, Te Po is not invoked as are some younger superhuman controlling powers. As far as the Maori is concerned the controlling power of Te Po is indirect, controlling those superpowers to whom we can relate directly.

The Tamariki of Rangi and of Papa

The tamariki [Tamariki translates as children][1] named are Tane, Tu, Rongo, Haumie and Tawhiri matea (Tawhiri for short). Tawhiri, son of Rangi, is half-brother to the others and is eldest. The tamariki perceive it is dark, their world consisting as it does of the valleys and hollows between the bodies of Rangi and Papa who are in close embrace. The feeling of cramp and a longing for light is general. There does not seem to be any prospect of change. Except for Tawhiri, the tamariki agree to a proposal to separate Rangi and Papa, the former to be removed afar off and the latter to be retained as nurturing parent. [Rangi potiki and Papa, supported by Tawhiri, resist separation. This is the first time in the korero tahito that there is opposition to differentiation or expansion, and the intervening factor is aroha (love, sympathy). The separation is physical only. Rangi sends his aroha down in the rains, which are his tears, to Papa, who responds by sending up her greetings at dawn in the rising mists. Although physically apart they are united in spirit, their aroha binding them as one. The saying that 'aroha is the one great thing' may have originated here, and it is tempting to suppose that some ancestors appreciated the process of condensation without which life on this planet as we know it would not exist.] The retention of one parent is the idea of Tane, as is also the advice that force only adequate to accomplish separation and no more should be applied. All four brothers in turn attempt to bring about separation but it is Tane's effort alone that brings success and in that role he gains the title of Tane-toko-Rangi (Tane who sets Rangi asunder). [Tane, Tane mahuta, Tane-toko-Rangi and so on is similar to Dad, Mr Chairman at the Rugby Club meeting, Major in the army and so on: the same individual wearing different hats.] With the change in role the name of Rangi becomes Rangi nui (the sky) and that of Papa becomes Papa tuanuku (the earth).

Tawhiri brooding over the maltreatment of Rangi and of Papa projects thoughts that assume material form as the clouds, rains, sleet, storms. In the spirit of revenge Tawhiri unleashes these upon his brothers. They wreak havoc with all except Tu who withstands their assault. Tu, who had urged the others to present a united front against the assault, and who had been ignored, now turns upon his brothers and uses them for food and for his other needs. The korero tahito ends.

The addition to intuitive perception of sensory perception proves expansive and the plot of complex interrelationships is seen to thicken. Expression of experiences now requires physical terms such as cramp, but also emotional terms such as aroha (sympathy, love) and the feelings that make for the spirit of revenge. Possession by the tamariki of human attributes provides a basis for assuming that, exalted as they are, they are sufficiently human as to be approachable by the Maori. Sometimes as themselves, but more often in their forms as manifestations, the tamariki are recognised superhuman controlling powers. Thus Tane manifest as Tane mahuta (trees and birds) is invoked by those who have business in the forest. Rongo manifest as Rangomaraeroa (sweet potato) is invoked during the cropping season.

The purpose of religious activity here is to seek to enter the domain of the superbeing and do violence with impunity: to enter the forest and do some milling for building purposes, to husband the plant and then to dig up the tubers to feed one's guests. Thus that activity neither reaches for redemption and salvation, nor conveys messages of praise and thanksgiving, but seeks permission and offers placation.

From this korero tahito together with the Te Po one we see that humans consist of a tangible and an intangible part. Implicitly both originate in Te Po. The intangible part is wairua (soul). There is also the mauri (essence or potential) but how it relates to wairua is unclear. The word 'essence' is appropriate in that it conveys the idea of that which cannot be analysed further. The word 'potential' is appropriate in so far as it refers to the unrealised. Mauri construed very briefly in terms of power is mana. The privileges and constraints that accompany the possession of mana are the tapu. And the dread or awe that surrounds the possession of mana is the wehi. A chief is often welcomed with the words: haere mai te mana te tapu me te wehi. 'Welcome to the powerful, the privileged and the awesome.' The Maori on the street of Ruatoria speaks of the mauri of carving, the mauri of oratory and so on. And by that he means the spiritual climate that surrounds the carver and his carving, especially during the creative process, the spiritual climate that surrounds the orator and his words, especially during the moments of delivery.

Tane and Hine-ahu-one (Earth Maiden)

Tane observed that the tamariki without exception were male and so set about redressing the imbalance. Using the female substance, the earth, Tane formed the first anthropomorphic female and mediated the spirit into her through his breath. He called this manageable female Hine-ahu-one and begat from her a daughter called Hine-titama. Tane took her to wife. One day she asked him who her father was, and his reply was that she might ask the walls of the house. [The walls of the house were of timber and Tane was referring to his many roles: the father, husband, giver of shelter and so on.] When she learned the answer she fled in shame and eventually arrived at Rarohenga, the underworld. [The shame did not, as is sometimes supposed, spring from the incest but from a violation by Tane of a fundamental principle of social relations, namely sharing. So long as there was only one woman Tane was entitled to her exclusively. As soon as there were more than one under his jurisdiction he was bound to share. This he failed to do.] Tane followed and implored her to return with him to the world of light. She declined, saying that she would remain to welcome their descendants into her bosom after the completion of their lives in the world of light and that he should return there and welcome them into it. Tane tearfully agreed. In her new role Hine-titama is called Hine-nui-i-te-po (Great lady of te po). The korero tahito ends.

The tamariki lack the generative power and on this account there is some sense of failure. The Maori on the street of Ruatoria has only vague notions about the whole thing. The power that the tamariki lack is possessed by Hine-ahu-one who transmits it to her daughter Hine-titama. Hine-titama bears children for whom it is clear for the first time that this life has an end. Henceforth it may be said that people are born only to die and because of this the womb has sometimes been referred to as te whare o te mate (the house of death). The Maori on the street of Ruatoria is disinclined to subscribe to this piece of inverted logic. As descendant of Maui he knows the myth that tells how his ancestor met his end: strangled while attempting to enter the womb of the slumbering Hine-titama in her role as Hine-nui-i-te-po. In his view it is an ignominious end. Some say Maui wished to return to the pre-born state and others that he wanted to obtain immortality. But the korero tahito about Ruaumoko tells us of man's innate wish to be born, and as for immortality, the wairua (soul) lives forever.

At the end of this life the physical part of the dead return, rather than proceed, to the bosom of the ancestress Hine-nui-i-te-po. The po in her name has made for an interpretation such as the 'grand lady of the night'. I wonder whether the reference is not Te Po - the 'great lady of Te Po'? If this is so then the boundaries of Te Po lie on the other side of conception and through the doorway that is death. This interpretation of that part of her name seems to be borne out in the addresses made to the dead in the form of farewells and travelling directions: haere atu ki ou tipuna te hanga tamoko kei Te Po (precede us to your ancestors, the tattooed ones at Te Po).

Tane and Tu

These two had contrasting personalities. Tane was peaceable and philosophic while his younger brother was aggressive and a man of action. The brothers clashed. For his part in that affair Tane was given the lordship of Tikitiki-nui-a-rangi - the fourth heaven - and with the role the title Tane-nui-a-rangi. [The creation includes many heavens and also basement levels. The numbers are in question; mention is made of twelve heavens and at least four basement levels. The higher the level the more spiritual the environment.] Tu for his part lost the power to travel to the different heavens. The korero tahito ends.

In retrospect we can trace the growth of expansion and can say that it is a propensity in the creation. It was present at the level of awareness or consciousness and then extended into the physical level; more specifically into the realm of bodily experience and of geographic realms.

In the Tane and Tu korero tahito the field of expansion is mana. The mana of Tu is in the temporal field; that of Tane-nui-a-rangi is in the divine field, with one foot nevertheless in the temporal field. This situation has not, however, been taken to mean that the flow of mana from the realm of Tane into that of Tu is more fluid than vice versa. This expansion is not expressed as a feeling or reaching toward a God or origin at this stage or for a long time to come. Emphasis is sometimes placed upon the element of confrontation, the situation that appears to have developed when the two mana came into contact. However this korero tahito is not mentioned among explanations of the rites invoked when different mana are brought together; as for example, the rites invoked when visitor and host come together on the occasion of a hui.

Tane-nui-a-rangi

An information release from Naherangi - the eleventh heaven - reached Tane-nui-a-rangi; that three baskets of knowledge had been made available at Naherangi for the taking. Competition would be intense. The chances that Tane-nui-a-rangi would win the baskets appeared slight indeed, but of those closely associated with man's genealogical tree he was the one with the greatest chances of success in that venture. It transpired that Tane-nui-a-rangi was successful notwithstanding fierce harassment by Whiro, lord of one of the infernal regions. Tane-nui-a-rangi has the three baskets with him at the moment in his fourth heaven. The ancient explanation ends.

The source of much knowledge, the difficulties that were faced in order to obtain it, the willingness of no less than Tane-nui-a-rangi to face those difficulties, the high motivations required of students before they are considered fit persons to come in contact with knowledge of a superior kind, all these are indications that knowledge should be prized.

(I had thought that the significance of the number three - the number of baskets - would have struck people not in a numerical sense but as representing a balance of knowledge to enable one to live a balanced life. Like the three-fingered hands on many carvings, the three represents a useful, balanced, piece of anatomy.)

Maui Tikitiki a Taranga

Taranga has a miscarriage and miscarriages are normally born dead. There was a social role for the dead foetus, and that was to provide the focal point for the rites to appease the soul thought to have been angered by this denial of the opportunity to live life. But this miscarriage has been born alive, and of course society has no role and therefore no place for the person whose time of arrival is not yet.

Taranga cut off her tikitiki - topknot - wrapped the foetus in it and flung the bundle into the sea. This is washed ashore in due course and morning finds the bundle entangled in kelp upon the beach. Sunshine causes the placenta encasing the foetus to shrink and strangulation is averted when a seagull pecks away the placenta. More dead than alive the foetus is espied by Tane-nui-a-rangi who removes it to Tikitiki-nui-a-rangi. The foetus survives as the child Maui-tikitiki-a-Taranga - Maui of the topknot of Taranga. Among other activities Maui delves into the three baskets of knowledge. When Maui is capable of deciding whether to remain in Tikitiki-nui-a-rangi or to return to the world of men he opts for the latter. The ancient explanation ends.

The abnormal circumstances in which Maui first sees light singles him out as unusual. The apparent withholding of his mother's personality to prop up his own during the first hours of life precludes him from being a social being. He is then denied a place on the breast of Papa tuanuku - a right of every human. Thus the gates opened to humans into this life have been shut in his face.

Physically too, the chances of enjoying life are waning. Nature itself seems to have reversed its function. The protecting placenta is threatening to strangle him, and the energy-giving rays of Tama-nui-te-ra (the sun) is threatening to deprive him of what scarce energy remains to him. Starved as well, it appears he is being discouraged from this life and forced to turn his face to the next. The reference to him as my mokopuna, by Tane-nui-a-rangi, confirms that Maui is indeed more of the next world than of this. One with such a disposition is ready to delve into the baskets of knowledge.

Conclusion

Sir Apirana Ngata, considering in 1930 doing a doctorate in Maori social organisation, left as the introductory part of rough notes the following:

> The thesis is that after 140 years contact with the kind of civilisation the English brought to these islands there are indications that the Maori is settling down to a regime under which he finds he can exist side by side with the Pakeha [European] or at some distance from the Pakeha, not merely physically but rather socially, economically, morally and religiously so as to make the Maori communal life possible in the same country.

This chapter bears out Ngata's thesis, in respect at least of the Ngati Uepohatus during the 1980s.

Note

1. The word in fact refers to persons of the group who belong in the generational category to which one's natural children do or would have belonged. The group can be as large a one as the tribe.

Further reading

Alpers, A., *Maori Myths and Tribal Legends*, London: John Murray, 1964.
Best, E., *Maori Religion and Mythology*, (2 parts), Wellington: Government Printer, 1976 and 1982, (first published in 1924).

Binney, J., Chaplin, G. and Wallace, C., *Mihaia - the Prophet Rua Kenana and His Community at Maungapohatu*, Wellington: Oxford University Press, 1979.

Metge, J., *The Maoris of New Zealand*, (rev. edn) London: Routledge & Kegan Paul, 1976.

Reed, A.W., *Maori Myth and Legend*, Wellington: Reed, 1972.

Salmond, A., *Hui - A Study of Maori Ceremonial Gatherings*, Wellington: Reed, 1975.

Schwimmer, E., *The World of the Maori*, Wellington: Reed, 1966.

Simmons, D., *The Great New Zealand Myth: a Study of the Discovery and Origin Traditions of the Maori*, Wellington: Reed, 1976.

Baha'i Faith

Bronwyn Elsmore

Members of the Baha'i faith follow the teachings of the Persian-born prophet who took the title Baha'u'llah (The Glory of God) and claimed to be the universal Messenger of God for this modern age. As a result of his religious activities and the declaration of his divine mission, Baha'u'llah, whose given name was Husayn Ali, was exiled first to Iraq, then to Turkey, and finally to the Akka-Haifa area of Palestine. The worldwide headquarters of the religion are therefore in Haifa, Israel, with the administrative buildings situated on Mount Carmel.

The Baha'i faith began in 1844 and is now represented in every region of the globe with, in 1990, an estimated five million members. The country with the greatest Baha'i population is India, where the faith has been spread rapidly in recent years.

New Zealand origins and growth

Baha'is (followers of the Glory) have been in New Zealand since 1913, when Miss Margaret Stevenson of Auckland accepted the teachings of Baha'u'llah. Her introduction to this faith was through reading accounts of the addresses given in London by 'Abdu'l-Baha, published in the British journal *Christian Commonwealth*. 'Abdu'l-Baha, the son of the Prophet, is regarded as the Exemplar of his father's teachings.

Numbers were small for many years, but the foundation of a firm national community was gradually built up. In 1926 the first Local Spiritual Assembly was formed, and in 1957 the first National Spiritual Assembly of the Baha'is of New Zealand was elected to administer the affairs of the Cause in New Zealand.

Since then, growth has been steady, with an increasing number of local administrative bodies forming throughout the country. The Baha'i pattern of development favours geographical coverage rather than the congregating of a few large communities in the main centres.

Between the 1981 and 1986 censuses, membership of the Baha'i faith in New Zealand increased by 44.4 per cent, an average rate of 9 per cent each year. This is affecting many areas of Baha'i organisation and practice.

Places

When numbers were small, meetings in most localities could be held in the homes of believers.

More commonly, now, larger premises are used. These are mostly rented rooms, though in several areas property has been obtained, usually a house or small hall. Meetings are for worship or business, children's and study classes, social gatherings, and perhaps administrative work. The buildings used are not regarded as sacred places in the way that churches and temples are.

The Baha'i faith does have its sacred buildings, however, which are known as Houses of Worship. At the present time there are only seven of these in the world, sited in different continents, each one being a symbol of the faith for a wide area. The closest to New Zealand are in Sydney, serving Australasia, and in Apia, serving the Pacific region. Others are in Europe (near Frankfurt), South America (Panama), North America (Chicago), Africa (Kampala), and Asia (New Delhi).

Brad Burch

Baha'i House of Worship, Apia

Houses of Worship are all constructed with nine sides, and a dome. Each of the nine sides contains a door, signifying that people can come to worship God from any religious background. Services, open to people of all faiths, consist of the reading of the sacred books of many religions.

The New Zealand national administrative centre is at Henderson, and the first House of Worship for this country will eventually be built on the same property, though this is not expected for many years.

The rise in membership has seen the number of local administrative areas increase. Wherever there are nine or more adult Baha'is living in a locality (at present determined by local government boundaries), a body known as a Local Spiritual Assembly is elected. These assemblies have an administrative function - they oversee the functioning of the local Baha'i community, ensuring that regular meetings are held, promoting the spiritual life of the community, assisting with personal matters when requested, and generally dealing with the business of the faith in that area.

In the same manner, a National Spiritual Assembly attends to the affairs of the national community. Local assemblies are elected yearly on 21 April, the anniversary of the day on which the prophet Baha'u'llah first announced his station and mission. The election of the National Assembly occurs during an annual convention held close to that date.

Baha'i elections differ from most others in that there are no nominations of candidates and no electioneering is permitted. Rather, the election process is conducted in a prayerful attitude. All adult Baha'is can vote and be voted for. The nine who poll the highest are expected to serve.

The New Zealand Baha'i community is strongly multi-cultural, as census figures show. Only 73 per cent are New Zealand born, against 84.5 per cent of the general population. While the numbers born in the United Kingdom and Europe are comparable to the general population, many times more than the usual proportions have come from the Pacific Islands, North America, and other countries. In recent years, for instance, increasing numbers of Iranian Baha'is have been accepted as immigrants. This is not to say that all Baha'is born elsewhere have chosen to come to New Zealand for religious reasons. Many have become Baha'is after they arrived and settled in this country.

This international multi-cultural character stands out in the way Baha'i gatherings are developing. Prayers are commonly offered in a number of languages - Tongan, Samoan, and Farsi, particularly, being added to English in many areas. Social occasions, too, are often marked by musical and cultural items from different countries.

Members' diversity

Maori membership, though small for most of the faith's early years in New Zealand, has also been increasing in recent times. In 1990 two of the nine members elected to the National Spiritual Assembly were Maori believers. National and regional gatherings are frequently held on marae, with Maori tradition forming an integral part of the proceedings.

The translation of Baha'i scriptures into Maori has been proceeding slowly over many years. Collections of prayers and extracts from the Baha'i writings are now available, as are some introductory books about the faith. Maori members frequently put prayers and passages of the writings to music and sing them at gatherings.

The Baha'i principle of the unity of humankind is reflected in the New Zealand community not only in the diversity of cultures but in the variety of marriages between different nationalities and races. And unlike most other religious groups in New Zealand, the Baha'i community is distinctive in that most of the members are first-generation believers. This is particularly true of those who are New Zealanders by birth - almost all were brought up in another religious tradition and have become Baha'is by investigating and accepting the beliefs of this faith for themselves.

A description of the social makeup of New Zealand Baha'is was obtained through a request for information published in the national newsletter.[1] Members were found to come from a wide range of former beliefs. Some identified these as Anglican, Catholic, Congregational, Jewish, Methodist, Open Brethren, Presbyterian, Ratana, or more generally as previously Christian, having no religion, or as atheist.

Some have gone through a period of religious searching which has included adherence to, or interest in, a number of different groups. One said she was brought up as Dutch Reformed, became a Catholic, married into the Presbyterian Church, and then became 'a fiery atheist until I found the faith'! One said his interests had included 'the new age-astrological-reincarnation-Buddhist-vegetarian-1960s thing'.

Overseas-born Baha'is listed most of the same beliefs, with the addition of the Episcopal Church of USA, Free Church of Tonga, Hawaiian Congregational Church, Islam, and the Mormon Church. Some of these too had followed several previous paths, one tracing his journey through a Presbyterian upbringing during which he attended 'various Protestant denominations, then short-term membership of various faiths - Mormon, Church of Christ, Buddhist, Krishna, and interest in comparative religions'.

The few who identified themselves as coming from a Baha'i background were from the USA, or were young members of Iranian birth whose families had been Baha'i for several generations. However, a growing number of second and third generation Baha'is of New Zealand birth are represented in the national community. Of the first-generation Baha'is who responded, more than half joined this faith when in their twenties.

In the Baha'i faith, the children of Baha'i parents should be brought up with full knowledge of that faith, but are free to choose whether or not they wish to continue as members after they reach fifteen - the time nominated as the age of spiritual maturity. Voting privileges begin at the age of adult membership, twenty-one. This means that membership lists for those older than fifteen can be quite accurate, without large numbers of fringe adherents being added. In mid 1989 records provided by the New Zealand National Spiritual Assembly showed that there were 1863 members over fifteen at that time, with a further 984 children being brought up in the faith.[2]

Reasons for becoming Baha'is

As most Baha'is have conducted their own personal spiritual search before becoming members, the questions that first led people to become attracted to the religion, and why they decided to make it their own, are popular topics of conversation at social gatherings.

A common reason given among New Zealand Baha'is is that they accepted and welcomed the doctrine that God has revealed knowledge through a continuing line of prophets throughout the history of the world. Consequently, all religions based on such revelation should be regarded as contributing to the divine education of humankind.

This includes the claim of Baha'u'llah that he is the Prophet and Messenger of God for this age. Baha'is are those who have investigated and accepted that claim, and become believers.

One woman, formerly Jewish, said, 'I had been searching for a long time. I knew there must be something more and my own religion had stopped somewhere. At last I had found a way of combining all faiths - I didn't have to choose between them.'

Another who became a Baha'i in her forties, after being fully involved in church membership, wrote:

> In my late twenties, because of involvement with a naturopathy course, I began reading about other religions and philosophies, plus New Age books. I had never before questioned that there was any other way to God but through Christianity. Now I realized that Christianity didn't have a monopoly on God and that there were other paths to spiritual attainment. Gradually I felt compelled to detach myself, and when I was about 40 decided to no longer belong to any religious group, believing there was a God, but distrustful of all religious teachings. [After this her daughter became a Baha'i and she read some Baha'i books.] It did not take very much to convince me that this was truth. The idea of progressive revelation was wonderful, because I'd already come to that conclusion.

Even more specifically, some say they recognised Baha'u'llah as the Return of Christ. Jesus Christ is specifically mentioned in the Baha'i Writings as a divinely-appointed Messenger of God. Others mentioned are Krishna, Buddha, Abraham, Moses, Zoroaster, and Muhammad.

> Beware, O believers in the Unity of God, lest ye be tempted to make any distinction between any of the Manifestations of His Cause, or to discriminate against the signs that have accompanied and proclaimed their Revelation. This indeed is the true meaning of Divine

Unity, if ye be of them that apprehend and believe this truth. Be ye assured, moreover, that the works and acts of each and every one of these Manifestations of God ... are all ordained by God, and are a reflection of His Will and Purpose.

Baha'u'llah[3]

Many Baha'is give as their reason for joining, the logical nature of the teachings. One said 'the principles rang true for me and confirmed many of my own beliefs.' 'Religious clarity', 'down-to-earth and sensible philosophy', 'relevant for today', were other views. Some say that though they agreed with the principles, they did not become members for some time, several years in some cases, till they realised that the principles must be channelled through an administrative structure if they are to be effective.

A very strong attraction is the Baha'i teachings on peace. Members put it as: 'the promise of world peace', 'a better world in which to raise children', 'the orderly system to bring justice and peace to a troubled world'.

One member told her story in this way:

> I was looking for a group that had the ability to unite the world so all the wars would be stopped. I knew that love was the key. One day I rang the Baha'i Centre in Dunedin to obtain a book and after three hours of reading I knew I had found the group. What I didn't know then was that I got heaps more than what I was looking for. Praise God!

A Tongan-born believer was going to school along the main street of Nuku'alofa when he was told by an old uneducated man:

> Going to school is not enough to reshape the world. The foundation of the Baha'i teachings is unity of mankind ... and Baha'u'llah's gift to mankind is justice ... if you become a Baha'i you will find better ways of changing this world....

This young man remembered the words and later became a fellow believer.

A good number were first attracted by the Baha'is they met, particularly their devotion. Typical responses were: 'the dedication and enthusiasm of the Baha'is', 'some Baha'is we both knew - their tranquillity and spirituality', 'a happy Baha'i and her happy family', 'they were doing something to change things peacefully'. As one young woman wrote, 'they drew me like a bee to a honeypot.'

For some, this was a very individual experience. From one, 'the personal transformation of a Baha'i woman who was dying of cancer.' From a man who emigrated from England:

> I transited Teheran in 1961 and met a Baha'i there who I considered the most trusting, considerate, and genuine person I had ever met. He explained the principles of the Baha'i Faith to me and they sounded relevant to today. I met another Baha'i in New Zealand and decided that I would become a Baha'i after reading some of the principles of the faith.

One believer said she was attracted by the Baha'i history and stories of the three central figures of the faith.[4] Another saw one of the Baha'i Houses of Worship and it inspired her to look into the teachings of the religion. For a Tongan man it was a Baha'i radio programme which was broadcast by Radio Tonga.

A man now in his mid-30s tells how he became a Baha'i at seventeen, but at that age was attracted more by the fact that it was 'different'.

> On hearing the name Baha'i I thought it sounded quite snappy, and I wanted to become one of them as it seemed to fit in with the image I was presenting - long hair, into surfing.... I was trying to find a lifestyle totally opposite to my Maori upbringing.... I wasn't really interested in the teachings, and it took me at least two years before I picked up a Baha'i book. But eighteen years on I'm still plodding along there.

Several members say they were particularly impressed by the multi-racial aspect of the Baha'i communities - 'I was drawn by the diversity of races' - and the principle of oneness of humankind which states that all people of every race have full equality with one another.

> It is not for him to pride himself who loveth his own country, but rather for him who loveth the whole world. The earth is but one country, and mankind its citizens.
>
> Baha'u'llah[5]

Equality of men and women

The strong emphasis on the full equality of women and men is another principle which is appreciated by the members of this faith. It is interesting to note that the membership figures (age fifteen and over), as at mid 1989, show 1010 (54%) women, and 853 (46%) men. Women's committees nationally and locally encourage Baha'i women to take a full place in the life and work of the Baha'i and wider communities.

> The world of humanity has two wings - one is women and the other men. Not until both wings are equally developed can the bird fly. Should one wing remain weak, flight is impossible. Not until the world of women becomes equal with the world of man in the acquisition of virtues and perfections, can success and prosperity be attained as they ought to be.
>
> 'Abdu'l-Baha[6]

One young woman who joined at the age of twenty-two says:

> My previous background was Christian. Although I always maintained a belief in God, as a feminist I was unable to reconcile my views on the equality of men and women with Christian thought, in particular biblical scripture. The principle of the equality of the sexes was one reason I was attracted to the faith.

One young man who replied to the request for information about Baha'is in New Zealand wrote that one of the things that attracted him was that there was no priesthood. The woman quoted above also added, 'I also felt that individual search for truth is essential - the non-existence of clergy appealed.' The teachings of the Prophet Baha'u'llah on this matter is that in this age it is the duty of everyone to come to an understanding of spiritual truth through their own investigation.

Activities

As stated above, Baha'i communities do not rely on professional orders of clergy. All activities and services are led by individual Baha'is. The central activity is the Nineteen Day Feast, a meeting held on the first day of each of the nineteen months which are each made up of nineteen days. (An additional four or five intercalary days makes the Baha'i calendar conform to the solar year.) On these occasions the members of the community gather in a meeting which includes worship, consultation on matters of interest to the community, and a social time when food is served.

> This Feast is held to foster comradeship and love, to call God to mind and supplicate Him with contrite hearts, and to encourage benevolent pursuits.
> That is, the friends should there dwell upon God and glorify Him, read the prayers and holy verses, and treat one another with the utmost affection and love....
> If this Feast be held in the proper fashion, the friends will, once in nineteen days, find themselves spiritually restored, and endued with a power that is not of this world.
>
> 'Abdu'l-Baha[7]

The format of each Nineteen-Day Feast follows broad guidelines set down by the Prophet, but otherwise is organised according to the wishes of the member or members hosting the meeting. Only Baha'is attend these spiritual feasts, but other meetings are open to anyone interested. The celebration of holy days is a time when non-members are welcome and often invited to attend.

Brad Burch

A Baha'i youth peace group

Baha'is are encouraged to be active in public life, though not in areas concerned with party politics. Because of the central teaching of unity, they often take a leading part in activities promoting peace.

> I charge you all that each one of you concentrate all the thoughts of your heart on love and unity. When a thought of war comes oppose it by a stronger thought of peace. A thought of hatred must be destroyed by a more powerful thought of love. Thoughts of war bring

destruction to all harmony, well-being, restfulness and content. Thoughts of love are constructive of brotherhood, peace, friendship and happiness....

If you desire with all your heart friendship with every race on earth, your thought, spiritual and positive, will spread; it will become the desire of others, growing stronger and stronger, until it reaches the minds of all men.

'Abdu'l-Baha[8]

Special holy days occur throughout the year, marking the anniversaries of significant events in Baha'i history. On the nine most important of these occasions, members try to take a day off from their employment in order to celebrate appropriately. There is no set way of commemorating holy days - each community decides on an activity that suits the occasion. On a joyful occasion it may take the form of a picnic or social; for the more serious anniversaries a special service may be considered more in order. But the manner of commemoration varies from community to community and from year to year.

Children are encouraged to attend Baha'i services, and most communities organise children's classes where religious instruction is given. This usually includes lessons on other world religions as well as on the Baha'i Faith. In many areas this broad-based viewpoint has prompted non-Baha'i parents to ask if their children may also attend.

For those over the age of fifteen, one Baha'i month is set down as a time of fasting when there should be no eating or drinking during daylight hours. These nineteen days are a reminder that it is our spiritual lives rather than physical wants which are most important. Children, those over seventy, those who are ill, pregnant, travelling, or nursing a baby, do not fast.

New Year comes at the end of the days of fasting, and falls on March 21. The Baha'i calendar began in 1844 with the announcement by the Prophet-Herald known as the Bab (the Gate) that the time had come for the appearance of the universal Messenger of God, Baha'u'llah.

Prayer

Baha'is are expected to pray daily. Three prayers are known as obligatory prayers, and every believer should recite one of these each day. This may take as little as twenty seconds. However additional prayers are encouraged, as well as reading from the sacred writings each day.

The obligatory prayers are binding inasmuch as they are conducive to humility and submissiveness, to setting one's face toward God and expressing devotion to Him. Through such prayer man holdeth communion with God, seeketh to draw near unto Him, converseth with the true Beloved of one's heart, and attaineth spiritual stations.

'Abdu'l-Baha[9]

Here are two prayers given by Baha'u'llah, a prayer of praise and a prayer for unity.

O Thou Who art the Lord of Lords! I testify that Thou art the Lord of all creation, and the Educator of all beings, visible and invisible. I bear witness that Thy power hath encompassed the entire universe, and that the hosts of the earth can never dismay Thee, nor can the dominion of all peoples and nations deter Thee from executing Thy purpose. I confess that Thou hast no desire except the regeneration of the whole world, and the establishment of the unity of its peoples, and the salvation of all them that dwell therein.

O my God! O my God! Unite the hearts of Thy servants and reveal unto them Thy great purpose. May they follow Thy commandments and abide in Thy Law. Help them, O God, in their endeavour, and grant them strength to serve Thee. O God! leave them not to themselves but guide their steps by the light of knowledge, and cheer their hearts by Thy Love. Verily, Thou art their Helper and their Lord.

Pilgrimage

When possible, Baha'is go to Israel to make a pilgrimage to the sacred places of their faith. There is no special ritual connected with the pilgrimage, but all will visit the holiest spot - the Shrine of Baha'u'llah at Bahji - and other places in the area associated with the Prophet's life. They will also visit the Shrine of the Bab on Mount Carmel.

Other buildings at the world centre include an Archives building which holds items connected with the early history of the religion, and another which is the Seat of the Universal House of Justice, the body which sees to the concerns of the whole Baha'i world community.

These buildings, like the Houses of Worship situated in each continent, have been built solely with the donations of believers. It is a principle of the Baha'i faith that no donations can be accepted from those who are not members, and this is true too of the activities of each local community. So Baha'is undertake no money-raising campaigns among the public. Money needed for the organisation of the faith is given by members on a freewill basis, or under a system whereby members can choose to give a set proportion of their assets after living expenses are deducted.

Occasional rites

Occasions such as marriages and burials are conducted by individual members of the faith under the jurisdiction of the relevant Local Spiritual Assembly. To satisfy New Zealand marriage laws, a number of Baha'i marriage celebrants have been registered. But it is the vows exchanged by the pair which are regarded as being the central and necessary part of the ceremony.

The couples involved prepare their own service, usually choosing excerpts and prayers from the Baha'i Writings, or any other readings or music. The marriage celebrant usually takes no part in the ceremony other than seeing to the signing of an official register.

Similarly, there is no set form of funeral service. On these occasions the family and friends prepare a suitable programme, the only requirement being that a specific prayer is read at the graveside. The Baha'i faith teaches that bodies should not be cremated. Nor should they be transported to a far-away place of burial, but interred in a cemetery close to the place of death.

The doctrines include belief in an eternal soul. Death is seen as a time when the soul is freed from the limitations of this earthly existence and can continue to progress in the world to follow. All souls enter the spiritual world, their level of spiritual attainment in this life determining their relative degree of understanding in the next.

> Consider how a being, in the world of the womb, was deaf of ear and blind of eye, and mute of tongue; how he was bereft of any perceptions at all. But once, out of that world of darkness, he passed into this world of light, then his eye saw, his ear heard, his tongue spoke. In the same way, once he hath hastened away from this mortal place into the Kingdom of God, then he will be born in the spirit, then the eye of his perception will open, the ear of his soul will hearken, and all the truths of which he was ignorant before will be made plain and clear.
>
> 'Abdu'l-Baha[10]

There is no Baha'i ceremony equivalent to either a christening or baptism in Christianity, or any rite at the time of maturity as in Jewish practice.

There are no special dress requirements which distinguish Baha'is from other New Zealanders, though some choose to wear items of jewelry incorporating symbols significant to this faith.

This design, referred to as the 'Ringstone Symbol', depicts the three levels of existence. The topmost of the parallel bars represents the level of God, the middle the Manifestation or Messenger of God, and the lower level humankind. The vertical line is the level of the Manifestation, repeated to show the link between the Divine and earthly realms by revelation through the Messengers.

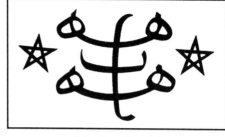

Ringstone Symbol

Greatest Name

Many Baha'i homes display the symbol referred to as 'The Greatest Name'. This is a stylised representation in Arabic of the invocation 'O Thou Glory of the All-Glorious'. Baha, meaning Glory/Splendour, is said to be the greatest of all the great names of God.

Moral injunctions

The Baha'i writings enjoin members to take up occupations which benefit humanity, and to follow a way of life based on high moral standards.

> It is enjoined upon every one of you to engage in some form of occupation, such as crafts, trades, and the like. We have graciously exalted your engagement in such work to the rank of worship unto God, the True One. Ponder ye in your hearts the grace and the blessings of God and render thanks unto Him at eventide and at dawn. Waste not your time in idleness and sloth. Occupy yourselves with that which profiteth yourselves and others....
>
> When anyone occupieth himself in a craft or trade, such occupation itself is regarded in the estimation of God as an act of worship....
>
> Baha'u'llah[11]

> O Divine Providence! Bestow Thou in all things purity and cleanliness upon the people of Baha. Grant that they be freed from all defilement, and released from all addictions. Save them from committing any repugnant act, unbind them from the chains of every evil habit, that they may live pure and free, wholesome and cleanly, worthy to serve at Thy Sacred Threshold and fit to be related to their Lord.
>
> 'Abdu'l-Baha[12]

Food laws

The only food prohibition is that regarding the taking of alcohol.

> The drinking of wine is, according to the text of the Most Holy Book, forbidden; for it is the cause of chronic diseases, weakeneth the nerves, and consumeth the mind.
>
> 'Abdu'l-Baha[13]

Mind-altering drugs are also prohibited.

Spreading the faith

Baha'is seek to teach their beliefs mainly by personal contact, and are happy to share their views with anyone interested. They often place advertisements in newspapers, or hold public meetings in order to explain their beliefs with anyone who responds.

> Consort with all men, O people of Baha, in a spirit of friendliness and fellowship. If ye be aware of a certain truth, if ye possess a jewel, of which others are deprived, share it with them in a language of utmost kindliness and good-will. If it be accepted, if it fulfil its purpose, your object is attained. If anyone should refuse it, leave him unto himself, and beseech God to guide him.
>
> Baha'u'llah[14]

Holy days of the Baha'i faith

The following special days are commemorated in the Baha'i calendar. Of these, nine are designated as 'work-suspended days' when members try whenever possible to avoid working at their occupation.

Festival of Naw-Ruz (New Year) - 21 March. The Baha'i day begins at sunset, so this is usually celebrated at sunset on the twentieth.

Festival of Ridvan - 21 April to 2 May. This commemorates the twelve-day period spent in a garden on an island of the river in Baghdad in 1863 when Baha'u'llah announced his mission as Messenger of God. Three days in this time are specially significant and regarded as work-suspended days.

First day, 21 April. The celebration takes place at 3 p.m., coinciding with the time of the announcement.

Ninth day, 29 April. On this day the Prophet's family arrived to join him.

Twelfth day, 2 May. On this day all of the gathering left the island and Baha'u'llah and his family set off on their long journey to Palestine.

Declaration of the Bab - 23 May. The anniversary of the time when the Bab (the Gate) declared his mission as the Messenger to herald the coming of the Promised One. Celebrated at two hours after sunset.

Ascension of Baha'u'llah - 29 May. The anniversary of the death of the Prophet. It is commemorated at 3 a.m.

Martyrdom of the Bab - 9 July. The commemoration of the death of the Prophet-Herald, the Bab, which occurred in 1850. It is observed at noon.

Birth of the Bab - 20 October.

Birth of Baha'u'llah - 12 November.

Other special anniversaries are also commemorated, but are not work-suspended days.

The Day of the Covenant - 26 November.

Ascension of 'Abdu'l-Baha - 28 November. Commemorated at 1 a.m.

Notes

1. This was not conducted as a representative study; it merely seeks to illustrate the diversity of the New Zealand Baha'i community. Religious or national affiliations listed should not be regarded as complete, but simply those nominated by the respondents. The first fifty replies were used to produce this picture.
2. Thanks to the National Spiritual Assembly of the Baha'is of New Zealand for supplying figures and some historical information.
3. *Gleanings from the Writings of Baha'u'llah,* Wilmette: Baha'i Publishing Trust, 1952, pp. 59-60.
4. The Bab, Baha'u'llah, and 'Abdu'l-Baha.
5. Shoghi Effendi, *The World Order of Baha'u'llah,* Wilmette: Baha'i Publishing Trust, 1955, p. 198.
6. *The Baha'i Revelation,* London: Baha'i Publishing Trust, 1970, p. 212.
7. *Baha'i Meetings : The Nineteen Day Feast,* Wilmette: Baha'i Publishing Trust, 1976, p. 19.
8. 'Abdu'l-Baha, *Paris Talks,* London: Baha'i Publishing Trust, 1969, pp. 29-30.
9. *The Importance of Prayer, Meditation and the Devotional Attitude,* Auckland: National Spiritual Assembly of the Baha'is of New Zealand, 1980, p. 10.
10. *Selections from the Writings of 'Abdu'l-Baha,* Haifa: Baha'i World Centre, 1978, p. 177.
11. *Tablets of Baha'u'llah,* Haifa: Baha'i World Centre, 1978, p. 26.
12. *Selections from the Writings of 'Abdu'l-Baha,* p. 149.
13. *The Advent of Divine Justice,* Wilmette: Baha'i Publishing Trust, 1973 p. 27.
14. *Gleanings from the Writings of Baha'u'llah,* p. 289.

Further reading

Scriptures

Gleanings From the Writings of Baha'u'llah, Wilmette: Baha'i Publishing Trust, 1952.

Baha'i World Faith (Selected Writings of Baha'u'llah and 'Abdu'l-Baha), Wilmette: Baha'i Publishing Trust, 1956.

The Baha'i Revelation (Writings of Baha'u'llah and 'Abdu'l-Baha), London: Baha'i Publishing Trust, 1970.

History and explanation

Effendi, Shoghi, *God Passes By,* Wilmette: Baha'i Publishing Trust, 1970.

Esslemont, J.E., *Baha'u'llah and the New Era,* London: Baha'i Publishing Trust, 1974.

Buddhism

Ajahn Viradhammo

For more than 2500 years the spiritual tradition known as Buddhism has inspired Eastern civilisation and been the source of some of its greatest achievements. It originated in Northern India in the sixth century BCE (before the Common Era) with the life and work of Sidattha Gotama, the historical Buddha. In time Buddhism spread peacefully over a large part of Asia, profoundly influencing the lives of its people.

Until recent times Buddhism has been thought of as a faith only for those from an oriental culture. But study and practice of the Buddha's teaching reveal it as a way of life which makes for the well-being and happiness of any person who undertakes it, regardless of nationality. Because Buddhism speaks directly to the most crucial concerns of humanity - the perennial problems of dissatisfaction in life, of birth and death, suffering, and the yearning for peace and fulfilment - it is now capturing the attention of many people all over the world, in the West as well as in the East.

The founder of Buddhism was neither a deity nor a prophet. He was a man who was awakened, through his own efforts, from ignorance to perfect enlightenment. That means liberation from any personal manifestation of greed, aversion or delusion through physical action, speech or thought; or more positively, perfect peace.

The title Buddha means 'the enlightened one'. The Buddha's teaching, known as the *Dharma* (or *Dhamma*) is taught on the basis of his own clear comprehension of reality, free from appeals to divine authority and demands for unquestioning faith. Open to reason and critical enquiry, the *Dharma* invites personal verification at every step. The Buddhist learns to develop truth-discerning awareness, casting attention directly onto the everyday experiences of human existence. The various forms of inner conflict and discontent are especially scrutinised, for these become a source of ennobling wisdom and understanding. Human suffering, the Buddha explains, is rooted in our self-centred attitudes and desires. Liberation from suffering, which is the goal of Buddhism, therefore requires a fundamental transformation in the way one perceives the world and hence the way one acts, speaks and thinks in the world. The cultivation of truth-discerning wisdom leads to the abandonment of narrow and limited self-perceptions and thus to the eradication of greed, hatred and delusion. With the lessening of selfish attachments there is then space for the manifestation of kindness, compassion, generosity and equanimity.

The means for that transformation is the Noble Eightfold Path, a teaching which addresses various aspects of human endeavour:

Right understanding
Right thought
Right speech
Right action
Right livelihood
Right effort
Right mindfulness
Right concentration.

Known as the Middle Way, the eightfold path, when correctly practised, lays a foundation of virtue and leads directly to an understanding of the way things really are, leaving aside the smog of delusion that blinds humanity. Buddhism emphasises personal responsibility as the key to right conduct, and personal experience as the gateway to truth. Integral to this teaching is a profound philosophy, a detailed and clear analysis of the mind, well-grounded ethics and tested methods of meditation. Cultivation of the Buddha's way bears fruit in serene understanding and equanimity amidst the vicissitudes of life and in the ability to act and relate in the world with wisdom and compassion. The growth of Buddhism throughout Asia was not only the promulgation of a religious philosophy but also the foundation of a civilisation. After his enlightenment, the Buddha spent the remaining forty-five years of his life going throughout the Ganges plain, expounding the Dharma to people from all walks of life who were ready to hear his teaching. He founded the *Sangha*, the earliest order of monks in the history of monasticism, and one which still continues intact today. A large body of supporting lay followers grew around his example and teaching. By the time of his death at the age of eighty, India had been deeply touched by one of her most compassionate and wise sons.

Buddhist history in New Zealand

As long ago as the 1850s and '60s the 6000 or more Chinese gold prospectors who came to Southland and the West Coast brought with them a folk religion which had elements of Buddhist influence. The occasional temple or 'joss house' was built (largely Taoist rather than Buddhist in function) but none have survived to the present day. Among those families who settled, often working as cooks or market gardeners, some kept up Buddhist practices and beliefs, maintaining household shrines but otherwise giving few outward signs of this religion.

It was in the 1950s and 60s that signs of interest in Buddhism by Westerners become apparent in this country and in Australia. While the 1945 official census records only twenty-nine Buddhists, by 1966 that figure had reached 652.

In 1956, the Buddhist Society of New Zealand was formed at Takapuna in Auckland. During the '60s, regular meditation sessions led by lay-people began to be held in several towns and cities. A branch of Friends of the Western Buddhist Order was founded in Mairangi Bay in 1970, and a Chinese Buddhist Society in Auckland in the following year.

Monks and lay-teachers from various Buddhist traditions (Theravadan, Western, Zen, Tibetan) were to visit the country regularly during the next few years, helping establish or strengthen such local organisations as the Sphere Group, Denkyo-ji Zen centres, and the Dorje Chang Institute (see below). With resident teachers, public meetings and regular study and meditation groups now available in several centres, New Zealanders had many opportunities to study the Dharma for themselves. Several New Zealanders went abroad for study and eventual ordination as monks.

Buddhist ceremonies featured on national television in February 1978, when visiting Tibetan lama Ven. Karma Thinley Rinpoche consecrated the site for the Karma Kagyu Trust's monastery.

Since the early 1980s, immigration has produced a steady increase in the number of South-East Asian Buddhist residents. (By the 1986 census, the number of Buddhists overall had reached 6255, a figure which had almost doubled the 3330 of the 1981 census.) Mostly Theravadans in tradition, the refugee and new-settler communities desired above all regular contact with monks, and the celebration of familiar festivals and rites. Theravada Associations formed in Auckland and Wellington, with associated groups elsewhere, bringing together Thai, Sri Lankan, Burmese, Chinese and other Buddhists (mostly resident here in professional or academic capacities or married to other New Zealanders) with the newly arrived peoples from Laos, Cambodia and Vietnam. With four temples (see details at end) and a number of resident monks, these now form by far the largest proportion of this country's practising Buddhists.

Bodhinyanarama Monastery

First ordination of Theravada Buddhist monk in New Zealand (26 March 1989)

Buddhist New Zealanders

Among followers of the Buddha's teachings in New Zealand, we must distinguish between those who have grown up within countries steeped in Buddhist civilisation, and those who are New Zealand born. The latter, mostly urban-dwelling and Western-educated, have often been attracted to Buddhism by its straight-forward teachings regarding personal dissatisfaction and dis-ease, maladies of the heart and mind. Their avenue of approach has perhaps been through books, travel, acquaintance with other Buddhists, or experience of a meditation retreat. Their search may come from a deep-down feeling that there is more to life than the usual choices offered by the contemporary modes of living, within which one still lacks personal understanding, and craves something more than momentary satisfaction. Here is the story of one New Zealand man who discovered Buddhism in that manner.

Robin's story:

My family have been Canterbury sheep-farmers for five generations. I was brought up the youngest child of parents who were married when they were well into their thirties, at the end of

World War II. My brother and sister being some years older than me, made growing up on the farm rather a solitary experience. At school I followed further solitary pursuits, like reading, and writing my own stories.

At nine, I was uprooted from my idyllic existence, separated from my mother, and sent off to boarding school like my brother and sister before me. This was naturally a traumatic event for a rather sensitive child. On balance, though, my four years at prep. school were happy enough. I had imaginative teachers who fostered an interest in history, literature and science, and encouraged me to take an interest in things beyond the school curriculum. I began to be fascinated with astronomy and the mysteries of the universe, and became an avid stargazer. By fourteen I was totally absorbed: lecturing to the Canterbury Astronomy Society on stellar evolution and cosmology, the main mover behind the formation of a junior section of the Astronomical Society, and elected onto the society's committee.

From prep. school I was sent as a day boy to Christ's College. This coincided with my parents selling the farm and moving into Christchurch. After positive encouragement by my teachers at prep. school, I was now expected to conform. As someone who was not a cricket player nor a rugby enthusiast, not brilliant academically but tending to question things rather than wanting to conform, things were made rather difficult for me. My extracurricular activities such as astronomy were discouraged.

From being quite religious at the age of twelve, I became by fifteen a committed atheist, refusing to take part in the compulsory chapel services. My interests now turned to history, particularly the history of the Soviet Union, encouraged by books and propaganda pamphlets I obtained from the Soviet embassy. My interest not only in Russian culture but in Marxist politics led to further ostracism.

At university, where I specialised in history and Russian language and literature, I shocked everyone by joining the Socialist Unity Party. Taking up the offer of a scholarship to study Russian in Moscow for a year led to my gaining a genuine respect for the Russian people and a more balanced picture of their political system. I came back cured of my communist leanings, but still an incurable romantic at heart.

A brief and unsuccessful marriage, followed by a drab, unsatisfied life of work and entertainment, left me with low self-esteem. Then came an event which changed my whole perspective on life; my mother's illness and death from cancer. I discovered how people avoid death and deny this fundamental reality of life. I felt privileged being able to share some of my mother's experiences during her illness, and to be with her in her final hours. I found that this direct confrontation with death itself was actually not as bad as the thought of death. This gave me a perspective on my own suffering. I came to understand that the source of suffering was within me and not the fault of other people. Consequently the strength to overcome my personal problems, also, was to come from within and not without.

A couple of years were to go by before I picked up the books that acted as catalysts for the beginning of my spiritual quest. One was Herman Hesse's *Siddhartha*, the other a book on yoga. I began to experiment with a vegetarian diet, and to practise yoga postures which helped me to become more aware of myself and my body. This led me to the practice of meditation. I really did not have any guidance in this, and wanted to search further.

Through a friend at work I was invited to a ceremony attended by Buddhist monks at the Stokes Valley monastery. This was something quite new - my first real introduction to an Eastern religion. I was immediately impressed by the serenity of the monks and the discourse given by the Achaan (teacher) was so simple, direct and relevant it was as if he was speaking directly to me. His words seemed to confirm what I already felt but could not express consciously. I now began to see how we create our own suffering through our unconscious reacting to sense stimuli, craving for the pleasant and avoiding the unpleasant. I began to visit the monastery regularly and to practise meditation. I decided after just a couple of months to make a break with my present way of life and to travel to Asia to study meditation and yoga. I arrived in Thailand and went to a famous forest monastery in the South, but found myself fleeing the boredom and discomfort and mosquitoes for the excitement of Bangkok, where I found a Dutch monk who was willing to teach me meditation.

After ten days of practice in Bangkok I went to a quieter temple out of the city, for intensive practice. The ten days I spent there must have been some of the most difficult, but also most rewarding, days in my life. When I went there to meditate I considered I would experience feelings of great peace and bliss but instead, with meditating for twelve hours a day, alternating sitting and walking practice, I experienced pain and discomfort greater than ever before. Rather than trying to avoid this discomfort, I was to watch the sensation of pain, to develop a patient abiding with and detachment from whatever arose in the body and mind. I found myself with doubts as to why I was submitting myself to such torture. But with gentle encouragement from my meditation instructor I managed to use the discomfort as an object of my awareness and just watch the sensation of pain itself and the mind-states it created; anger, restlessness, and then drowsiness, boredom. There were intervals when I was able just to be whatever was there, to let go. In these moments I experienced a space in the mind and a realisation that by letting go one could be free of conflict.

Then there would be more pain in the knees, I would be restless and tempted to leave to find a place on the beach of one of those idyllic Thai islands. My mind wandered off to India and other places, planning, judging, remembering. However I stuck through to the end of the retreat, and left feeling more at peace and more aware not only of myself but also of things around me.

From that point there was no looking back. Fourteen months of travel followed, a forest monastery in Northeast Thailand, a meditation centre in the beautiful hill country of Sri Lanka, a yoga ashram in India. Then the return to New Zealand and the humdrum of everyday existence.

Life is outwardly no more exciting than it was before, but I have developed a greater ability to find contentment with what is, and to use life situations as an opportunity to learn more about myself. Buddhism appeals to me as a religion for the very reason that it does not provide all the answers, does not tell me what I must do or point to a separate God that I should believe in and turn to for help. Rather, it teaches one to be responsible for oneself and provides the frame of inquiry and a path of morality, wisdom, and mental development one can follow, and by which one can realise true inner freedom through one's own effort.

Of the Buddhists whose upbringing has been within the Buddhist civilisation, the vast majority now resident in New Zealand have come from South-East Asia and Sri Lanka. These include refugees from Laos, Cambodia and Vietnam, as well as those who have come more freely from Thailand, Sri Lanka, Burma, Malaysia, Hong Kong and Singapore. For these people, Buddhist culture is at the heart of life itself. No amount of academic reflection on the Buddhist teaching can convey the way their hearts respond to it.

As Buddhism has few dogmas, and has grown up hand in hand with popular beliefs and practices in the various cultures of Asia, different individuals may express themselves rather differently. Thus a Chinese-Cambodian funeral might involve chanting of Pali scriptures, Chinese ancestral worship, Taoist ritual, and various other observances which have evolved out of the Buddhist way. The lay practitioners themselves may not know which of these rituals is in fact Buddhist. This does not matter to them, however much it may be confusing to the casual observer, or the scholar seeking to neatly categorise the array of cultural practices.

Usually the elders will be the most natural in the expression of their traditions, and will take the role of organising and directing their ceremonies. Those who are younger may at times feel somewhat uncomfortable or a little perplexed, trying to relate ancient cultural background to the totally new and often contrasting Western environment. Children of new settlers do not always understand the profundity and pertinence of their cultural roots, so that for them the religious functions of traditional Buddhism may at times seem an anachronism in present-day New Zealand. Theirs is often a search for security and identity as Kiwis in their new environment, though some do feel motivated to understand their own traditions at a deeper level as well.

Here is the story of Ramini, an ethnic Buddhist woman now living in New Zealand.

Ramini's story:

I was born in September 1947 on the eve of Sri Lanka's independence from British rule in February 1948. I would grow up free to speak my language and be a Sinhalese, and most of all, to be able to practise, openly and with pride, the religion my people had treasured and protected for over 2000 years.

Those of preceding generations had been forced to study in English, most often in Christian mission schools, for there were few Buddhist schools. Though not forced to convert to Christianity (as were thousands in the sixteenth century when the Portuguese ruled) they were made to feel that their faith was inferior. It was the Christian who was viewed favourably, and many converted for the advantages being a Christian brought.

My grandmother told tales of how her businessman father would wear a crucifix when out on business, and on returning home would hang it on a nail outside the house. At home, like the vast majority of Sinhalese, they were devout Buddhists, nurturing a faith born of conviction, studying the teachings of Buddha and supporting the Sangha, the guardians of the Dhamma.

I, and those of the post-independence generation, would be educated in our mother tongue, Sinhala or Tamil. And no one, Buddhist, Christian, Hindu or Muslim, would be forced to study a religion other than their own.

I attended Visakha Vidyalaya, the leading Buddhist girls' school. At school the day started with paying homage to the Buddha and observing the five precepts:

Refrain from - taking life
- theft
- sexual misconduct
- lying
- intoxicants

Buddhist values were learnt along with the usual school subjects. Discipline was firm, never harsh. Modesty and decorum were insisted upon, especially in the 1960s when the miniskirt sent uniform hemlines up! We were taught not only to respect our teachers, elders and each other, but education itself. Even a book was respected, never thrown carelessly on the floor, to be stepped on or over. The standard of education was extremely high, and Visakha competed not only with other girls' schools but with the best of the boys' in the numbers admitted to universities. Women in our society, while knowing and accepting limits and limitations, were never considered intellectually inferior. After all, we achieved universal franchise in the 1930s and produced the world's first woman Prime Minister!

The schools reinforced the Buddhist way, which had been 'our way' since the third century BCE. Buddhist ethics and principles influenced all who lived in Sri Lanka. Generosity and sharing are qualities that are very much a part of our lives. No one dropping in close to mealtimes is allowed to leave without sharing your meal. No self-respecting housewife will prepare a meal that will not feed an extra mouth. And as Buddhists we take special joy in offering alms to the monks as well as the poor and destitute.

Most Buddhist households have a set day each month to send alms food to the temple. Birthdays and anniversaries are celebrated not with parties, but by auspicious chanting ceremonies followed by the offering of alms to the monks. Family and friends get together with relations, close and distant, strengthening family ties.

Very early in life we learnt of rebirth and *karma*. We grew up with a healthy fear of the law of karmic retribution. We were told that naughty children who misused their limbs to hit and kick would be reborn without the limbs. 'You spit on people; you'll be reborn a snail, leaving a trail of saliva.' 'Those people, the poor and beggars, haven't been generous in previous lives.' 'See that pretty lady? She would have offered flowers to the Buddha with a pure heart. It is reflected in her face in this life.'

As in most Buddhist households we'd wake to the chanting over the radio. We'd fall asleep to the soothing sounds of a parent reciting *sutras* (scripture). In a moment of fear, *itipi so bhagava* comes to mind, recounting the noble qualities of the Buddha: 'like a warrior gone to war, looking up at the banner of his leader he is filled with courage, and is not afraid.'

But our home differed from the typical Buddhist home in that we didn't have a shrine where offerings were made and sutras were chanted daily. My father didn't believe in ritual or the efficacy of 'blessings' to ward off misfortune. He lived (and lives) an exemplary life, strictly adhering to the dhamma. He was patient, kind, loving, generous and full of humour. Only once have I seen him giving in to anger. He taught by example. He influenced without imposing. When my brother wanted to study medicine my father was not happy thinking of all the animals whose lives would be sacrificed. My brother saw his point of view and decided to study engineering instead. He discouraged me from studying law as he believed lawyers lived off others' misfortunes for the most part. He wanted us to pursue careers that were *samma ajiva* (right livelihood). Our lives must always work towards Nirvana. 'There would be no doctors or lawyers if all thought as you did,' people scoffed. But he'd smile and say nothing, knowing very well that this was not a possibility.

My mother insisted that children needed some outward form of practice. So on *poya* or observance days we'd go to the temple. Often we'd observe the eight precepts. My father rarely took part, but would wait on us instead. Even now it is my mother who points out our shortcomings, constantly exhorting us to make an even greater effort. During Wesak she'd help us make lanterns and decorate the house with flags and streamers.

Ah Wesak, that glorious festival of light, of goodness, of caring and sharing! The dawn of Wesak is greeted by temple bells and thousands of white-clad devotees going to temple to observe the eight precepts. And the moment it grows dark, oil lamps, paper lanterns candle-lit, and electric bulbs light up, making the country a fairyland of light. The streets come alive with people thronging to see *pandals*, huge constructions depicting various aspects of the Buddha's life, decorated with a million dancing lights. Folk theatre blossoms, with plays and puppet shows enacting the Buddha's birth stories being performed on makeshift stages by the roadside. Special stalls are set up to distribute free food and drinks to the sightseers. There are processions with elephants, dancers, drummers, flag and torch bearers weaving their way along the streets escorting holy relics in special expositions.

When after eight years of marriage I had to leave Sri Lanka to join my husband in Singapore, I was determined that my children should not lose our Buddhist values and cultural heritage. We were delighted to find a thriving and active Buddhist community and a temple 'Sri Lankaramaya', with Sri Lankan monks for whom I would take *dana* (gifts of food) as I had done at home.

Our social life centred around the temple. On Sundays we'd all be there, me teaching at the Dhamma school, the children following the lessons, and my husband making himself useful where needed. But before long I started to realise why my father distanced himself from temples and monks. I too had his (almost puritanically) high expectations of the monks' ideals. Disillusionment sets in when you find your idols have clay feet; when you feel their standards and expectations are not as high or idealistic as yours. I began to see the corrupting influence of materialism, and the gifts of money the Chinese devotees showered on the monks, changing their outlook. But I'd remember my father saying, 'Good and bad, it is the monks who have preserved the Dhamma for us to practise today. It is the duty of every lay Buddhist to support the Sangha.'

It was in Singapore that I began to experience the true essence of Buddhism: that there is *dukkha* (inner conflict), and that there is a way out of it. Living in a country where there is poverty and want, you become immune to it, accepting it as *karma*. It is in a rich materialistic environment that the contrast between the haves and the have-nots becomes apparent. Being separated from family and loved ones, living among cold uncaring strangers, *tanha* (craving) developed in shops loaded with gorgeous things one can't afford. I started understanding what *dukkha* was!

Then Venerable Dhammika, an Australian monk who had lived many years in Sri Lanka, introduced us to meditation. In Sri Lanka, meditation is practised almost exclusively by the monks of the forest tradition. Save on an observance day, when we would observe the eight precepts, meditation was not part of the Buddhist way for the lay-person. Regular meditations with Venerable Dhammika brought tranquility and peace to my restless, worrying and dissatisfied mind.

Then we moved to New Zealand. Thinking that I was going to a spiritual desert I brought along Dhamma books and tapes to help me in my practice. But it was our good *karma* indeed that led us to New Zealand. For, at the Wellington monastery, I found monks who taught meditation as a way of life, monks who, I could see, practised well, directly, insightfully (as the stanza I often chanted said they ought) to the best of their ability.

Practising meditation under the guidance of the monks, especially over ten-day retreats, brought fresh insight and understanding. I started to see the Dhamma in all its purity and beauty, through the eyes of those whose vision was not clouded by the trappings of ritual and tradition; the Dhamma as the Buddha taught, direct and straightforward. I started believing that the Dhamma is 'here and now'. The aspiration of Buddhists in Sri Lanka in performing meritorious deeds is, 'May I, by this deed, become enlightened in the time of the next Buddha.' I realised that without meditation and a constant effort to train the mind, I could not become enlightened even in the time of a future Buddha.

Though enlightenment is not near at hand, I have faith and confidence that I have at last started trekking the long and rigorous path that leads to the 'stream' (of enlightenment). My aspiration is: 'that wherever I am born, may there be an upright mind, mindfulness and wisdom, austerity and vigour. May harmful influences not weaken my efforts. Until I attain liberation, whatever faults I have, may they quickly perish.'

Those personal reflections from Ramini are especially poignant considering the violent decay in Sinhalese culture in the past few years. Ramini's nostalgic description of a wholesome childhood within the framework of a healthy Buddhist environment offers the reader some idea of what often underlies the deeper feelings of other Asian Buddhists (Cambodian and Laotian, for instance) in New Zealand, when they speak of their Buddhist heritage.

Monastery and monks

Among adherents to Buddhism in New Zealand there are those who enjoy the more traditional forms of religious congregation - forms which include a rich variety and texture of ritual and ceremony. There are also those who live by Buddhist principles and are quite diligent in their investigation of the teaching yet who do not feel drawn to the traditions that have grown in Asia. This creates no problem, as the external manifestations of religious convention are seen merely as tools that can be used skilfully to realise the Buddhist vision of freedom. What counts is whether the use or non-use of religious conventions is conducive to success in the spiritual quest.

To understand traditional forms of Buddhism popular in this country it will be helpful if we consider the role of the monastery and its monks in the life of a Buddhist congregation. (A trip to Southeast Asia, Tibet or Japan would help our inquiry and give us some insight into the importance of the monastery or temple.)

In secular New Zealand there is little emphasis on spiritual traditions and the indications of religion are mostly rather peripheral to the main concerns of society. In Asia, however, religion and culture have always been synonymous. The great festivals and observances that punctuate each yearly cycle are celebrations in which the monastery and the monks play a central role. Because, in Asian cultures, the importance of the group is stressed more than that of the individual, these festivals are opportunities to express the joy of great communal gatherings.

The rites of passage common to all - birth, marriage and death - are given due recognition in ceremonies performed at the monasteries under the auspices of the monks. Even when there is no event of particular significance, the monastery offers serenity and refuge; even if only for a brief respite from the market-place.

The monks provide an example of human aspiration to spiritual understanding. Each morning they walk through the village or town, moving silently past the houses. Alms-food, prepared by the faithful layfolk, is placed into their bowls. This daily activity, involving generosity and humility, is an ever-present but quiet reminder of the religious side of life. Since the monk's life is based on simplicity, morality, and a concern for human suffering, a noble standard of conduct and aspiration is constantly available to the local community.

Buddhist monks are the teachers, counsellors, psychologists, religious guides and spiritual friends of the community. The inevitable confusions and troubles which any community faces are brought before the monks for consideration. Much of the spiritual teaching manifests itself from these situations, so that life's problems become sources of edification. The schools of primary and secondary education are often found in the temple grounds. Although the monks no longer play such an important role in teaching secular subjects, their mere presence, and the atmosphere of these religious sanctuaries, have a significant effect on the children.

The monastery is an open place, and one of the primary duties of the monk is to be available for the needs of the lay community. Visitors are always welcome. For those interested in deepening their spiritual understanding, the monasteries provide opportunities for the study of religious texts and the practice of meditation. Among those who are keen to develop the more contemplative aspects of Buddhism, there are the forest monasteries somewhat removed from village life, which offer the tranquility and spaciousness that are so conducive to silent reflection.

Another aspect is that of *punya*. This word has no direct equivalent in English but is sometimes, rather awkwardly, translated as 'merit'. From this comes the idea of 'merit-making', which to the Western ear sounds like spiritual materialism. One Buddhist commentator has translated the word as 'grace'. Most simply we might say that *punya* is the opening of the heart to goodness, and thus is the cause of happiness. This then entails generosity, morality, devotion, gratitude, reverence, self-sacrifice, kindness, serenity and wisdom - and thus no simple word of translation suffices.

Some explanation of the monk's life is necessary at this point. Strictly speaking, the monk is an alms mendicant who has no salary, cannot use money, and cannot grow or store food. His is a life of renunciation and as such his daily sustenance is dependent on the generosity of the lay community. Thus where there are no generous lay people, there are no monks.

As the monks each day walk silently through Southeast Asian villages and towns receiving the generous offerings of the laity, *punya*, the manifestation of goodness, is displayed. Because monks are considered the spiritual guides and counsellors of the local community, making offerings to the monastic order is a very special kind of *punya* - one of the most important acts of devotion in the Buddhist way. This creates a unique relationship between the monks and the laity; a relationship which would not be possible if the monastic communities were closed orders or if they charged for their services. The occasions of giving to the monks, ranging from their daily meal to the grand annual festivals of offering robes, have always been very important in Buddhist cultures.

The manifestation of goodness or *punya* can occur in many ways. The observance of moral precepts, generous actions, meditation, contemplation - all of these involve *punya*. But one of the highest forms is the giving of the teaching. It is said that the gift of truth excels all other gifts. To be able to give the gift of truth, that is, to be able to teach with real understanding, requires considerable dedication to study and meditation. If an individual is willing to make the necessary commitment, even for a short time, then the Buddhist community is most enthusiastic in giving its support. Admission into the novitiate or into monkhood, often for as little as three months, has always been considered most auspicious and, hence, great *punya*.

These many occasions of *punya* are thus a way of uplifting the heart to the joy of goodness, and so a way of letting go of the inevitable fears, doubts and uncertainties that beset the human mind. The Buddhist monastery, then, is a place where those of faith can go to regain their confidence and inner serenity.

All the above-mentioned functions (refuge, spiritual inspiration, moral example, education, counselling, community centre, *punya*, meditation, religious study, rites of passage) make the Buddhist temple or monastery indispensable to the health and well-being of typical Asian Buddhist societies. But what is the relevance of the monastery in New Zealand? Obviously to those who have been nurtured in this ancient tradition the monastery or temple is a great source of comfort and serenity. But what will happen in two or three decades? Will the monasteries still be relevant, or will they die out, like the joss-houses of the old Chinese gold diggers?

No clear answer can be given, and time will allow for a natural development to take place. But a possible future role for the Buddhist temple or monastery could be compared to that of the marae. Like the marae, the temple is a place of refuge where traditional values are honoured and where the community finds a common ground. There the individual takes second place to the group. The elders feel confident and at ease and are treated with respect and kindness. It is a place where the most important aspects of cultural maintenance - morality, generosity, compassion, serenity and wisdom - are encouraged and praised. These things are indispensable to the well-being of any society.

Rather than being thought of as an alien intruder or an anachronism, the Buddhist temple or monastery will then be seen as beneficial to New Zealand's culture, complementary to existing social structures with similar concerns. Because it is steeped in a profound and practical wisdom, which has been of benefit to society for over two millennia, the Buddhist monastery can significantly contribute to this country's spiritual growth in the future.

The practice of Buddhism is in no way restricted to the life of the monastery or temple. For many people the primary contact with Buddhism has been through meditation retreats, both here and abroad. From this has come a commitment to carry the practice of meditation into ordinary life. Like-minded people have formed informal groups which meet weekly in someone's home to practise meditation and discuss the Buddha's teaching. Having formed an association of meditators they have then organised weekend and ten-day retreats. From these retreats a personal daily life practice of morning and evening meditation has evolved, depending of course on the diligence and commitment of each individual.

For those who live near a monastery or temple and who find the traditional forms inspiring, the practice would be enhanced by contact with the monastery. Most common would be a weekly visit to the monastery for meditation and reflection on the Buddha's teaching. As the monasteries have an ongoing programme that includes meditation instruction, many beginners would go to receive instruction in some basic form of meditation. For many of these beginners there would be no intention (and from the side of the monastery no need) to become Buddhist, but rather the wish to enhance their own spiritual endeavours by developing some practical means of achieving inner serenity.

One of the interesting aspects of Buddhism in New Zealand is the harmonious gathering of Asian and Western peoples at the monastery. For the Asian Buddhist the monastery is a haven of sanity and peaceful reflection. For them it is a great joy to go to the temple with the family, offer food to the monks and imbibe the peaceful atmosphere. Meditation, however, is in the eyes of many Asian folk only for the monks, not the laity. They see their function as the generous supporters of the monastery so that the monks can get on with the training, and be available for the various needs of the lay community.

On the other hand the Westerner initially approaches the monastery with a view to developing some understanding and proficiency in meditation. After some time of visiting the monastery a sense of gratitude begins to arise, and thoughts of helping the monastery become important. The Westerner then notices the Asian folk diligently preparing a meal or helping in some other way. Thus the lesson that the East gives to the West is that of generosity, service and gratitude.

At the same time, however, the Asian folk notice the Westerners diligently practising meditation and questioning the teaching. This stimulates both curiosity and surprise among the Asian Buddhists, and they begin to look more deeply into their own roots. Thus the lesson the West gives to the East is one of investigation, application and meditation. Where such mutual support and encouragement take place it is most inspiring and indicates how the values of people with different cultural conditioning can enhance each other's appreciation and understanding of life.

In conclusion we might note that the expressions of traditional Buddhism vary all the way from the baroque richness of a Tibetan monastery to the austere elegance of a Zen temple. The commitment to the teaching varies from individual to individual. Some feel drawn to ancient traditional forms and the mutual support of large groups. Others feel no attraction to ritual and ceremony, preferring to develop the Buddha's path on their own or with a small group of friends. But it is safe to say that the path of Buddhist practice begins as an inner journey in the context of the world around us. Whatever the external trappings of that world might be, the important issue is inner understanding from which a compassionate and wise response to the world is possible.

Buddhist monasteries and centres in New Zealand

Theravadan

The way of Buddhism practised in Burma, Cambodia, Laos, Thailand and Sri Lanka (and to some extent Malaysia and Vietnam) is known as *Theravada*, or 'the way of the elders'. New Zealand has four monasteries and various affiliated organisations which follow this tradition.

Cambodian Buddhist Temple - Island Bay

The temple is in Wellington's Island Bay and serves as the focal point for the Cambodian community throughout New Zealand. There are regular meditations and religious services at the temple as well as classes in the Cambodian language for the youngsters. The spiritual head is Venerable Ajahn Maha Suthep, a Cambodian monk who trained in Bangkok and taught Buddhist scripture in Thailand for many years. He travels to Dunedin, Christchurch, Auckland, Palmerston North, Hamilton and other centres serving the needs of this far-flung community.

Bodhinyanarama Monastery - Stokes Valley

Bodhinyanarama is a Buddhist community situated in forty-five acres of bush land at the end of Stokes Valley about thirty minutes by car from Wellington. It is affiliated with monasteries in Thailand, England, Australia and Switzerland. At present there are four monks in residence, Ajahn Viradhammo, Ven. Karuniko, Ven. Thanasilo, Ven. Nyanapalo. All the monks speak fluent English and because they are well versed in the traditions of Theravada Buddhism, the monastery is a meeting of East and West; multi-culturalism in action.

Regular meditation is held each Thursday and Sunday evenings at 7.30pm. Sunday mornings have become a time when families like to come to the monastery. It is an occasion to offer food to the monks; share a meal with others; listen to teaching; and generally uplift the heart with the goodness of the occasion. Meditation retreats are held regularly and the great festivals are observed during the year. Weekly meditations are led by the monks from Stokes Valley every Monday evening at the Quaker meeting house in Mount Victoria, Wellington.

Auckland Buddhist Vihara

Affiliated with Bodhinyanarama monastery is the Auckland Theravada Buddhist Association at whose *vihara* (meditation centre) are held similar activities to those of the Wellington monastery. Each Thursday and Sunday evenings there is a meditation evening commencing at 7.30pm. On the fourth Sunday in each month commencing at 10am there is a family day similar to that held at the Wellington monastery.

The Auckland *vihara* has a peaceful shrine room where people may go to meditate and perform traditional religious observances. This centre also has one of the better Buddhist libraries in New Zealand, and books can be taken out on short-term loans.

Laotian Buddhist Temple - Mangere

The new settlers from Laos have banded together to purchase a house in Mangere which now serves as their religious centre. There are usually two monks in residence, both of whom were born in Laos. This centre has regular religious services and offers a venue for the various Buddhist festivals throughout the year.

Mahayanan

The other major tradition of Buddhism, known as *Mahayana* ('Great Vehicle') is represented in New Zealand by a number of organisations.

Dorje Chang Institute- Auckland

Dedicated to the practice and preservation of the Gelugpa tradition of Tibetan Buddhism, this centre for advanced Buddhist studies is situated in Herne Bay, Auckland. It has a meditation hall, bookstall and book and tape library. The institute's resident Geshe (teacher) is Kensur Rinpoche, who gives weekly instruction and leads meditation retreats at the Institute and in other centres throughout the country. Annual Buddhist celebrations including Wesak are observed, and seasonal festivals according to the Tibetan lunar calendar. High lamas such as the Institute's Spiritual Director Lama Thubten Zopa Rinpoche (who received initiation and teachings from His Holiness the Dalai Lama) are regularly brought to New Zealand.

NZ Karma Kagyu Trust - Kaukapakapa

The Karma Kagyu tradition of Tibetan Buddhism emphasises the oral transmission of teachings through recognised teachers. At Kaukapakapa, near Albany, the Trust is constructing Karma Chokhorling (shortened name, Karma Choeling), a monastery and retreat centre with amenities which include Tibetan-style *stupas* (commemorative and symbolic structures), a seven metre high Buddha statue, a temple with shrine room, meditation hall and accommodation for *lamas*, and huts for residents and visitors.

Ven. Lama Karma Samten has been resident teacher at Karma Choeling since 1982. Besides daily *puja* (worship services) and meditation, regular courses are held at this and other Karma Kagyu centres (Whangarei and Wellington) with frequent visits by noted lamas and teachers who specialise in communicating the relevance of Buddhist perspectives and insights in today's world.

Dhargyey Centre - Dunedin

This centre was established recently as a teaching base for Venerable Geshe Ngawang Dhargyey, formerly principal teacher at the Tibetan Library in Dharamsala, India, for many years. Geshe Dhargyey, through his teachings and books, has gained an international reputation as one of the greatest living masters of Tibetan Buddhism. His teaching programme at the centre covers the great Mahayana

Jan Crawford

Tibetan-style stupa at Karma Choeling

scriptures, as well as instruction in meditation and integrating Buddhist practice in daily life. The centre's library includes a complete collection of the Buddha's teachings (the *Kangyur*) as well as the collected works of the great Tibetan master Tsong Kharpa and his two disciples, Khedrup Je and Gyalsap Je.

Kwan Yin Buddhist Society - Auckland

Non-sectarian and keeping in close touch with other Buddhist organisations, this Auckland society mainly follows the Mahayana tradition, specifically Chinese Buddhism, as members are overwhelmingly immigrant Chinese. Weekly services are held for chanting of *mantras* and for *dharma* discussion.

Friends of the Western Buddhist Order

The Friends of the Western Buddhist Order was founded in 1967 by Ven. Maha Sthavira Sangharakshita, an English-born Buddhist monk who spent many years in India. Drawing on all the main traditions, the FWBO has its own distinctive approach to the Buddha's teaching, communicating it to the West through more than thirty centres worldwide. The FWBO's Auckland Buddhist Centre teaches the principles and practice of meditation, holds regular retreats, and celebrates the main Buddhist festivals. There is a similar centre in Wellington.

Zen Society of New Zealand

Zen Buddhism was established in China by the enlightened Indian monk Bodhidharma in 528 CE and today is transmitted to the West particularly by Korean and Japanese masters. The Zen Society coordinates Zen Buddhist groups and practitioners throughout New Zealand. Emphasis is placed on *zazen* (Zen meditation) with groups sitting regularly in the main centres, and on *sesshin* (five-seven day meditation retreat) currently held once a year. One-day sittings, lectures and weekend retreats are also organised.

Other Buddhist organisations and societies are coming into existence, to meet diverse needs and interests. Some (like the Vietnamese and Sri Lankan Buddhist Associations) are organised along ethnic lines. Some are meditation-centred (like the Vipassana groups) or, like Shorinji Kenpo, practise martial arts drawing on Zen traditions. Others, like the study and retreat centre at Wangapeka, near Nelson, are inspired by Buddhist teachings but embrace other spiritual traditions as well. As Buddhism is increasingly established within contemporary New Zealand, the range of organisations will no doubt continue to grow.

Further reading

Buddhist Scriptures, selected and translated by Edward Conze, Harmondsworth: Penguin Books, 1959.
Goldstein, Joseph, *The Experience of Insight*, New York: Unity Press, 1980.
Khantipalo, Bhikkhu, *Calm and Insight*, London and Dublin: Curzon Press, 1981.
Rahula, Walpola, *What the Buddha Taught*, New York: Grove Press, 1959.
Saddhatissa, H., *The Life of the Buddha*, London: George Allen & Unwin, 1976.

Christianity:
Eastern Orthodoxy

Raymond Oppenheim

When the tiny Eastern Christian community of New Zealand uses the term 'Orthodoxy' in describing itself, it believes it has an historical right to do so. In fact, it has more of a right to use such an all-embracing title than the Church of Rome has to call itself 'Catholic'. For, in a very real sense, Orthodoxy is the original church, from which all the others broke away.

Today, even in such a remote land as ours, the Orthodox seek to maintain a faith and a religious life which have changed very little in many centuries. In an era of liturgical change for Catholics, Anglicans, and Protestants, the Orthodox pride themselves on the antiquity of their style of worship. For they are a church which claims that it has never had a reformation. The Orthodox Liturgy (the name they give to their equivalent of the Catholic Mass or Protestant Communion) is celebrated in New Zealand in virtually the same form as it was a dozen centuries ago. No style of Christian worship is more elaborate, more artistic, or more time-consuming. It is designed in such a way that all the senses are involved - it is a worship which the believer can hear, see, touch, taste, and smell. There is intellectual challenge, emotional catharsis, and aesthetic enrichment - all in forms which are rooted in the context of national culture and ancient heritage. The language of worship varies, as does the art and music, with each Church using a distinctive national style. The rich polyphony of Russian harmony contrasts with the almost Oriental sound of Greek chanting. And yet, the service itself is virtually the same throughout the Orthodox world.

But outsiders are bemused by what they find. People wander around in the services, come late, leave early, chat with friends in a corner, or step outside for a smoke if they find the priest boring. To the Orthodox Christian, worship is something you be, rather than something you do. For them, worship is perpetual, the church is already crowded with angels before the service begins, and they come to 'tune in and turn on'. It is impossible to sit back and be passive - as they see it; participate if you like, but don't pretend. If an Orthodox worshipper loses interest in what is going on at the altar, it is perfectly acceptable to withdraw into a corner, near a favourite icon, to pray for a sick uncle. But individual involvement is required.

There is constant use of the sign of the cross (right to left, rather than the Western left to right) and a great deal of individual physical response (prostration, bowing, kneeling). Much attention is shown to the icons (religious paintings), depicting Christ, the Blessed Virgin Mary, feasts of the Christian calendar, and seemingly countless saints. The icons become trysting places for the believers, windows through which they can encounter the spiritual meaning of the subjects.

Affection is lavished upon them - they are kissed, candles are lit before them, and they are adorned with flowers. It is clear in the mind of the Orthodox that these are objects of veneration, not worship. But to the more reserved Protestant visitor, the distinction is unclear, and the normal Orthodox style of worship may appear to be bordering on the idolatrous.

If the Westerner finds the Orthodox style of worship peculiar, rest assured that the Orthodox feels the same way about Anglican Mattins. In the Liturgy, the worshipper rarely uses books, even more rarely follows the service word for word, and is never given page numbers by the celebrant. The only unison activities are the Creed, the Lord's Prayer, and an occasional hymn. Otherwise, everyone does his or her own thing. As a concession to the West, some of New Zealand's Orthodox churches now have pews, but many worshippers still follow the old tradition of standing throughout the service.

Most of our nation's Orthodox Christians have roots in one of the traditionally Orthodox countries. The dividing line between Eastern and Western churches follows roughly the ancient boundary between the Eastern and Western Roman Empires. Italy is West and Greece is East. Albania and Yugoslavia are divided. Hungary, Czechoslovakia, Poland, and the Baltic states are West. Bulgaria, Romania, and Russia are East. Changing borders, over the centuries, have left the Ukrainians divided, and some representatives of each family remain stranded on the wrong sides of borders.

Each national church is autocephalous, meaning 'self-headed'. In a traditionally Orthodox country, there is a single Orthodox church, but although each church is a member of the larger family, there is no central authority over them all. In Greece, there are only Greek Orthodox churches, although there are parishes within that jurisdiction which may have the occasional service according to the Russian or Romanian tradition. What is important to the Orthodox is the unity of the church family within a region, under its bishop. There are not meant to be any competing jurisdictions.

A parallel with the Anglicans can be seen in the fact that all Anglican parishes in New Zealand are part of the same jurisdiction. There isn't an Australian Anglican parish in one part of the city and an American Episcopalian parish in another, while the rest are parishes of the Church of the Province of New Zealand. In the same way, a decision by the Australian Anglicans not to ordain women to the priesthood has no bearing on the Anglican Church in New Zealand. The Orthodox follow exactly the same pattern. Each national church makes its own decisions, and the fact that the Romanian church has deaconesses does not require the Greek church to do so.

The Orthodox have a central figure, the Ecumenical Patriarch of Constantinople, based in Istanbul (the modern Turkish name for the ancient Byzantine capital). Like the Archbishop of Canterbury, he exercises a unifying rather than a governing role over the family of national churches. His is a primacy of honour, as the first among equals. Within each Orthodox Church, there is a titular head, and in the major churches he is given the title of Patriarch. His traditional jurisdiction is only within the borders of his nation, and to communities of his own people overseas, in non-Orthodox countries.Throughout the Orthodox family, this pattern has been maintained until the twentieth century. Mission offspring were always the responsibility of the missionary church. For example, the Russians had authority in America, because of their missions in Alaska and California. The Ecumenical Patriarch has always had responsibility for remote congregations, in the same way that the Archbishop of Canterbury has responsibility for the Anglicans in Korea or Bermuda or the Falkland Islands. But this system broke down early in the twentieth century, much to the confusion of all parties. As international migration increased, different ethnic groups sought to preserve their traditions. This was further complicated by the Russian Revolution and two world wars. Communication was difficult, administrative ties were often impossible or undesirable, and swarms of refugees made the preservation of Orthodox unity in the diaspora a forlorn hope. Today, the unity of Orthodox jurisdictions within individual countries is maintained only in the homelands. Overseas - in Europe, in America, and in Australasia - a multiplicity of jurisdictions overlap. Rather than a single Orthodox Church in New Zealand, we find five different churches - one small and four tiny.

The Orthodox in New Zealand

Orthodox Christians represent less than two tenths of one per cent of our population, compared with two per cent in the USA and three per cent in Australia. Most New Zealand Orthodox are Greek and come under the jurisdiction of the Ecumenical Patriarchate of Constantinople. Three other Patriarchates are represented - Romania, Serbia (in Yugoslavia), and Antioch (in Syria). The fifth group is under the Russian Orthodox Church Outside of Russia, an exile Synod. According to ancient tradition, the Ecumenical Patriarchate of Constantinople should have authority in New Zealand, as our Orthodox are a transplanted colony in the diaspora, rather than a mission church. And it is the Ecumenical Patriarchate which has sent New Zealand's only Orthodox Bishop - Metropolitan Dionysios Psiachas. But he does not have jurisdiction over the non-Greeks. The other four groups look to bishops in Australia for their oversight.

Raymond Oppenheim

Metropolitan Dionysios censing an icon of the Virgin and Child in the Greek Cathedral, Wellington

The Antiochian Orthodox

Individual Eastern Christians came to New Zealand in the early colonial days, but the first Orthodox community was made up of several Lebanese families, who settled in Dunedin in the 1880s. They looked to the Patriarchate of Antioch, based today in Damascus, Syria, as their source of authority, but Syria was very far away. For a period of years, there was a Russian Archimandrite (a senior monastic priest), living in exile in Dunedin, but this small community has never had a priest from the Near East. In 1911, their Church of St. Michael was consecrated as New Zealand's first Orthodox Church, and today is one of three in our country under the jurisdiction of Bishop Gibran, the Antiochian bishop in Sydney, Australia.

The Dunedin community is under the care of the South Island's only Orthodox priest, a former Anglican vicar who has converted to Orthodoxy. Also under the same jurisdiction is the Church of St. Simon and St. Jude, in Ashley, north of Christchurch. It is a former Anglican church, in a rural setting, and it is hoped that it can become the centre of an Orthodox farming community. Many of the Dunedin congregation, and virtually all of the small Ashley congregation, are converts to Orthodoxy, and the Antiochian parishes represent the only group of New Zealand Orthodox with a substantial percentage of converts from other traditions. The third parish is the

Church of St. Ignatius, named after the great second-century martyr-bishop of Antioch. It is in a rented Anglican hall in Waterview, Auckland. The parish dates from 1978, and is based on the local Lebanese community, although the majority of its members are converts, as is its recently ordained priest. This tiny Christian community of only three small parishes and less than one hundred faithful nationally, is a member of the Conference of Churches in Aotearoa New Zealand. Its two clergy participate in many ecumenical events, and its vision is one of growing numbers of New Zealand converts to Orthodoxy.

The Greek Orthodox

The second jurisdiction historically is by far the largest - the Greeks. Australia's substantial Greek community has meant the gradual influx of Greeks into New Zealand. Melbourne is now the second-largest Greek city in the world, with more Greeks than any city but Athens. As family-minded people, the Greeks have tended to colonise in groups, and most of New Zealand's Greeks live in Wellington, where the colourful Greek Fair (on the Sunday following 25 March) is an important annual event. There are about four thousand Greek Orthodox Christians in the Wellington area, more than two thirds of the nation's total. As the original migrants were mostly fishermen from the Aegean Islands, they settled primarily in Seatoun and Island Bay. The census of 1878 includes twenty-nine Greek Orthodox, but the first Greek parish was founded only in 1935. As has often been the case overseas, the Greeks of Wellington formed a parish on their own, without the supervision of a bishop. Official ties were with the Ecumenical Patriarchate, via Australia, but local Greeks established their own administration and finance. The isolation of the much smaller Greek community of Auckland, numbering now only about 400, has produced a stronger sense of local autonomy.

In 1970, Constantinople appointed a bishop for New Zealand, with the extra responsibility of supervising the scattered Greek parishes of south and east Asia. The hierarch based in Wellington is also Exarch (to use the proper title) of Greeks and local converts, from India all the way to South Korea. For nearly twenty years, the same man has held the post, and he now bears the honoured title of Metropolitan. Needless to say, with the great deal of travel required, it is convenient that all Greek bishops are celibate monastics. He has a heritage of local independence, resulting from decades without a resident bishop, and it has not been easy for him to assume administrative authority over his congregations.

As soon as he arrived in New Zealand, Metropolitan Dionysios undertook quite a programme of expansion. On 19 December 1971, he consecrated the Church of the Annunciation of the Virgin Mary, situated at the foot of Wellington's Mt. Victoria. It is a handsome building, constructed in traditional Byzantine ecclesiastical style. In contrast to most Western churches, the building is virtually cube-shaped, under an impressive dome, and the interior is decorated with modern Greek icons. It was built to be an Orthodox church, whereas most New Zealand Orthodox churches formerly belonged to the Roman Catholics,

Raymond Oppenheim

Baptism in the Greek Cathedral

Anglicans, or Protestants. Based at this church is the only full-time Orthodox priest in New Zealand, Fr. Polikarpos Neonakis, who came to New Zealand from Greece in 1977. In 1972, the Metropolitan established as his domestic chapel the small Church of St. Andrew, near Wellington Airport. Officially, it is the Greek Orthodox Cathedral.

During the 1970s, a school and a magazine were founded in Wellington. New parishes appeared: Dormition of the Virgin Mary (Christchurch), Holy Trinity (Auckland), St. Nectarius (Petone), Nativity of John the Baptist (Palmerston North), and Transfiguration in Masterton. Most church buildings have come from other denominations - i.e. Baptist, Methodist, Seventh-day Adventist. It has been difficult to attract priests from Greece, and even more difficult to hold them in New Zealand, as the lure of the much larger Greek communities in Australia has been tempting. Services in parishes outside Wellington have been irregular, and there has not been a Greek Orthodox priest resident in the South Island for nearly a decade. Only among the Greeks of Wellington has Orthodoxy in New Zealand found a sufficient population base to create a real community life, and it is only here that non-Orthodox observers can come into contact with Orthodoxy as a living religious unit in society.

The Romanian Orthodox

Among the Displaced Persons who arrived in New Zealand in the late 1940s was a contingent of Romanian Greeks. Since they represented a more educated group than the previous settlers from the Greek Isles, they assumed positions of leadership within Wellington's Greek community. Among the couples who came to New Zealand from Romania were mixed marriages - Romanian and Greek. As the years passed, there was growing pressure for the establishment of a Romanian parish. In 1971, the congregation was registered, and in 1974, a priest arrived from Romania. He has remained in Wellington, holding down secular employment while ministering to his small flock. Of a community of about 300, only a few are actually Romanians. A former Masonic Lodge in Berhampore was purchased with Roman Catholic assistance in 1977, and in 1980 it was consecrated as the Church of the Dormition of the Virgin Mary. Although the church is rather

Raymond Oppenheim

Carved iconostasis in the Romanian Church, Berhampore, Wellington

nondescript from the outside, it boasts a lovely carved iconostasis (the wall covered with icons which separates the altar from the body of the church), sent from Romania. The parish is under Bishop Iosif, the Romanian Bishop of Sydney, an appointee of the Patriarch of Romania, in Bucharest.

The Serbian Orthodox

As noted above, Yugoslavia is divided ecclesiastically between the Eastern and Western Churches. New Zealand's relatively large Yugoslav population is well-known, particularly in the wine industry, and has been prominent in both sport and politics. But the substantial majority of our Yugoslavs are from Croatia and the Dalmatian coast in the west, solidly Roman Catholic districts. The Serbs in the east, who represent the largest nationality within Yugoslavia, are very sparsely represented in this country. They may not be numerous, but they have become well-established and affluent. In Wellington, a group of about thirty families formed a parish in the 1960s, got the use of a former Roman Catholic church in Island Bay, brought a priest from Yugoslavia, settled him into a secular job, and consecrated their church in honour of St. Savas, the Patron Saint of Serbia.

For a tiny church, New Zealand's Serbs have had surprising success, even though they have only the single church in Wellington and a dozen families in Auckland. The Serbs can claim New Zealand's only Orthodox monastic community - the Skit of the Dormition of the Blessed Virgin Mary. Fr. Ambrose and Fr. Nicholas are both converts from Roman Catholicism, and through them, other converts have now gone abroad to test their monastic vocations in larger communities. Their skit (the traditional name for a small monastery) was based first near Feilding, then on the Coromandel, and now at Reikorangi, near Waikanae. Fr. Ambrose, who is a priest-monk, exercises a nationwide ministry, serving congregations of both his own jurisdiction and the Russian. This involves more than just the services and sacraments of the church, as Orthodox believers look to their clergy as important community and cultural figures. To add to his burden, monastics have always been sought for spiritual direction. The Serbs are proud that they are in communion with all four of the other jurisdictions, forming a bridge among them and allowing Fr. Ambrose to cross all the boundaries. The Serbian hierarch to whom they look for oversight is Bishop Longin of Sydney, Australia.

The Russian Orthodox

Throughout the world, Russian Orthodox Christians are divided, as a result of the Russian Revolution. Many countries in the West have competing Russian hierarchies, loyal to the Patriarchate of Moscow or strongly opposed to it. And in America, there is a third, which claims self-rule (autocephaly). A single Russian jurisdiction is represented in New Zealand - the Synod of the Russian Orthodox Church Outside of Russia. This extra-canonical jurisdiction was formed among Russians who were exiled at the time of the 1917 Revolution. Since it was originally based in Karlovtsy, Yugoslavia, under the protection of the Serbian Patriarchate, New Zealand's Serbs are the only local Orthodox who are in communion with the Synod. As the only Russian priest in New Zealand is now elderly and infirm, the Serbian priest-monk Ambrose takes services for the three Russian congregations.Christchurch has the only Russian Orthodox Church, the tiny but beautiful Church of St. Nicholas, built in Waltham as a labour of love by a handful of refugees who had reached Christchurch through China, Persia, and the Displaced Persons camps of postwar

Germany. Wellington has only a house chapel on Mt. Victoria. In Auckland, the small congregation is without facilities. There are no more than fifty to seventy-five members in each of the three. They also look to Sydney, to Archbishop Paul, but were it not for Serbian assistance, they would be virtually without pastoral care, since so much of their religious life requires the participation of a priest.

Orthodoxy's contacts with other churches

With the exception of the Antiochians, New Zealand Orthodox Christians seek to maintain ethnic traditions, brought with them from their home countries. Part of the ethos of Orthodoxy are the distinctive styles of music and iconography associated with each national church. Only Antioch has moved beyond its ethnic roots, but, in doing so, it has become a haven for dissident Anglicans and Roman Catholics. The only alternative path for involvement with the rest of New Zealand Christianity appears to be through ecumenical contacts.

After a rather tentative start, the Orthodox Churches have become deeply involved in the New Zealand ecumenical movement. The Greeks joined the National Council of Churches in 1947, but rarely took part in any of its activities and were seldom represented at meetings. The Antiochians joined the NCC in 1982, but also kept a low profile. With the launching of the new Conference of Churches in Aotearoa New Zealand in 1987, the Orthodox assumed a prominence far outweighing their numbers. One of the founding Presidents was Prof. Barbu Niculescu, retired Victoria University economist and lay leader in Wellington's Romanian Orthodox parish. Four of the five jurisdictions are now members - the Greeks, Romanians, Serbians, and Antiochians. The same four are now involved in an on-going dialogue with the Anglicans, under the co-chairmanship of Prof. Niculescu.

The past few years have seen a growing awareness among mainstream Christians in New Zealand that the Orthodox Church is a source of spiritual treasures. Russian and Greek icons are now to be seen in many Anglican, Protestant, and Roman Catholic churches. Classics of Orthodox spirituality are available in paperback. But it is often disappointing to discover that most of the worshippers in our Orthodox churches appear to know relatively little about the richness to which they have clung so tenaciously. It is taken for granted - just part of their ethnic baggage. For this reason, many intellectual searchers, who have turned from mainstream New Zealand Christianity towards Orthodoxy, have found the ethnic congregations unsatisfying. To gain knowledge of Orthodoxy, many have sought out knowledgeable amateurs within the Roman Catholic and Anglican traditions, as they have made the effort to explore the treasures with which the Orthodox Christian lives every day.

Within the Orthodox family, a cycle of yearly celebration unfolds, and whereas the West stresses Christmas as the great family celebration, Orthodoxy maintains a sounder theology in making Easter the high point of the year. The central event is the Midnight Liturgy, in which the Resurrection is dramatically recreated. As midnight approaches, the church itself becomes the tomb of Christ, while the clergy play the role of the women on the way to the tomb, solemnly circling the outside of the building. At the stroke of midnight, the doors are flung wide with cries of, 'Christ is Risen!' The first liturgy of Easter is celebrated and everyone goes home for a feast. All the foods forbidden during a strict Lent are served, along with baskets of red Easter eggs.

The dining-room table is a focus for religious life, as it is in the Jewish home, with special seasonal feasts. In the corner of the dining-room in a traditional Orthodox home will be the family's icons, its greatest treasures. Christ is indeed a guest at the table, and the presence of the icons reinforces this teaching. The sign of the cross plays a constant role at the table, as it does elsewhere in Orthodox life, for Orthodoxy places strong emphasis on the idea of transfiguration - every object, every gesture, can be transfigured by the in-dwelling of Christ, making everything sacramental, a source of blessing and of grace.

Orthodox from other traditions

As was noted at the beginning of this chapter, Orthodoxy has never had a reformation. This is not to say that it has been without schisms. In five distinct periods, groups have broken away from the Eastern Church, and all of these are represented in New Zealand.

The Assyrians

At the Council of Ephesus, in 431, the so-called 'Nestorian' heresy led to the expulsion of the majority of the Christians on the Eastern borders of the Roman Empire - modern Syria, Iraq, and Iran. This 'Church of the East' (they call themselves 'Assyrians') spread all the way to China during the seventh century, and planted a thriving church in South India. Today, numbers have shrunk to less than a quarter of a million, many of whom are refugees in North America or Australia.

In 1985, New Zealand opened its doors to Assyrian refugees from northern Iraq. An initial group of twenty-five families has now grown to about 200 persons, most of whom are in the Wellington area. Their nearest priest is in Sydney, and they rarely have a visit. They use the ministry of Greek Orthodox or Anglican churches for baptisms or funerals. An ancient people, their spoken language is Syriac, a modern version of the Aramaic spoken by Jesus. Their liturgy, the Qurbana, is one of the oldest in Christendom, and it is chanted without instrumental accompaniment. Worship is long and elaborate, but church buildings are always without religious art. As the Assyrians become established, it is hoped that a priest can be brought to New Zealand, so that this community may carry on its traditional religious life here.

The Oriental Orthodox

The second schismatic group represented here is the so-called 'Oriental Orthodox Churches' - those who broke with the Orthodox at the Council of Chalcedon in 451. The representatives of these five churches - Coptic, Ethiopian, Armenian, Jacobite, and South Indian Jacobite - are so few in New Zealand that they are usually encountered only as individuals. The exception is the Armenians, who are fervently nationalistic and enthusiastically practise what they can of their traditions in music and art and hospitality, no matter how few they may be. With only a couple of dozen scattered throughout the country, they still maintain community contact, and have even had a priest over from Australia for a visit.

The Uniates

In the third group, we find those Christians of Eastern Orthodox tradition who have entered into union with the Roman Catholic Church. These 'Uniate' Rites are allowed to continue their liturgical style and many of their customs (such as married priests, their own language for worship, and their individual versions of the Creed), but their loyalty is to the Bishop of Rome. Many of these Rites are represented in Australia, in particular: the Ukrainian, the Maronite (Lebanese), the Syrian, and the Melkite (Arab). From time to time, the Roman Catholic Church in New Zealand has provided ministry according to Eastern Rites, usually with the help of visiting priests, but this is now rare, except for the occasional Ukrainian Liturgy. Most of our Uniate Catholics now attend Latin Rite parishes.

The Old Believers

In the middle of the seventeenth century, a portion of the Russian Orthodox Church refused to accept a series of reforms. These conservatives became known as the 'Old Believers'. In order to protect an old-fashioned way of life and worship, many of them sought isolation in Siberia. Later, to escape the Russian Revolution, some then crossed into Manchuria or Sinkiang Province (in western China). In 1965, eighty of the latter group were allowed to leave China, and eventually reached New Zealand as refugees. They found the climate of Southland congenial, and settled in Gore, Invercargill, Dunedin, and even as far north as Christchurch. Others joined them over the following decade. As the years have passed, many have moved on to Oregon, Alaska, or Canada, joining larger communities, and few of them remain in New Zealand. Private almost to the point of secrecy, they have kept a seventeenth-century Russian Orthodoxy, but they have done it without priestly ministry or the Eucharist.

Modern schisms

Finally, there are those Orthodox who have broken away from their mother churches in the twentieth century, often for political reasons. To some extent, this would describe the Russian Church in this country. But two other groups should be mentioned. In 1958, the Macedonian part of the Serbian Orthodox Church seceded. Although this act officially involved only south-east Yugoslavia, the Macedonian people actually live in south-western Bulgaria and northern Greece as well. There are over two hundred Macedonians in New Zealand, and although they are not organised as a church, they identify with the schism in their own minds. The present community spirit and their nationalism may well result in some future developments ecclesiastically.

The second group is based on the refugee Ukrainian community, which came to New Zealand following the Second World War. In recent years, a 'priest' of the Ukrainian Autocephalic Orthodox Church was resident in Petone. This church is not recognised as canonical by the other jurisdictions, and its orders are considered to be completely invalid. Services were held for some time in an Anglican church, but since the return of its leader to Australia, the community appears to have disbanded, with worshippers attending either the Russian Orthodox or the very occasional Ukrainian Rite Catholic services.

Conclusions

Orthodoxy holds an important position in New Zealand Christianity. It is a church which knows what it believes, and clings to its positions with tenacity. In a time of theological and ecclesiastic uncertainty, there is something quite attractive about this ancient religious family. It is sure of itself to the point of arrogance, and revels in self-satisfaction with its own tradition. And yet, it approaches its conception of God with a sense of awe virtually unknown in other Christian families. No other church has developed worship into such an elaborate art form, and a well-celebrated Orthodox liturgy is a deeply moving experience. Contemporary Christians from other traditions often find guidance for prayer and spiritual development in the treasures brought to this land by the Orthodox Church.

And yet, this tiny community is dwindling. Without the Orthodox population base to be found in America or Australia, it is difficult for our Orthodox to build the kind of nurturing community that will attract and hold a younger generation. Converts have been relatively few, and much of the religious life of New Zealand's Orthodox is merely as a part of the ethnic baggage brought to our shores by immigrants. Exploration of the spiritual treasures of Orthodoxy is more likely to be found among enthusiasts from other traditions than among our Orthodox themselves. The exception has been the small Church of Antioch, but its growth has been very slow indeed. The greater involvement of the Orthodox in the Ecumenical Movement may improve this situation, however, as more 'mainstream' Christians come into contact with the riches of Orthodox tradition.

Further reading

Meyendorff, J., *The Orthodox Church,* London: Darton, Longman and Todd, 1962.
Waddams, H., *Meeting the Orthodox Churches,* London: SCM Press, 1964.
Ware, T., *The Orthodox Church,* Harmondsworth: Penguin, 1964.
Ware, T., *The Orthodox Way,* Oxford: Mowbrays, 1979.
Zernov, N., *The Russians and Their Church,* London: SPCK, 1978.

Christianity:
Mainline Denominations to the 1960s

Colin Brown

The diversity of contemporary Christianity is blatantly proclaimed by the church notices in our Saturday newspapers. There are advertisements for Roman Catholic, Anglican, Presbyterian, Methodist, Baptist, Brethren, Lutheran, Quaker, Salvation Army, a variety of Pentecostal services and often many more. Diversity extends into the denominations. Anglican worship, for instance, ranges from the restrained elegance of cathedral-style liturgy to the ebullience characteristic of the modern charismatic movement.

Although the number and diversity of the Christian denominations present on the New Zealand scene have increased in recent years there was some variety from the early days of European settlement. Methodists, Presbyterians, Catholics, Baptists and Anglicans were present by the 1850s. By the end of the century Churches of Christ, Congregationalists, Quakers, Brethren, Seventh-day Adventists, Lutherans and Mormons had joined them. Such variety reflects the time at which the European settlement of New Zealand took place.

Christianity: origins and divisions

During the early centuries of its life Christianity took three main directions, shaped by geography and culture but united, more or less, in one community of belief. There were the largely Syriac-speaking communities centred on ancient Edessa (Urfa in modern Turkey); the Greek-speaking Christians with, from the fourth century onwards, Constantinople (now Istanbul) as their major centre; and Latin Christians in the West, who looked to Rome.

Christianity became divided in three main stages: first, two groups separated from the main body in the wake of the Council of Chalcedon, 451. They included the Nestorians, whose missions were later to reach as far as China, and the Coptic Christians found today in Egypt and Ethiopia. Second, on a larger scale and more significant generally, was the East-West schism of 1054, the rupture of a relationship that had long been strained. Third, Western Christianity was divided in the sixteenth century when demands for 'reformation' separated Roman Catholicism from several varieties of Protestantism, which in later centuries diversified still more (Quakers in the seventeenth century, for instance; Methodists in the eighteenth).[1]

Shaping and reshaping

All these varieties of Christianity are derived, ultimately, from a movement which began in the first century of the Common Era within Palestinian Judaism. Christianity was characterised by its recognition of Jesus as the Messiah longed for by Jews; the earliest believers eagerly awaited Christ's return from heaven, the end of the present age and the consummation of the Kingdom (rule) of God. When events did not turn out as expected, belief in a last and general judgment associated with Christ's return was retained but death, the 'particular' judgment believed to follow it, and the nature of a life after death loomed larger in Christian concerns. Meanwhile what had begun as a community of eager expectation settled down for 'the long haul of history' and shaped its institutional life accordingly.

At first persecuted by the Roman imperial authorities as a threat to the Empire's well-being, by the fourth century Christianity had become the state religion. Important consequences followed for Christianity's life and ethos. Where war was concerned, Christians had hitherto been pacifists. This continued only as a minority opinion. Church leaders attempted to distinguish between 'just' and 'unjust' wars and to alleviate their evils. A new perspective opened on relations between the church and the state - a matter on which Christians have continued to hold divergent views. The wider question was raised, too, whether the Christian stance is to be world-affirming or world-negating. Monasticism, which had its beginnings about this time, arose, in part, as one way of resolving that tension.

In reflecting on the human condition - what is it that prevents humans from realising their full potential? - Christianity developed elements found in its Jewish heritage. The fundamental evil was identified as 'sin'. By this was meant not specific wrongful acts so much as the alienated condition of human life, disordered in its relationship to God, and consequently in all other dimensions and relationships also.

In the story of Adam and Eve (Genesis 2) the allegedly historical origins of this alienated condition were discovered. For Western Christian thought the detailed exposition by Augustine of Hippo (354-430) of the drama of creation, fall, and redemption was especially important. Augustine depicted 'original sin' as a disorder transmitted by the normal processes of human generation.

Christians believe, however, that in Jesus as the Christ, salvation has been made available to humankind in accordance with the loving purposes of God. To explain how this comes about, early Christian thinkers adopted one or more of the following images or models: Christ as teacher, as sacrificial victim, as offering deliverance from the corruption of time and change and, most popular of all, as triumphing over all the forces of evil. If, however, so great a salvation had become available through Christ, who was he? What was his relationship to God?

Christians had inherited, again from their Jewish past, a strong insistence on monotheism. They thus felt compelled to explore their belief in the resurrection of Christ and their continuing experience of his power and presence, in ways compatible with monotheism. As a result of quite complex, protracted and sometimes bitter controversies, Christianity had, by about 500, come to fairly general agreement on two main points: Christ was conceived as a divine-human reality, the Word of God incarnated in a genuinely human life; and God was envisaged as trinitarian (Father, Son, and Spirit) in activity and nature.

Much of the reasoning behind such doctrines and even their final statement probably only found its way down to the grassroots in very generalised and imprecise forms. More significant, at that level, were developments like the cult of saints, especially the Virgin Mary, and the emergence of a sacramental system which made divine power available and touched human lives at their major turning-points.

Christianity began with two main ritual observances: baptism (a ceremonial washing or bathing), and a sacred meal (celebrated weekly from quite early) originally anticipatory of the messianic banquet in the Kingdom of God. Both observances were believed to have been sanctioned by Christ himself. By about the end of the fifth century baptism had become, predominantly, an infant initiation rite designed to remove the guilt of original sin and to counter its effects. The ritual meal, called Eucharist (thanksgiving) or Mass, had become very much the liturgical heart of the Church's life. It was increasingly spoken of as a sacrifice, and the sacred bread and wine were regarded in realistic but varied ways, as 'the body and blood of Christ'.

In seeking to regulate the conduct of its members the clerical leadership of the church required public confession of wrongdoing in certain instances. This gradually developed into sacramental confession to a priest. Increasingly the Church became a community in which clergy and laity were sharply differentiated and the ordained ministry was conceived hierarchically. The sacrament of ordination, then, served to regulate and legitimate such hierarchical arrangements as well as to endow those concerned with a sense of spiritual power (grace) bestowed on them for their tasks. Ordained persons became the ministers of the sacraments including the anointing of sick persons with holy oil, and, somewhat later, holy matrimony - the sacrament of marriage.

In the early centuries of its existence the Christian community had to shape and maintain its identity against various rivals: Judaism, the Mystery religions, and especially Gnosticism.[2] Moreover Christianity itself did not emerge from the pages of the New Testament as a tidy entity; orthodoxy was created out of dispute and conflict, not bestowed as an initial endowment.

In establishing a sharper identity for Christianity three developments were especially important. One was the emergence of Christian creeds, notably the so-called Apostles' and Nicene Creeds. A second was the creation of a canon of sacred writings. (The New Testament, for Christians, joined the Hebrew Bible - appropriated from the Jews and re-named the Old Testament to signify the Christian estimate of it.) The third development was the exaltation of the office and role of bishop so that the holders of this office became, in the words of one of them, 'the glue of the church'.

Bishops were the principal sacramental and administrative officers, with each bishop responsible for a given area (a diocese). Bishops of key cities were given special precedence (e.g. Jerusalem, Constantinople). The bishop of Rome had by about 500 largely acquired actual jurisdiction over the church in the West.

In its earliest phase, Christianity was a relatively egalitarian movement in which women played important roles.[3] Quite soon, however, women were almost totally excluded from the ordained ministry which became a male preserve. Under the influence of ascetic notions from largely non-biblical sources, the stress on Eve's actions in the Garden of Eden, and a form of symbolism in which 'male' symbolised reason/rule, and 'female' body/fragility (and worse), women were not only excluded from teaching, decision-making and ordained ministry with all its sacramental functions but, especially in the West, a deep distrust of women and human sexuality was engendered. Here, as with ideas about original sin, Augustine of Hippo was particularly influential.

This, then, was Christianity as it was transmitted to the Middle Ages of Western Europe. There were, of course, subsequent changes in liturgy and piety in this period. The sacramental system became even more important, the church more hierarchical and clericalised, and the Mass a sacrifice performed in the presence of an audience with infrequent lay reception of the sacred bread and wine. The traditional doctrines concerning human nature, sin, and Christ went largely unchallenged; the general shape of the Church remained intact.

The Reformation of the sixteenth century did not change everything. Roman Catholicism, it can be said, largely retained the status quo, sought to reform abuses and, in the process, created an even more tightly knit, centralised organisation. Protestants, in varying degrees, made more sweeping changes. But most, while they repudiated the Papacy and, in some cases, bishops, retained some form of ordained ministry and continued to restrict it to males.

The number of sacraments was reduced from the traditional seven to, basically, two only - Baptism and the Lord's Supper. But, the Quakers apart, sacraments as such were retained. As far as the major doctrines were concerned these were largely maintained save by some marginal groups. In this respect Christian orthodoxy went unchallenged until the eighteenth and nineteenth centuries.

That, then, in outline, is the Christianity, in its unity and diversity, which arrived in New Zealand with missionaries and with European settlement. What impact has it had on the Maori? What happened to Christianity transplanted from its homelands to a new land? To what extent, if at all, has Christianity helped to shape New Zealand life and society?

Christianity and the Maori: the early missions[4]

Missions among the Maori began with Samuel Marsden's 1814 Christmas Day sermon at Rangihoua, Bay of Islands. But only from the late 1820s onward were missionary efforts under the auspices of the Church Missionary Society (Anglican) effective. By then Methodists also were active in the North; Presbyterians made insignificant beginnings in the Manawatu from 1843.

To most Europeans, especially missionaries, Maori culture (including its religious aspects) was at best opaque, at worst repugnant. In principle and to some extent in practice Catholic missions were more sensitive than Protestant missions to Maori culture and values. Bishop Jean Baptiste Pompallier (1801-71) inaugurated Roman Catholic missions in 1838. But Anglo-French rivalry, anti-Catholicism, and the withdrawal of the Marists to Wellington (as a consequence of tension between their Superior and Pompallier) undermined early Catholic efforts.

In time, numerous Maori converted to Christianity. The fascination of literacy, the role of the more effective missionaries and their wives, and evangelistic activities of Maori themselves, were the main causes of this growth. But despite the part played by Maori catechists and the extensive use of the Maori language in services, evangelism and education, European missionaries were slow to foster Maori leadership in church life. The first Maori ordained as a deacon in the Anglican church was Rota Waitoa in 1853. Europeans devised that church's constitution in 1857. Among Catholics and Methodists, likewise, control remained firmly in missionary hands.

From the first the Maori received Christianity on their own terms. Indeed literacy increased both their capacity to do so, and their independence relative to the missionaries. Increasing availability of translations of the Bible, anxiety over the inroads of disease, and concern over land issues all assisted in generating various religious responses among the Maori.[5]

The first of such movements was Papahurihia, led by Te Atua Wera. This significant movement in the North from 1833 was merely the first of such movements seeking to blend Christian and Maori elements. Missionaries tended to see such responses in clear-cut terms, as deplorable reversion to paganism, and anti-Christian in intent. It seems clear that Maori saw the matter rather differently. They were seeking to create syntheses which would blend the new and the old and meet the changing needs of Maori more effectively than mere retention of undiluted traditional culture.

One other event in the initial period gained significance in the light of later developments. The attitude of the various missionaries concerned with the Treaty of Waitangi was mixed, but most were either benevolently neutral or, moved by dual concerns for Maori interests and law and order, positively sought its enactment and signature. Admirable as this stance may have been, it linked the credibility of the churches and clergy to the honouring of the treaty. Subsequent events diminished that credibility, with important consequences for Christianity among the Maori people.

Land, war and disillusionment

By around 1850 about seventy-five per cent of the Maori population had been baptised into one or other of the Christian denominations. But during the following decade disenchantment with the churches and European culture set in. The ravages of disease took their toll - physically, mentally and spiritually. Disputes over land were festering, and there was some disillusionment with Europeans and their ways generally. These developments reflected on the missionaries who, in some cases, had problems of their own. Increasing multiplicity of denominations was a handicap, and Anglicans specifically were hampered by the death of early leaders and disputes with Governor Grey and Bishop Selwyn.[6] More and more, too, missionaries were drawn away to minister to the growing number of European settlers, and in so doing came to identify with their interests rather than with Maori concerns.

Thus when armed conflict came it made an already worsening climate even bleaker. Missionaries, moreover, were not of a common mind on Maori and land issues. John Whitely, a Methodist minister at New Plymouth, and the Anglican bishop Selwyn, held divergent views over the highly contentious Taranaki land issues. Although not all missionaries panicked in the face of the Maori King movement, many tended to see in it a threat to British sovereignty, law and order, and the continued advance of Christianity. The fact that some ministers acted as chaplains to the troops was offensive to many Maori. Most tragic of all was the dilemma of Christian Maori, especially ministers and catechists, who were trapped in a bewildering conflict of loyalties.

The effects of war went well beyond the destruction of Maori property, serious though that was. Personnel were withdrawn and Maori mission work declined drastically or collapsed entirely in many areas. Distrust and widespread alienation from Christianity ensued, fed by large-scale confiscation of Maori land, and war injuries done to non-combatants.

Statistics do not tell the whole story but they are highly suggestive. In 1855 Methodists reckoned Maori members at 3070, but by 1874 this number was only 375. During the same period annual attendance at worship fell from 7590 to 2434.[7] Equally suggestive is the vigour and variety of such Maori movements as Pai Marire and Ringatu. The events of the war years cast long, dark shadows over Maori-Pakeha relationships and Maori attitudes to Christianity and the churches.

Assimilation, integration and biculturalism

From the 1880s onwards Anglicans, Methodists, Catholics and Presbyterians all revived their missionary efforts in a variety of areas. An effective newcomer from 1881 was the Church of Jesus Christ of Latter-day Saints (Mormons). Unhampered by any link with British colonialism, assisted by their interest in genealogy, relatively open as regards (male) Maori in positions of responsibility in church life, and effective in inculcating a serviceable work-ethic, the Mormons prospered. By 1936, 6.4 per cent of the Maori population identified with Mormonism, although this figure has scarcely varied since that time.

As with government and public policy generally, the major churches have edged only slowly away from the goal of assimilation, towards integration and, much more recently, in the direction of biculturalism. This last involves granting a greater degree of autonomy to Maori groups and organisations within the larger framework of church life. Though accepted officially by the churches, biculturalism is only partially understood and widely distrusted at the grassroots level of church life.

In 1882 the Church Missionary Society gave notice of its intention to withdraw from New Zealand in twenty years' time. In that year also a move was made to secure a suffragan ('assistant') bishop for Maori in the Anglican diocese of Auckland. The General Synod withheld approval, and when bodies were created to oversee missions and ministry to the Maori they were, initially, not represented on such bodies. Significantly the bishopric of Aotearoa was created in 1928, towards the end of a decade in which the Ratana movement had registered gains in numbers, power and influence.

The powers of the bishop were circumscribed. Technically he was little more than an assistant to the Bishop of Waiapu, covering roughly the area from Tauranga and Rotorua to Napier. Only with the permission of the bishops concerned could the Maori bishop enter dioceses other than Waiapu. For some years from 1940 on, this access was denied in Auckland and Waikato because the bishops concerned regarded it as transgressing their episcopal authority in these dioceses.

In Methodism and Catholicism Pakeha control persisted. Presbyterian missions among the Tuhoe began in 1895. Especially important was the role played by two women, Annie Henry from 1917 to 1948 and Edith Walker from 1914 to 1949, and the Reverend J.G. Laughton. The last-named (superintendent of the Presbyterian Maori Mission from 1935 to 1955 and Moderator of Te Hinota Maori from 1956-62) was pre-eminent for nobility of character, linguistic expertise, and his role in securing greater autonomy for Maori Presbyterians.

Talk of integration as a goal did not confer much in the way of autonomy on Maori Christians. During the 1960s, for instance, Maori participation in the early stages of prayer book revision by Anglicans, and ecumenical discussion about church union, was minimal.

But some changes had already occurred; others followed. The Presbyterian Maori Synod was given full powers in 1956. In 1964 and subsequent years the Anglican bishopric of Aotearoa gained greater status and enhanced powers, while Methodists replaced their Maori Mission with a Maori Division in 1973. Among Catholics a Maori priesthood was slow in developing, and only in 1944 was the first Maori priest ordained. The Reverend Takuira Mariu was consecrated as the first Catholic Maori bishop in 1988. From 1983, however, Catholics had met in conference under the auspices of Te Runanga Hahi Katorika ki Aotearoa. The Maori Section of the National Council of Churches,[8] begun in 1947, was replaced in 1982 by Te Runanga Whakawhanaunga I Nga Hahi o Aotearoa - a constitutionally separate Maori council of churches with, unlike the NCC Maori Section, full Catholic, Ratana and Ringatu participation. Like the Maori Section before it, the new body has already shown a concern for the totality of Maori life. One expression of such wider concern was the convening in 1984 of a major hui on the Treaty of Waitangi.

Such structural changes are important and point to other changes also. There have been some attempts to develop Maori theologies.[9] These interpretations of Christianity are the work of those seeking to go beyond mere translation of European Christianity and to draw more creatively than before on Maori spirituality. The recently issued Anglican prayer book has the alternative title *He*

Karakia Mihinare O Aotearoa. It provides an order of service for the Eucharist which is not a mere translation into Maori of an originally English rite, but an original Maori production.

The contrast between such developments and earlier missionary attitudes to attempts to blend Maori culture and Christianity in any substantial manner is interesting and instructive. Yet some conservatively minded Christians are deeply suspicious of any such moves, regard Maori spirituality as pagan, and seek to have its study excluded in public schools.[10]

Will biculturalism in its various aspects genuinely transform church life and meet the needs of Maori Christians? There are signs that Maori allegiance to the mainline churches is diminishing. Whether moves towards autonomy, together with Maori theologies and liturgies, will help arrest that apparent drift from the churches in the years beyond 1990 is very much an open question.[11]

Settlers and churches

Anglicanism, Methodism and Catholicism all began in New Zealand as missions. Increasingly, however, along with other churches, they turned their attention also to the non-Maori population which grew rapidly, from 26,707 in 1851 to 297,654 by 1874, and 701,090 in 1896. The churches each coped with this challenge, some more effectively than others, in ways related to their distinctive structure and ethos.

Anglicans and Catholics extended their traditional diocesan and episcopal structure. By 1869 there were six Anglican dioceses; a seventh (Waikato) was added in 1926. Anglicans did not find at all easy the change from an 'establishment-type' situation in England to one where they were one denomination among others and dependent upon members for voluntary financial support. A constitution adopted in 1857 made the Anglican Church in New Zealand a 'voluntary society'. In matters of church government, this gave representative rights and legislative functions to clergy and laity, thus modifying episcopal autocracy which then prevailed in England. In other ways, however, the church in New Zealand remained tied to the formularies, faith and prayer book of the parent body. Then, as now, Anglicans looked to the Archbishop of Canterbury as spiritual though not jurisdictional head of their church.

Bishop Pompallier arrived in 1838, and by the end of the century the Catholic church in New Zealand was organised into four dioceses (two more being added in recent years). While this structure conferred a measure of local autonomy, ultimate authority was (and remains) vested in the Pope, as both spiritual and jurisdictional head, and in the bishop within the diocese. Because of its emphasis on sacraments administered by an ordained ministry only, the advance of Catholicism was often hampered by a shortage of priests. From the first, religious orders (both men's and women's) made significant contributions to the church's work. The provision of education was an early priority. As early as 1842 the first Catholic priest resident in Auckland established a school there.

Methodists were best placed to respond effectively to the needs of settlers. While the (Anglican) Church Missionary Society was, as its name implies, committed to missionary work, early Methodist ministers readily acted as both missionaries to Maori and pastors to Pakeha. Methodism, too, had strong traditions of evangelism and lay involvement. When the Reverend Samuel Ironside visited Nelson in 1842 he found that lay preachers had already organised services there. Methodism was exported to New Zealand in four main varieties: Wesleyan, Primitive, United Free Methodist Church, and Bible Christian Church. (This last was notable for its use of women preachers.) By 1913, however, Methodism in New Zealand was a united and autonomous body.

Other than the Manawatu mission already mentioned, Presbyterianism opened its New Zealand career by ministering to settlers. It was present on the Auckland scene from 1842 (although not effectively so until the following decade), and in Wellington from 1840. It received its most notable accession of strength with the arrival of Scottish settlers in Dunedin in 1848, and during the 1850s and 1860s spread widely in other areas. Lay initiative played some part but was less evident than among Methodists. Especially in Dunedin, education was a major concern - the first university established was the University of Otago (1869). Two main varieties of Presbyterianism persisted for some time, but reunion moves, which faltered in the 1860s, succeeded in 1901.

Other denominations present in New Zealand by that date included Baptists, Churches of Christ, Brethren, Congregationalists, Lutherans, Quakers, and the Salvation Army, along with Mormons and Seventh-day Adventists. Where lay initiative was usual, such churches took root quite early. Brethren Assemblies appeared in the Motueka area from the early 1850s. The first Baptist church was established in Nelson in 1881, and by the following year, when the Baptist Union was created, there were twenty-five congregations. The Salvation Army, which was launched in England in 1877, reached Port Chalmers in 1883. With its military-style command structure, its lively (and sometimes criticised) style of evangelism, and its concern for the destitute, it spread quickly and effectively.

For a more complete view four facts must be noted about the nineteenth-century religious spectrum. First, Anglicans were much the largest in numbers, among Pakeha. In 1886 they constituted about 40 per cent of the population, with Presbyterians next at around 23 per cent (according to census figures). However, Anglicans carried a large nominal membership, and even with it were not so dominant that they could operate as a sort of unofficial establishment.

Second, by no means all who expressed their denominational allegiance in the census attended church on any regular basis. A careful investigation of this topic observes: 'Usual attenders in 1886 formed 28 per cent of the New Zealand population.'[12]

Third, Christianity in Europe, including the British Isles, was experiencing the inroads of scepticism and secularism as well as some indifference and hostility, and these quickly found expression in this country. While among Pakeha in 1886 less than 1 per cent labelled themselves as having no religion or as 'Freethought', there was a vigorous Freethought tradition. (It included among its members Sir Robert Stout who had a distinguished career as a reformer, politician and Chief Justice from 1899 to 1920).[13]

Fourth, sectarian bigotry persisted, most notably in Protestant-Catholic tensions. In riots on the West Coast in 1868, and in Timaru in 1897, religious differences were one element. Tensions were heightened when Peter Charles Chiniquy, a former Catholic priest turned anti-Catholic publicist, visited in 1880. Protestant-Catholic tensions were kept alive by agitators on both sides down to the 1920s.[14]

At the same time there was much cooperation among Protestants, in interdenominational societies such as the YMCA and the British and Foreign Bible Society. In smaller communities, also, goodwill often bridged the Catholic-Protestant divide.[15]

There are still many visible reminders of nineteenth-century New Zealand Christianity. While in pioneer society services were held in a wide variety of settings, church buildings appeared early in the readily available material of wood. Christ Church at Russell (c.1836) is the best surviving example of an early (and severely functional) design. More elegant and eloquent are buildings such as St.John's College chapel Auckland (1847) and Old St. Paul's, Wellington.[16] But well before the century ended, stone and brick were used for building churches, some impressive but imitative like the Anglican cathedral in Christchurch, and others more strikingly original, like the Catholic cathedral in the same city.

Most of the churches relied heavily on the services of an ordained (male) clergy. The quality varied greatly. Anglicans, Presbyterians and Catholics did a great deal of recruiting overseas, but some importations, especially from the Church of England, did not adjust easily to colonial life. At the same time these denominations, and the Methodists also, sought to establish institutions to train clergy. Arguably the Presbyterians achieved the most, with Knox College's Theological Hall in close relationship with the University of Otago.[17]

Emphasis on the importance of an educated, professional ministry identified the churches concerned largely with the middle and professional classes. Efforts were made to reach other sections of the population and the unchurched generally. It was not only the Salvation Army which went in for revivalism. There was considerable local interest in evangelist Dwight Moody's ministry in the United States and Great Britain. Some evangelists from America visited New Zealand, e.g. William (California) Taylor and R.A. Torrey. Among Catholics, Father O. Henneberry was a pioneer in New Zealand of parish-based missions which stressed both temperance and sacramentalism. Then, as now, such revivalism, which owed a great deal to overseas techniques and practitioners, had both its backers and its detractors.[18]

Churches: dependent or independent?

How far have New Zealand churches relied on overseas inspiration and resources? Has a kind of ecclesiastical colonialism operated to stunt Christianity in New Zealand? New Zealand has had political independence for some time. This did not automatically confer independence in the realms of mind and spirit.

In religious matters dependence has been reinforced by a variety of factors. Except by Maori and Catholic Irish, Great Britain was not seen as an oppressor nation but as 'the source of religious enlightenment, and culture, scholarship and spiritual leadership'.[19] More recently the United States has seemed to many to be a fountainhead of inspiration in fields as diverse as fund-raising, pastoral theology, and theological scholarship generally. The Charismatic renewal and Fundamentalist resurgence also have significant links with that country.

In financial and human terms New Zealand is a small society with slender resources. This makes dependence on overseas sources a continuing fact of life, and penetration by foreign influences an ever-present fact of church life. In addition, however, Christians in varying degree and a variety of ways, are inevitably conscious of being members of international communities with long-standing traditions. There are two sides to that awareness. It can help to stave off parochialism, but it can also lead to uncritical adoption of imported ways and ideas.

Denominational links with parent bodies overseas are in some cases formalised and involve a fair degree of central control (eg. Catholic Church, Salvation Army). Others are less formal but still powerful and enduring. Especially during the earlier years of European settlement, dependence on overseas resources was clearly unavoidable. If we go on to ask whether that dependence has sometimes smothered local initiative, the evidence points in more than one direction.

In matters of doctrine, Anglicans and Presbyterians early went on record affirming their resolve to share with their respective parent bodies a common version of the Christian faith.[20] For long, Anglicans, Methodists, Presbyterians, and Catholics drew heavily on imported ministers, thus helping perpetuate overseas influence. When training institutions were established they became further channels for imported personnel, methods and attitudes. At the top leadership levels, too, change away from dependence was slow - although, of course, the churches have not been unique in that respect.

Hymns, liturgy and architecture testify to dependence as both a past and present reality: for good and ill. Inception of the reforms that led to the new prayer book for Anglicans (1989) owed much to overseas examples as do the contents of the new book. In church architecture there are, unhappily, all-too-permanent reminders of local inability to pass beyond slavish imitation. In the realm of theological thought a well-informed commentator remarked in 1966 that 'Theology must be one of New Zealand's least indigenous activities'.[21]

On the other hand there are instances where the New Zealand churches have chosen to go their own way, sometimes against the wishes of parent bodies. New Zealand's relatively small size, the seeming irrelevance to the local scene of some imported denominational divisions, and the need to pool limited resources have all helped facilitate reunion moves and inter-denominational co-operation.

Presbyterians and Methodists both arrived internally divided, and by 1901 and 1913 respectively had reunited, in both cases earlier than their parent bodies. In terms of ecumenical developments world-wide, a national council of churches emerged relatively early (1941). The local context also shaped some responses to ministry. Presbyterians decided in 1875 to place some students in 'charges' while expecting them to continue their studies. Methodists made similar moves, while Anglicans made more extensive use of lay readers than in England.

From the 1920s onward the Bible Class movement was very influential in the non-Catholic churches. It began among Presbyterians in 1888 and was widely adopted by other Protestant and Anglican churches. Likewise especially prominent is the wide variety of inter-denominational or non-denominational movements found among conservative, evangelical Protestants. These include movements for young people (e.g. Navigators), or professional groups (e.g. nurses) and for disabled persons. Such groups nourish a piety based on Bible study rather than on church liturgies and sacraments.

In constitutional matters Baptists, Congregationalists, Methodists and Presbyterians were able quickly and easily to create self-governing churches. The Anglicans' 1857 constitution created a self-governing, autonomous church; but theologically and liturgically it forged so close a link with the Church of England that in 1928 empowering legislation had to be passed by the New Zealand parliament to 'free up' the situation.

In some other respects Anglicanism in New Zealand has moved in different directions from its parent and some of its sister-churches. The ordination of women to the priesthood, and the marriage of divorced persons, are now established features of local church life. (In England the church is still locked in acrimonious disputes over both issues.) Most recently, in 1989, Anglicans in Dunedin diocese chose a woman (the Rev. Dr Penelope Jamieson) as bishop and became the first Anglican

Ed Higbee

Bishop Penelope Jamieson with bishops and laywomen at her ordination in June 1990

diocese in the world to do so. (Bishop Barbara Harris, elected in 1989 by the diocese of Massachusetts, is an assistant, not a diocesan bishop.) Similarly both Methodists (1959) and Presbyterians (1965) acted to ordain women before their parent bodies did so.

All these instances, it might be said, are typical of New Zealanders' pragmatism. This is only partly true, since the ordination of women involved theological issues which were canvassed quite thoroughly over some years. Other signs of theological independence, though, are recent and limited. Some Maori and Pakeha have tried their hand at more distinctively 'local' theologies but, like liturgical reform, the 'indigenisation' or 'contextualisation' of theology is itself an international, not a home-grown, phenomenon.[22]

In summary, then, during the short history of the churches in New Zealand there are instances of sensible dependence, slavish imitation, and innovative adaptation or invention. Some degree of dependence is likely to continue given the slender local resources, the international links between churches and para-church bodies, the important role of tradition and continuity in Christianity, and the capacity of modern media such as tapes and videos to spread messages world-wide in a very short time.

A woman's work ...

From New Testament times onwards women have usually made up the larger part of Christianity's active membership, and in religious orders and voluntary associations have supported and extended the work of the churches. At the same time, however, they were early excluded from positions of leadership and decision-making, especially the ordained ministry. This situation has only begun to change in the present century and then only slowly and fitfully where the larger churches are concerned.[23]

In New Zealand the wives of some of the early missionaries extended their activities into teaching and nursing. (Marianne Williams, wife to Henry Williams the leading Church Missionary Society missionary, is a good instance in this regard.)[24] Missionary activity and interest on the part of women have continued and found two main outlets. Some have been notable as workers among the Maori - whether Roman Catholic nuns like Mother Mary Joseph Aubert or Protestants like the noted Presbyterian Annie Henry who ministered to the Tuhoe from 1917 onwards.[25]

Many have served as missionaries beyond New Zealand. Local Presbyterian, Methodist and Baptist women's organisations throughout this century have supported such missionaries as their principal concern. (In more recent years these organisations have widened their range of interests to include social service and public issues, as well as pastoral care in parishes.) In addition to denominational organisations, churchwomen were active in the Women's Christian Temperance Union and the YWCA from their inception.

Religious orders for women in the Catholic Church early moved into the care of the urban poor as well as education, a more traditional concern. Mother Aubert and the Sisters of Compassion, after missionary and nursing activities in Hawkes Bay and at Jerusalem on the Wanganui river, moved to Wellington to care for its destitute. Concern for such was a principal work also of Anglican religious orders for women which were founded in Christchurch and Auckland early in the twentieth century.

But neither women in religious orders nor deaconesses in the Presbyterian (from 1902) and Methodist (1912) churches enjoyed the equality of leadership and ministry of the Salvation Army. In 1892, for instance, of 262 full-time commissioned officers, 146 were women who also commanded units of the Army in the four major cities and in Invercargill.[26]

But in addition to all these 'professionals', laywomen have been the main and largely unpaid labour-force in teaching Sunday Schools, participating in Bible-in-Schools programmes, parish visiting, and church cleaning and catering.

Women's formal exclusion from decision-making in the life of the churches has only slowly been modified. Generally, smaller denominations made the first moves. Despite there being no constitutional barriers in the Methodist church where women were concerned, there, as in other churches, they moved into the newer roles only gradually. The Congregational Union made women eligible for the membership of their assembly in 1893; the Baptists did likewise in 1909. By the time women were admitted to the Presbyterian eldership in 1955 most other lay positions in that church had been opened up to them. Until 1919 Anglican women could not even vote at parish meetings! Three years later the General Synod (the national governing body) resolved to admit them on equal terms to men in all representative church bodies. But here and elsewhere women only began to be an effective presence in decision-making bodies from about the 1960s.

On the matter of women's suffrage there was some ecclesiastical equivocation also. A New Zealand branch of the Women's Christian Temperance Union was formed in 1885. It campaigned for female enfranchisement in the belief that, if women had the vote, there would be greater pressure on politicians to control the drink trade. Congregationalists, Baptists, Methodists and the Salvation Army all backed both causes. Anglicans, Catholics and Presbyterians were somewhat divided although some individuals supported female suffrage - e.g. Bishop Cowie (Auckland) and Bishop Churchill Julius (Christchurch) - both of them Anglicans.[27]

Admission to the ordained ministry was, likewise, a protracted business. Where the Salvation Army and the Catholic Church were concerned there was no problem, but for different reasons. The former put women officers on the same basis as men; the latter excluded women from the priesthood (and still does). Those churches which have admitted women to the full exercise of the ordained ministry have done so only since the 1950s - Congregationalists 1951, Methodists 1959, Presbyterians 1965, Baptists 1973, and Anglicans 1976.

It is, perhaps, significant that this change followed on the heels of a softening up of the long-held line on the domestic and familial role of women. From the late nineteenth century bodies such as the Plunket Society (founded 1909) were joined by churches in stressing that the place of women - an exalted role it was emphasised - was in the home. The Anglican Mothers' Union was especially to the fore in this regard. The first New Zealand branch was founded at Avonside, Christchurch in 1886 and during the years 1892-97 the New Zealand organisation was under the active patronage of the Countess of Glasgow whose husband was governor-general during the years 1892-97. (Ironically, then and later, the very active more highly placed officials of the organisation, often bishops' wives too, were out of their homes and away from families a good deal!)

The Catholic Church, in its official opposition to birth control, expressed similar views about the domestic role of women.[28] When the National Council of Churches Women's Committee was established in 1945 it quickly moved into the production of studies on 'home and family' issues.[29]

That did not exclude, however, the slow liberalising of attitudes to divorce and re-marriage, in the Protestant churches first of all. Anglicans moved more slowly, but when they did, they involved the local Mothers' Union in tensions with its parent body. The rules of the organisation excluded divorced persons from membership and the desire to modify them was one cause of the establishment, in 1969, of the locally based Association of Anglican Women.[30]

By 1970 newer influences were beginning to make themselves felt from the twin and inter-related sources of the feminist movement and changes in family and work patterns. They affected women and the churches in important ways; their effect is still being worked out.

Church, society and nation

Christian churches have had a considerable role in fostering both ethnic and national identity. Especially in the earlier phases of settlement, ethnicity and religion are often mutually reinforcing as immigrants seek, on the one hand, to retain old ties and, on the other, to face up to the challenges of life in a new land. In New Zealand there have been several instances where such links have been especially strong. Of the early settlements Christchurch (Anglican), and Dunedin (Presbyterian), are well-enough known. Other settlements with explicit religious connections were Dannevirke (Scandinavian and Lutheran), Waipu (Scottish and Presbyterian), and Albertland (Scottish and English Non-conformists). The predominance of the denominations concerned was soon watered down but still today there linger traces in these places of this early connection and particular ethos.

Irish-Roman Catholic links were rather more important and were strongly maintained by ecclesiastics like Bishop Moran (Dunedin 1871-95) and Bishop Liston of Auckland. But this Irish/ Catholic tie, stronger perhaps among clergy than laity, has gradually dissolved. It has been eroded by population mobility, the laity's desire to win acceptance in the wider community, increasing social homogeneity, growth in the proportion of New Zealand-born and foreign-born non-Irish Catholics, partial resolution of the question of state aid to church schools (long an issue overheated by the joint efforts of ecclesiastics and secularists) and the changed ecumenical climate since the Second Vatican Council.

But among one more recent group of immigrants, the link between religion and ethnicity remains very important indeed. Polynesians in New Zealand numbered 7000 in 1959 and 88,824 by 1981. The various churches represented among these newest immigrants, especially the Pacific Islands Presbyterian Church, provide public worship in native languages, links with island communities, advice and assistance of various kinds, and warm fellowship to new settlers in sprawling urban areas. In this instance ethnic and religious identities interact, are mutually reinforcing, and show no immediate signs of dissolving.

In addition, however, the churches have interacted with various images of the meaning of national identity, playing their part in the on-going search for a national identity for Aotearoa/New Zealand. In this process we can distinguish three main concepts which have been taken up by the churches although not successively. There is what can be termed 'New Zealand as a Christian country'; the 'liberal imperial ideology'; and most recently, the vision of 'biculturalism'.

Firmly rooted in the ethos of some of the churches which came to New Zealand was the notion of shaping a Christian social order. A more general concern for matters of morality worked in the same general direction. This type of vision suffered early setbacks. Dunedin quickly resisted attempts to create a theocratic society, and leading Anglicans quickly discerned that their church was one denomination among others, not, as in England, an established church with a pre-eminent right to shape the national life.

The dream of New Zealand as a 'Christian country' has long persisted and has informed a whole series of moral campaigns. The years 1880-1920, for instance, saw a number of attempts to ensure that what were taken to be Christian standards should prevail; where appropriate, through legislation.[31] Over those years many Christians, especially Protestants, campaigned for such causes as prohibition of the manufacture and sale of alcoholic beverages, restriction of gambling, and Christian teaching in state schools. All those campaigns failed in their set purpose, partly because of division within and between the churches over the stands taken, partly because of opposition from other sources. But the vision survived this first round of campaigns.

Soon after the National Council of Churches was founded in 1941 it launched a Campaign for

Christian Order - with rather mixed results.[32] The major churches began to get some sense of their position in a secular and plural society. More recently, some conservative Christians resurrected the old battle-cry in the campaign against homosexual law reform in 1984-85 and in the activities of the Coalition of Concerned Citizens in their build-up to the General Election of 1987.

Equally beguiling for some of the churches, especially in times of war, has been the attraction of what has been called 'the liberal imperial ideology'. Loyalty to Queen and Empire was often expressed in various church contexts in the late nineteenth century and at the time of the South African war. 'The strain,' said the Anglican *New Zealand Church News*, for January 1900, 'has banded us together one indivisible people.' With some interesting exceptions, the general consensus of church opinion identified strongly with the cause of Britain in the First World War. The Methodist Conference in 1915 boomed forth: 'We regard the British Empire, with all its defects, as being, in practical righteousness, the largest instalment of the Kingdom of God that has yet arisen among men'.[33]

During the years between the two world wars countervailing tendencies operated. The 'Anzac tradition' took strong root in the wider community, but at the same time a degree of anti-militarism and pacifism found some support in the churches. When World War II came the sense of identification with Britain was still very close. 'Where she goes, we go' said Prime Minister Savage, and many church leaders strongly affirmed that view. At the same time, however, there were more openly expressed doubts, more criticisms of naive patriotism and national self-righteousness, than during the preceding World War.[34] Since then, where New Zealand is to 'go' is much less clear. The Vietnam War, South Africa and apartheid, and the collapse of ANZUS have divided the churches as deeply as the community in general.

Most recently, the notion of biculturalism has been fostered as a key element in the on-going search for national identity, and officially the mainline churches have taken up this rallying-cry and sought to embody it in the life of their own organisations in a variety of ways.

Evidence for the churches' wider influence in shaping national life is complex, conflicting and in some areas under-researched. 'Churches' is, after all, an umbrella word. Crowded uncomfortably under it are clerical hierarchies, representative assemblies, editors of church newspapers (and writers of 'letters to the editor'), committees and organisations, and 'grassroots' laity. For this reason alone, any estimate of the extent and depth of Christian influence in New Zealand's history must be tempered with care and caution. Such estimates frequently dwell on the negative aspects.

The evidence suggests that, by the 1960s, the churches were beginning to become increasingly marginal to New Zealand society. Sabbatarianism, the struggle to legislate prohibition into effect, opposition to gambling and to birth control by various sections of Christian opinion, resistance to liberalisation of laws relating to divorce and homosexual acts have all helped create an image of organised Christianity as negative and illiberal. Then too, with some exceptions, the larger churches have had a mainly middle-class constituency and others have felt alienated in consequence.

It is hard, too, to point to any major reform for which church backing was decisive. On the contrary, some in the churches have an impressive track record for resistance to almost all change. The most recent evidence indicates that the major churches (except the Catholic) have an aged and aging constituency and, anyway, do not seem to be uniformly successful in shaping the attitudes of their members.[35]

That is not all that can be said about the past, present and future of the churches concerned. Their charitable efforts have sometimes been paternalistic, unimaginative and focused on symptoms rather than causes. All the same, work undertaken by such bodies as city missions and the Salvation Army has rightly won wide respect. Education, too, has been an area in which Christian participation has sometimes been a 'mixed blessing', but has been important nevertheless. Thus the role played by Te Aute College in the education of Maori leadership is only one story of solid academic and social achievement by church-based institutions.

Then there have been Christian individuals, committees and other organisations whose well-informed criticisms or submissions to government have played some part in effecting change. Rutherford Waddell, a Presbyterian minister in Dunedin, played a leading role in agitation against 'sweated labour' during the closing years of the nineteenth century. At another level and in more recent years the Inter-Church Commission on Immigration and Refugee Re-settlement has worked closely with government agencies.

The churches too have had a range of international links through which they have been able to keep the government and the general public aware of sectors of overseas opinion which might otherwise be overlooked or smothered. Church links with Asia and Africa have been significant in this regard in recent years. Then at the individual level there have been politicians, members of the caring and teaching professions, those in commerce and a few in trade unions, those in public and municipal service, whose notions of service and integrity have been rooted - as far as one can tell - in Christian faith and practice.

At the most basic level of day-to-day life there has been the quality of life of those 'ordinary Christians' whose faith expresses itself in acts of unostentatious courtesy, thoughtfulness and kindness. Through acts such as these above all, Christians believe, their task is to be 'the salt of the earth'.

Notes

1. For an excellent survey of Christianity's main 'families' in their rich variety see Andrew Walls, 'Christianity', *A Handbook of Living Religions,* edited by John R. Hinnells, Harmondsworth: Penguin Books, 1985, pp. 56-122, esp. 96-113.
2. On Mystery Cults and Gnosticism see entries in *The Penguin Dictionary of Religions,* edited by John R. Hinnells, Harmondsworth: Penguin Books, 1984.
3. See, esp., E.S. Fiorenza, *In Memory of Her; a feminist theological reconstruction of Christian origins,* London: S.C.M. Press, 1983.
4. For Christianity in New Zealand see especially: *Transplanted Christianity: documents illustrating aspects of New Zealand Church History,* edited by Allan K. Davidson and Peter J. Lineham, Palmerston North: Dunmore Press, 2nd edn. 1989, and Allan K. Davidson, *Christianity in Aotearoa,* Wellington: Education for Ministry, 1989. The latter will be re-published in 1991 in a revised form as *Christianity in Aotearoa: a history of Church and Society,* Wellington: Education for Ministry.
5. See Bronwyn Elsmore, *Mana from Heaven: a century of Maori Prophets in New Zealand,* Tauranga: Moana Press, 1989.
6. Davidson, pp. 23,26; Davidson and Lineham, 2nd edn., pp. 53-4, 62-5.
7. Davidson, p. 38.
8. See Colin Brown, *Forty Years On: a history of the National Council of Churches in New Zealand 1941-1981,* Christchurch: N.C.C., 1981, chs. 10, 11.
9. See further, e.g. James Irwin, 'Towards a Maori Theology', *Colloquium 16/1* (1983), pp. 13-21; M. Shirres, 'The Maori Contribution', in *Towards an Authentic New Zealand Theology,* edited by J.M. Ker and K.J. Sharpe, Auckland: Univ. of Auckland Chaplaincy Publg. Trust, 1984, pp. 3-9.

10. e.g. Michael L. Drake, *The New Maori Myth,* Auckland: Wycliffe Christian Schools, 1988.

11. See Davidson and Lineham, pp. 172 and 176.

12. Hugh Jackson, 'Churchgoing in Nineteenth-Century New Zealand', *New Zealand Journal of History,* 17/1 (1983), p. 52.

13. P.J. Lineham, 'Freethinkers in Nineteenth-Century New Zealand', *New Zealand Journal of History,* 19/1 (1985), pp. 61-81.

14. See, further, Colin Brown, 'Church, Culture, and Identity', in *Culture and Identity in New Zealand,* edited by David Novitz and Bill Willmott, Wellington: G.P. Books, 1989, p. 245 and references there.

15. H.R. Jackson, *Churches and People in Australia and New Zealand 1860-1930,* Wellington: Allen and Unwin/Port Nicholson Press, 1987, p. 97.

16. See, e.g., Margaret Alington, *Frederick Thatcher and St. Paul's; an ecclesiological study,* Wellington: Government Printer, 1965, and C.R. Knight, *The Selwyn Churches of Auckland,* Wellington: A.H. and A.W. Reed, 1972.

17. See further, Ian Breward, *Grace and Truth: a history of Theological Hall, Knox College, Dunedin 1876-1975,* Dunedin: Theological Education Committee, Presbyterian Church of New Zealand, 1975.

18. See further, Jackson, ch.3 and Davidson and Lineham, pp. 193-201.

19. Ian Breward, 'Have the Mainline Protestant Churches Moved Out of their Colonial Status?', in *Religion in New Zealand Society,* edited by Brian Colless and Peter Donovan, Palmerston North: Dunmore Press, 1985, 2nd edn., p. 67.

20. Brown, 'Church, Culture and Identity', pp. 238 and 240.

21. F.W.R. Nichol, 'Theology in New Zealand', *Landfall,* 20/1 (March 1966), p. 49.

22. Brown, 'Church, Culture, and Identity', p. 241 and references there.

23. On women and the churches, see, briefly, Brown, 'Church, Culture, and Identity', pp. 242-4 and references there.

24. Davidson, pp. 65-7 and references there.

25. Davidson, pp. 72 and 120.

26. Brown, 'Church, Culture, and Identity', p. 242 and references there.

27. Davidson, p. 70.

28. Jackson, *Churches and People,* ch. 7 and references there.

29. A forthcoming doctoral thesis by Jane Simpson (Otago) will explore these developments fully.

30. Brown, 'Church, Culture, and Identity', p. 240.

31. Davidson and Lineham, pp. 225-40.

32. Brown, *Forty Years On,* pp. 34-8 and Davidson, p. 107.

33. Davidson and Lineham, pp. 292-3.

34. Peter Lineham, 'The Religious Face of Patriotism: civilian church people in World War Two', unpublished MS.

35. Alan C. Webster and Paul E. Perry, *The Religious Factor in New Zealand Society,* Palmerston North: Alpha Publications, 1989, pp. 22-3, 120-1, 137, 139, 142.

Further reading

On Christianity in New Zealand, besides the works by Brown, Davidson, Davidson and Lineham, and Jackson, mentioned in the notes above, the following are suggested:

Lineham, P.J. and Grigg, A.R., *Religious History of New Zealand: a bibliography,* Palmerston North: Department of History, Massey University, 3rd edition, 1989.

Oliver, W.H. (ed.), *Oxford History of New Zealand,* Oxford/Wellington: Clarendon Press/OUP, 1981.

Brief introductions to Christianity are:

Walls, A., 'Christianity', in *A Handbook of Living Religions,* edited by John R. Hinnells, Harmondsworth: Penguin Books, 1985, pp. 6-122.

Frankiel, S.S., *Christianity: a way of salvation,* San Francisco: Harper and Row, 1985.

Smart, Ninian, *The Phenomenon of Christianity,* London: Collins, 1979.

Wiggins, J.B. and Ellwood, R.S., *Christianity: a cultural perspective,* Englewood Cliffs N.J.: Prentice-Hall, 1988.

Christianity:
Catholics Since the 1960s

Elizabeth Isichei

The Catholic Church, spiritual home of nearly two-thirds of the world's Christians, has undergone immense changes, especially in the West, partly as a result of the Second Vatican Council (1962-65), and partly as a result of events which occurred in the sixties and seventies. 'The 1960s Revolution of Expressive Disorder ... was essentially an attack on boundaries, limits, certainties, taboos, roles, systems, style, form and ritual.'[1] This was bound to affect a church which laid such emphasis on external authority. Its position is now one of profound paradox. The stresses caused by rapid reform and change are well illustrated from the church's recent history in New Zealand. According to the 1986 Census, 496,158 New Zealanders describe themselves as Catholic - making it the third largest religious denomination.

In 1989 a long-lived Catholic who arrived in New Zealand as a child in 1923, wrote of the Catholicism he remembered in the Timaru of his youth:

> Besides a beautiful church, impressive convent and schools in the charge of religious, we had a Catholic football club, a Catholic cricket club and a Catholic tennis club. We had our own hall which featured billiards, snooker and small-bore rifle shooting. We had a Catholic glee club and a Catholic drama club.
>
> Everyone seemed to go to one of the three masses on Sunday, the last being a High Mass with the splash of the Asperges, clouds of incense and a splendid choir singing the sacred works of Mozart, Gounod and company. Rosary, sermon and Benediction marked every Sunday evening, the First Sunday featuring a Procession of the Blessed Sacrament, with the Hibernians holding the canopy, flower girls scattering petals in the way of the Lord, followed by the Sodalities with their colourful banners - the Children of Mary in white and blue, the Sacred Heart Sodality and St. Anne's Guild of charitable women, the Knights and Handmaids of the Blessed Sacrament and the regiment of the Holy Name Society.
>
> Add to all this the deep devotional life of the parish - evening devotions every Wednesday and Friday; queues outside the confessionals every Saturday night.... A Catholic could live and die in the Timaru of my youth without making an intimate friend of anyone who was not a Catholic.[2]

This is a picture immediately recognisable to one who looks back on the Catholicism of the 1950s: its clear and cosy sense of social identity, the comfort of its majestic certainties. But the picture is very different today, whether we look at worship, clergy and religious orders, or the concerns and life-styles of Catholic laymen and women.

Worship

Before Vatican II, mass was always said in Latin. Few people understood it, but with its familiar phrases and long silences it was much loved. It became essentially a context for individual contemplative prayer, not unlike the 'Jesus Prayer' of the Eastern church. There was a vast number of devotional practices - scapulars of various hues, and medals, and pious societies - which Catholic intellectuals tended to look down on (as they did on plaster statues and 'holy pictures'), but which were a great source of consolation in many people's lives.

Some non-Catholics found the church's element of mystery extremely attractive. Some were drawn by the very pious paraphernalia which others despised. I remember how I strayed into the Cathedral of the Blessed Sacrament in 1958. I was nineteen, and a fervent Anglican. The church was in half-darkness, apart from a blaze of candles around the altar of Our Lady of Perpetual Succour. The congregation thundered the second part only of the Hail Mary (they were saying a Rosary in turn with an inaudible priest). I was enchanted, and became a Catholic soon after.

Now, in 1990, the church's worship has changed almost beyond recognition. Despite moves which are clearly 'reforms' - such as the replacement of Latin by a vernacular liturgy and increased lay participation in Sunday services - mass attendance continues to decline. Various estimates suggest that approximately one third of those who call themselves Catholics attend Sunday mass.[3] This is partly a concomitant of the decline of a belief in Hell (mass having been compulsory, under pain of mortal sin), but is also partly because, in the view of many, church services have become not more but less attractive.

Michael King, one of New Zealand's Catholic intellectuals who drifted away from the church during these years, spoke for many when he said:

> Oddly the few reforms in the Catholic church that have taken place seem to me to be the wrong ones. Aggiornamento had resulted in the beauty and suggestive mystery of the Latin rite being replaced by simplified litany in English that seemed prosaic and flat, utterly lacking in the feel of antiquity, continuity, mystery and divine reverberation that I had experienced at school. The sense of awe had been replaced by that of the commonplace, and to me the whole process felt like one of impoverishment, subtraction rather than addition.[4]

A twenty-two year old woman graduate, with a history of exceptional dedication to the church, said: 'Mass. It is totally irrelevant. It is not worth going to.'[5] An older Catholic suggested that the problem was due to the poor quality of sermons.

> In my youth we were constantly threatened with hell. Nowadays, nobody mentions hell.... Without hell, youngsters leave school and give up going to Mass because of boredom. And the prime cause of boredom is the Sunday sermon.[6]

In 1988, somewhat in the accents of Canute commanding the waves, the New Zealand bishops issued a statement that Sunday mass was obligatory.[7] A Dominican nun replied with an analysis of some categories of non-attenders:

Women, who have become aware of the patriarchal nature of language, expression of liturgy and symbols that hold them bound.... People of other cultures - who find the liturgy does not speak of God present in their lives or their symbols, but speaks of division and not belonging. People who find that the liturgy is in no way related to their daily lives....[8]

Not all lay Catholics feel this sense of alienation of course. Many find satisfaction in roles which did not exist in 1960 - distributing communion, reading scriptural passages to the congregation, or leading congregational prayer. But many parishes have lost their once-excellent choirs.

During the 1970s, attendance at confession dropped dramatically - a worldwide trend which is still imperfectly understood. Was it due to the declining fear of hell, or to a new inner authority, a new robustness of conscience?

Suddenly and unexpectedly confession was no longer valued. The people did not want it. Neither, for that matter, did the priests.[9]

Rechristening 'confession', which became 'reconciliation', changed nothing. It came to be felt 'confession could ... be producing that kind of oppressive guilt in people'.[10]

Priests and religious

Priests and religious (i.e. members of religious orders) were enormously esteemed in the culture of the 1950s. A vocation was seen as a kind of tangible gift from Heaven. Religious dominated the educational system, and the uniquely impressionable adolescent naturally took them as a role model, as well as absorbing the nuns' reverential esteem for the parish priest. Priests and religious undoubtedly struggled with areas of unhappiness and uncertainty in their own lives. But these were not on general display or matters for public debate. The occasional priest did abandon his vow of celibacy and marry, but became 'in Catholic circles, a social leper of the lowest order'.[11]

Pre-Vatican II women religious were often lonely in the middle of a crowd. Their consciousness had not yet been raised to a resentment of their inbuilt position of subordination in a profoundly hierarchical church. 'The life was always a paradox: there was both pain and peace, heaviness and humour, formality and informality, justice and injustice.'[12] An old nun told me, 'I remember a couple of times I was hauled over the coals for something or other, and I wasn't at fault. I felt so hurt and angry about that. I suppose I could have explained fully but you weren't encouraged in those days to explain fully.'[13]

One of the most striking indices of the present malaise in the church has been a massive exodus from the priesthood and religious life. This has two facets: the departure of existing members, and the lack of new recruits. Religious and priests, though overlapping, are best considered separately.

Ironically, it all began with Vatican II's call to religious to re-examine their calling in the light of the charism of their founders, and to meet the needs of the modern world. Pauline O'Regan's autobiography gives us a moving picture, from within, of how the Mercy Sisters gradually abandoned their black serge habit, and a multitude of restrictions as well. She remembers when she first held Vatican II's Document on Religious Life: 'Little did I know that I was actually holding a time bomb ... a new and startling word entered our vocabulary - polarisation'.[14]

This process of re-evaluation meant that many sisters came to have misgivings about their work in schools and hospitals - among fee-paying pupils and fee-paying patients. Some felt drawn to work among the poor or in the mission field, or in a pastoral role. Some have found creative new spheres - Sister Jean Sinclair runs GIFT, a workshop in Auckland for the intellectually handicapped, which caters for 800 people. Sister Dominica Knox teaches personal growth techniques at Anawim House in Wellington. However, many gave up work in what they were trained for, and have failed to find a satisfactory, new avocation.

Strangely enough, as nuns experienced greater autonomy, the calling became less attractive to the young. As the average age of nuns increased, a further obstacle developed - new recruits could find themselves in the role of caregivers. As feminist consciousness has developed, many have come to resent their exclusion from the priesthood - they have travelled far from the traditional subservience of sisters to priests in the pre-Vatican II church.

Male religious went through the same questionings. Some Marist Fathers were anxious to give up teaching for work in the Pacific or Latin America.[15] In 1988 several left St. Patrick's College to work in the Wellington suburb of Strathmore which includes considerable state housing.

The priesthood went through the same process of change. On average only seven new priests have been ordained each year over the past fifteen years.[16] In 1989, New Zealand's national seminary had twenty-two students in the first year, nine in the second, eight in the third, three in the fourth and three in the fifth.[17] Many left the priesthood. One source suggests that over twenty diocesan priests have left in Christchurch since the mid-sixties - more in Auckland and Wellington, fewer in Dunedin.[18] Often they have left to marry. In the seventies priests were laicised and received permission to marry with relative ease. Under the present Pope, it has become virtually impossible. Many do not even apply, unwilling to face not only years of delay but humiliating interviews. But if not laicised, they are excluded from the sacraments. Ironically, at a time when the clergy are a shrinking and ageing body, the church makes no use of the talents of its married priests, many of whom have no desire to leave the ministry.

Not all clergy, of course, experience an identity crisis, or a failure of purpose in middle age. Some find ministry fulfilling, and light a candle in many darkened lives. Optimists point out that religious life has been through crises before (for example many religious orders collapsed during the French Revolution: in the nineteenth century an unprecedentedly large number of new orders were founded). They point out too that orders which have lost their first inspiration may gain a new lease of life by being refounded. It has even been suggested that orders which lost their original charism early are being founded for the first time.

An example of a New Zealander who has been acclaimed as a 'refounding personality' is Father Bernard Ryan who, in 1977, went from being the headmaster of a Hastings school to become the elected Superior General of the entire Society of Mary throughout the world. He 'courageously pointed to the obvious gaps between the founder's vision and the reality of Marist life' and stressed 'the themes of conversion, a deeper knowledge of the institution's charism, and emphasis of the new global mission policy'.[19] When his period of office was over, he went to work among the Australian aborigines. Father Gerald Arbuckle, a Cambridge-trained anthropologist and New Zealand Marist, has made major intellectual contributions which include a pioneering study of the pastoral needs of Maori Christians (1976),[20] and two books on the contemporary crisis in religious life.

Education

The pre-1960s church was committed to its own system of schools. It was considered gravely sinful for Catholic parents to send their children to state schools if Catholic schools were available, and some children had to make extraordinarily long daily journeys to comply with this requirement. There were no state subsidies and church schools were maintained by the sacrifices both of parents and of the virtually unpaid religious teachers. Convents in country towns often subsisted largely on the earnings of an overworked piano teacher.

Until 1966 religion was taught in the form of catechisms - questions and answers to be memorised. The architect of the religious education system which replaced it said:

> Rules and rituals, formulas and the threat of church punishment were all that many picked up. The children saw much of it as classroom knowledge, not to be integrated in their lives.[21]

The desirability of Catholic schools was a 'given' which could not be questioned - although the occasional thinker pointed out that they were not necessarily the best preparation for life in a pluralistic society, and that much of the time was spent studying subjects like chemistry(!) which could not have a specifically Catholic interpretation.[22]

The Catholicism in which those up to the fifties were schooled was very difficult to leave. To leave the church was to resist the known truth, certainly to plunge into mortal sin, and perhaps even to commit the sin against the Holy Ghost (an unforgivable iniquity to whose identity Catholic schoolchildren devoted almost as much awestricken speculation as they did to the identity of the non-disclosed Fatima predictions!).

Attendance at Catholic schools ceased to be compulsory in the 1960s, an apparent volte-face which many found deeply disconcerting.[23] The increasing use of lay teachers created a financial crisis, so that Catholic children were sometimes positively encouraged to attend state schools. Now 50 per cent of Catholic children do so. The proportion of religious on their staff has fallen dramatically (to 15 per cent) partly because New Zealand religious are a shrinking and ageing body, and partly because many of them have turned to other callings. The 'Catholic character' has inevitably diminished: a third of the teachers are non-Catholics, and probably only a minority of the rest have the degree of religious commitment typical of religious.

Since 1975 the state has borne the running costs of Catholic schools, making the lay teachers' salaries possible. School fees, however, continue, justified in terms of debts incurred in building costs. (State aid was dependent on acceptable buildings: this often meant expensive alterations.) There is a high degree of non-payment, perhaps suggesting that the fees are resented in an era of state support and of great economic difficulty.

The content of religious education changed dramatically in the sixties. 'Caring and sharing became the whole law and the prophets.'[24] It is deeply ironical that this was the work of Felix Donnelly, who later became the *enfant terrible* of New Zealand Catholicism, and who was silenced (that is, forbidden to preach or hear confessions) in 1980. It is also ironical that he did it with the wholehearted support of the ageing and autocratic Archbishop Liston. It is now generally accepted that the pendulum swung too far the other way, so that Catholic teenagers could leave Catholic schools with singularly little understanding of what Catholics believe. The stress on human relations - common to much of the community as a whole - suggested no reason for being specifically Catholic. Greater doctrinal content has since been introduced.

Marriage, divorce, sex

The Catholicism of the 1950s engendered an incalculable amount of human pain, most obvious in the people whose life condition made them irretrievably marginalised - the gay and the divorced and remarried. The murderer or rapist could repent and be restored to the odour of sanctity, but someone divorced and remarried was excluded from the sacraments. This could not change unless the first partner died, or the first marriage was annulled (a complex and lengthy process, with uncertain outcome), or the second marriage abandoned.

Nor was married life a cosy haven of licit sex. The church's embargo on birth control destroyed the spontaneity of sexual relations which most non-Catholic couples took for granted. Many couples had far more children than they had intended or could afford, and were locked into a situation of relative poverty and stress. An anonymous woman remembers:

> As a direct result of not being allowed to space my family, I suffered poor physical health, extreme depression, loneliness, suburban neurosis and alcoholism. I was not the only one - the number of Catholic women suffering breakdowns was high.[25]

It is possible that *Humanae Vitae*, the encyclical of 1968, affected lay Catholics more than Vatican II. Some openly challenged the Pope's endorsement of the traditional prohibition, but more widely it was simply ignored. A well-informed Australian estimate, probably true also of New Zealand, suggests that 85 per cent of practising Catholics under forty-five use contraceptives.[26] Others pointed out that the church's opposition to abortion was easier to sustain if it was not accompanied by a rigid prohibition of contraception, particularly of the pill.

This was, however, the beginning of a much more radical change. Some Catholics found it impossible to live in daily disobedience to the authority of the church, and left it. Some obeyed *Humanae Vitae*, often at the cost of much personal suffering and with a feeling of a deep and very understandable resentment of those Catholics who ignored it and continued to frequent the sacraments, appearing to have the best of both worlds. But many used contraceptives or were sterilised, and in all other respects led a Catholic life. They had made a radical discovery that it was possible to disobey the Pope on a matter on which he had spoken explicitly, and yet to remain a practising Catholic. It was this that empowered priests to marry, the divorced to remarry, gay Catholics to live openly with their partners and so on.

The divorced and remarried, like ex-priests and the gay, continued to be extremely marginal in the church. It was a major concern of the 1989 Auckland synod that 'the church should show more care and support for the divorced, separated and widowed'[27] - though, at the same time, glowing tribute was paid to workshops catering for their needs.

Gay Catholics, like the divorced and remarried, experience a gap between theory and practice. In theory, gay sexual behaviour is regarded as gravely sinful. (Felix Donnelly was silenced in 1980 for questioning this.) Cardinal Thomas Williams opposed the decriminalising of homosexuality in 1985,[28] and it was not on the agenda of the archdiocesan synod. Bishop Meeking caused a furore in late 1988 when he asked Compassion Sisters to stop working with the AIDS Foundation. But there is also an organisation called Ascent, with its own chaplain for gay Catholics, and masses are held in gay couples' homes. Not all can live with this kind of ambiguity. Many voted with their feet and left the church.

Women in Catholicism

In the years that followed Vatican II, many women struggled to reconcile insights absorbed from the feminist movement with their Catholic inheritance. Some concluded that the church was irremediably sexist and left. Some formed a Catholic feminist organisation called Sophia. A basic difficulty for Catholic feminists was abortion, to which most Catholics, at least in theory,[29] are opposed, and for which most non-Catholic feminists is a basic human right.

Some women reacted strongly against the feminist critique. In 1988, 2240 lay Catholics, many of them women, petitioned the bishops unsuccessfully not to proceed with a study of sexism in the church. A conservative counter-group was formed, called Magnificat.[30] Meanwhile, women were being admitted to liturgical roles such as special minister of the Eucharist, despite being prohibited by Canon Law, although admittedly 'in somewhat devious and de facto ways', as one speaker at the Wellington Archdiocesan Synod pointed out.[31]

There is no doubt that more roles are open to Catholic women than existed twenty-five years ago. They are prominent in pastoral work and in church offices and ministries, and may find satisfaction in roles such as chairperson of the parish council. But they play very little part in decisions about the use of resources, and often feel excluded from liturgy and worship, by the use of non-inclusive language.

The major area of discrimination is that women are excluded from ordination, an exclusion probably felt most intensely by women religious. That sexism is still alive and flourishing was shown when a regular *Tablet* columnist told an inquirer that women 'are as incapable of ordination as animals' - a response gleefully seized on by the secular press.[32] It is worth noting that the traditionally conservative Catholic Women's League is generally accepted as the church's strongest and most influential lay body.

Maori Catholicism

Until the late 1940s, Maori Catholics tended to live in rural communities. Their priests were religious: Mill Hill fathers of continental extraction, and usually in an unwittingly paternalistic relationship. Church attendance was part of the life of the local community. Ranginui Walker recaptures it vividly:

> You imagine going to the Waiaua church on a Sunday. That was what made going to church - meeting your cousins, having lunch at the marae with the priest, going down to the river to swim in the afternoon. You go to church here and there's nothing like the sense of belonging....[33]

The Dominican Michael Shirres suggested in 1988 that only 2-3 per cent of Maori are happy in the church.[34] Shirres sees traditional Maori religion as a foreshadowing of Christianity. Maori gods 'were created spirits under the authority of Christ, like angels'. But when prayers at Christchurch cathedral gave thanks for Maori gods, such as Tane Mahuta and Tangaroa, a clerical columnist told an inquirer, 'Pagan gods are quite simply not real beings.... The angels are real persons.'[35]

Maori theology will be done by Maori people, and not by Pakeha, however well intentioned. The appointment of Father Takuira Mariu as first Maori bishop was an important step in the direction of discovering a distinctive Maori Catholic identity. Maori Catholic theology done by Maori people is only in its early stages. But it must be remembered that the extent of autonomy in the local church is limited. Major decisions, whether on faith or practice, morality or liturgy, are made in Rome.

Like other New Zealanders, Catholics have had to think through their position on biculturalism, the ideal of equal partnership between tangatawhenua and manuhiri: people of the land, and later immigrants. Biculturalism was strongly supported by the Commission for Evangelisation, Justice and Development (founded in 1978, and renamed Commission for Justice, Peace and

New Zealand Tablet

The Bishop of Hamilton, Bp. Edward Gaines, with Bishop Takuira Mariu.

Development ten years later). It is led by a Maori layman, Manuka Henare. Biculturalism was endorsed in 1988 by the Major Superiors of religious orders.[36]

The Commission was intended to speak with a prophetic voice, but has often had a divisive effect. Third or fourth generation New Zealanders found themselves profoundly threatened by the idea that they were 'visitors'. Some preferred the concept of multiculturalism, fearing that biculturalism made non-Maori minority groups invisible. In all this, Catholics mirror divisions within the wider community.

Politics

During the last thirty years, Catholics have often been divided over issues of foreign and domestic policy. In this, too, they mirrored divisions in society as a whole. It was perhaps Vietnam which cracked their complacency. Pauline O'Regan remembers how Vietnam divided the Christchurch Mercy sisters:

> Many of us were strongly opposed to New Zealand's involvement in Vietnam. It was bewildering to many nuns. Wasn't America fighting communism? Might not the communists overrun New Zealand if they were not stopped in Vietnam? Wasn't the Catholic church the chief opponent of communism?[37]

Archbishop Liston thought the same. The editor of *Zealandia*, Father E.R. Simmons, was a journalist with a national reputation. He censored President Kennedy for jeopardising world peace during the Cuba crisis. Liston could not understand how a Catholic newspaper could criticise a Catholic president, and in 1969 demoted Simmons, and the able deputy editor who succeeded him. His actions led to an unprecedented protest, and pickets outside his residence. *Zealandia*, which in its heyday had a paid circulation of 30,000, virtually collapsed in 'the year of the three editors'. The question of Springbok tours was later to divide Catholics similarly; and so, later still, was the decriminalisation of homosexuality.

In the mid-eighties the bishops, and Cardinal Thomas Williams in particular, have been increasingly vocal on political issues: supporting New Zealand's anti-nuclear policy, opposing the purchase of frigates, and attacking the social and economic consequences of the Labour Government's policies. Williams' sincerity was patent; he was a parish priest at Porirua before he became a cardinal.

Critics pointed out that cardinals are not necessarily experts on economics or defence. But there was a much more fundamental criticism to be made. It was made on a talkback show, when the cardinal was asked why the proceeds of the sale of prize church real estate - Loretta Hall, or the Redemptorist Monastery in Oriental Bay - did not benefit the poor.[38] A sympathetic Presbyterian noted, 'the churches are so deeply involved as beneficiaries of the existing social and economic order that they are timid in the questions which they raise.'[39] I discussed this question with the national bursar of a women's order which has sold similar real estate. She pointed out that their nuns live simply, following a budget, and donate any surplus to charities espoused by the international order as a whole: 'We would never be able to sit back and say, "We're millionaires!"'[40]

Father John Curnow is one who has expressed a radical vision, which owes much to liberation theology. 'It would be a real conversion if we threw in our lot with the marginalised.... Is the church visible up there at the top, or down there at the bottom?'[41]

Meanwhile in 1988 the bishop of Waikato, Edward Gaines invited Opus Dei into his diocese. Founded in 1929, it is deeply controversial, criticised by liberals for its right-wing role in countries such as Spain and Latin America. It was strongly denounced in a recent book by an Australian priest.[42] Gaines was undoubtedly motivated by the exodus of no less than five religious orders from his diocese in a single year. But the move caused disquiet among some New Zealand Catholics.[43] It remains to be seen what impact this secular institute will have on the New Zealand scene.

Theology

There has been more debate about social and political issues than about theology, despite the attempts that have been made to make the clergy, nuns and others involved in the new Christian doctrine courses more au fait with modern theological thought.

In 1972, Father Hubert Richards was invited to lecture in New Zealand. The conservative *Tablet* published not his own words, but summaries from two hostile conservatives.[44] Richards replied mildly, 'I was trying to do no more than make available ... the agreed conclusions of respectable Catholic scholars'.[45] Two bishops then issued public statements, energetically defending Richards and reproving his critics. 'It is becoming horribly clear to me,' wrote Bishop Ashby, 'that the church in New Zealand today needs to be saved as much from its friends as from its enemies.'[46] He went on to make the interesting point that sisters and Christian doctrine teachers were already familiar with much of what was said, and that they 'have left a number of us priests far behind'.

There was a similar clash when the Cambridge Catholic theologian, Nicholas Lash, visited in 1974. In an interview he spoke of 'the thoroughness of the anti-intellectualism of New Zealand Catholics'.[47] Michael King recalls how one of the episodes that alienated him from Catholicism was clerical condemnation of a Dutch visiting priest, Jacques Vink.[48]

In 1988 Matthew Fox visited New Zealand, invited by an interdenominational committee. His creation theology with its stress on Original Blessing appealed to many Catholics, freeing them from a guilt-ridden spirituality. So did his concern for ecology and global peace and justice, and his sympathy with feminism. *The Tablet* denounced him for associations with witchcraft (since the faculty of his Californian college includes Starhawk, the best-known Californian witch!).[49]

In 1987 *Accent* published a New Zealand Stations of the Cross. The Second Station was

'Mosgiel: Theology'. (Mosgiel is the home of Holy Cross Seminary.) Neil Darragh wrote, 'To do theology is to accept the burden of our misunderstanding.... We have to search through the rubble of other people's ruins and our own deceit.'[50]

In the past, Catholics knew exactly what they believed. They knew that only God was adored - the saints were venerated. Sins were either venial or mortal. Mortal sin (which could include eating meat on Friday) qualified one for Hell, unless one repented. They believed that Jesus was truly present in the bread and wine at mass; to go to communion in a state of mortal sin was sacrilege. Some have all these certainties still. The present writer, reviewing a book by Lloyd Geering, stated that only in eternity would the answers to various questions be known. She was smartly rebuked by Father George Duggan; he knows the answers with certainty now.

Most Catholics, however, are less certain, partly because in some respects the rules have changed (for example the rules forbidding meat on Friday). The belief in Hell is less immediate and terrifying. Most still believe in a core of doctrine - the divinity of Jesus, the Trinity, the physical resurrection - while being vaguely aware that modern theologians have questioned this inner core. The saints are, in practice, venerated less - there is more emphasis, perhaps, on a relationship with Jesus.

Theological conservatism on the part of many has been matched with conservatism regarding the liturgical and other changes of post-Vatican II years. Liturgical changes meant changes in church design. In particular, the priest now said mass facing the people, from the far side of the altar, so that if a church had a high altar his back was turned to it. The logical removal of the high altar in the Cathedral of the Blessed Sacrament in Christchurch led to an unprecedented, though unsuccessful, explosion of protest which showed the depth of conservative feeling.[51] (Appeals were made both to the Pope, and to the Municipal Planning Authority!)

Some conservatives left the church. A few joined a variety of little splinter groups, inside or outside it.[52] Those who left faced a basic contradiction: they were trying to retain the church of the past, but rejecting the obedience to Pope and bishops which was one of its chief elements. A few New Zealanders - 500 at the outside - are followers of Archbishop Lefebvre. His Society of St Pius X, with a seminary in Switzerland, existed in a state of virtual schism for years. The breach became irreparable when he ordained his own bishops, thus ensuring that the movement would survive his death. A young Lefebvrist priest, who was tragically killed in a car crash at twenty-three, wrote a summary of their position which was published posthumously. It is interesting for the many insights it gives us into the conservative case.

> Worst of all, Catholics no longer pray like Catholics but more like Protestants. As a result they end up believing like Protestants....
> You all collectively allow the EJD... to finance communist organisations in the Philippines, or to push what is pagan in Maori culture. Perhaps if we adore the rising sun or a statue of Buddha you would invite us to a prayer meeting.[53]

One remembers the words of Dr Johnson, 'a convert from Popery to Protestantism gives up as much of what he had held as sacred as anything that he retains: there is so much laceration of mind in such a conversion, that it can hardly be sincere and lasting.'[54] But if the church itself is perceived to have 'become Protestant'...?

The Catholic church indeed drew closer to other Christian churches. The key turning point was in 1987, when it joined the Conference of Churches in Aotearoa New Zealand. Catholics acquired a deeper appreciation of the value both of other churches and of non-Christian spiritual traditions

- changes rooted in the decrees of Vatican II. The old hostility to 'mixed marriages' and to Catholic attendance at non-Catholic services faded away.

Those who admit to ennui and boredom in church worship (and some improbable informants admit to this, including elderly nuns) sometimes find more satisfaction in smaller groups. The conservative, especially, find satisfaction in the little congregations at daily mass. Parents group together to prepare their children for their first communion and reconciliation. RENEW, which began in 1985, consisted of several intense periods of small group study and discussion. Many participants found these small groups satisfying; the problem is that they were not geared to permanent existence. A couple I interviewed who feel very positive about the state of New Zealand Catholicism, believe that the future lies with small groups, but that to endure, these groups need a focus in study.

A considerable number of Catholics, especially the young, have joined fundamentalist and often pentecostalist churches, a local manifestation of a worldwide phenomenon. They are attracted by their religious certainties, a lively form of service and a warm and welcoming community. Within Catholic church life the Charismatic Movement which flourished in the 1970s has left its mark in some places, with its emphasis on personal experience, lively services and warm fellowship. The congregational life of the tiny mid-city chapel of Holy Cross in Christchurch, for instance, with a strong charismatic input, is strikingly vital.[55]

Women religious in particular have been active in organising a great variety of personal growth courses. The Myers-Briggs' personality-type indicator, first used in New Zealand Catholic circles by religious, is now 'on the programme of pastoral centres along with the Enneagram, dream workshops, journal keeping, creative expression and the odd therapy'.[56] Some Catholics are drawn to yoga, or to the eastern-style spirituality of *Sadhana*, written by an Indian Jesuit.

Conclusions

Many people reacted to the Second Vatican Council with an enthusiasm which has been compared to first reactions to the French Revolution![57] Some of those who were once so hopeful have been alienated by the conservatism and authoritarianism of the present Pope. The extent of this alienation was reflected during his visit to New Zealand in late 1986. Attendances were far lower than anticipated; the souvenir booklet and memorabilia remained largely unsold, and the church experienced a large financial loss.

Later that year, the New Zealand church had a striking experience of Roman authoritarianism. The bishop of Christchurch died; his successor was appointed two months later, while the process of consultation was in full swing. His successor, Basil Meeking, had been working in Rome since 1969....[58]

We have spoken of the stresses caused by rapid change. They are nothing new to Christianity. Church history reflects a constant pattern of ebb and flow. Tension and crisis rather than security and contentment have always been the lot of people of faith. A widely cited paradigm isolates successive responses to a period of rapid change.[59] The first response may be euphoric (the French Revolution), but there is some disorientation. In the second, people respond to disorientation with major or minor changes. In the third, where these changes seem to produce no positive results, they experience 'chaos, malaise, anger, fear of the future, even despair'. In the fourth phase, people begin to explore their own identity. Sometimes they seek an escape from this into the past (the followers of Lefebvre) or 'cult movements and fads of various kinds'. In the fifth phase, 'people achieve varying levels of cultural integration. The new integration must not remain something static'.

Most New Zealand Catholics are somewhere between stages three and five. Some will react against these perplexities and leave. Some will emerge at a new place of discovery, like the religious congregations which began in the nineteenth century and are now founded for the first time.

> We shall not cease from exploration
> And the end of all our exploring
> Will be to arrive where we started
> And know the place for the first time.[60]

Many people of faith have continued to find fulfilment in New Zealand Catholicism; many New Zealand Catholics have led inspiring lives. When Ernie Simmons ceased to be editor of *Zealandia*, he did not leave the priesthood. What lay ahead of him were years of ill health, and activity on a smaller scale as an archivist and chaplain to nuns. He continued to write a much-loved column in *Zealandia*. When he moved into the convent, he signed his column Sister Mary Ernest!

Gerard Crotty died in 1988, aged thirty. He was a Marist brother, and an outstandingly gifted composer. Interviewed in his last months, he spoke with the greatest enthusiasm of God, of his religious vocation, of his music, of his work as a teacher:

> Sometimes I have the feeling that I've already made the move into heaven, to paradise. There's still a journey to make; but the journey I'm making now is within paradise.[61]

Ida Corrigan was another Catholic who died in 1988; in her case, at the age of ninety-three. When nearing retirement age, she and her husband went to work in the Solomons, for the Leprosy Trust Board. Her husband died in 1954. In her seventies and eighties she embarked on epic journeys 'to mission stations in canoes and boats of all sizes...'.[62]

It is possible for a Christian to have a transforming influence on others without being conventionally holy. It has been said that New Zealand has produced three prophets: the nineteenth century Maori leader Te Whiti, the painter Colin MacCahon (who was not a member of any church), and James K. Baxter.[63] Baxter died in 1972 at the age of forty-six. He had been a convert, first to Anglicanism; later, in 1958, to Catholicism. He overcame his alcoholism with the help of Alcoholics Anonymous, and struggled, not always successfully, to follow the church's stern teachings on sexual morality. The struggle, and failures, are mirrored with remarkable honesty in his poems.[64] They mirror, too, his basically traditional piety - his love of rosaries, scapulars, statues, and most of all, confession.[65]

Baxter was beyond doubt New Zealand's greatest poet, and his work reflected an ever-deepening concern for the poor, both in New Zealand and abroad, and an ever-stronger sense of identification with the tangata whenua. But perhaps his poems were less prophetic than his life. From 1968 until his death he lived wholly among the poor and marginalised; first in Grafton, then at Jerusalem on the Wanganui river, then in Auckland again. He sacrificed the many rewards life offers to the literary lion,

> having nothing to lose,
> not even hat or shoes -
> wife, home, reputation,
> that too is gone.[66]

He died in 1972, prematurely old, oppressed with a sense of spiritual failure. 'Lord Christ, I do not know you. My bones are taking me towards the grave.... Though I do not know you, in my heart I find a small secret hope, hidden like a seed in the winter ground, that at the moment when I die, you will reveal yourself to me....'[67] He was, as his biographer says, one of those 'who blaze like the sun/between our thoughts'.[68]

Churches have chequered pasts, for their ideals are filtered through imperfect people. But 'holy is the true light, and passing wonderful, lending radiance to them that endured in the heat of conflict'.[69]

Notes

1. Gerald A. Arbuckle, *Strategies for Growth in Religious Life,* Homebush, NSW: St Paul Publications, 1987, p. 6.
2. Father Frank Durning SM, 'A lifetime of breathless change', *Zealandia,* 23 April, 1989, p. 10.
3. Figures for the six New Zealand dioceses range from 20.66 per cent for Hamilton to 36.25 per cent for Dunedin. (Paul Shanahan, *150 Years.* Leaflet issued by the Catholic Inquiry Centre, Wellington, 1988.)
4. Michael King, *Being Pakeha: an encounter with New Zealand and the Maori renaissance,* Auckland: Hodder and Stoughton, 1985, p. 101.
5. 'Teresa' in 'A Voice Crying in the Wilderness', *Zealandia,* 6 December 1987, p. 8.
6. S.O. Melmoth in *Zealandia,* 31 July 1978.
7. Pastoral letter, 'The First Day'. October 1988 - to omit Sunday mass 'is a serious fault which requires the healing of the Sacrament of Reconciliation'.
8. Sr. Mary Horn O.P., *Zealandia,* 18 December, 1988, p. 8.
9. Fr. Neil Darragh in *Zealandia,* 18 September 1988, p. 10.
10. Ibid.
11. Tony Peterson and Michael Parer, *Prophets and Losses in the Priesthood,* Sydney: Allela Books, 1971, p. 13.
12. Pauline O'Regan, *A Changing Order,* Wellington: Allen & Unwin/Port Nicholson Press, 1986, p. 82.
13. Interview in Wellington, 13 June 1989. The present writer is currently engaged in conducting interviews among present and former Catholics.
14. O'Regan, pp. 89 and 92.
15. *The New Zealand Tablet,* 23 March 1988, p. 8 and 27 April 1988, p. 10.
16. C. Brett, 'Priests No More', *More,* January, 1988, p. 79.
17. *Tablet,* 12 April 1989, p. 7.
18. Brett, p. 79.
19. Gerald A. Arbuckle, *Out of Chaos, Refounding Religious Congregations,* New York: Paulist Press, 1988, p. 165.
20. G. Arbuckle and J. Faisandier, 'The Church in a Multi-Cultural Society', (privately circulated), 1976.
21. Felix Donnelly, *One Priest's Life,* Auckland: Australia and New Zealand Book Company, 1982, p. 67.
22. D. Kolston, 'Are Catholic Schools Desirable?', *Insight,* Jan-Feb 1967, pp. 15-20. In Kawerau, Father Tom Ryder decided not to build a parish school. 'It seemed to me that New Zealand society is quite open and that Catholics should identify and belong.' (Peterson and Parer, pp. 46-7).

23. Interview on 19 July 1989 with a former Catholic, born 1931, describing the reaction of his mother.

24. Durning, p. 11, cf. the widely accepted comments of Bishop Basil Meeking, *Tablet*, 26 October 1988, p. 7.

25. 'Anne' in *Zealandia*, 6 November 1988. She refers to a period 'thirty years ago'.

26. Paul Collins, *Mixed Blessings, John Paul II and the Church of the Eighties*, Ringwood: Penguin Books, 1986, p. 185.

27. *Zealandia*, 12 March 1989.

28. *Wel-com*, March-April 1985, '...I oppose the Bill...'

29. Donnelly, *One Priest's Life*, p. 146 says of SPUC, 'it has concerned me to learn that there have been a few of its active members who have used abortion services ...' Cf. *The Bulletin*, 2 May 1989, p. 75 (concerning America), 'Roman Catholic women are more likely to have an abortion than either Protestant or Jewish women'. (Source: Alan Guttmacher Institute.)

30. 'Sexism project - a critic answered', *Zealandia*, 5 February 1989, p. 8. Cf. *Tablet*, 4 January 1989.

31. Hilary Mitchell, address summarised in *Zealandia*, 5 February 1989, p. 9.

32. 'Answerman', *Tablet*, 21 September 1988, pp. 11-12. Cf. *Evening Post*, 1 October 1988, p. 56.

33. Ranginui Walker, *Nga Tau Tohetohe, Years of Anger*, Auckland: Penguin Books, 1987, p. 18.

34. *Tablet*, 9 March 1988.

35. 'Answerman', ibid., 27 January 1988, p. 29.

36. In a statement published in ibid., 5 October 1988, p. 8.

37. *A Changing Order*, p. 98.

38. Summary of replies made by Cardinal Tom Williams and (Anglican) Archbishop Brian Davis to questions on Radio Pacific, summarised in 'The Bishops Talk Back', *Accent*, June 1988, pp. 8-9.

39. Bruce Hacker, 'Churches Question Economic Policy', ibid., pp. 11-12.

40. Interview in Wellington on 10 June, 1989.

41. Address at Hui Whanau, January 1988, in *Tablet*, 17 February 1988, pp. 11-12.

42. Collins, *Mixed Blessings*, pp. 103-110.

43. 'Opus Dei', *Accent*, September 1988, p. 14.

44. Fr. G.H. Duggan and Fr. P. Durning, In *Tablet*, 2 August, 1972, pp. 28-31.

45. Hubert Richards, ibid., 9 August 1972, p. 7.

46. Reginald Delargey, Bishop of Auckland in ibid., pp. 7, 30; cf. Brian Ashby, Bishop of Christchurch in ibid., 16 August 1972, pp. 27-30 and 23 August 1972, p. 3.

47. *Zealandia*, 22 September 1974, p. 11.

48. King, *Being Pakeha*, p. 100. On this (earlier) occasion, the critics included 'several New Zealand bishops, including Archbishop Liston'.

49. *Tablet*, 11 May 1988, p. 4. G.H. Duggan in ibid., 20 July 1988.

50. *Accent*, April 1987, p. 9.

51. *Tablet*, 6 March 1974, pp. 7-31. Cf. M. O'Meeghan, *Held Firm by Faith: a history of the Catholic diocese of Christchurch 1840-1987*, Christchurch: Catholic Diocese of Christchurch, 1988, pp. 306-7.

52. I discuss this in more detail in a forthcoming paper.

53. Father S.C. Abdoo, 'An Open Letter to the Catholic Bishops of New Zealand', (full page advertisement) in the *New Zealand Listener*, 26 September, 1987, p. 105.

54. Quoted in Garry Wills, *Bare Ruined Choirs; Doubt, Prophecy and Radical Religion*, New York: Doubleday, 1972, p.2.

55. 'Holy Cross Chapel', *Tablet,* 16 March 1988, pp. 23-4.

56. *Zealandia,* July 1989, p. 19.

57. This imagery is used (of post Vatican II converts) in David Lodge's novel, *How Far Can You Go?* (1980), and also in Durning's recollections (n.2 above).

58. Bob Consedine, 'Conservative bishops being imposed by Vatican: Why was consultation aborted in Christchurch?', *Accent,* October, 1987, pp. 17-18.

59. A.F. Wallace, 'Revitalisation Movements', *American Anthropologist,* 1956, pp. 264-282, adapted in Arbuckle, *Strategies,* pp. 25-8.

60. T.S. Eliot, *Four Quartets,* London: Faber and Faber, 1954, p. 59.

61. Fr. John Weir, interview with Gerard Crotty, *Zealandia,* 9 October, 1988, pp. 10-12.

62. *Wel-com,* May 1988, p. 9.

63. Ron O'Grady in *Accent*, August 1986, p. 38.

64. 'Jerusalem Sonnets' 32, (1969), in *Collected Poems, James K. Baxter,* edited by J.E. Weir, Auckland: Oxford University Press, 1988, reprint, p. 470; also p. 494, 'Brother I am like a dead man'. Cf. also his 'Confession to the Lord Christ' (1972). 'Certainly I have loved more women in my life than the Law of Moses commonly allowed', in Frank MacKay, *The Life of James K. Baxter,* Auckland: Oxford University Press, 1990, p. 278.

65. Oliver, W.H., *James K. Baxter, A Portrait,* Wellington: Port Nicholson Press, 1983, pp. 75-6; cf., pp. 149-50 on his less orthodox last years.

66. 'He Waiata mo taku Tangi (For Eugene)',(1971) *Collected Poems,* p. 505.

67. 'Confession to the Lord Christ', in Mackay, p. 278.

68. Mackay, p. 290.

69. From the Salisbury Diurnal, cited here from the score of Herbert Howells, *Hymnus Paradisi.*

Further reading

No one book covers the theme of this chapter, though several listed in the footnotes shed light on aspects of it. The present author has written on 'Australia and New Zealand' in *Modern Catholicism, Vatican II and after,* edited by Adrian Hastings, London/New York: SPCK/Oxford University Press, 1990, pp. 336-345.

Christianity:
Protestants Since the 1960s

James Veitch

The influence of Christianity on New Zealand life until the mid-sixties was extensive. It was a rare family who did not have some connection with the church. Women and children in particular used the church and its extensive social activities. It was in the Sunday School that children received a moral education, and most parents (or at least one parent) went to church in support of this. Confirmation or joining the church was an important rite of passage, and the clergy ran a series of talks two or three times a year in preparation for this event. Before packed congregations, teenagers made their professions of faith, or were baptised into membership. This was the way the church ensured its influence on young people.

Christian influence still dominated Sunday and holidays, shaped attitudes to books and entertainment, and even controlled the language people used. While religious jokes existed, sexual references were seldom heard, or when they were, were regarded with strong disapproval. Swearing rarely extended to the use of religious expressions; 'God', 'Christ', even 'Crikey' or 'Jeeze' were frowned upon. The moral principles of Christianity - the Ten Commandments and the Golden Rule - were sufficiently well known in the community to provide business, industrial and community leaders with a broad ethical framework. Honesty, hard work and thrift were admired and rewarded. It was rare for leaders of any section of the New Zealand community to be without church connections of some kind.

The 1959 Billy Graham evangelistic crusade had made a significant impact on churchgoing in the mainline communities. The invitation to Graham was issued by Alan Brash, General Secretary of the National Council of Churches, and brought all the Protestant churches together. The crusade's venues were planned as major thrusts into the unchurched community, and as a catalyst to activate many with nominal Christian links. Graham's meetings were well attended and the use of landline connections took the evangelist to a number of centres neither he nor his associates could visit in the time available. At the conclusion the organisers were well pleased with the impact.

From the sixties onwards things changed rapidly. Television began an Auckland transmission in 1960, and within six years had spread into the majority of homes throughout the country. This innovation brought New Zealand into contact with the rest of the world, and drew the country together in new ways. In 1964 the jet plane revolutionised overseas travel. More and more New Zealanders set out to visit 'the old country', often visiting the United States, travelling round Europe and touching down in Asia on the same trip.

By the mid-sixties, complacency had been ripped aside, and young people in particular began to destroy the community mould of the fifties, the suburban life style and the material prosperity of their parents. Their counter-culture movement can be seen beginning with the growing popularity of Bill Haley and the Comets. His film, *Rock around the Clock*, released in 1955, caused cinema riots all over Britain and created tremendous interest among young people in New Zealand. In the sixties the Beatles took over that role. Bob Dylan became the prophet of the new age, and one of the creators of the new quasi-religious folk music movement. 'The times they are a-changing,' Dylan warned.

Churches had grown in the fifties to accommodate young people born in the immediate post-war years, as well as their parents. This growth committed churches to rebuilding, extending and refurbishing existing plant, and thrust the denominations into extension work. They founded new congregations, particularly in new housing areas. But in the sixties fewer people went to church, and the expansion turned into a slow, physical contraction. Other leisure activities began to take the place of the church. Attendance at evening services began to fall away, and the family began to create alternative Sunday agendas. There was more for children to do. As the sixties passed, Sunday sport crept in.

Changing attitudes towards sex, individual freedom and morality took the church by surprise. Young people discovered a new world in which the church many had experienced as Sunday School children did not seem to have a place. In fact, the church was seen as the institution which had kept this new world hidden, and when it did emerge, condemned both the new world and the young who had discovered it.

The sixties' generation was born during the War and the years immediately following, so they experienced Christianity, but by 1965 many considered it totally irrelevant. These teenagers carried this attitude into adulthood and, by and large, they have not encouraged their children to experience the church. As adults and parents they thought the church had nothing to offer in terms of a moral education or worthwhile human experience. The following figures drawn from Presbyterian church statistics illustrate this:

	1960	1990	Decline
Attendance at Worship	119,041	45,613	61.7%
Membership (includes Presbyterians in Union/co-operating parishes)	85,080	63,522	25.3%
Sunday School Roll	76,030	10,948	85.6%
Youth	20,507	5,569	72.8%

Since 1960 there are fewer children and young people in New Zealand society, but according to statistics from the Sunday School Union, the percentage of children in primary schools who are caught up in the life of the church at some level has still fallen dramatically. This decline, I suggest, is consistent with their parents having, in the sixties, rejected the church as teenagers.

The same point can be illustrated not only by looking at the Presbyterian figures above, but also by noting the following statistics from the same source.

	1960	1988	Decline
Confirmations	4,617	1,257	72.7%
Baptisms of Children	11,543	2,896	74.9%

A shift in era

Why did the teenagers of the sixties move away from the church? The fundamental reason is a shift in era culminating from changes taking place over several centuries. The decline in the influence of the Protestant Church can be traced back to the beginning of modern science when Copernicus and then Galileo showed that, in contrast to what the Bible held, the earth did circle round the sun. The emergence of an historical consciousness applying to the Bible brought about a revolution in the understanding of the Scriptures. Protestant Christianity faced a crisis. Its starting point was the authority of the Bible for all matters of faith and conduct. With the Bible becoming a new and different sort of sacred scripture, Protestantism itself was forced to change.

Further signs of the new era came early in the twentieth century with Einstein's theory of general relativity. It was followed by the creation and the use of atomic bombs in 1945, and the subsequent development of nuclear weapons. The mid-fifties saw first Sputnik and then satellites in place round the earth, and this was capped off in the sixties with humans visiting the moon.

The year 1960 is often called the watershed in American religious history. Catholic politician J.F. Kennedy became President. There was an upheaval in black civil rights led by Martin Luther King Jnr. New ethical attitudes were worked out and began to affect the thinking and living of many people. In the wider world the election of Pope John XXIII created a revolution in the Catholic church, spawning a whole rethinking and re-examination of traditional Catholic belief. A new era burst over the western world and began to sweep away cherished values and beliefs, thrusting the whole human family into three decades of change and new dimensions.

In Protestantism crucial theological debates got under way about this time, often startling church members with the audacity of the thinking involved. Bishop John Robinson's small paperback *Honest to God*[1] popularised radically new ways of making sense out of traditional Christian imagery and ideas. Paul van Buren's *Secular Meaning of the Gospel*[2] tried to rework Christian belief using secular language. *Time Magazine* on 25 October 1965 ran a cover story on the 'death of God' movement entitled, 'Christian Atheism'. Harvey Cox produced *The Secular City*[3] the same year, and carefully charted the course of the noisy revolution then shaking the foundations of Protestant Christianity.

New Zealanders snapped up these books as they became available, and with mixed feelings followed news of the debates overseas. Many were alarmed by what they read and nervous about the ideas being tossed about. Robinson was thought irresponsible with his media-catching criticisms of the church, and in danger of undermining the authority and credibility of Christianity. The 'God is Dead' theologians were outright unbelievers. When Knox College principal Lloyd Geering reviewed Robinson's further book *The New Reformation?*[4] in the Presbyterian *Outlook* on 25 September 1965, it was not surprising that it aroused disquiet. Critics saw him as an advocate of the new theology and regarded him as unnecessarily provocative and even dangerous. As if sensing a major revolution about to burst on the religious scene, Presbyterians began to affirm and clarify some basic beliefs clustering around the Christian hope - like the return of Christ and the final judgement.

The Geering controversies

By Easter 1966 the revolution hit the Christian community in New Zealand. Lloyd Geering, in writing about the Resurrection, stated: 'the bones of Jesus [may] lie somewhere in Palestine.' (He was quoting the professor of Divinity at Glasgow University, Ronald Gregor Smith, in his book *Secular Christianity*[5]). There was a stormy reaction and a vigorous debate engulfed New Zealand churches and flowed over into the wider community. Was this a denial by Christian theologians themselves that Jesus ever really rose from the dead?

At their annual Assembly, Presbyterians played safe by producing statements on key beliefs in the language of classical theism. But the next year emotions flared. Again Lloyd Geering was at the centre. In March 1967 at Wesley Methodist Church in Wellington, Geering delivered the address at the beginning of the Victoria University academic year. He spoke from Ecclesiastes and in the course of his sermon remarked, 'Man has no immortal soul'. A reporter from *The Dominion* newspaper, sitting in the church, grasped the significance of the phrase, and next morning Wellington woke to these words on newspaper billboards: MAN HAS NO IMMORTAL SOUL - says Lloyd Geering.

There was an immediate reaction from the church. A Laymen's Association (itself an innovative development) had formed within the Presbyterian Church the previous year, led by Robert Wardlaw. It immediately spoke from Auckland of the seriousness of the theological situation in the Presbyterian Church, and called for Lloyd Geering's resignation from his position at the Theological Hall, Knox College. This was the beginning of more than eight months of debate, leading ultimately to formal charges of doctrinal impropriety against Lloyd Geering, heard at the General Assembly in November 1967. After a lengthy debate, a resolution was eventually passed recording the Assembly's majority decision that Geering had not stepped out of line so far as the church's thinking was concerned.

A.C. Moore

Prof Lloyd Geering, at conference of NZ Association for the Study of Religions, August 1989

As a consequence of the controversy the Presbyterian Church went on to draw up contemporary formulations of a number of its fundamental doctrines. On the subject of 'life after death' the statements sidestepped any definition of what the resurrection of Jesus actually was, and simply underlined its crucial importance to faith. As far as Christian hope for the future was concerned, instead of talking about immortality, statements emphasised the significance of eternal life.

By 1969 the church had a feeling that all these issues had been satisfactorily resolved. Then in 1970 the whole issue was raised again. Lloyd Geering went to Brisbane to visit the church of which he had been a member when he taught at Emmanuel College, and while there, was interviewed on TV station Channel Nine. The interviewers explored the same issues that were present in the debates of 1966 and 1967, and he replied to the questions in much the same way as he had on the previous occasion. The interview was taken down in shorthand and a copy sent to one of Geering's sternest critics in New Zealand. When that person realised the significance of the television programme an official transcript was requested. Once received it was circulated quite widely in New Zealand amongst those who were known to have been uncomfortable with the decisions of 1966 and 1967.

When the General Assembly met in 1970 it had before it a proposed resolution asking the Assembly to disassociate itself from the Brisbane interviews and, by implication, the thinking of Lloyd Geering. There was a sharp debate. Geering himself, present at the Assembly, was not once asked to contribute to the discussion or explain himself. The resolution was eventually passed by a substantial majority.

When the Assembly finished there was discussion amongst his critics about the steps that might be taken to persuade Geering to resign his position of Principal at the Theological Hall. All this became unnecessary when Victoria University announced his appointment as the foundation Professor of Religious Studies. By April 1971 Lloyd Geering was in Wellington on the staff of Victoria University. The church heaved a deep sigh of relief that the person who had raised the issues and the questions of the modern age in the New Zealand setting had removed himself.

The controversy produced its own homegrown literature. Lloyd Geering had published in 1968, *God in the New World*.[6] This was the New Zealand parallel to Robinson's *Honest to God*, and was a remarkably clear account of how the more liberal side of Protestant Christianity came to hold the views Geering echoed. The vicar of Ngaruawahia, R.J. Nicholson, wrote a sharp rebuttal, *Empty Tomb or Empty Faith: the Geering debate*[7]. Hodder and Stoughton who published *God in the New World* contracted E.M. Blaiklock, then Professor of Classics at Auckland University, to examine Geering's arguments in the wider context of the 'New Theology', and

Challenge Weekly

The late Prof E.M. Blaiklock, New Zealand's most-published biblical scholar

produce a rebuttal. This he did with *Layman's Answer: an examination of the New Theology*.[8] The book was, as the publishers indicated, a reply 'from the standpoint of informed conservatism'. It was a great pity that the two 'standpoints' never met either in debate or dialogue, but passed each other by. This was regrettable because Blaiklock was, in addition to being a classicist, a conservative evangelical biblical scholar of international standing, with an established reputation and an impressive list of publications. (Indeed, Blaiklock is the most published New Zealand biblical scholar of the post-war period.)

The Presbyterian Church published monographs containing articles and correspondence from their journal *Outlook* dealing with the resurrection and, in a separate publication, the speeches of the 1967 Assembly debate. A further stage in the widespread discussion sparked off by the controversy was the publication of two further titles. Robert Blaikie, one of the two who laid charges at the Assembly, wrote *Secular Christianity and the God who Acts*.[9] He touched upon Geering's standpoint only briefly, and then showed in dialogue with an impressive array of established theologians, how it was possible to hold the classical, central doctrines of the Christian faith in a secular age, without having to rethink these beliefs or capitulate to secularisation. Three years later Blaikie died, leaving behind a deep respect for his scholarship and ability to defend and expand the meaning of the Christian faith in a turbulent era.

Lloyd Geering followed up his earlier study with a book entitled *Resurrection - Symbol of Hope*[10]. It did not, at the time, receive the attention it deserved - the controversy was closed, and Geering was then a Professor at Victoria University in Wellington. So far as the churches were concerned, he had moved outside and could be disregarded. He went on to write a small study of Martin Buber, a volume dealing with religion and change entitled *Faith's New Age*[11] and, in retirement, sets of lectures published by the St. Andrew's Trust in Wellington.[12] In addition, there were numerous articles and, for many years, regular columns in the newspapers. He became the ordinary person's guru, more accepted outside the churches than inside.

The Presbyterian Church's experience of the 'Geering controversies' shows that anyone raising crucial issues within the New Zealand church community runs a considerable risk. The churches are only indirectly concerned with rethinking Christianity in terms acceptable and meaningful to the non-church community. For the most part Christians in New Zealand wish to retain and reinforce the classical statements of Christian belief and, on this basis, make their appeal to non-Christians. Despite considerable liberalism in other matters, when it comes to the doctrines held to be essential to the Christian faith, New Zealand Protestantism is predominantly conservative.

Further ferment

If the church community thought that ferment was over when the theological debates concluded, they were mistaken. From the late sixties the Charismatic movement began to appear, affecting Anglicans first and then spreading into all the mainline churches. 'Life in the Spirit' seminars, healing services, speaking-in-tongues and words of prophecy gradually assumed a role in worship. Public prayers were personalised, new hymns appeared, fervent study groups sprang up; in some cases the character of whole congregations changed.

Charismatic Christians, whether Catholic or Protestant, are deeply and enthusiastically committed to the Christian faith. They talk about the intimate relationships they have with Jesus, and often have a daily message from God to give to others. The return of Christ to this earth is expected sooner rather than later, and they watch developments in international events with great interest. For many in the Charismatic movement, support for Israel is quite crucial, as the return of Jesus the crucified, risen Messiah is expected in Israel following major conflicts between competing ideologies and religions.

Initially the Charismatic movement was divisive in many congregations and churches, but this has moderated over the decades as its leadership encouraged people 'filled with the Spirit' to stay on in their congregations, and witness to the power of changed lives.

New ecumenical initiatives were born out of the Charismatic movement, as Christians from right across the denominational spectrum met together in conference and convention. Even Catholics and Protestants came together, unofficially at least, in shared celebrations of the Eucharist. Charismatics tended to hold denominational loyalty lightly, but were often involved in leadership in local congregations, trying to steer the direction of its religious life.

Charismatic Christianity has enabled the churches to discover a fresh understanding of the Holy Spirit, and has put new life into many communities. It emerged as an alternative to the 'rethinking Christianity' agenda of the radical theologians. Over more than thirty years it has helped reshape the Christian community worldwide, largely replacing the evangelistic rallies of previous generations as a way of trying to revitalise dying congregations and present Christianity's way of salvation to the outside world. By 1990 it has a strong hold and influence on mainline churches, and exerts tremendous influence on the leadership and on policy development. It is a movement which has brought minister and laity closer together in a concerted action to stem the tide of political and religious liberalism.

The seventies - many changes

The seventies seemed less turbulent than the sixties, but nevertheless saw many changes and developments. New Zealand troops were withdrawn from Vietnam. The churches managed a goodwill visit from an ecumenical team prior to the American withdrawal, but it was a gesture too late to do any good. However, it was an important gesture from the churches in New Zealand, for at the time the deputation visited there was no sign that the Americans would be defeated in Vietnam.

Surprisingly New Zealand has followed the United States in its attitude towards Vietnam, and has treated that country and neighbouring Cambodia in such a way that their isolation in the world community became inevitable. The churches have followed suit. Contacts that did exist, particularly with Vietnam from the Presbyterian Church, faded in the years subsequent to the closure of the Vietnam war. In 1985 a tentative contact was made by the Protestant community in Vietnam to the Presbyterian Church in New Zealand, but this has not been reciprocated. A shortage of money in the churches in New Zealand and involvement with many other areas in the world community have largely prevented the churches from exploring possible avenues of assistance to Vietnam and Cambodia. Within this country, however, churches and individual Christians have played a large part in the task of resettling refugees from those lands.

The 1973 Springbok rugby tour to New Zealand was cancelled largely due to public pressure. The churches had lobbied for the cancellation unless the team members were selected on merit rather than on racial grounds. When a Springbok tour took place in New Zealand in 1981, Christians were strongly represented in the protest movement and in attempts to disrupt and stop games being played. In 1984 the Methodist and Presbyterian Churches declared apartheid a heresy, and in 1985 it was Christian support for legal pressure which brought about a High Court decision to prevent the All Blacks from touring South Africa. This was one crucial area of success for the church presence in the public arena.

The Labour Government of Norman Kirk in 1973 sent the HMNZS *Otago* into the Mururoa test zone, protesting against French nuclear testing. This too was hailed by the churches as a significant step in the struggle to establish a nuclear free Pacific. But by 1990, while little has changed at Mururoa, the church protests have mostly been taken over by conservation activists (though New Zealand churches do continue to affirm their solidarity with their Pacific neighbours on this issue).

Church union moves

Five churches enjoyed a long interest in union plans. Methodist, Presbyterian and Congregational churches had been meeting together since 1951. Four years later, representatives from each had joined together in a united Act of Witness. That same year the Associated Churches of Christ joined the Union Committee. A vote in the churches was taken in 1957, showing overwhelming support for union. As a result of this, the first plan for union was published in 1960. Following the Faith and Order Conference (organised by the National Council of Churches on the theme 'What is our Gospel?' and held at Massey University in 1963), the four were joined in 1964 by the Anglican Church in a serious effort to explore the question of wider union. The churches were able to work together well in developing chaplaincies to hospitals, prisons and industry and, with a wider grouping of churches, in the area of religious education.

In 1967 an Act of Commitment to the search for union was entered into by what became known as 'the five negotiating churches'. In 1969 the National Council of Churches began to develop closer relationships with the Catholic Church, and preliminary steps were taken to explore ways of working together.

The year 1971 saw the five negotiating churches putting forward a plan for union which, in theory, found a measure of acceptance. However, in practice, there was a growing and widespread resistance to an organic union, and a preference for working together loosely in an ecumenical movement like the National Council of Churches.

Five years later the Anglican Church rejected the plan for union. Associated Churches of Christ congregations also began to express mixed feelings. Methodists remained enthusiastic, but Presbyterian membership approval was more reluctant than that of its ministers. The Congregational Union, which had been largely decimated by a merger of sorts with the Presbyterian Church in 1969, began to feel less comfortable with structural union.

The plan might well have succeeded if Presbyterians, Methodists, Congregationalists and the Associated Churches of Christ had remained in negotiation. But the coming of the Anglicans into the negotiations enlarged the movement and intensified the search, only to leave it at the end without any sense of fulfilment. The 1981 vote on union showed the Presbyterians evenly divided, and the Methodists keenly in favour. The other churches were not involved. From this time onwards, any prospect of a union became less and less likely.

In 1982 Anglicans and Catholics conducted some combined services throughout the country. The bishops of the two churches had been meeting since 1979 to discuss matters of commonality and possible areas of co-operation, and these combined services were seen as an act of commitment to explore togetherness a little further at parish level. The churches have continued to develop good relationships locally with combined bible studies being held nationally. In 1990 the combined bishops hosted a seminar/symposium on the future of New Zealand, attended by parish representatives from throughout the country. This was very successful. But divisions over the authority and role of the Pope within organised Christianity, and differences over admission to each other's mass/eucharist, continue to keep the two churches apart and on parallel courses.

From 1983 onwards the Methodist Church committed itself to a bicultural programme with the Maori community, and over seven years to 1990 has developed this with changes to structures and decision making. There was less room than ever in this programme for union with other churches. The Anglican Church also took this direction with similar changes. They, too, were no longer interested in union but were taking steps to firm up their own identity and sense of mission. In 1984 the five churches involved in the original union did take steps to consolidate work done in producing union parishes by forming the Negotiating Churches Unity Council. A major conference of union representatives in 1989, and widespread discussions about union in such parishes, led in 1990 to the modification of the structure of this Council. One of its major steps forward was to provide union parishes with representation on this new body. But there was no sign of any real interest in union. The time for such a move was long gone. There was even some talk in churches of the union parishes linking back to a founding church, and thus moving away from a union identity. But many union parishes had gone too far and were faced with the loneliness and frustration of independence. The mainline union movement had been a disaster.

The closure of the National Council of Churches, and the formation of the Conference of

Churches in Aotearoa New Zealand (CCANZ) in 1988, heralded a major step forward in general ecumenical co-operation, as distinct from any organic union. The members of the existing National Council were joined by the Catholic Church in this new venture, although the Congregational Union and the Associated Churches of Christ had reservations about the developments, and the Baptist Church voted to withdraw.

By 1990 the national forum was working well, bringing together the representatives of all the churches involved in the CCANZ and thus drawing on a broad cross-section of Christian experience. But the local forums which had been promised in the new structure have, by and large, failed to emerge. The reality may well be that in spite of an initial willingness to work together in a broad community of witness, the energy of each of the participant churches has been syphoned off in the directions of self-preservation.

Protestant concerns in the 1980s

In order to put the church union question into perspective, it is necessary to chart some of the more important characteristics of life in the 1980s.

Elected with a considerable majority in 1984 the Labour government led by David Lange set about 'opening the books' on expenditure. Leaders of the community representing a diversity of interests were called together to seek a consensus upon which to introduce urgent social and economic reforms. Then the government launched a series of quite startling economic reforms in a programme which became known as 'Rogernomics', after the Finance minister, Roger Douglas. The radical nature of these changes, and the implications for restructuring the public service, government departments and the private sector, were not immediately recognised.

The bombing of the Greenpeace ship *Rainbow Warrior* by French special agents, and the subsequent furore, stole the headlines and diverted attention from economic developments. The government's move declaring New Zealand nuclear-free, and the banning of naval ship visits unless they were non-nuclear, also caught media attention. But by 1986 the economic changes were affecting the farming community. The next year saw unemployment leap ahead, and in October of that year the sharemarket crashed. Although major government-sponsored social legislation on adoption information, abortion, and homosexuality went through Parliament, it was the economic-driven reforms, designed to make industry and the commercial areas more competitive in world markets, which forced the pace of change and saw bankruptcy grow in the farming and business sectors.

As a country, New Zealand had lived beyond its means for decades. New Zealand society had been held together since the 1930s by government-provided social benefits and a support system which was the envy of other countries. But all this living by credit and dependency on the Government came to an abrupt end. The pain of change was severe and, in the second term of the Labour Government, people became angry and bitter. Not even the 1990 Auckland Commonwealth Games, royal visits, and the celebration of 150 years of nationhood, could replace the pain and dissatisfaction with pleasure and security. Aotearoa/New Zealand, it was recognised, would never be the same again.

Education was radically overhauled in an effort to prepare young people to live and work in an economic-driven, technological world. Although the idealism was impressive, the path of change has been strewn with bad drafting of legislation and poorly conceived plans for new structures forced upon the country's educators and the public by government decisions.

Christian moral concerns have also been aroused by the social and legal reforms. While the adoption legislation did not attract a great deal of comment, homosexual law reform incited sections of the church. A petition taken up in 1985 (with the largest number of signatures ever presented to Parliament) summed up the attitude of many - the reforms have gone too far. A minority disagreed. The Presbyterian General Assembly, by a majority decision, declared its belief that homosexual acts were sinful.

Abortion divides the country, the churches included. Many see legalised abortion as placing a woman's 'right to decide' above the rights of the unborn foetus. Interfering with the gift of life, and protecting this by legislation, seems an obvious sign of a declining Christian influence on society. But for other Christians the issue is not so clear.

Methodist and Presbyterian churches led the way in the antinuclear movement, declaring churches and worship complexes nuclear-free zones. However, with the passing of legislation, the churches have taken a back seat on further developments. It is left to activists to continue the nuclear debate with the government.

With enormous changes taking place in the structure of New Zealand society, and redirections taken in economic matters, there is less money in the community to spend on voluntary agencies, including the church. The mainline churches, with a declining membership, have to face the reality of economic difficulty. The economic hardship of small parishes makes it difficult for congregations to put money into national programmes. Often they have barely enough to sustain themselves.

In this new environment, each of the churches is obliged to look towards ways of surviving and maintaining its own influence and traditions in a threatening secular environment. The ideal of ecumenism or inter-church organic union looks more fragile in 1990 than any other point since 1960. The direction is to look inward and shore up the buttresses of traditional belief.

By 1990, however, Charismatic Christianity has continued to grow in strength throughout all the churches, and become a major factor in maintaining the life and vitality of individual congregations. Flowing over traditional barriers between Protestants and Catholics, and bringing together Christians from fringe and mainline churches, it has become a 'new ecumenical movement' - a movement of the spirit drawing Christians together in new ways in order to be the Church in new times. It is a movement which values conviction and certainty, characterised by a conservative theology and an authoritarian if not always 'fundamentalist' attitude towards the Bible.

Charismatic Christians in the mainline Protestant churches are increasingly joined by 'Evangelical' Christians (particularly Baptists and Brethren) and 'Pentecostal' churches (Assemblies of God, New Life Centres and the like) to form strong alliances on moral and political matters. Such Christians combine, for instance, in opposing homosexual law reform and in the anti-abortion campaign, and many have held reservations about the anti-nuclear stance of the Government and the promotion of Maori interests in the name of the Treaty of Waitangi.

Thus the 1980s saw something like a New Zealand version of the American 'Moral Majority' emerging, committed to influencing the election of candidates to Parliament, local government and school boards of trustees. They highlight the protection of the family as a social unit, and what they regard as the high moral standards of personal behaviour demanded from the Christian in the Bible. In challenging the 'liberal' or 'secular humanist' forces in society they represent a decisive movement within contemporary New Zealand Protestantism from a sometimes passive 'mainstream' to an active 'sectarian' point of view. Thus the 1990 election saw candidates representing a 'Christian Heritage Party' standing in some electorates.

A further important contribution made by the Charismatic movement to Christian life and worship has been in the area of new hymns and music. The hymn book *New Zealand Praise* (1988) offers congregations extra resources for worship, supplementing *With One Voice* (1982), a hymn book shared with churches in Australia (first published in 1977) which many had been using. Plans were announced towards the end of the eighties for a New Zealand hymn book that would bring together some of the best hymns available in the New Zealand church setting, and draw in others from the world community.

What has consistently been avoided, however, is any attempt to restate the Christian faith and to rethink it in the language and thought-forms of the late twentieth century and in the environment of growing secularity. Independent and Charismatic congregations often restructured themselves along lines that were thought to be attractive to the interests of the current 'baby boom' generation. Evangelists from overseas, particularly from the United States, continued to bring to New Zealand some of the more glitzy approaches to this generation of young people, with a very different lifestyle and expectation from their parents. But by 1990, it is not clear that any of these approaches has been any more successful than that offered by the traditional mainline churches - and still the issue of rethinking the Christian faith remains an untried and avoided option.

The Women's Movement emerging in the community from the early seventies has also had its influence on the mainline churches. Traditionally, in these churches, women belonged to organisations which supported fundraising and provided the catering services in congregations. However, as women went to work, fewer and fewer were represented in these organisations. Conscious of a leadership gap between the women who sat in the pews in churches and the decision-making bodies, all the mainline churches were forced in the seventies and eighties to ensure that women took a more equal place with men in the organisation of local congregations, and in the leadership of national churches. The theory was fine, but it was actually very hard to find women willing to take leadership positions, when they had been trained and encouraged to take secondary roles. Then too, it was difficult to encourage women to find the time for leadership positions in the churches, when they were already being offered such positions in other parts of society.

The year 1990 saw the election of the first woman bishop in New Zealand, the Reverend Dr Penelope Jamieson, who was consecrated Bishop of the diocese of Dunedin in June. Women have been ordained as clergy in all the mainline Protestant churches including the Baptists, and serve increasingly in decision-making positions. But the movement towards inclusive language in liturgies, hymns, Bible translations, sermons and reports, is much slower in developing. So too is the struggle to achieve equality of opportunity and economic independence for women, and the willingness on the part of men to acknowledge and deal with violence in the family and in society as largely their problem. Despite their good intentions, then, the churches clearly have a long way to go to find appropriate Christian responses to these issues, arising from what is clearly the greatest social revolution in recent times.

Major contributions in public and private life

In other areas Protestants have made considerable contributions to present day New Zealand life. The social service organisations of Anglican, Presbyterian, Methodist and Baptist churches, and of the Salvation Army, in addition to aged care homes and hospitals, have established family counselling centres and maintained social work amongst children, women and men at risk. These are multi-million-dollar concerns. The Methodist Central Mission in Otago recently took over the Cromwell hospital from the area health board and will run it as a hospital caring for the aged - a move which might be followed elsewhere.

Anglicans, Presbyterians, Methodists, some Baptists, Reformed Churches, Congregational and other congregations and Protestant groups are also active in independent private education. Anglicans and Presbyterians in particular are strongly represented by the number of schools and colleges they have established, helping maintain a Christian ethos and environment for education. Middleton Grange School in Christchurch is an example of an independent Protestant foundation which is thriving. More young people nowadays attend such schools than are found in Protestant Bible Class and youth groups on a Sunday morning, so the influence of Protestant Christianity in these areas is extensive.

Wanganui Newspapers Ltd

Scripture Union children's holiday programme

The work of Scripture Union and the Inter-Schools Christian Fellowship, with school meetings and a wide range of holiday camps and programmes, brings thousands of young people throughout the country each year in touch with the evangelical forms of Protestant Christianity. Where 'Bible-in-schools' classes are supported by local school boards of trustees, the churches seize the opportunity to present the Christian faith to children in a lively and attractive way.

Tertiary Students Christian Fellowship, Navigators, Campus Crusade for Christ and Youth for Christ are all active in spreading the Christian faith amongst students and young people. Radio Rhema broadcasts are listened to extensively throughout the country. A Christian Broadcasters' Association produces quality programmes for use on the state radio network. Companies also exist to provide quality programmes for public television. Christian bookshops, usually well supported by local groups, can be found in most towns and cities. Interdenominational Bible reading and study courses are offered by several organisations, and the Bible College of New Zealand, based in Henderson, conducts off-campus courses in other centres. Protestant churches have played a large part in the formation of the Auckland Consortium for Theological Education, through which theology degrees for ministers and laypeople are from 1990 being granted by the University of Auckland. This may markedly change the focus of New Zealand theological education, which previously has been on the Faculty of Theology at Otago University, in existence since the late 1940s.

Conclusion

There is one decade left in the twentieth century, and all Protestant churches have been involved in some way in launching plans for a decade of evangelism. For many Christians the greatest gift they could collectively bring to their Lord at the beginning of the third millennium is a nation won over to Christ. Specialists in mission and church growth are analysing New Zealand society and preparing to proclaim the Gospel in effective ways. Modern methods of communication and strategies borrowed and adapted from the commercial world will be considered. In some denominations, Presbyterians and Anglicans for example, the target group is the nominal census person. In others the aim is to 'claim for Christ' New Zealanders who have had no contact with the church.

Mainline churches, as we have seen in this study, are in numerical decline. The fifties was a decade of expansion and development, the sixties of decline, the seventies of partial recovery, and the eighties of further shrinkage. Among the smaller churches it is the Baptist, Elim, Apostolic, Christian and Missionary Alliance, and Pacific Island Independent churches which are growing. The Baptist Union has set itself the goal of '40,000 members and 300 churches by the year 2000'. Recent analysis done by researchers at the Department of World Religions at Victoria University suggests that in order to achieve stable growth of such proportions, a large turnover is needed. Looking back over forty years the research shows churches appearing to lose two out of every three people gained. The loss is often to other denominations; but even then there is a noticeable attrition rate.

A church-planting growth strategy, combined with a strong charismatic and evangelical thrust, appears to be more successful at gathering in Christians from other churches than at attracting non-Christians. But even then the main problem is how to keep the people who become members. So far, this growth in numerical strength is fairly small, compared with the size and growth of the New Zealand population. Little attention in the decade of evangelism has yet been given to rethinking the Christian faith in a language and forms of expression which might be attractive to those outside the church. The emphasis is on brushing up the traditional language, so that the existing ideas of the Christian faith can be represented to people who have lost touch with the church.

Protestant Christianity in New Zealand attempts to play its part in a world which faces enormous problems as it turns into the last decade of the twentieth century. Tension in the Middle East and the Third World - civil unrest, military conflict, crop failure, bad water, disease, malnutrition and starvation for millions - endangers international peace. Unexpected changes in the ideological structure of Europe are a positive but not unproblematic sign of fresh political initiatives. And looming above any hopeful signs are serious threats to human survival caused by massive pollution of the earth's surface and atmosphere. Conservation of the planet we all live on becomes an urgent necessity, calling for further radical changes to the way we live.

Besides the issues already mentioned, the churches have to follow through the implications of their commitments to the Treaty of Waitangi and biculturalism. They have to find ways of properly accommodating the different cultural emphases of Pacific Islander Christians in their midst. As well, they are faced with decisions about how to relate to the rising number of representatives in this country of other world faiths.

Against this global background, and with whatever plans their church leaders may be making for the coming decade, Christians from the Protestant traditions will be continuing their daily tasks seeking the ways of God, guided by the Spirit of Christ. Clergy and laity alike will be consoling the bereaved, comforting the sick, rejoicing with those who marry and counselling those who separate. They will be doing unpaid work for the needy, giving unrecorded hours of assistance to the helpless and dependent, coping with poverty and unemployment and old age. They will be trying, where they can, to start their children off on paths of truthfulness and virtue, and hoping and praying that they will not turn to drugs and self-destruction. Whether in church meetings or in homes they will be offering forgiveness to one another when they fail and hope when they are discouraged, just as Christians throughout their history (not always the most prominent or conspicuous ones) have always done.

As the country moves into a new stage of its history we can expect many of the churches identified with Protestantism (with an eye on the millennial clock, perhaps) to attempt to launch major outreaches amongst the 'unchurched'. Besides such efforts at evangelism, there will still be those who wish to grapple rather with the world's social problems, and those for whom the greatest priority will be personal spirituality, prayer, or Bible study. There will be those who are impatient to re-think their church's teaching and traditions, and those who continue to work away at forms of co-operation and bridge-building with others. How far any or all of these efforts will be successful, we shall have to wait and see. In any event, while organised Protestant Christianity may be numerically in decline at the moment, the diverse contributions it will continue to make, in public and in private, to New Zealand life and society are likely to be far from insignificant.

Notes

1. London: SCM Press, 1963.
2. London: SCM Press, 1963.
3. London: SCM Press, 1963.
4. London: SCM Press, 1967
5. London: Collins, 1965.
6. London: Hodder and Stoughton, 1968.
7. Auckland: G.W. Moore Ltd., 1968.
8. London: Hodder and Stoughton, 1968.
9. London: Hodder and Stoughton, 1970.
10. London: Hodder and Stoughton, 1971.
11. London: Collins, 1980.
12. *In the World Today*, Wellington: Allen & Unwin/Port Nicholson Press, 1988; and see also *Faith in An Age of Turmoil, Essays in honour of Lloyd Geering,* edited by James Veitch, London: Oriental University Press, 1990, (especially James Veitch, 'The Lloyd Geering Story: a biographical essay', and Lloyd Geering, 'A Contemporary Expression of Faith').

Further reading

In addition to the further reading suggested by Colin Brown (chapter five, above) see also *Presbyterians in Aotearoa 1840-1990*, edited by Dennis McEldowney, Wellington: Presbyterian Church of New Zealand, 1990.

Christianity:
Alternative Churches

Brian Colless

Besides those who belong to mainline denominations (and those who, for various reasons, simply write 'Christian' on their census form) thousands of Aotearoa's Christians declare allegiance to what we shall here call alternative churches. These are the people or churches commonly designated (in order of numerical size) Latter-day Saints (Mormon), Jehovah's Witness, Pentecostal, Assemblies of God, Seventh-day Adventist, Apostolic, Indigenous Pentecostal, Exclusive Brethren, Spiritualist, Elim, Christadelphian, Quaker (Society of Friends), Christian Fellowship, Worldwide Church of God, Nazarene, Christian Scientist, Church of Christ (Life and Advent), Church of Christ (Non-Denominational), Full Gospel, Commonwealth Covenant, Unitarian, Liberal Catholic, Reorganized Latter Day Saints, Bible Students, Swedenborgian, Unificationist (Moonies), Metropolitan Community Church.

Many and varied as they are, these alternative churches have at least one characteristic in common, namely their relationship with Jesus Christ. Their similarities and differences will be examined in sections entitled American Connections, Identity Duplication, Characteristic Types, and Lifestyle Features.

American connections

Most of the alternative churches were either founded in the United States of America or have long been established there. In both respects this is true of the largest of them, the Church of Jesus Christ of Latter-day Saints, commonly known as the Mormon church, which was founded in New York state by the prophet Joseph Smith (1805-1844) and has had its centre in Salt Lake City, Utah, since 1848; its missionaries came to New Zealand in 1854.

The Seventh-day Adventist Church arose in the eastern states after the Great Disappointment of 1844 (when Christ's expected second coming failed to eventuate). This church is based on the visions and teachings of Ellen Gould White. Adventist evangelists were sent to Australasia in 1885, and Mrs White herself visited New Zealand in 1893.

Christadelphians name John Thomas (1805-1871) as the founder of their sect (a word they seem happy to apply to themselves). He was an English physician who migrated to Brooklyn, New York, and lived through the Great Disappointment; his book *Elpis Israel* (The Hope of Israel, 1848) is an interpretation of Bible prophecies; his movement grew in America and England, and reached New Zealand in the 1880s.

Jehovah's Witnesses are incorporated as the Watch Tower Bible and Tract Society, which was founded in Pennsylvania in 1884, under the leadership of Charles Taze Russell, and which now has its headquarters in Brooklyn, New York; representatives of the society first came to New Zealand in 1904.

Christian Scientists, members of Churches of Christ, Scientist, declare that their foundation was laid in Boston in 1879, by their teacher Mary Baker Eddy, who sought to reinstate spiritual healing in the church; New Zealand's first Christian Science congregation was formed in 1907.

The year 1907 also saw the formation of the Church of the Nazarene in the United States, as a merger of numerous bodies which stemmed from the nineteenth-century Wesleyan Holiness Movement, including the Association of Pentecostal Churches of America. Originally named the Pentecostal Church of the Nazarene, it dropped the term Pentecostal in 1919, because it implied 'speaking in tongues', a practice not followed by the Nazarenes, who concentrate on Christian holiness. The Nazarene headquarters are in Kansas City, Missouri, and the church now has a strong following in Auckland.

The Pentecostal groups which make up the Associated Pentecostal Churches of New Zealand, notably the Assemblies of God, the Apostolic Church, the Elim Church, and the Indigenous Churches of New Zealand (New Life Centres and Christian Fellowships), seem to have an American style. Certainly the Pentecostal World Conference has its headquarters in the United States, and the Assemblies of God are the largest Pentecostal group in America, as also in New Zealand. However, the Pentecostalism of New Zealand (first planted in 1922) owes more to Britain and its evangelists than it does to America and its missionaries: its charismatic characteristics, including 'divine healing', 'baptism of the Holy Spirit', and 'speaking with tongues' (glossolalia), are said to stem from the Welsh Revival of 1905, and the British preacher George Jeffreys.

The Worldwide Church of God (originally the Radio Church of God) was founded by Herbert W. Armstrong in 1935, and it has its headquarters in Pasadena, California; it first reached New Zealand through his radio programme entitled 'The World Tomorrow', and is also widely known through its magazine *The Plain Truth*.

The Christian Spiritualist Church (or the Greater World Christian Spiritualist Association) was founded in 1931 on the teachings given through the mediumship of Winifred Moyes by a spirit named Zodiac, who had been a contemporary disciple of Jesus Christ. The headquarters are in London, and branches of this church were established in New Zealand in the 1930s. The beginnings of modern spiritualism are usually traced to a farmhouse in New York State, where, in 1848, the medium Kate Fox communicated by a rapping code with the spirit of a man claiming to have been murdered in the house. The Spiritualist Church of New Zealand is another association in this tradition, but its links with Christianity are not strong.

The Unification Church (or the Holy Spirit Association for the Unification of World Christianity) was founded in 1954, by Sun Myung Moon, hence the name Moonies applied to his followers. Although the church (as also its founder) was born in Korea, it has established itself in America, with a seminary in Barrytown, New York. At present its membership in New Zealand is not large enough for it to be listed by name on the census table of religions.

The Unitarian Church traces its roots to the Reformation in Europe, and remembers such martyrs as Francis David, Unitarian bishop of Transylvania, imprisoned for denying the doctrine of the Trinity. The Unitarian Church is more British than American (having its world headquarters in London), but five early presidents of the United States (Jefferson, for example) were Unitarians. This church sees itself as theologically liberal. Its first minister in New Zealand was William Jellie, who arrived from Britain in 1901.

The Religious Society of Friends, whose members are popularly known as Quakers, came out of the religious turmoil in England around the middle of the seventeenth century, when George Fox (1642-1691) sought to rediscover essential Christianity, without the ecclesiastical trappings. The migration of many of his followers made the state of Pennsylvania a stronghold of Quakerism, and Quaker Oats part of the American way of life. Meetings for worship by Friends have taken place in New Zealand since 1853.

The New Christian Church, or the Swedenborgian church, was founded in England, late in the eighteenth century, and was based on the visionary writings of the Swedish scientist Emanuel Swedenborg (1688-1772). James Glen took Swedenborgianism to the Quaker city Philadelphia in 1784. Swedenborgians name Helen Keller as an admirer of their teacher, and they reveal the truth about Johnny Appleseed (he distributed Swedenborgian tracts as he went round planting trees) in books published by the Swedenborg Foundation, New York. There is a New Church congregation in Auckland, and the history of the Swedenborgian church in New Zealand is traced back as far as 1842; the congregation had its first minister in 1917, a New Zealander trained in America.

The Liberal Catholic Church was established in 1916 as a Theosophist church; its main connections are with Sydney and London, but it has an American branch with legal headquarters in Baltimore, Maryland, and ecclesiastical headquarters and publishing house in Ojai, California. The founder, Bishop James Ingall Wedgwood, came to New Zealand in 1917 and ordained two priests in Auckland.

The main Churches of Christ in New Zealand, denominational and non-denominational, stem from Thomas and Alexander Campbell, Irish Presbyterians who emigrated to the United States of America. The beginnings of the denominational Churches of Christ in New Zealand are dated to 1844. The non-denominational, 'non-instrumental' churches of Christ were established in New Zealand by American missionaries, in the 1950s. They are differentiated by their unaccompanied singing of hymns, a practice they share with the first Christians and the present-day Exclusive Brethren.

The Exclusive Brethren are a self-isolating group which originated in 1848, when John Nelson Darby (a former clergyman of the Church of Ireland and a dominant figure in the Brethren movement in England, Ireland, and Europe) withdrew his flock from contact with other churches and other Brethren, and led them along a path of exclusivism. He came to New Zealand in 1876 to inspect Brethren assemblies (churches). After his death in 1882, the leadership eventually passed to America, where James Taylor held sway from some time after 1908 until his death in 1953; his son directed the organisation from 1959 to 1970; and then J.H. Symmington took up this role. In the New Zealand census the Exclusive Brethren are distinguished from Brethren (that is, Open Brethren, or Plymouth Brethren, so named because an early congregation was established there in 1831, under the leadership of Benjamin Wills Newton and others).

A remarkable phenomenon of modern times is the Metropolitan Community Church, which has a special ministry for homosexual Christians; it was founded in Los Angeles in 1968 by Troy D. Perry. There are branches of the Universal Fellowship of Metropolitan Community Churches in New Zealand. The mainline churches have a similar outreach in the Auckland Community Church.

Identity Duplication

Because of the propensity of new religious movements to hive off into factions, there are often two or more groups claiming to be the same thing. By way of illustration, Jews and Christians alike profess to be the true Israel. This is a case of 'identity duplication'.

The main examples of this phenomenon can be viewed on the accompanying chart (Table One: Cognate Groups, 'cognate' meaning 'descended from a common ancestor, akin in origin'). It should be noted that the members of the first six sets disassociate themselves from each other in each case, but this does not apply to the other groupings.

For example, the Church of the Nazarene stands on the same foundation as the Methodist Church, namely the writings of John Wesley, the founder of the Methodist Church, and there is no real antipathy between the two churches. On the other hand, the two Latter Day Saint churches do not recognise each other, even though they both acknowledge the prophet Joseph Smith and the *Book of Mormon*. Note also that the Methodist and Mormon churches have other sects stemming from them, but these are not significantly represented in New Zealand. As a matter of interest, the Mormon leader Brigham Young was a Methodist, as also were William and Catherine Booth, the founders of the Salvation Army.

Table One: Cognate Groups
Church of Jesus Christ of Latter-day Saints (Mormons) Reorganized Church of Jesus Christ of Latter Day Saints Seventh-day Adventist Church Reformed Seventh-day Adventist Church Jehovah's Witnesses Dawn Bible Students 'Open' Brethren (Plymouth Brethren) 'Exclusive' Brethren Associated Churches of Christ Churches of Christ (non-denominational) Worldwide Church of God (Herbert W. Armstrong) Church of God, International (Garner Ted Armstrong) Christadelphians Christadelphians (Old Paths) New Christian Church (Swedenborgian) General Church of the New Jerusalem Spiritualist Church Christian Spiritualist Church Theosophical Society Liberal Catholic Church Methodist Church Church of the Nazarene Elim Pentecostal Church Assemblies of God Apostolic Church

Jehovah's Witnesses and Dawn Bible Students are another case in point: both see their origins in Charles Taze Russell and his writings, but they are completely separate and distinct organisations. The local Jehovah's Witnesses churches (ecclesias) are strictly controlled from the centre, by the leaders of the Watch Tower Bible and Tract Society in New York, while the Bible Student ecclesias are directed (less rigidly, they allege) by the Dawn Bible Students' Association in New Jersey.

Christadelphians, who are also ardent students of Biblical prophecy and who likewise congregate in ecclesias, have had schisms; but the two groups were happy to be together under one entry as Christadelphians, 'Brethren in Christ' in Massey University's *Beliefs and Practices in New Zealand: A Directory.*

This is in contrast to the relationship between the Open Brethren and the Exclusive Brethren. Open Brethren 'assemblies' (churches) are autonomous and led by local 'elders'. Exclusive Brethren assemblies are controlled by the central leader (for most of the twentieth century the heads of the church have been resident in America); until 1970 they were under the dynastic rule of James Taylor Senior and Junior. There are also assemblies of Reading Brethren in New Zealand (standing somewhere between Open Brethren and Exclusive Brethren on the scale of openness).

Reformed Seventh-day Adventists (Rowenites) are found in New Zealand, as an offshoot of the mother church of Ellen White. In 1916 Mrs Margaret W. Rowen claimed to be the successor of Mrs White as a prophetess conveying messages from God, but her claims were rejected, and in 1919 she was disfellowshipped from the South Side SDA church of Los Angeles, of which she had been a member. She retained a group of enthusiastic followers. In 1923 she predicted that the Lord would return on the clouds of heaven on 6 February 1925. This prophecy failed, and the orthodox Adventists are at pains to point out that they have never (not in 1844, nor in 1925, nor at any other time) predicted a date for the Second Coming. (In saying this, they are also contrasting themselves with Jehovah's Witnesses, who have made such a prediction more than once.)

The two main Latter Day Saint churches ('Mormon' and 'Reorganized') exemplify some key factors in the duplication (or multiplication) of new religious groups. First, personality conflict: personal rivalry and antagonism arises among the leadership, with one leader going his or her own way, and perhaps taking their own followers into 'the wilderness', as Brigham Young did with the Mormons, migrating to the inhospitable salt lake region of Utah, and leaving the wife and son of the deceased founder to carry on as the Reorganized Church. Second, doctrinal differences: disagreements arise over the basic teachings, causing schism, as when Brigham Young supported polygamy for Mormons, but Joseph Smith's widow and her son Joseph rejected plurality of wives in the Reorganized Church. Third, dynasty formation: the leadership is kept in the family of the founder, but another leader with charisma forms a rival group, again as in the Mormon case, where the son of Joseph Smith was in competition with the dynamic leader Brigham Young.

The case of the Worldwide Church of God is similarly instructive: Herbert W. Armstrong and his son Garner Ted Armstrong used to share the radio programme ('The World Tomorrow') by which the teachings of their church were propagated; but the father disinherited the son over a question of morals, and so he went out into the wilderness to form his own Church of God, International. The deceased father's church (under new leadership) remains the greater of the two (as in the case of the Mormons). A dynastic succession has been established, but it runs outside the main body, and history will show whether it can continue. In New Zealand the Worldwide church has a far greater profile than the International church.

One of the teachings of the Armstrong churches is that the Anglo-Saxons are related to the

Israelites, and thus have a special place in God's plan of history. This is also taught by the British-Israel-World Federation, whose fundamental belief is that the British are descended from the lost tribes of Israel. W.F. Massey, a prime minister of New Zealand, was a supporter of British Israelism. This group does not appear in the census, because it is not a Christian denomination or sect, but a para-ecclesiastical association. Presumably its members would put themselves down as 'Christian' or would state their particular Protestant denomination. Members of the Commonwealth Covenant Church (founded in New Zealand in 1939) hold the same British-Israel doctrine, but they are also Pentecostal.

Pentecostal Christians belong to another parachurch organisation, the Associated Pentecostal Churches of New Zealand, covering a multitude of entities such as Assemblies of God, Elim Church, Apostolic Church, New Life Centres, Christian Fellowships, and Open Door Mission. The growing Christian Revival Crusade should also be mentioned here. Thus, although there were factors in the past which led to their divisions, the various Pentecostal churches have found a form of unity.

The various Churches of Christ make up a complicated picture. The main body is the Associated Churches of Christ, a denomination, which distinguishes itself from the non-denominational (or non-instrumental) group of churches of Christ. They all acknowledge Thomas and Alexander Campbell (Irish Presbyterians who migrated to America) as founding fathers. The Associated Churches were originally called Disciples of Christ. The other group, the churches of Christ (with a small initial c), regard themselves as more conservative and closer to the New Testament pattern. That is why they sing hymns without accompaniment (hence the epithet non-instrumental applied to them by outsiders). These two groups are unrelated to other New Zealand 'Churches of Christ'. Thus, the Churches of Christ (Life and Advent) began in New Zealand in 1880 in response to the preaching of G.A. Brown, a former Baptist pastor from England; and in 1882 an association of Life and Advent Churches of Christ was formed. The Church of Christ New Zealand is an independent evangelical Protestant church, established in Auckland in 1950 by F.A. Wilson (1909-1982).

The relationship between the Theosophical Society and the Liberal Catholic Church was not based on schism but on complementarity. The church was established by members of the Theosophical Society, notably Charles W. Leadbeater (presiding bishop from 1923 to 1934), as a church that would be liberal enough to administer the Catholic Sacraments to Theosophists. John B.S. Coats (of cotton-yarn fame) was a bishop of the Church and president of the Society (and in this capacity he visited New Zealand in the 1970s). However, not all members of this church are Theosophists, and not all Theosophists are members of this church.

Among New Zealand Swedenborgians, the New Church and the General Church coexist happily enough, as is shown in Edith Jarmin's short history, *The New Church in New Zealand (1842-1983)*, in which the last chapter is devoted to the General Church.

The numerous offshoots of the Spiritualist movement in New Zealand have reasonably harmonious relations. The Christian Spiritualist Church and the Church of the Golden Light are specifically Christian. The various branches of the Spiritualist Church observe Christmas and Easter, and they hold Sunday worship services followed by seances and spiritual healing. The New Zealand Church of Spiritual Healing (which was constituted in 1978) does likewise. All these and other Spiritualist groups (such as The White Eagle Lodge, founded in 1936) are loosely related to the whole movement, and contribute to the *New Zealand Psychic Gazette*.

Characteristic Types

Each of the alternative Christian churches can be characterised according to one or more of the twelve types set out on Table Two. These types will be considered one by one and applied to appropriate churches in each case.

Table Two: Characteristic Types		
Accessibility: SEPARATIST	EXCLUSIVIST	UNIVERSALIST
Evangelism: CONVERSIONIST	INTROVERSIONIST	REFORMIST
Supernatural: CHARISMATIST	GNOSTICIST	SACRAMENTALIST
History: ADVENTIST	SPIRITUALIST	POST-ADVENTIST

The four lines list related categories: first, degree of openness and access; second, attitude to evangelism; third, approach to supernaturalism; fourth, sense of history.

(The three columns also tend to contain kindred types: first, fundamentalist and zealous; second, esoteric and mysterious; third, cosmopolitan and gregarious.)

Separatism

This means primarily separation from the world and its worldliness, its secularism. 'Come out from among them and be separate, says the Lord, and touch nothing unclean' (2 Corinthians 6:17). To be 'in the world but not of the world' is the stance taken by Seventh-day Adventists, Mormons, and Exclusive Brethren. They will be found in the business world (the Sanitarium Health Food Company, for example, is run by Adventists), but they are unlikely to be seen as spectators in theatres or sports arenas, as their spare time will be largely devoted to church activities. The same applies to Jehovah's Witnesses, but they are less prominent in business, being constantly engaged in missionary work, preaching the imminence of the War of Armageddon and selling religious literature from door to door.

Adventists and Mormons try to establish separate schools for their children. The Witnesses and the Exclusive Brethren send their children to state schools, but forbid them to take part in a number of school activities, especially religious instruction. Exclusive Brethren are not permitted to eat with outsiders, at school or at work. As their founder J.N. Darby taught: 'Separation from evil is God's principle of unity'. Pentecostal and other Fundamentalist Christians likewise take a stand against worldliness. They also seek to put their children into Christian schools.

Exclusivism

This is the special mark of the Exclusive Brethren, and it means that membership is restricted to the chosen people. In one sense it is a basic doctrine of Christianity: 'You are a chosen race' (I Peter 2:9), but if taken to extremes it could engender racism. Thus the Mormon church has tended to discriminate against blacks; only in recent times have they been permitted to hold priestly offices (formerly restricted to white males), after the prophet-president of their church was given a revelation by God.

With their British-Israel emphasis, the Commonwealth Covenant and Worldwide churches would appear to be in danger of racial exclusivism, but this is not really so.

Universalism

In Christian theology the term universalism technically means the belief that all will eventually be saved. In this sense the Worldwide church of H.W. Armstrong is somewhat universalist, believing that all who have ever lived will have an opportunity to accept salvation. The Mormon practice of baptism on behalf of the dead (see I Corinthians 15:29) is in the same vein; the aim is to offer salvation through vicarious baptism to everyone who has ever lived on earth, and that is why Mormons are such ardent compilers of genealogies.

The word universalism will be used here in the additional sense of all nations and races united in God: 'People will come from east and west, and north and south, and feast in the kingdom of God' (Luke 13:29). This idea is typical of the Baha'i religion. It can also be seen in the Unification church of Reverend Sun Myung Moon, who chooses a spouse for each of his followers, and in the process he deliberately fosters inter-racial marriage, as part of his church's unificationist and universalist plan.

The Metropolitan Community churches are somewhat unique in their universalism, extending their ministry to homosexuals and heterosexuals alike, to transvestites and transsexuals, to rich and poor, and to people of all skin colours. The Liberal Catholic church fits here because of its Theosophist recognition of truth in other religions. The Unitarian church promotes ideas of unity and it uses scriptures of all religions. The ability of Quakers to find 'that of God in every person' (and 'to be open to new light from whatever quarter it may come') demonstrates their universalism. The Swedenborgians affirm that God's New Church embraces within itself all who live by the truth of their own religion, whether Christian or not. Christian Spiritualism aims for a spirit of world-wide kinship without barriers of race or creed.

Such universalism, in respect of other religions and scriptures, is found in some of the parachurch groups also. The Moral Re-Armament movement aims to unite people above the divisions of race, class, and creed (it is not a religion, but includes people of all faiths). The Association for Research and Enlightenment, Focolare, Higher Thought, Infinite Way, Sutcliffe Schools of Radiant Living and Unity School of Christianity all have this spirit of openness.

Conversionism

Conversionist here means seeking to change people's life and character and to draw them into a church; this involves religious conversion of individuals, achieved through evangelism and proselytising techniques. Evangelistic fervour and the desire to win souls for Christ is shown, in different ways, by the Assemblies of God (and other Pentecostals), Open Brethren, churches of Christ, Church of the Nazarene, Christian and Missionary Alliance, and the parachurch organisations Agape Force, Navigators, Youth for Christ, Youth with a Mission. Their methods involve preaching, witnessing, tract distribution, audio cassettes and correspondence courses (two features of the evangelistic outreach of the Pentecostal Open Door Mission in Palmerston North), and broadcasting (Radio Rhema, a Gospel-proclaiming station, is supported by Pentecostal churches and charismatic Christians in mainstream churches).

Mormons and Jehovah's Witnesses are possibly the most zealous conversionists, carrying out their campaign on every doorstep in the country. Mormons have audio-visual showings at their information centre, right next to their splendid white temple, near Hamilton, and their full-time missionaries (mostly young 'elders' from America) take similar educational programmes into the homes of people who express interest in their church. The Witnesses rely on the written word, offering householders their two magazines (*The Watchtower* and *Awake*) and books attacking the theory of Evolution or predicting the end of the present age; they also conduct Bible studies in the homes of inquirers, using their own *New World Translation of the Holy Scriptures*. Seventh-day Adventists distribute by post a glossy magazine called *Signs* (formerly *Signs of the Times*), which has articles promoting healthiness, cleanliness, godliness, and marriage, with occasional allusions to the Book of Daniel and the

Watch Tower Bible and Tract Society of NZ

House-to-house ministry of Jehovah's Witnesses

Revelation of John. They have in the past employed colporteurs for their house-to-house evangelism, and the best-known of their books are the series of Uncle Arthur's bedtime stories, every one of which has a moral. The early Adventist evangelists in New Zealand held revival meetings in large tents, in which they preached prophecy and prohibition. These days the approach is to offer a series of vividly illustrated lectures on Biblical archaeology, in which the truth of the Bible's predictions is defended.

Christadelphians occasionally put tracts in letter boxes, inviting the reader to a talk on 'World Countdown: Christ is coming' ('Our speakers will show that the Bible signs of the countdown are being fulfilled and that the return of the Lord Jesus Christ is very near'). Dawn Bible Students are responsible for the radio session known punningly as 'Frank and Ernest', in which two men discuss Bible prophecies and doctrines, and seek to convert the listener to their beliefs.

The Worldwide Church of God, the Armstrongian church, proclaims its message by all available media (notably its radio and television programmes entitled 'The World Tomorrow', and its free and widely available magazine *The Plain Truth*); yet you will not find its meetings advertised on the church page of your local newspaper; it claims that it does not proselytise, but simply baptises those who are led to it by God.

Though there will be differences in the theological interpretation of the rite, all the groups named above have baptism as the means of entry into their church. The Worldwide view is that the act symbolises the person's faith in Christ's atoning sacrifice, and the death of the old self, to be replaced by a new life devoted to keeping God's laws. Pentecostals insist that converts must be 'born again believers' and be baptised with water and the Holy Spirit. Jehovah's Witnesses see the baptismal rite as a symbol of the new believer's dedication to God's service.

Unificationists (Moonies) also have a reputation for being ardent seekers of new members for their church, but they do not baptise their converts. Marriage, preceded by a Holy Wine ceremony, is their initiation rite, for removing original sin and setting the person on the new path.

Introversionism

This category seems severe, but when a group closes its ranks, becomes withdrawn, and turns inwards on itself, then introversionism is an applicable term. Exclusive Brethren find a place here, because of their relative lack of evangelistic activity. They do stand on street corners to proclaim judgement on the world and salvation from sin, but entry into their closed community is normally gained by being born into it. The ghetto experience of Jews in Europe (though this lifestyle was not always of their own choosing) shows a similar loss of desire to proselytise ('proselyte' being originally a Jewish word). However, living in the ghetto by choice and among the chosen people (with daily forays into the world to gather food and goods) can give satisfaction and security, and that is how the Exclusive Brethren feel; but to those who disturb the equilibrium, they mete out ostracism and excommunication.

Jehovah's Witnesses are certainly zealous in their endeavours to rescue the perishing and to enfold them into the congregation at their local Kingdom Hall. However, because they are also keen to protect the cleanness of the congregation, they expel ('disfellowship') members who deviate from the Bible-based path laid down by the central leadership in the Bethel headquarters building, Brooklyn, New York. There are introversionist aspects to their church, despite their high public profile.

However, our best example would be a Christian counterpart to the Centrepoint commune in Auckland, something like the Amish and Hutterian communities of the Mennonite (Anabaptist) tradition in North America. The Riverside Community (near Nelson) comes to mind in this regard, founded in 1940 as a Christian (largely Methodist), pacifist, self-supporting commune; but it would not see itself as introversionist ; it is more reformist, seeking to set up a utopian model for the outside world to copy, an image of life based on non-violence, caring, and sharing.

Then there is Camp David, by the Waipara River, north of Christchurch, the headquarters of the Full Gospel Mission (nicknamed the God Squad by the hostile communication media in the 1970s). The Mission originated in 1920, in Wellington and Christchurch, around the time when the evangelist Smith Wigglesworth came to New Zealand. Many of their members live in this Christian Co-operative Community, which has a farm and a 'fortress'. However, a fortress mentality is not really in evidence here; this group is separatist but not isolationist (visitors are permitted to enter and inspect the premises), and it is certainly conversionist.

Elsewhere in Canterbury, at Rangiora, a group known as the Christian Community was founded in 1970 by Neville Cooper, formerly an Australian Pentecostal evangelist. It is isolationist in its attitude to the world and most other churches, having withdrawn into its own introversionist commune to avoid contamination from them. As God's chosen people its members are exclusivist, and their belief that the end of the world is nigh characterises them as adventist. Another example of introversionism seems to be the Stone Kingdom Trust (an object of media attention in the 1980s), originating in Auckland but reappearing in Karamea (west coast of the South Island), and withdrawing from secular society into its own realm, where its members could live in obedience to the commandments of God.

Reformism

The reformist is intent on social activism, and desires 'to proclaim good news to the poor' (Luke 4:18): 'Blessed are you who are poor, for yours is the kingdom of God' (Luke 6:20). Amongst denominational churches, this reformist approach is typical of the Methodist Church and the Salvation Army (though there may be theological differences in their motives).

Despite its quietism and pacifism, the Society of Friends (Quakers) is socially active and constantly working against evil in the world. Similarly, though Christian Science could be categorised as gnosticist, it publishes an international newspaper which is respected for its integrity and social concern.

Moral Re-Armament, a parachurch movement, aims to bring dynamic Christianity into the world, to bring about a moral and spiritual revolution, beginning with each individual, as a foundation for world peace. Belonging to this same family are the Focolare movement and the Taize Community, which are both likewise dedicated to putting the Beatitudes into practice,

Charismatism

This category covers the charisma aspects: the leader's capacity to arouse devotion and enthusiasm, and the spiritual gifts (Greek *kharismata*) imparted by God (I Corinthians 12), such as healing power, prophecy, and speaking in tongues (glossolalia). Foremost in this regard are the Charismatic Christians of the Pentecostal churches; glossolalia is their distinguishing mark.

Mormons are also to be labelled charismatist (though not Charismatic): first because they claim to have all the spiritual gifts of the early church (Latter-day Saints constitute the Restored Church), and second because their founder Joseph Smith was a divinely inspired prophet.

The Seventh-day Adventist church has a prophet at its source, in Ellen White, but although Adventists accept her revelations as inspired, they have not institutionalised the prophet-role, as the Mormons have done in the person of their President.

Gnosticism

Gnosticist is the appropriate epithet when esoteric knowledge (gnosis) is involved. The word 'science' (Latin *scientia*, knowledge) will be one clue for finding instances of this type. Thus, by its special interpretation of the Bible, through Mary Baker Eddy's *Science and Health with Key to the Scriptures* (1875), the Christian Science church shows itself to be gnosticist. The Swedenborgian churches see a new revelation in the books of Emanuel Swedenborg, notably his *Arcana Coelestia* (Heavenly Secrets, 1747) in which, 'dictated to him from heaven', the spiritual sense of Genesis and Exodus is expounded in Latin in some three million words and seven thousand pages.

The presence of arcane knowledge and revelations in Joseph Smith's *Book of Mormon* and *Pearl of Great Price* makes the term gnosticist applicable to the Church of Jesus Christ of Latter-day Saints. Similarly, in the Unification Church, the *Divine Principle* of Sun Myung Moon is placed alongside the *Holy Bible* as a source of revealed truth; Unificationists (like Mormons with their *Book of Mormon*) receive as part of their conversion experience the conviction that the *Divine Principle* is true.

Some parachurch organisations have gnosticist features. The Association for Research and Enlightenment holds 15,000 discourses of the American psychic Edgar Cayce, delivered while he was in a state of altered consciousness and covering almost every facet of life. In 1946 Joel Goldsmith received daily illumination over a space of two months, and out of this experience came the Infinite Way, which involves a Christ consciousness similar to that found in the teachings of

Herbert Sutcliffe's Schools of Radiant Living and Charles and Myrtle Fillmore's Unity School of Christianity.

The doctrine that identifies the Anglo-Saxon people with the children of Israel (as espoused by the British-Israel-World Federation, the Commonwealth Covenant Church, and the Worldwide Church of God) is rather arcane and apparently in the nature of a special revelation.

Sacramentalism

Sacramentalism means attaching great importance to the sacraments, the sacred rites of the Church, especially Baptism and Eucharist. Churches which do not have these two sacraments presumably do not qualify for this category (Religious Society of Friends, Unification Church, and Church of Christ Scientist, as also the Salvation Army). The best example in this section would be the Liberal Catholic Church, which was set up precisely for the purpose of making the Catholic Eucharist available to Theosophists.

Roseanne Jones

Young members of Aaronic priesthood in Church of Jesus Christ of Latter-day Saints (Hastings second ward) about to pass sacramental emblems to the congregation.

The Mormons have a number of distinctive sacramental rites, of which some are performed openly in chapels, and others are enacted secretly in temples. Baptism (by immersion), consecration of marriage, and the Sacrament of the Lord's Supper (with water replacing wine, because of the Mormon prohibition of alcohol) are administered in the churches. In the temples three additional rituals are carried out: baptism for the dead (immersion in a font on behalf of ancestors), celestial marriage (sealing a couple in wedlock for eternity), endowment (an 'ordinance' in which the initiate is anointed with oil, wears special temple garments, and witnesses a dramatic performance).

Adventism

Adventist, as in Seventh-day Adventist, means awaiting the (imminent) second coming of Jesus Christ: 'The kingdom of heaven is at hand' (Matthew 4:17); 'Behold, I am coming soon' (Revelation 22:20). The term adventist is relevant to Latter-day Saints (Mormons) and Latter Day Saints (Reorganized), who see their churches as belonging to the time of the end. Finding fulfilment of Biblical prophecies in current world events has been a distinctive mark of Seventh-day Adventists, Jehovah's Witnesses, Christadelphians, the Worldwide Church, and the Pentecostal churches. The Nazarene church also has a firm conviction that their Lord will return to judge the world.

The Watch Tower view on the Apocalypse and the Last Judgement will serve as an illustration, though it has some distinctive features: the wicked will suffer permanent death and not eternal punishment in hell fire, while the faithful Christians (Jehovah's Witnesses) will enjoy everlasting life in the new heaven and earth, but only 144,000 of them will be allowed to enter the heavenly kingdom.

Spiritualism

Spiritualism is here placed between Adventism and Post-Adventism because Spiritualists are not excited about the second advent: they tend to lack a sense of history, and they are continually receiving visitors and messages from the spirit world, through spirit mediums in seances.

The Bible forbids necromancy (Leviticus 19:31, Deuteronomy 11:1), so there will be a distinct reluctance by most churches, especially Pentecostals and Jehovah's Witnesses, to be classed as spiritualist. Swedenborg's clairvoyance and communion with the angels in heaven, Joseph Smith's encounter with angels who were formerly humans, and Sun Myung Moon's visions are therefore not regarded as spiritualist experiences. And the Association for Research and Enlightenment has a psychic medium at its source, in Edgar Cayce, but it affirms that it does not include spiritualism in its practices.

Post-Adventism

This label adheres to Christians who have some form of 'realised eschatology', whereby the Second Advent has already happened: 'The kingdom of God is in your midst' (Luke 17:21). The New Christian Church sees the Second Coming of Jesus Christ as having occurred in the revelation of the spiritual sense of the Word through Swedenborg's writings. Christian Scientists have a similar conviction about Mary Baker Eddy's book, *Science and Health*.

In the Unification Church the Messiah is not expected to come on the clouds of heaven, but be born in the East, in a land where many religions are known (since he does not come to save only Christians), where God and Satan are in confrontation (democracy versus communism), and which has prepared the way for him with a prophecy. The *Divine Principle*, the book written by the founder, reveals that Korea is that country, with Shamanism, Buddhism, Confucianism, Christianity, and other religions; also a 500 year-old book of prophecy entitled *Chung-Gam-Nok*; and its struggle between democracy and communism. The Messiah was to be born in Korea between 1917 and 1930; Sun Myung Moon was born in northern Korea in 1920; in 1936 Jesus appeared to him and told him to establish the Kingdom of Heaven on earth.

Lifestyle Features

These churches offer alternative lifestyles, which are different from the way of the world and divergent from the path followed by the conventional churches. Some striking features of their lifestyles will be noted here.

Health and healing

The healing of sickness has been a part of the Christian religion since Jesus first went about 'preaching the kingdom, and healing every kind of disease and illness among the people' (Matthew 4:23-24). The miraculous cures performed by Jesus were repeated by his apostles (Acts 3:1-8). The charismatic gift of healing through the Holy Spirit was present in the early church (I Corinthians 12:9, 30), and the new Christian churches have usually sought to restore this healing power to their armoury. Foremost in this regard are the Pentecostal churches, who have practitioners of this gift working in their congregations and at public meetings.

The teachings of Mary Baker Eddy on the 'science' of healing are in the same Biblical tradition. She had an experience of sudden physical healing in 1866, while reading the New Testament; Christian Science healing is therefore said to be based on prayer and spiritual inspiration, not on psychological therapeutic techniques or simple positive thinking. Christian Scientists also abstain from tobacco, alcohol, and drugs (including medicines). Spiritual healing is also offered by the Christian Spiritualist Church and some parachurch groups, especially Charles and Myrtle Fillmore's Unity, Joel Goldsmith's Infinite Way, and Higher Thought.

In 1863 the prophetess Ellen White had a divine vision about human health, and since then Seventh-day Adventists have seen it as their duty to live healthily. They pay some attention to the Old Testament dietary laws, and they tend to be vegetarians. They have founded medical schools: in Chicago the American Medical Missionary College, and in Michigan the Battle Creek Sanitarium. The Sanitarium, where the Maori leader Maui Pomare studied, was directed by John Harvey Kellogg, whose name became famous on packages of breakfast cereals. Nowadays the SDA food supplier is the Sanitarium Health Food Company, marketing Weet-Bix, Corn Flakes, Muesli, and Marmite. Adventists frown on alcohol, tea, coffee, and tobacco; and they organise courses to assist members of the general public to give up smoking.

Mormons have a similar concern for maintaining personal health, by avoiding the socially accepted drugs and stimulants. They follow 'The Word of Wisdom', which advocates a healthy diet of grains, vegetables, and fruits, with sparing use of meat, and rejection of harmful substances. The aim is to keep the body healthy and pure, as a temple in which the Spirit of the Lord may abide (see I Corinthians 6:19).

Jehovah's Witnesses have no strict dietary rules, but they do not allow blood transfusions, in line with the Bible's prohibition on eating blood. And they often say that their hygiene is so meticulous that there are no stomach aches or food poisoning at their regular mass meetings of believers.

Camp meetings

The 'camp-meeting' (an open-air or tent meeting for evangelism and revivalism, often lasting several days) was a feature of the American religious scene from which many of the alternative churches emerged. In Auckland in 1882 the Church of Christ (Life and Advent) used a tent for a revivalist meeting. In 1886 Seventh-day Adventists constructed a tent, fifty feet long, and set it up in Auckland for evangelistic campaigns, over two successive summers. It was then taken to other North Island towns. They used to hold annual conventions and camp in tents at a different place each time. When they broke camp, that place would invariably have the nucleus of an Adventist church established in it. Quakers have an annual 'summer gathering', at which the Friends camp together in tents, or cabins, or dormitories, for mutual encouragement and instruction (rather than for evangelism of the unconverted). Jehovah's Witnesses have large convention meetings, often in stadiums and sports grounds (places they would not normally frequent). They take the opportunity of baptising converts, hiring a public swimming pool for the occasion.

Moonies gather for huge open-air meetings in stadiums in Korea and America (in New York's Yankee Stadium and Madison Square Garden, for example). At these mass rallies thousands of couples have been married, receiving Mr Moon's blessing and being sprinkled with holy water; as noted earlier, this ceremony has apparently taken the place of Christian baptism in Unification-ist practice. This church also organises large conferences for scholars (whatever their persuasion) to discuss religious questions.

The Full Gospel Mission has its headquarters in a 'camp', Camp David by the Waipara River, with a fortress and ramparts on which the flags of Medieval chivalry fly. Three times a year all its baptised men assemble at Camp David to appear before God, in accordance with the divine injunction in Deuteronomy 16:16. They thus follow Jewish festivals, and reject Christmas and Easter as unbiblical. They worship on the Sabbath Day, not on Sunday.

Sabbath observance

At some point in their early history Christians made Sunday their weekly holy day instead of the Jewish Sabbath Day (Saturday). The idea of the Sabbath (as a day for resting from work and for worshipping God) was transferred to Sunday; but some churches have insisted on keeping Saturday as their Sabbath. The reason for this is sometimes stated thus: a Christian should keep all of the Ten Commandments, including 'Remember the Sabbath Day, to keep it holy' (Exodus 20:8).

Seventh-day Adventists, who hold their worship services on Saturdays, are the most prominent example of a sabbatarian church. They follow the Jewish practice of starting their Sabbath observance at sunset on Friday and completing it at sunset on Saturday; thus Saturday night is not part of the Sabbath. The Seventh Day Baptist Church is an older Sabbath-keeping group, going back to the English Reformation in the seventeenth century.

More recently, Herbert W. Armstrong's Worldwide Church of God has adopted the Saturday Sabbath as its day for congregating (usually in hired halls). It also observes the seven annual holidays laid down in the Old Testament; this is a reasonable thing to do if a church wishes to emulate the early Christians, and there is some sympathy for this idea in Pentecostal circles also.

Jehovah's Witnesses meet for worship on Sundays. They do not include the Eucharist in their weekly worship, but have it once a year at the time of the Jewish Passover, as the only memorial ceremony that Jesus asked his disciples to keep. The Church at Auckland, an autonomous local organisation founded in 1951, should be cited as our final example: it meets for worship on the Sabbath, not on Sunday.

All these details have only given us a glimpse of the varieties of lifestyle and worship practised by the alternative churches (some of which have not even been mentioned here). But it can be seen that each of them adds its own spice and flavour to the multicultural feast enjoyed by the people known as 'Kiwis' or New Zealanders.

Further reading

For further information on alternative Christian groups, see the relevant sections of *Beliefs and Practices in New Zealand: A Directory*, Massey University, Palmerston North, 1985 (available in public libraries). In this book each group speaks for and about itself. This book has been the chief source for writing the above presentation, supported by forty years of personal encounter with Christians of alternative churches. Other relevant books are:

Ballis, Peter H., *In and Out of the World: Seventh-day Adventists in New Zealand*, Palmerston North: Dunmore Press, 1985.

Barker, Eileen, *The Making of a Moonie: choice or brainwashing?*, Oxford: Oxford University Press, 1984.

Colless, B. and Donovan, P., (eds.), *Religion in New Zealand Society*, (2nd edn.) Palmerston North: Dunmore Press, 1985, pp. 99-118 (Colin Brown, 'The Charismatic Contribution'), pp. 119-142 (Michael Hill, 'The Sectarian Contribution').

Hunt, Brian W., *Zion in New Zealand: a history of the Church of Jesus Christ of Latter-day Saints in New Zealand, 1854-1977*, Temple View: Church College of New Zealand, 1977.

Lineham, Peter, *There We Found Brethren: a history of Assemblies of Brethren in New Zealand*, Palmerston North: Gospel Publishing House, 1977.

Worsfold, J.E., *A History of the Charismatic Movements in New Zealand*, Bradford: Julian Literature Trust, 1974.

Christianity:
Maori Churches

Manuka Henare

Maori Christianity today has its roots in the traditional religion developed by nga tupuna (the ancestors) over thousands of years in that part of the world known to Maori as Aotearoa and te Moana Nui a Kiwa (the Pacific ocean region). I refer to this early religion as 'traditional Maori religion' and, consistent with Maori thinking, argue that it is the basis of maoritanga (Maori culture). Christianity, together with all its new insights - a Creator God intervening in human history, the Son of God as Redeemer, new notions of salvation - and its own long tradition of ritual, denominationalism and division, is a relatively recent addition and has been accepted as an integral part of Maori culture.

While Maori refer to Christianity as whakapono (faith and beliefs) it would not be correct to assume that Christianity has therefore supplanted the world view of traditional Maori religion or many of its rituals and customs. Despite the endeavours of the settler churches and the respective settler governments to direct Maori away from such belief-systems, they continue to be the foundations of a resilient Maori culture, where Christ and his teachings have become part of the world view, the kinship system and the culture. Maori religious life and spirituality cannot therefore be defined outside the definition of maoritanga, because religion is not an abstract concept for Maori. Rather it is a lived experience which is elaborated in the culture.

Maori acceptance of Christianity

The introduction to Christianity for Maori may have begun nearly 200 years ago, because it is clear from Maori sources that we came in contact with Christianity before the end of the eighteenth century. This is in contrast with the commonly held view that Christianity was introduced by the Reverend Samuel Marsden and other missionaries from Europe. Many whalers, sealers and traders belonged to various Christian denominations and had already introduced elements of Christian belief and practice among the hapu and iwi with whom they worked and lived.[1]

The written records of Maori acceptance of Christianity as part of their belief system begin from 1814, and up to the 1830s, according to missionary accounts, Christian influence was minor.[2] It is clear that Maori in general approached the new religious force with understandable caution. However one notable example from this period was a sign of what was to come. In 1830 Rawiri Taiwhanga of Te Uri o Hau section of Nga Puhi became one of the first rangatira (hapu and iwi leader) to accept Christianity as part of his own and his whanau life.[3] The new commitment followed dramatic changes in the ways he exercised his political, economic and social roles as rangatira. He had in the 1820s become a farmer, then later a preacher and a teacher, and was known as a man of quick discernment. He obviously used scripture as a basis for critiquing the life of his people and culture, but at the same time he maintained his traditional responsibilities as a rangatira.

Eventually signing the Treaty of Waitangi, Rawiri Taiwhanga together with other important Christian rangatira such as Patuone, Waka Nene and Hone Heke, all from Te Tai Tokerau, recognised the treaty as 'he kawenata hou', a new covenant. They believed it to be a covenant like that of the New Testament.[4] They all appeared to have a remarkable understanding of some aspects of scriptural theology and as early Maori Christian patriots they were the forerunners of generations of other prophets. These latter, drawing on traditional Maori religious and Christian beliefs, led their peoples into a rapidly changing world.

According Te Pakaka Tawhai's account of Aotearoa's spiritual heritage (above, chapter one) Maori conceive of creation as a great kin unit which has a genealogical structure. This genealogy begins with Te Kore (the Nothing) which through aeons evolved into Te Po (the never-ending beginning) which also evolved through generations to the human person to the stage of Te Ata (the Dawn). The beginnings are in a spiritual world and according to contemporary Maori Christian writers and speakers like Maori Marsden, Tawhao Tioke and Hemi Potatau, the spiritual order is the basis of the social and temporal order.

Maori Marsden says that Maori have never accepted a mechanistic view of the universe; rather it is conceived as a two-world system in which the material proceeds from the spiritual, and the spiritual interpenetrates the material physical world.[5] The cultural milieu is thus rooted in both worlds and te tangata (the human person), te whanau (extended family), te hapu (the extended families) and te iwi (the genealogically linked hapu) are involved in an intimate relationship with nga atua (spiritual powers) and the universe. Tawhao Tioke also says that the universe is conceived as a two-world system in which the material proceeds from the spiritual.[6] Potatau has written that all things come from nga atua and adds a further dimension, when he says that there must be karakia in all human action to nga atua.[7]

The theological and anthropological research of Fr Michael Shirres on aspects of over 400 karakia and ritual collected in the 1840s to 1860s is a window into Maori appreciation of the centrality of religious insights and practices and how they are a way of understanding and interpreting the meaning of life. Nga karakia are a variety of forms of ritual chants which 'often invoke the atua and are a means of participation, of becoming one with the ancestors and events of the past in the "eternal present" of ritual'.[8]

Karakia are human actions which involve the power of spoken or sung words. And through speaking the words of nga tupuna this power is the work of people rather than of an individual. This participation in ritual means that Maori continue to take part in the whole movement of creation 'from the nothingness, to the night, to the full daylight'. The function of karakia is to express this participation whereby the person is identified with the people, both living and dead, speaking the words of nga tupuna and taking on their world view. Ritual and therefore karakia has been a major factor in establishing this world view and Maori cultural values. In such a framework, the domains of nga tupuna and nga atua were not separated absolutely from the world of everyday life and activities. The two worlds were linked and all activities in the everyday world were seen as coming under the influence of nga atua and nga tupuna. Karakia links the people of today with the ancestors and events of the past and takes us into the eternal present life.[9] Ritual time is thus the eternal now and at the same time a level of historical consciousness.[10] In these ways the Maori relives history.[11]

According to Wiremu Te Rangikaheke of Ngati Rangiwewehi, a Christian scholar of last century whose written accounts of Maori history covers the evolution of the universe to the life of hapu in Aotearoa, nga karakia were the means of bringing every aspect of creation under control. However because the mana or power of the karakia came from the atua (the spiritual source), their effectiveness depended on the faith of the people using the chants and not just on reciting the words. This faith was to be a faith in the atua.[12]

What we can see here can be described as 'implicit faith', an interesting and helpful appreciation of the fact that there are levels of faith. According to Aylward Shorter modern theologians have explored the connotations of implicit faith in which they reverse the order of a supernatural love that follows and depends on supernatural faith.[13] Instead the proposition is that the virtue and habit of faith are born of love, in which God is the source and faith is to be compared to the judgements of value and commitments of a person in love. This is a very different point of view from those held for centuries in European Christianity and from conservative and evangelical Christians today. The notion of implicit faith is easily understood by Maori because the rituals and karakia were points of entry into the spiritual world. Over time, as Maori knowledge of Christian insights deepened and additional rituals and new types of karakia from the churches were accepted and incorporated as part of the culture, a more explicit Christian faith emerged.

A Maori notion of faith includes tradition and the past, with its own understanding of truth and its own commitment of faith. The early Maori Christians came to their respective Christian churches with their own understanding of truth, salvation and faith. These continue to be the bases for much contemporary Maori Christian theological discussion, the search for effective liturgies and appropriate church structures in and through which Maori evangelises Maori and others. The problem for Maori of last century and most of this century has been that European notions and judgements concerning faith and salvation were understood in very narrow, ethnocentric terms. Salvation, understood in terms of European and Middle East experience, was not possible outside the church, and truth was something that the enlightened and civilised cultures of Europe held. While many Maori would say this linkage of salvation with civilisation is erroneous, most have learnt to live with it. Europe's own historical experience and values also permeate and are reflected in church institutions and structures.

The types of church structures such as parishes, dioceses, synods, general assemblies and so forth which are consequences of European experience and values have not proved appropriate for Maori expressions of faith and cultural development.

Tradition and the idea of the past in this context and frame of reference, is another important element of the world view. For Maori the past is not something that is behind but instead is seen as nga ra kei mua (the days immediately in front). Muru Walters says that not only is the past in front of us but so is the present because the past and the present are considered to be one.[14] What is present is not an illusion but the facts concerning Maori history. This world view, where the past and the present are both seen as a continuum, is an essential part of Maori Christianity, and can be contrasted with the western world view of Christianity.

Maori Christianity today

Today Maori Christianity is acknowledged by Maori as the religion of their culture. However the journey leading to this acknowledgement was a traumatic one. Christianity as an organised religion and as a set of moral, ethical and religious beliefs and practices, has had a profound effect on nga tikanga me nga ritenga (values and customs).[15]

According to one Maori Christian scholar, Maharaia Winiata:

The Christian missions were sources of the most powerful forces of change in the early interaction between the chiefs and European society. The Christian church was, in effect if not in form, a totalitarian organisation both in its purpose and policy. It directly initiated and controlled vital agencies such as schools, literature, modes of religious activity and belief, systems of behaviour, and technical training schemes. The missions set out deliberately to change Maori society and its personnel, for the dynamic had always been the conviction that the Christian revelation was unique and that this fact imposed an absolute obligation on the bearers of the gospel to bring the heathen into the Kingdom of God.[16]

Maori attitudes towards religion (specifically Christianity), its function and its relationship with society, are interesting. According to Apirana Ngata and I.L. Sutherland, the Maori initially identified Christianity with the British law of the Pakeha. This identification was consistent with the Maori holistic understanding of the place of the social order in religion.

[the] Maori was used to thinking of religion and the civil law as one. The functions of religion took the place of what the Pakeha calls civil law as the restraining and controlling force in the Maori commune. Western civilisation, when it reached New Zealand, presented a combination of Christianity and British law.... He [the Maori] assumed the law and the gospel to be one.[17]

This Maori understanding of the unity of the spiritual and temporal orders can be exemplified in the events of 150 years ago at the signing of the Treaty of Waitangi in Paihia. The rangatira had confidence in missionary advice and the good faith of the British Crown. As described earlier many Christian rangatira saw the treaty as the making of a covenant between themselves and the British Queen, and this compact was witnessed by God. The assumption was that this covenant demanded of both sides certain honourable behaviour.[18]

Maori have learnt through the bitter experience of colonisation that there is a difference between the message and the messenger. Like so many other peoples in Asia, Africa and the Pacific they found the Christian churches came as part of the colonising cultures who believed themselves to have a divine commission to civilise and evangelise the so-called native peoples of the world. Maori found that:

Pakeha religion, Pakeha trade, Pakeha agriculture, and Pakeha government were not all woven of one cloth, as was the case in their own society. They found that the Pakeha God was often neatly separated from more mundane pursuits and that Pakeha order and justice were not all they were cracked up to be.[19]

In the face of all this hypocrisy the Maori Christian response was to further internalise Christian faith in terms of maoritanga and to continue the dynamic interaction of gospel and culture. This acculturation or inculturation process continues today because a religious understanding of reality is at the heart of culture.

Historically, Maori incorporated Biblical texts as part of whaikorero (speech making on the marae), and in iwi discussions biblical quotations were used as authoritatively as the sayings from iwi traditions. Biblical names were adopted and bestowed, at baptisms, on children and in some cases on Maori communities.[20]

Because of settler government aims of assimilation and the demise of many Maori customs and practices, Maori Christians identified with the sufferings of the Children of Israel in the Old Testament. Many Maori prophets emerged from among the people: Te Ua Haumene, Te Kooti, Te Whiti and Tohu Kakahi, Tawhiao, Rua Kenana, Wiremu Ratana all explaining an oppressive world and giving messages of hope. Often prophetic movements developed around them, such as Papahurihia, Pai Marire, and Tariao. In the case of Te Kooti and Ratana two independent Maori Christian churches were established.[21] The Maori theologian Ruawai Rakena has described these as messianic movements which followed the orthodox missionary teaching yet represent indigenous churches.[22]

On the other hand, while large groupings of Maori joined or participated in these movements, it is as well to remember that the large proportion of Maori continued their involvement in the Methodist, Anglican, Presbyterian and Catholic Churches, albeit in some tension. And while these latter churches largely failed to address the racist and assimilative activities of the new Pakeha culture and politics, Maori Anglicans and Catholics were very active in the Maori solidarity movements such as Te Kotahitanga and Te Kingitanga. The prophets, their movements, and the Maori in the Churches all found identification easy. Ngata and Sutherland have said, 'The promised land was Aotearoa restored.'[23]

New Testament qualities of peace-making, humility, good will, charity, service, law-abidingness, obedience and faith provided a new concept of rangatiratanga (authority and mana). Adopting these new ideals was assisted by the fact that some of these qualities were also inherent in the traditional concept of rangatiratanga.[24]

Today many Maori make a distinction between Pakeha churches, and Maori churches, where the fundamental Christian beliefs and values of faith, hope, charity, justice and peace are expressed according to each group's cultural norms and practices. A Pakeha church is one which was established when the early missionaries of all denominations changed their mission policies from about the 1850s. The missionaries initially worked among Maori and saw this as their primary mission. When the influx of settlers from Europe began after the 1850s and Maori became a minority people in their own land, the priorities of the churches' mission

Anne Manchester, *Crosslink*

Tuhoe carver Maha Tepoono works on poupou (panels) for Te Kakana o te Aroha, the Presbyterian Wellington Maori Pastorate's church marae.

policies changed to that of a mission to the settlers. This in effect added to the marginalisation of Maori in society. Like the experience in society, Maori Christians were relegated to the periphery of church life. Society became European and the Churches became settler churches or as Maori describe them, Pakeha churches.

These same churches, says Allan Davidson, were struggling at the beginning of the twentieth century to try to find ways to re-establish their 'Maori work', and throughout this century and only in recent times have church structures begun to change in order to accommodate this.[25] This accommodation was certainly the agenda of the Pakeha church leadership and some Maori, but many Maori Christians wanted more than accommodation, they wanted to establish Maori churches which at the same time reflected the various denominational options taken up by hapu and iwi.

Maori churches are of two types. First are those synods, divisions or more appropriate structures within the mainline churches which are more or less controlled by Maori Christians. The largest grouping of Maori belong to these churches. According to the 1981 census figures some 53 per cent of the Maori population identify themselves as belonging to the Anglican, Presbyterian, Catholic, Methodist and Mormon churches. The three largest are Anglican (21 per cent), Catholic (15 per cent) and Mormon (7 per cent).[26]

The second type are the Ringatu and Ratana churches. Both have Maori founders, Te Kooti and Ratana, and in 1981 some 13 per cent of Maori identified themselves as members. The largest grouping was Ratana with 11 per cent of the Maori population. These churches are independent Maori Christian churches and operate in a Maori milieu. Each has developed its own types of karakia and rituals. For Ringatu the content of karakia is decidedly scriptural, with prophecies of Te Kooti and the form of expression traditional. Ratana is a mixture of scripture with elements of tradition and they have developed their own specific liturgies. Both churches attempt to address the specific needs of Maori in terms both of a spiritual and a material salvation.[27]

A.C. Moore

Ratana Temple and band

But what of the relative strength and influence within the churches? What we see is that most Maori Christians were a minority group within their church. Nearly 90 per cent of the total membership of Ratana and Ringatu were Maori, meaning that the milieu is Maori. This cannot be said for the other churches, where the milieu and the structures come from a Pakeha world. Maori Anglican are only 7 per cent of the total Anglican membership, Maori Catholic are 9 per cent, Maori Methodist are 10 per cent, Maori Presbyterian were 1 per cent. The exception are Maori Mormon who are 51 per cent of the membership.

Winiata has observed that initially certain features common to both Christian and Maori religion eased the propagation of the gospel.[28] Later, Maori re-interpreted the gospel in the light of their fundamental values, thereby giving rise to particular Maori cultural expressions of Christianity which are evident. Maori traditional values and those values inherent in Christian teachings have come together in a continuing dynamic interaction. Increasingly it is Maori who determine their hierarchy of values and, particularly in the mainline denominations, seek their own Maori churches.[29]

Te Hahi Mihinare: The Anglican Church

In 1877 the Anglican missionary T.S. Grace and Hemi Matenga both asked a question about a Maori leadership within the Anglican Church, when they asked about a Maori bishop for Maori Anglicans. Then in 1880 the Native Church Board of the diocese of Auckland tried to appoint a suffragan bishop for Maori in the diocese. This was rejected by the General Synod because it might split 'the oneness' of the Church. What followed was years of struggle by Maori Anglicans for representation on diocesan synods, although in 1898 Waiapu diocese made provision for Maori. At the same time a college called Te Rau Theological School at Gisborne trained Maori ministers from 1833 to 1920, when it was closed and students moved to St John's Theological College in Auckland.

In 1925 the General Synod approved the establishment of a Diocese of Aotearoa for Maori. However it required the approval of each diocesan bishop and the legislation was never given effect. Then when a Pakeha, Herbert Williams, was nominated by the bishops, Sir Apirana Ngata and others refused to accept the nomination and insisted that a Maori be appointed. Finally in 1928 the General Synod reached a compromise and agreed to the appointment of a Maori but as a suffragan bishop of Waiapu with the title of Bishop of Aotearoa. F.A. Bennett was consecrated in 1928 but the limitations of his position became evident. The position held little effective power and limited resources. The existing diocesan structures proved impediments to the blossoming of a Maori Anglican faith. Frustration was to continue into the 1960s, until finally the bishop was given a place in the General Synod.

Finally after more organising and planning by Maori Anglicans the Bishopric of Aotearoa was established in 1972, but the Bishop remained a suffragan bishop of the Bishop of Waiapu, and diocesan approval was still required in order to work in each part of the country. Then in 1978 Te Pihopatanga o Aotearoa with its own council was established and the bishop shared with each diocesan bishop the episcopal oversight of Maori.[30] The decisive moment came in November 1990 during the 150th commemoration year of the signing of the covenant called the Treaty of Waitangi. A special General Synod accepted a new constitution for the whole church. It had the effect of acknowledging the cultural strands and history within the Church. Te Pihopatanga O Aotearoa was recognised as a local Anglican Church in its own right and would stand alongside the Anglican dioceses in full partnership. The Synod acknowledged that the Treaty of Waitangi embodied two matters important to Anglican life in Aotearoa New Zealand. The insight was, that the Treaty encapsulates both Gospel values and the principle of partnership. And together these implied certain rights and obligations for Maori Anglicans and the wider Church. After more than 150 years Te Pihopatanga was now in place and a partner in the mission of the Church. The new constitution was to be tested among the Anglican dioceses who must agree or disagree with it and the changes by 1992. Maori Anglicans now have control of their own affairs and can address other important issues related to developing Maori Christianity.

An added dimension to the changes was the affirmation that the Diocese of Polynesia was no longer a missionary diocese. This new diocese, centred in Fiji, is a diocese in its own right with its particular set of Pacific customs and values and full authority over its affairs.

Te Hahi Weteriana: The Methodist Church

From the 1860s Maori Methodists have also struggled for their own identity and belonging within the church.[31] As early as 1839 the Wesleyan lay-preacher Minarapa Rangihatuake of Taranaki was responsible for the first Methodist Church in Wellington.[32] While Maori involvement seemed to be a common pattern there was little effective decision-making given to Maori. All Maori mission work was controlled by the Home Mission Department. Attempts to establish new approaches and an autonomous Maori Synod in 1897 and 1913 failed and a commitment was made to keep Pakeha supervision. Maori ministers and lay representatives were only admitted to district synods and the Annual Conference in 1919, but Maori could not vote on the reception of Pakeha ministers. Finally in 1973 after years of organising by Maori Methodists the Maori Division was inaugurated with Ruawai Rakena as first superintendent. Since that time the division has sought to realise 'Maori styles of Christian life, witness and service, or a Maori response to the Gospel'.[33]

Te Hahi Katorika: The Catholic Church

Like other Christians, Maori Catholics have struggled to be Maori inside the Church. The initiative to be members of the Catholic Church belongs to rangatira in Tai Tokerau who in 1835 sent young people to Poihakena (Sydney) for study and training as catechists, a form of lay ministry. These youth returned to work among their people. It was in 1838 that the first official Catholic representative arrived to formally establish the presence of the Church. Bishop Jean Baptiste Pompallier came with a group of priests and brothers to the Hokianga. The Catholic Church arrived some twenty-four years after the Anglicans and Methodists. The mission policy change referred to earlier, when the Church's priorities moved to take up the care of new European settlers, had a dramatic impact on its work among Maori. It was a consequence which was to hamper the effective evangelisation of Maori. Internal differences within the Church over areas of competence added to the difficulties for the Church, and in the long run it was Maori who suffered. The Maori missions were poorly provided for during the Land Wars and right into this century.

In the 1880s an early attempt by Maori and others to seek the appointment of a Bishop with specific pastoral responsibilities for Maori almost succeeded. The Vatican had chosen Fr James McDonald for the job, but there was disagreement among the Bishops in New Zealand who had other priorities involving Irish and English Catholics and the appointment somehow lapsed. However throughout the turbulent years a strong Maori catechist movement maintained the faith, with the support of a small dedicated band of missionaries. The appointment of Maori priests suffered many setbacks, from a time when the seminary in the 1860s in Auckland was full of candidates. War and internal difficulties in the Church saw all the candidates leave; one was sent to the Vatican for study, but he returned home unsuitable for the vocation. It was not till 1948 that the first Maori was ordained a priest and since then a small number have followed. Maori sisters have been active since 1840 till today.

The assimilationist tendencies of society in general were reflected by church policy and behaviour. However Catholic lay people maintained the requests for more autonomy and more responsibility within the church. In 1983 the Bishops' Conference established Te Runanga o te Hahi Katorika ki Aotearoa, a national Maori agency of the Bishops. Te Runanga consulted widely and prepared the submission requesting the appointment of a Maori bishop. This led to a Maori Catholic delegation of Te Runanga going on a pilgrimage to the Vatican with a request for a Maori bishop to be responsible for the pastoral care of all Maori Catholic. The Bishops' Conference sent

Cardinal Thomas Williams of Wellington to support the application. This culminated in 1988 in the consecration of Takuira Mariu as the first Maori Catholic bishop. Together the Bishop and Te Runanga are exploring ways of enhancing Maori Christianity, using culture and theological reflection as the driving forces behind all initiatives.

This brief review of the main Maori Churches hopefully gives some insights into the world view and history of Maori Christians, and their determination to address the challenge of culture and gospel. It will be on Maori terms, and there is much more yet to be done. It is within each denomination and then within the now strong Maori ecumenical body, Te Runanga Whakawha-naunga i Nga Hahi o Aotearoa (the Maori Council of Churches, constituted in 1982), that progress will be made. The story of the development of Maoritanga and that of Maori Christianity is the same story, with the churches some of the key actors in the drama.

Notes

1. Manuka Henare, 'Nga Tikanga Me Nga Ritenga o Te Ao Maori: Standards and Foundations of Maori Society', in *Report of the Royal Commission on Social Policy,* vol. III, part one, Wellington: The Royal Commission on Social Policy, 1988, p. 33.
2. Bronwyn Elsmore, *Like Them That Dream: The Maori and the Old Testament,* Tauranga: Tauranga Moana Press, 1985, pp. 12-13.
3. C. Orange, and O. Wilson, 'Rawiri Taiwhanga', in *The Dictionary of New Zealand Biography,* edited by W.H. Oliver, vol. 1, 1769-1869, Wellington: Allen & Unwin/Department of Internal Affairs, 1990, pp. 417-418.
4. Claudia Orange, *The Treaty of Waitangi,* Wellington: Allen & Unwin/Port Nicholson Press, 1987, pp. 49-50.
5. Maori Marsden, 'God, Man and Universe: A Maori View', in *Te Ao Hurihuri,* edited by Michael King, Wellington: Hicks Smith & Sons, 1975, p. 215.
6. T. Tioke, 'Pre-Christian Maori concept of Spiritual Reality', cyclostyled notes (not for publication), Te Hinota Maori, Presbyterian Church, Whakatane, n.d., p. 1.
7. H. Potatau, 'The Maori and his background, an account of Ngati Kahungunu', cyclostyled paper, Department of Maori Studies, Victoria University, Wellington, n.d., p. 5.
8. M. Shirres, 'An Introduction to Karakia', unpublished doctoral thesis, University of Auckland, 1986, p. ii.
9. Shirres, pp. 18,20,21.
10. F. Allan Hanson, 'Maori Religion', in *The Encyclopedia of Religion,* editor-in-chief Mircea Eliade, vol. 9, New York: Macmillan, 1983, p. 293.
11. J. Pritz Johansen, *The Maori and His Religion in its Non-ritualistic Aspects,* Copenhagen: E. Munksgaard, 1954, p. 161.
12. J. Curnow, 'Wiremu Maihi Te Rangikaheke', in *The Dictionary of New Zealand Biography,* vol.1, p. 495; Shirres, pp. 22-24.
13. A. Shorter, *Toward a Theology of Inculturation,* London: Geoffrey Chapman, 1988, p. 94.
14. M. Walters, 'An investigation of archaeology in New Zealand as a means of establishing views about the past', unpublished MA thesis, University of Otago, 1979, p. 4.
15. Henare, p. 32.
16. M. Winiata, *The Changing Role of the Leader in Maori Society,* edited by M. Fraenkel, Auckland: B. & J. Paul, 1967, p.49.

17. Sir Apirana Ngata and I.L.G. Sutherland, 'Religious Influences', in *The Maori People Today,* edited by I.L.G. Sutherland, Wellington: NZ Institute of International Affairs and the NZ Council for Educational Research, 1940, pp. 344-5.
18. Henare, p. 33.
19. Hans Mol, *The Fixed and the Fickle: Religion and Identity in New Zealand*, Waterloo, Ontario: Wilfrid Laurier University Press, 1982, p. 27.
20. Ngata & Sutherland, pp. 341-2.
21. Bronwyn Elsmore, *Like Them That Dream*, and *Mana From Heaven: A Century of Maori Prophets in New Zealand,* Tauranga: Moana Press, 1989.
22. Rua Rakena, 'The Maori Response to the Gospel' in *Wesley Historical Society Proceedings,* vol. 25, nos. 1-4, 1971, p.28.
23. Ngata and Sutherland, p. 351.
24. Winiata, p.51.
25. Allan K. Davidson, *Christianity in Aotearoa*, Wellington: Education for Ministry, 1989, p. 115.
26. The latest (1986) census no longer contains this information.
27. Rakena, pp. 28-9. See also chapters by Wi Tarei on the Ringatu Church and Moana Raureti on the Ratana Church in *Tihe Mauri Ora*, edited by Michael King, Wellington: Methuen, 1978.
28. Winiata, p. 50.
29. Henare, p. 35.
30. Davidson, pp. 117-8, 123.
31. Rakena, 'The Maori Response to the Gospel'.
32. J. Roberts, 'Minarapa Rangihatuake', in *The Dictionary of New Zealand Biography*, vol. 1, p. 357.
33. Davidson, pp. 119, 123.

Christianity:
Pacific Island Traditions

Betty K. Duncan

The migration of Pacific Islanders to New Zealand has occurred in a series of waves. During the 1940s the new arrivals were mainly young, single, transient Cook Island and Niuean workers. As citizens of New Zealand since 1901, they have free entry into this country. The 1950s saw family groups, including Samoans, settling here. The leadership from these older people gave the new communities direction and stability. Tokelauans, New Zealand citizens since 1948, have also been arriving since the mid-1960s. But the greatest influx took place in the late 1960s and early 1970s as a response to the growing labour shortage in urban New Zealand. Also because of their rapidly growing populations many Pacific Islanders were looking to New Zealand for better educational and economic opportunities.

However the 'oil shock' of 1973 and growing recession led to a restriction on all immigrants entering New Zealand. Western Samoa gained independence in 1962. Samoans are admitted to New Zealand according to an annual quota system. There is no quota system for Tongans but over the years they too have come on six-month work schemes and visitors' permits. But, since the 1973-1974 'dawn raids' by police on potential overstayers many new migrants, for reasons of economic pursuit and family reunification, have shifted their destinations to Australia or the United States of America.

The national churches of the Pacific were becoming independent during this period.[1] As the migrants came to New Zealand they brought with them their vigorous religious faith. Already of London Missionary Society/Congregational background, it was natural that they would worship at a Congregational Church. In the early 1940s a small group of Cook Islanders, attending the Beresford Street Congregational Church in Auckland, attracted the attention of the Reverend Robert Challis, an LMS missionary to the Cook Islands, 1933-47. It was decided to create a Pacific Island Church as part of the Beresford Street Church and in 1944 Pastor Tariu Teaia and his wife came from the Cook Islands to minister to the migrant community. In 1947 the Congregational Union of New Zealand Assembly formally accepted responsibility for the Pacific Islanders' Congregational Church (PICC). That same year saw the Auckland Niuean Group formally instituted and a PICC branch started in Wellington.[2]

During the following two decades there was a rapid growth of branches throughout New Zealand.[3] In the beginning European leadership was essential as new migrants were educated in European ways. However, as the numbers of Cook Islanders and Samoans grew, they took an active role in church government and decision-making for they already had many years of experience running their island church councils and committees. The vernacular language services became the focus of the new communities and the venues progressed from private houses or rented halls and churches, to church buildings owned by the Pacific Island groups. The first ministers and pastors travelled vast distances to visit their congregations at least once a month and initially their load was lightened by theological students. However by 1967 there were eleven full-time ministers. For many the church became the sustaining focus of their religious and social life. Here they could indulge in their own cultural activities and catch up on news from home. The church community replaced the loss of the island village community.[4]

In 1969 the Congregational Union of New Zealand united with the Presbyterian Church of New Zealand. The PICC officially became Presbyterian and its name was changed to Pacific Islanders' Presbyterian Church (PIPC).[5] While the churches were pressing towards union, and the integration and assimilation of migrants was still a conceptual ideal,[6] divisions were already taking place.[7] In 1963 a group of Samoans had broken from the Auckland PICC church and established a branch of the Congregational Christian Church of Samoa (CCCS), a second one being formed in Wellington the following year. For these people the CCCS provided a religious and cultural environment much closer to that with which they were familiar. Of special significance was the use of the Samoan language and the supplying of ministers from Samoa. In retrospect it is possible to see that these splits from the PICC, and the continuing growth of new island churches in New Zealand such as the Samoan Methodist Church and the Cook Islands Christian Church, are part of an overall trend of Pacific Islanders to take responsibility for the spiritual care of their people.[8]

It has indeed been the general policy for Tongans and Fijians to join the Methodist Church of New Zealand. But in New Zealand, Tongan religion has experienced divisions paralleling the history of the church in Tonga.[9] Vital religions always experience tensions and dynamics. Since the 1970s the ideal of integration has given way to the reality of cultural and religious pluralism. Sitting within this cultural and religious pluralism is the phenomenon of ethnic mobilisation. One of the distinctive marks of this concept is the shift made by a migrant group from the church of the adopted country to a church imported from the country of origin.[10]

Today in 1990, the Pacific Island people worship, serve and minister in churches which reach across the full range of a continuum.[11] At one end are the monocultural indigenous churches which are responsible to the Conferences in their island nations. Their services and activities are conducted in their traditional languages and most of their ministers are trained in the islands although a number are taking the opportunity to further their theological studies in New Zealand. These churches include the Congregational Christian Church of Samoa, the Samoan Methodist Church, the Cook Island Christian Church, the Assemblies of God (Samoan, Fijian, Tongan and Cook Island), Seventh-day Adventists and several Tongan Churches. At the centre of the continuum are the multicultural churches, especially those of the Pacific Islanders' Presbyterian Church which caters for Samoans, Niueans, Cook Islanders, Tokelauans, Tuvaluans and some Europeans. Their ministers include both island and New Zealand born whose theological education has been in New Zealand. The Methodist Church of New Zealand includes Tongan, Fijian and Samoan ministers and holds services in the vernacular, as does the Roman Catholic Church for its Cook Island, Samoan and Tongan communities. Also in this area are the Mormons and Baha'is.

The other end of the continuum includes the predominantly European parishes which are ministered to by Pacific Island born ministers while at the extreme end of the continuum there are a few New Zealand born Pacific Islanders who have one hundred per cent European congregations. The presence of a Tongan, Samoan or Cook Island minister can attract others of their ethnic group to their church. In some parishes bicultural activities have been initiated by the ministers and through these shared experiences a mutual trust can develop and flourish. Because none of these divisions is rigid, given the strongly communal nature of the Pacific Islanders, there is a great mobility and intertwining between the migrant churches. Close relations, even brothers, serve as ministers in different churches across the continuum, while the congregations are well informed about and take part in combined activities with other churches in their region.

So what are some of the activities which contribute to the distinctive character of the Pacific Island Churches in New Zealand? These churches have a shared religious heritage from their common Wesleyan or LMS backgrounds. And because of Samoan missionaries the Christianity of Niue, the Tokelaus and Tuvalu closely resembles Samoan Christianity. However each of the Pacific Polynesian nations has its own distinctive culture. Therefore they should not be generalised or lumped together, any more than New Zealand European culture should be confused with Australian, English or American.[12]

A calendar of events and festivals

Although the following descriptions provide an overall picture there are differences and variations between the churches, denominations, different island groups and areas of settlement in New Zealand. The activities I describe have come mostly from a Samoan Presbyterian church in Auckland. This church has been selected first because it sits within the middle of the continuum and second because of the numerical strength of the Pacific Islanders' Presbyterian Church (PIPC).

Events and festivals are community-orientated. During the summer holidays some people visit families in their home islands or other parts of New Zealand. For others, Boxing Day or New Year heralds the start of games competitions between churches. Every year one to two weeks are set aside for the *ta'ologa* (games) including such sports as *kilikiti* (Samoan cricket), volleyball, tug-of-war, marching (CCCS churches) and athletics. The teams of each denomination are organised by their parish committees which also arrange the choir and culture competitions, the venues and prize-givings. The teams compete in different grades and wear distinctive uniforms with the spectators providing much vocal and entertaining support as the glory of their church is fought for on the sports fields.

Competitions also take place in the secular arena - for example, the Crown Pacific Cricket competition. Churches become involved by hosting village teams from the islands. Smaller and more scattered communities may meet together in the new year for fellowship, sports activities and cultural competitions. For example, one year the CCCS churches of Invercargill, Dunedin and Christchurch will meet in one of these centres while in another year a church sponsored group will visit Samoa for such activities. Similarly at Easter isolated people often travel to a town where a minister from their home country is stationed.

The focus of March or April is Easter. Some churches have camps or manage to send a number of their youth to combined Easter camps. Others join with European congregations for Good Friday and Easter Sunday services. Then again for some special occasion or fund raising one church may put on an evening performance lasting three to four hours. The Easter story is presented through items of choir singing, and action songs interspersed with acted dramas. The evening can close with the host church providing a large meal in the middle of the night for their supportive audience.

The second Sunday in May is Mother's Day. This is one of the highlights of the year. The churches are beautifully decorated with fine mats, tapa and garlands of white flowers. The mothers conduct the service and lead in preaching and praying. It is an emotional time with many tears and deep feelings expressed. At the end of the service, in a descending order of rank and age, the mothers are called one by one to the front of the church to be greeted by their children who show their love in kisses and the placing of *ulalole* (necklaces of lollies) around their mothers' necks. All mothers are included whether present or absent, while a deceased parent will be represented by another family member. A parallel ceremony takes place after the Father's Day service in September and again all fathers are honoured, even fathers-in-waiting.[13]

Traditionally June is the time when the thirteen PIPC churches in Auckland come together for their annual competitions. Taken in yearly rotation the competitions include choir singing, Samoan culture and Bible plays. While these competitions are mainly for older youth and adults, June-July is also a busy time for the Sunday School teachers and children as all age groups are prepared for the New Zealand Sunday School Union Scripture exams. The minister oversees the teaching and the supervision of the exams. Not only are classes conducted on Sundays but also three or four nights each week for two hours during the weeks of preparation beforehand.

For the children the climax of the church year is White Sunday. The CCCS and Samoan Methodist churches usually celebrate this on the second Sunday in October as this is the traditional date for Samoans. Some PIPC churches choose Labour Weekend. The Cook Island name is Gospel Sunday - also observed at the end of October, but dates can be flexible. In the Wellington PIPC parish of Newtown, Gospel Sunday has been brought forward to May so as not to compete with the Samoan White Sunday in October. First Church in Dunedin also prefers May as this eases the workload on the university students preparing for final exams later in the year. And for the Tongans, their children's Sunday, *Fakame*, is traditionally celebrated on the first Sunday in May. On White Sunday, roles are reversed. It is the one special day in the year when parents formally acknowledge and honour the contribution their children make to their family, and instil in them a love of God and the Church. During the preceding weeks many practices are held as the children learn hymns, scriptural passages and Bible plays. At home too the parents prepare their children for family items which are also performed during the service.

Betty K. Duncan

Rev. Setu Solomona with grandchildren on White Sunday, 1989

The dominant colour on White Sunday is white - white with touches of red. White symbolises the purity of the church and the flesh of Jesus while red is for the blood of the Saviour. Churches are decorated with such things as fine mats, tapa or lacey white cloths featuring scriptural texts in red, or red crosses. Red and white streamers of crepe paper, garlands of green leaves highlighted by red flowers and vases of red and white flowers are also used. Sometimes a large banner depicting a devotional picture is dedicated and hung in a prominent place in the memory of a beloved child who has died during the last year. All children are dressed in new, radiant white clothes. The girls' dresses are often covered in masses of frills, laces and ribbons while the boys wear white shirts and trousers or lava lavas. Sometimes headbands of flowers are included and the girls may have a single red flower or bow pinned to their dresses while the ties of the boys are usually red or black. (Although white is the traditional colour, I have seen all the children and adults at Tongan *Fakame* services dressed in a full range of colours. None have been in white.)

The actual service can start with the children walking in procession to the church. The service lasts several hours, often finishing in mid-afternoon. Each Sunday School class and Bible Class presents items of religious songs, and acted dramas alternating with groups of individual family presentations. A few older teenagers may deliver mini-sermons. For the children it is an exciting and nerve-wracking time but their final reward comes when they are served first at the special Sunday meal after the service, either all together in the church hall or in their own homes.

The final festival of the year focuses on Christmas. Again the churches can be involved in rehearsals and fundraising performances, often of a lighter more secular nature, as groups are organised to travel either to the Pacific Islands or other parts of New Zealand in the New Year.

However, for Cook Islanders, New Year's Eve is *uapou* night. For this occasion the Cook Islands Christian Churches combine with the Cook Island Presbyterian parishes and other invited friends. In response to the chairperson's questions about selected verses from the Bible, each church group sings, answers the questions, dances, and debates on the Bible. New hymns are composed for the occasion and humour is added whenever possible. Finally the two or three leaders give their answers to the questions, followed by more dancing and feasting. Earlier in the year a national activity is conducted by the Uapou Cook Island Fellowship. At this festival a considerable amount of money is raised to be distributed to retired ministers and their wives and to school and theological students.

Sunday services, family devotions and prayers

Further proof of the commitment of many Pacific Islanders to their church is the time involved in weekly and monthly meetings, and Sunday services. If more than one ethnic group is using the church buildings then different language services take place on Sundays. A typical programme is: 9.30 a.m. Sunday School, 11 a.m. English, 12.30 p.m. Cook Island Maori, 3 p.m. Samoan and Tokelauan. In another area the timetable may be: 9.30 a.m. Sunday School, 11 a.m. English, 1 p.m. Niuean, 3 p.m. Cook Island Maori, 5 p.m. Samoan and 7 p.m. Youth Service.

At the combined service in English there can be two women's choirs (for example, Samoan and Cook Island), sitting in two separate groups in the front pews. The hymns from the *Pacific Islanders' Church Hymnary* will include one in each language of the church members, for example: Samoan, Cook Island Maori, Niuean, Tokelauan and English. (For the half hour before the commencement of a Tongan service the people sing their favourite hymns unaccompanied and often in complicated harmonies. During the service, each verse of the hymns is read aloud before being sung by the congregation.) Pacific Islanders are enthusiastic Bible readers and the scriptures may be read aloud simultaneously in each person's own language by all those present. As Holy Communion is served on the first Sunday in the month it has been necessary for the larger parishes to hold two combined services on these days.

Built into the timetables around the set services is a whole rotation of other groups having their own special services each month. For example, Christian Endeavour, women's fellowship, the *autalavou* (youth groups), bible classes and other groups have their special occasions.

But seldom does a service end without some meeting of a committee, of elders, or a choir practice, taking place afterwards. Where the Island traditions are very strong the form of worship as received from the early missionaries is still practised. The traditional Samoan service order is: introit, call to worship, hymn, prayers of thanksgiving, confession and intercession, notices, offering, hymn, sermon and final hymn. The Sunday School or choir sings while the elders collect the offerings. Every Sunday after the third hymn the church secretary announces the notices for the coming week. Then the treasurer gives a report of the previous week's offerings. The amount given by each family is read out. This is another practice begun by the missionaries. Originally to support not only the local mission but also the London Missionary Society, funds were collected in the form of coconut oil.[14]

One senior minister told me that he believes that through the sermons the minister is able to give something special to the congregation for the whole week. He knows from surveying the people that to explain a Bible text is not of the same value to them as preaching a sermon, especially when they need encouragement and reassurance that someone who is greater than them loves them - that God loves them. At times this means that the set text from the lectionary has to be abandoned while he selects a more appropriate text. Because the congregations are such avid Bible readers he knows that when he announces the text they will think seriously about what he is going to talk about. For their main thoughts are based in the life they are living, with, at the centre, the Cross of Jesus Christ. For example, after a disturbing movie on Saturday night's television the minister will take the opportunity to preach a sermon clarifying the Christian view on, say, 'The soul after death'. And it is effective. The words of the sermon do travel home with the people and are discussed in detail over Sunday dinner. Should the minister be absent, the service will be conducted by the session clerk and lay preachers. Those months which contain a fifth Sunday also provide an opportunity for lay preachers to take part in the services.

The practices of worship carry over into the home in the form of family devotions. But it must be remembered that in pre-Christian days, time was regularly set aside to honour local spirits and ancestors. Thus although such practices now have a Christian form and are focused on the Christian goal, the observances are ancient in origin.

When family members gather together for a meal a senior person present, usually the father, offers a grace. This is not a set verse as said by Europeans but rather a prayer which covers the following points. First, the generalised 'God in Heaven' is addressed. If it is the first meal of the day, thanks will be offered to God for looking after all during the night and maybe a confession of faith in the form that 'we know God exists because we are alive on this beautiful morning'. Next God is thanked for the food, the availability of food, and for the people who have prepared the meal. Grace ends with an acknowledgement of Christ with such words as 'Thank you for all things in the name of Jesus Christ, the Lord of the family and everything'.

The structure of the family prayers is similar to that of Grace. These are the devotions which are held at home in the early evening. Originally in the islands family worship took place both in the early morning and evening. This is rare now but in the villages there are still curfews in the early evening when families gather together to sing hymns, read scriptures and pray. This may not be a daily occurrence for most families in New Zealand but there are many occasions when they do gather to worship together. Of special note are times of family crisis or rejoicing, such as illness, death, travel, birth, marriage or exams. The hymn and bible readings are followed by prayers which always begin with addressing 'Our Father in Heaven'. Prayers of thanksgiving are followed by prayers dealing with the welfare of family members, the village and loved ones at home or overseas. Visitors too and their families are included. In this privacy emotions are released and many tears are quietly shed as the migrant families feel only too sharply their separation from loved ones. God too is asked for specific things and assistance. Towards the end of the prayer a request is made for the remission of sins and finally a kind of general invocation is made for God's care of the immediate night through Christ the Son. Samoan prayers often end with the singing of a favourite refrain which everyone knows.

On the evening before their departure to begin a new academic term in another city, students with their families may gather at the minister's house for family devotions and a meal. So not only do they leave with the physical support of their families and a solemn reminder as to why they are going to study, and to strive for success in the forthcoming examinations, but also with much spiritual reinforcement. And in times of achievement God is always at the centre of the Pacific Islander's life. For example, immediately after the university graduation ceremony, the newly capped Samoan students in full regalia are joined by their families and friends in one of the local churches for a special service, followed by a meal. In smaller settlements the community joins together in the celebratory service while in areas of larger populations such services are arranged in the student's home church.

Finally, all functions of a public nature, whether religious or secular, commence with a prayer, a short devotion or a service of perhaps fifteen to twenty minutes in length and conclude with a few moments in prayer. These include such occasions as twenty-first birthdays, sports meetings, conferences, cultural competitions, independence celebrations and balls, fundraising concerts, feasts, haircutting ceremonies and title bestowals and departing groups of people. We have already noted services in homes and churches but they also take place in halls, sports grounds and departure lounges at airports. And each time thanksgiving is offered to God - perhaps for the safe arrival and the good health of relatives. Next a specific request is made to God for his presence at and help in the success of the function. 'May it be a lesson for everyone.' For example, may the success on the rugby field be used to a positive effect in the lives of the people. In conclusion God is asked for the forgiveness and remission of sins. In every case actions are related to the spiritual life so that it is enriched and as a means of strengthening the faith through Jesus Christ the Son.

Church organisation

The minister is the head of the church. He is assisted by a session clerk/secretary, a treasurer, elders, lay preachers and youth leaders. In some combination or other these people meet at least once a week. The minister is responsible for the spiritual and physical well-being of his congregation. As God's representative he is highly respected.[15] In the islands it is traditional for the minister to visit his congregation on Saturdays and take services on Sundays. In New Zealand newer Samoan migrants still expect their minister to visit on Saturdays. This too is the time when the minister receives donations of money from the people. Both in the Islands and in New Zealand many families also provide the minister's household with gifts of food, especially a surplus of prepared meals on Sundays. A highly respected and much-loved minister receives many gifts.

Another Island practice which is repeated in New Zealand has been for the minister to stay in the same parish for most of, if not all, his ministry. However, in New Zealand the minister's role has expanded greatly to meet the needs of the ever-increasing number of migrants. The ministers have become a source of expertise and information concerning a wide range of subjects. It has been estimated that two thirds of their time is consumed by social work in matters such as meeting planes, finding accommodation and employment, assisting with immigration and social welfare, conducting language classes and acting as translators for the courts, police and hospitals. The PIPC churches initiated many social services in response to these needs and in doing so formed the foundations of their large congregations.[16]

In the areas of older settlement, especially Auckland and Wellington, some of these tasks have moved into the secular area and are covered by private companies - especially the work of translation - while the preparation of people for exams or tests such as for drivers' licences, is carried out either by schools, polytechnics or classes run by institutions such as Auckland's Pacific Islanders' Educational Resource Centre.

Even after many years in New Zealand, some people who are still not very fluent in English need the personal reassurance of the minister when facing bureaucratic processes, banks, social welfare or finding their way around new buildings. Thus the ministers in all areas of New Zealand play a very important role as key co-ordinators of information and sources of communication.

The women's fellowship is always headed by the minister's wife as president. This organisation has its own secretary, treasurer and committee as do the bible classes, the Sunday school, the choir and the *autalavou* (youth group). Throughout the week there are regular meetings. For example evening meetings in one church could be, Monday, elders' session; Tuesday, lay preachers; Wednesday, *autalavou*, which includes bible studies and lessons in culture and language; Thursday, bible class; and Saturday, choir practice. But should there be a contest date approaching, then every evening is practice night.

The elder's role in the church council parallels that of the members of the village council. In New Zealand the Samoan church elder does not have to be a titled person. It can be anyone of mature age. The church council parallels the village council. It is involved in the decision-making of the church. Some elders are more ceremonial leaders. They make speeches of welcome and farewell. Some play a liturgical role. They are active in the church services, serving communion, lay preaching and visiting the sick. Then there are those with a more secular role working in the community. They may be the choir managers, the church accountants, and lawyers. Some will never attend the weekly meetings but their opinions are canvassed by other elders and the ministers.

In Samoa the *autalavou* is made up of the younger people of the church. It is a group which functions in a cultural and secular way. If the minister wants a cricket team (or a dance group) to play a team from another village then he asks the *autalavou* to arrange it. In New Zealand the range of people involved in the *autalavou* depends on the size of the church membership. In the larger churches the *autalavou* is for the Samoan-born, Samoan-speaking young people. This group has a parallel group of English-speaking New Zealand-born youth. But when the congregation is small in numbers, or perhaps for other reasons, older people are also included in the *autalavou*. The presence of the elders is encouraging for the younger people. The *autalavou* has a president, (the minister) vice-president, secretary, treasurer and committee. The whole church may be divided into three or four groups with individual family members scattered through the groups. In many ways it is like the school house system. Each group has a name - for example: Ioane Uiliamu (John Williams), Savali ole Filemu (Messenger of Peace - the name of John Williams' boat) or Penina ole Pasefika (Pearl of the Pacific). Each of these divisions has its own leader, secretary and treasurer.

Special events

A *malaga* is a visiting party. A group of perhaps thirty to fifty people is led by a chief, minister or minister's wife and is made up of supporting orators, elders and people of all ages. The *malaga* travels with a specific purpose in mind. For example the doctors' wives' *malaga* came from Western Samoa to Auckland in 1989 to raise money to buy essential equipment for the hospital. A village sports team may travel to New Zealand for a competition. New Zealand church groups or village groups also travel out of New Zealand. The journey may include several places and last a number of weeks.[17] We see the mobility between churches and denominations when a PIPC church hosts a CCCS *malaga* from a particular Western Samoan village. Not only that, but one church may host three or four *malagas* in a single year. This requires a certain devotion, energy and stamina as hospitality and generosity are demonstrated through the gifts of food, goods and money. When the whole church makes up the *autalavou* it is practicable for each division to be responsible for one particular day. This includes the buying, preparation and serving of food and the planning of all activities for that day. The visiting *malaga* may be cared for by the church for five or six days before the group breaks up and individual members leave to stay with relatives in other parts of the city.

The visiting group is normally met at the airport from where the people and many large bundles of luggage are transported to the church buildings. They are welcomed and fed before being taken to the homes of their billets. They come together again in the evening for a service, meal and perhaps a rehearsal. On the second day, preferably a Saturday morning, the formal meeting lasting two to three hours takes place in the form of a *'ava* (kava) ceremony, the presentation to the hosts of many *ie toga* (fine mats), and money from the hosts to the guests. Now for the first time the communities of the two churches join together for a meal, the people being free to go home by mid-afternoon - that is except for those preparing the evening meal for the *malaga* who are themselves preparing for the evening's *fiafia* (celebration). This consists of several hours of entertainment made up of traditional songs and dances, acted dramas of histories and legends supported by a chorus of singers, and comedy items.[18] The audience is also invited to participate in dances supporting different people. Appreciation is shown in the form of donations of money deposited in a bowl. The amount for each item and dance is carefully recorded, the results being announced later in the evening. Supper is served and the evening closes with devotions.

On Sunday, the morning service is followed by the traditional Sunday feast, the *to'ona'i*, in the church hall. The afternoon or evening activities may include a bible study.[19] For this everyone sits in rows facing a leader at the front. The leader asks them to discuss a Bible text (for example, Matthew 5:3 - 'Blessed are the poor in Spirit') or a concept such as 'Three in One'. For the next half hour or so a dialogue takes place between the leader acting as chairperson and the rest of the group. One by one the people stand and express their ideas and understandings of the meaning of the text. Finally the minister moves to the front and addresses the whole group for perhaps twenty minutes, giving his teaching on the subject and clarifying all the points made by the people. The same method is used when taking a culture class.

For the final evening the hosting group usually plans something special. The hall is decorated with streamers and balloons. The women serving are uniformly dressed in pretty floral lavalavas and matching blouses. The activities could include a service conducted by the host minister at 6.15 p.m., 6.45 p.m. dinner, 7.30 p.m. band and dance, 10 p.m. supper, 10.30 p.m. the formal exchange of gifts and final speeches, 12.45 a.m. prayers. In this final exchange thousands of dollars worth of materials, linen and money are given to the *malaga* who in turn present the hosts with hundreds of fine mats.

A European observer could be forgiven for thinking that the whole operation seems to be a rather unfair exchange of mats for money. But one of the key features of Pacific Islands culture is the continual cementing of relationships between families, villages and churches through the collecting of and the redistribution of resources, be they food, skills, labour, materials, fine mats or money.

So far we have noted the call on the congregation's talents, both physical and monetary, in the form of the activities associated with the annual calendar, donations of food and money to the minister, church collections and the hosting of *malagas*. As well as these there are a number of other planned events which are a source of great pride for the church community. These include the planning, fund raising, building and dedication of new church buildings and ministers' houses, not only in New Zealand but also in the home islands.[20] Then there are weddings, birthdays (especially twenty-firsts and sixtieths) and anniversaries of the arrival of Christianity or the establishment of the churches. Today nearly all special occasions, festivals or church services are recorded on video tapes. These contribute to the easy transmission of new hymns, songs, dances and whole performances between communities not only within New Zealand but also between islands. As the video tapes are viewed over and over again, the Pacific Island traditions are continually being reinforced and preserved.

Finally there are funerals. Among Pacific Islanders an individual's illness and approaching death is very much a community affair.[21] Many friends and relatives travel the necessary distances to farewell the dying person and in each case the appropriate plans and rituals are attended to.[22] In the islands it is normal for the funeral and burial to take place within a day of death. However, in New Zealand because of the cooler climate and embalming techniques the funeral is often delayed for a number of days. Whenever possible a vigil is kept over the body of the deceased in his or her own home. The practice has developed of holding a family service the night before the funeral either at the home or at the church. If the latter, the body is conveyed to the church for the service and then returned to the home for the night. This is the time, for all who wish, to pay their last respects to the deceased. The service is conducted by the minister and sometimes is divided into a number of sections when prayers, hymns and remembrances are conveyed by groups from neighbouring churches. This is yet another demonstration of the ecumenical nature of the migrant communities. Family members and friends, individually or in groups, come forward to kiss the deceased, sing songs of farewell and reminisce on their relationship with the loved one.

The next day after the funeral service and burial the gratitude of the deceased and his or her family is expressed to the community in the form of a feast. This day will always be remembered by the way it was conducted with ceremonial beauty and dignity. For the bereaved family, despite the tears and sadness, because of the many expressions of love, comfort and support, not only in words but also in the very generous gifts of flowers, food, fine mats and money which lift all financial burdens from the relatives, it is also a time of family pride and solidarity for their sorrow has been shared by so many well-wishers and friends.

Conclusion

In this chapter I have tried to demonstrate the nature of the constant opportunities for involvement which are offered to the congregation throughout the year. Many Pacific Islanders display a great enthusiasm for Christianity. From their pre-European rituals they have inherited the practice of focusing their religious expressions through actions. For many there is a very high input into church activities of time, labour, talents, creativity, organisational skills, money, devotion and sheer hard work. The social organisation allows for individual development of many skills to a high degree of competence. But always the individual is submerged within the community experience. It may be necessary for a person to take a day off work to assist with the hosting of a *malaga* or to bow to the collective wish of the congregation when they are selected as a candidate in an election. For some, the term 'Pacific Island traditions' means the way things were in pre-European practices. Others interpret tradition as the way things are done in the islands. The Pacific Island migrants have brought to New Zealand their cultures which are inseparable from the church, the expressions of which are at the heart of their religious experience. And like the migrant, the migrant churches are also in transition as they adapt to their new environment.

At the same time the Pacific Island form of worship and church practices has proved to be quite a challenge to the New Zealand European understanding of the church. The ministers and theological students are aware of how a 'coconut theology' which is still being developed with relevance to a tropical island situation is yet again having to be adapted to the New Zealand situation.[23] Some are experimenting with the order of the service, or substituting taro and coconut milk for the bread and wine of the communion service. Other ministers with the experience of ministering to European congregations watch the clock and keep their services within the European concepts of time. For some people the demands, especially the monetary demands, have become too great a burden. They have not abandoned their Christianity. Some have shifted to the Pentecostal movements. Others have become Mormons. The Church of Jesus Christ of Latter-day Saints has annually contributed large amounts of money to the islands and offers the opportunity of higher education in Hawaii or mainland America. Then again ministers with the European parish experience are trying to accommodate the financial needs of their people by making church donations a private affair. Women ministers in the church bring another new challenge to Pacific Island traditions.[24]

Finally, the children of the first post-war migrants are now parents themselves. Many feel caught between their island culture and the New Zealand European culture. Daily they face a private internal struggle between the individualism of European values and the community values in which their parents give priority to the role of Christianity. Many of this new generation spend far less time involved in church activities. Yet at the same time they provide the support system which allows other members of their families to participate fully in the church. And because of the communal nature of their societies most people are linked to the Pacific Island religious traditions in one way or another.

Notes

1. For a detailed coverage of the independence process of the churches see Charles W. Forman, *The Island Churches of the South Pacific: emergence in the twentieth century,* Maryknoll, New York: Orbis Books, 1982. For the history of missionary activity in the Pacific see the following works, and further references therein:
   John Garrett, *To Live Among the Stars: Christian origins in Oceania,* Geneva and Suva: World Council of Churches in association with the Institute of Pacific Studies, University of the South Pacific, 1982; Niel Gunson, *Messengers of Grace: Evangelical missionaries in the South Seas 1797-1860,* Oxford: Oxford University Press, 1978; Ron and Marjorie Crocombe, eds., *Polynesian Missions in Melanesia: from Samoa, Cook Islands and Tonga to Papua New Guinea and New Caledonia,* Suva: University of the South Pacific, 1982. Recent information on the Pacific Islands may be found in Ron Crocombe, *The South Pacific: an introduction,* Auckland: Longman Paul Ltd in association with the University of the South Pacific, Suva, 1989; and on cultural and religious ceremonies in Tokelau, Tonga, Cook Islands, Western Samoa and Niue, see 'Focus on the Pacific' series by Jennifer Wendt, Auckland: Longman Paul, 1987.
2. For a detailed study of the PICC and especially the regional development in Auckland, Tokoroa and Wellington, see: Uili F. Nokise, 'A History of the Pacific Islanders' Congregational Church in New Zealand 1943-1969', M.Th. thesis, University of Otago, Dunedin, 1978.
3. Nokise, p.11, lists twenty branches by 1969, including eight in the Auckland region plus Tokoroa, Rotorua, Hamilton, Hastings, Wanganui, Porirua, Petone, Wellington, Christchurch, Dunedin, Invercargill and Bluff.

4. 'In seeking links of kinship and common interest Samoans in New Zealand stress church membership where in Samoa they would stress village affiliation.' Joan Metge and Patricia Kinloch, *Talking Past Each Other: problems of cross-cultural communication,* Wellington: Victoria University Press and Price Milburn, 1978, p.16.

5. Today it is more common simply to use the initials PIC in speech.

6. Nokise, p.249, says that the Rev. Challis 'had a tendency to enforce among the leaders of the church an idealistic view of integration based on the notion that "in Christ, there is no Jew or Greek". The majority of his sermons had this particular theme running through them. Not that he minimised the reality of the diverse composition of the church; rather, he tended to encourage and emphasise European forms of worship which the average Pacific Islander often found difficult to understand and relate to his Christian upbringing. For instance, he stressed the importance of migrant children learning English to be their mother tongue. This had the adverse effect of Pacific Island parents encouraging their children to speak English all the time, with the result that the children neither spoke good English nor good island dialects.' This is a reality which New Zealand-born Pacific Islanders identify with and are still coming to terms with as adults in the 1990s.

   Challis's own words on the church at this time can be found in 'The Place of the Church in Polynesian Society in New Zealand', R.L. Challis, *Pacific Islanders in New Zealand,* A Bulletin for Schools, Wellington: School Publications Branch, Department of Education, 1970, pp. 71-74.

7. Nokise, chapter 6, 'The Split within the Samoan Group of the PICC', pp. 216-244.

8. In 1905, when Lauaki and nine other Samoan chiefs and their families were exiled to Saipan by the German rulers, the church sent with them a Samoan pastor. Forman says that as Samoan colonies grew up in Hawaii, California and New Zealand, 'the Samoan churches were the only ones that tried to expand with their adherents to these new abodes.... Other churches, less imperial than the Samoans, relinquished the emigrants to the churches of their new lands, but were still concerned for them.' Forman, pp. 198-99. For a fuller picture of other Samoan settlements: Paul T. Baker, Joel M. Hanna, Thelma S. Baker, eds., *The Changing Samoans: behaviour and health in transition,* New York and Oxford: Oxford University Press, 1986.

9. Sifa Hingano, in 'Religious Movements Amongst Tongans in New Zealand,' S.Th. Thesis, submitted to the Joint Board of Theological Studies, 1983, examines the struggle within the Tongan Methodist Fellowship in Auckland and the Free Wesleyan Church of Tonga and the New Zealand Methodist Church. Other religious groups include: the United Church of the Tongan People in New Zealand, the Maama-Fo'ou (New Light) religious movement and the Free Church of Tonga.

10. Hugh R. Campbell, 'Ethnic Mobilisation Theory and the Dunedin Tongan Community', M.A. thesis, University of Otago, Dunedin, 1988.

11. Although now out-of-date the best co-ordination of lists of the Churches is in *A Directory of Organisations in New Zealand with relevance to Pacific Islanders 84-85,* Auckland: Pacific Islanders' Educational Resource Centre, 1985. Some idea of the numbers of members can be gauged from the census figures. *1986 New Zealand Census of Population and Dwellings* Series C Report 14, Table 2, pp. 14-15, Table 4, pp. 24-25.

12. For example Nokise, p.2, notes the different social groupings as: Cook Islands - individual islands; Niue - the village; Samoa - the extended family unit; Tokelau - islands and family units.

13. In Tonga the whole of the month of May is focused on family activities. The first Sunday in

the month is Children's Sunday, the second Sunday is Mother's Day and the third is Father's Day.

14. With reference to this practice Malama Meleisia in *Lagaga: a short history of Western Samoa*, Suva: University of the South Pacific, 1987, p.55 says that: 'This practice introduced the custom of making public the donations of money to the church; before people had money to give, the family heads would call out the amount of oil their family had made for the church. Families, villages, and districts competed for the honour of giving most to the church.'

15. At the present time there are three ordained Samoan women. Of the five Pacific Island women studying for the ministry at Trinity Methodist Theological College, Auckland, one is Samoan, while at Knox Theological Hall, Dunedin, there are two Samoan, one Cook Island and one Tokelauan woman. It must be noted, too, that in the Pacific Island Churches the ministers' wives play a very important role.

16. David Pitt and Cluny Macpherson, *Emerging Pluralism: the Samoan community in New Zealand*, Auckland: Longman Paul Ltd., 1974. Chapter 4, 'Church', in particular details the social welfare activities of the church.

17. I remember, in 1984, a *malaga* from Hawaii presenting superb performances of Pacific Islands dances at both Kanana Fou in American Samoa and a few weeks later at Sale'imoa, Western Samoa. I was told that the *malaga* was travelling on to New Zealand before returning to Hawaii.

18. A great favourite observed at one *fiafia* was Mrs Noah sending Mr Noah among the audience to search for three elephants (the fattest people) and four overstayers to take on the ark; the hilarity became too much for the local dog which proceeded to attack Mr Noah's heels.

19. This appears to be a simplified version of the Cook Islands' *uapou*.

20. Until the 1920s many church buildings in the Pacific were built in the indigenous styles and materials. However, after the Roman Catholic missionaries put up large churches reflecting European styles and especially after they built the cathedral in Apia, 'Samoa became the great area for large, even mammoth, church buildings constructed with cement in a bewildering variety of Western styles.' Forman, p.71.

In New Zealand the practice of building large churches has continued, with indigenous features also being incorporated. The most notable example is the fale-shaped church and hall of the Newtown CCCS, Wellington.

21. Patricia Kinloch, *Talking Health But Doing Sickness: studies in Samoan health*, Wellington: Victoria University Press, 1985.

22. *The Undiscover'd Country: customs of the cultural and ethnic groups of New Zealand concerning death and dying*, Wellington, Department of Health, 1987.

23. Dissertations written by some of the Pacific Island students at Knox Theological Hall, Dunedin show the way these topics are being addressed - for example:

Asora Amosa, 'The Lordship of Christ and the Matai Concept', Dissertation in Christian Thought and History, 1988.

TeAkatauira T. Ben-Unu, 'Parables of Jesus: as Interpreted by Cook Island Clergy, for Cook Island Audience', Dissertation in Biblical Studies, 1987.

Ionatana M. Faamausili, 'Interaction of Christianity and Samoan Tradition', Dissertation in Pastoral Studies 3, 1988.

Tafatoluomalua Filemoni, 'Ethical Challenges in a Multi-Cultural Society', Dissertation in Pastoral Studies 3, 1979.

Ngatokotoru Ine, 'A Theology of Migration (Israel and Pukupukan Migration)', Dissertation in Biblical Studies, 1989.

Afele R. Paea, 'A Study in Niuean Christianity and Its Theological Thought', Dissertation in Church History: History of Doctrine., 1977.

Tautiaga Senara, 'Samoan Religious Leadership: Tradition and Change', Thesis submitted for the Degree of Master of Arts at the University of Otago, Dunedin, 1987.

Maua B. Sola, 'A Theology of Respect', Dissertation in Old Testament, 1987.

Keri Soti, 'The Translation and Critique of K.T. Faletoese's *History of the Samoan Church (LMS)*', Chapters I-IX, partial translation, Exercise in Historical Theology, 1975.

Liva Tongalea Tukutama, 'A Basic Guide for Niuean Teachers in Religious Education', Dissertation in Pastoral Studies 3, 1988.

24. The *Presbyterian Church of New Zealand's Year Book 1989* lists 817 ministers, (including 236 ministers emeriti) of whom 51 are Pacific Islanders. Of these Pacific Islanders, two are women. The Methodist Church of New Zealand for *The Connexional Year 1990* names 430 people as deacons, minita-a-iwi, presbyters, students in training and those engaged in supply ministries. Of these 33 are Pacific Islanders. An approximate breakdown of these figures is Presbyterians: 35 Samoans, 8 Cook Islanders, 7 Niueans, 1 Tokelauan/Samoan, 1 Tuvaluan, 1 European; Methodists: 16 Samoans, 14 Tongans, 3 Fijians.

Esoteric Religions

Robert S. Ellwood

The word 'esoteric', according to the *New Zealand Pocket Oxford Dictionary*, means 'intelligible only to those with special knowledge'. Derived from a Greek word bearing the sense of 'within', esoteric teachings are therefore doctrines comprehensible only to people with a wisdom, or an initiation, not granted to everyone.

The esoteric tenets may have been deliberately kept secret so they could be transmitted only under the right circumstances, perhaps in an impressive initiatory ceremony. Or they may in principle be accessible to all, like the pages of Helena Blavatsky's massive Theosophical work, *The Secret Doctrine*, but of their own nature beyond the grasp of the masses of people not 'ready' for them. An esoteric teaching, then, is one based on the idea of this sort of special teaching and on practices to go with it.

New Zealand has long been a remarkably fertile field for esoteric religion. While attendance at conventional churches is low by world standards, per capita membership in groups we shall here designate esoteric - Spiritualism, Theosophy, Hermetic orders - is as high as, or even higher than, in any similar modern 'western' society. To be sure, religious membership figures are not always comparable, but the conclusion seems unavoidable. Membership in the Theosophical Society, for example, is reported fairly reliably and calculated in the same way in most countries. At the time of writing, it is about 1,700 in New Zealand and 5,000 in the United States. Given that New Zealand's population is 1/80th that of the U.S., this means there are more than twenty-five times as many Theosophists per capita in New Zealand than in the North American nation. (More, in fact, than in any other country in the world with the possible exception of Iceland, which in some ways oddly parallels its southern hemisphere counterpart.)

Results on much the same scale can be derived for such other standbys of alternative or esoteric spirituality as the Liberal Catholic Church, Anthroposophy, and probably - though figures are much less dependable - Spiritualism. The same can be said for the newer generation of esoteric and Eastern movements brought in by the 1960s 'counter-culture', and also, if observation and news media accounts are any guide, for the late 1980s 'New Age' vogue.

In this chapter we shall use the term 'esoteric religion' to embrace Spiritualism, including all Spiritualist churches and related organisations such as the White Eagle Lodge, and UFO groups such as the Aetherius Society which have many Spiritualist characteristics; the Theosophical Society and its kin, such as Anthroposophy, the Liberal Catholic Church, and the Arcane School;

Kabbalistic and Rosicrucian groups; and the Hermetic Order of the Golden Dawn and related groups in New Zealand.[1]

In some cases definitions had to be made arbitrarily. We recognise that not all groups discussed in this chapter would describe themselves as 'esoteric' or even as 'religions'. Nothing lies behind inclusion here except the organisational requirements of this book, which have sometimes meant that such terms have had to be employed in a very broad, non-technical sense. Other groups that might have been cited have had to be left out for reasons of space.

Spiritualism

We shall commence with Spiritualism, the oldest of this set of groups in New Zealand, and the 'grandfather' of many of them world-wide. Spiritualism in its modern form began in New York State in 1848 when the Fox sisters, three young girls living in a farm house near Rochester, heard mysterious tappings which they came to believe were encoded messages from a deceased peddler. The excitement generated by news reports of this phenomenon swept the country by storm. Circles engaged in spirit mediumship (communication from a spirit through the voice of an entranced medium) and related practices such as the popular table-turning sprang up everywhere. Needless to say, high-decibel controversy and accusations of fraud followed in their wake, but at first that only generated more interest. By the 1860s - the decade of Civil War - however, Spiritualism had begun to subside in the United States as a mass enthusiasm, though smaller groups and churches were to keep it alive down to the present.

Spiritualists believe in God, the immortality of the soul, and the reality of communication between the living and those 'on the other side of life'. They have been divided over the issues of reincarnation, and on whether Spiritualism is Christian or another religion. It is important to note also that Spiritualism has tended to align itself with 'progressive' social causes and to see itself as a new 'scientific' religion (because its phenomena were allegedly subject to empirical investigation rather than depending on authoritarian scriptures or priesthoods); spirits often gave lengthy discourses on the abolition of slavery, the rights of women, and the need for radical social and economic reform. In particular, in the nineteenth century Spiritualism afforded women one of their few opportunities for public speaking and the exercise of spiritual leadership. In an age when most churches and educational institutions were thoroughly dominated by male professionals, at least half of Spiritualist mediums and ministers were female, some of whom travelled the world lecturing and teaching. This is still the case, in New Zealand as elsewhere.

Spiritualist churches in New Zealand

Let us visit a typical New Zealand Spiritualist church, like those that advertise in the *N.Z. Psychic Gazette*. It may belong to the Spiritualist Church of New Zealand (a denomination incorporated in 1924 by act of parliament), or the smaller Spiritualist National Union or Greater World Christian Spiritualist League, both based in England. Or, like a large number of Spiritualist churches, it may simply be unaffiliated.

Here is an account of a Spiritualist service the writer visited on the evening of January 31, 1988. It took place in a rented hall; many New Zealand Spiritualists, of course, have their own churches, characteristically small but neat and furnished in bright, cheerful colours, with cross, Bible, and flowers on an altar in front. About thirty-five were present, more young people among them than I had expected. The presiding officer, however, was an elderly man, dressed informally in shorts and knit shirt. Casualness and a sense of happy enthusiasm, in fact, were keynotes of the evening.

The chief speaker was a pleasant man of part-Maori descent, a minister of another denomination who was also interested, and active, in Spiritualism. His brief sermon followed an opening hymn, a prayer, and a reading, the last not from the Bible but the White Eagle teachings, to be discussed later.

In the address, the clergyman talked about a piece of driftwood sculpture he had been given, a rather interesting work presenting enigmatic faces looking in opposite directions. He felt that the wood had come from the west coast of the South Island, and had been carved by a young couple - apparently a typically Spiritualist extrasensory perception. He then talked of his Maori mother, who had possessed clairvoyance though she would not have used that Spiritualist term, but a Maori expression meaning depth of sight. Unlike most westerners save for Spiritualists, he went on, the Maori spoke easily and naturally of those who had gone ahead on the path of life, communing with them just as with those remaining on this side of the divide.

Then came the direct clairvoyant readings which are the heart of Spiritualism as they are of most Spiritualist services. The minister singled out successively five or six members of the congregation, asking if he could 'come' to them. After a favourable response, he told each of things he 'saw' around him or her: a trip, a change of jobs, spiritual problems, a 'hassle' that could be overcome. In some (though not all) cases the 'reading' was clearly 'on the mark' for the recipient and undoubtedly helpful. The service ended with offering and hymn, and was followed by refreshments and an opportunity for people to receive private healing through prayer and laying on of hands.

Sometimes Spiritualist mediums do trance communications as well as clairvoyant reading. At sessions called seances, the medium, usually seated in a chair, will go into an apparent trance to give a 'direct voice' message from persons beyond the grave, both departed loved ones and high spiritual teachers; the latter have been particularly favoured in the late-1980s vogue for 'channeling', a modern version of Spiritualism. But while frequently public, seances are generally distinguished from regular Spiritualist church services like the one described.

Spiritualism has a long and active history in New Zealand. Its fortunes in the public eye, at least, have tended to wax and wane with the work of highly visible Spiritualist figures, often lecturers from abroad who generated an interest their New Zealand colleagues were, in the end, unable to sustain on a large scale. In 1873, for example, the country was visited by two Americans, Mr J.M. Peebles and Dr E.C. Dunn, whose Spiritualist lectures and healings were widely reported and debated in the Otago press.

They were followed in 1879 by another redoubtable American, Emma Hardinge Britten, in the course of a world lecture tour. Both Maori and Pakeha Spiritualism are described in the New Zealand chapter of her subsequent book, *Nineteenth Century Miracles* (1884). Among other forays, she made much of an emergent alliance between Spiritualism and the Rationalism or Freethought which, under the leadership of persons like Robert Stout, was also making waves in Dunedin. Both Spiritualism and Rationalism, she claimed, were in vehement opposition to the bigotry and intellectual tyranny of the established churches, and looked toward a new day of spiritual freedom and democracy based on a scientific approach to religion. However, the alliance did not prosper as Rationalists soon began to suspect that Spiritualists were insufficiently rational.[2]

In 1884 remarkable Spiritualist phenomena - table-turning, rappings, and blindfold readings as well as voice mediumship - were reported from the Wairarapa area. The correspondent was W.C. Nation, then newspaper editor in Greytown, and subsequently a leading figure in New Zealand Spiritualism for nearly fifty years. His account, first presented in a lengthy article in the *New Zealand Mail*, was later published in book form.[3]

In the 1890s another important Spiritualist personality emerged. This was Jane Elizabeth Harris-Roberts, affectionately known as 'the Mater'. Until her death in 1940 at the age of ninety, she lectured, wrote, and helped found churches on behalf of the cause. She particularly exemplified the connection between Spiritualism and radical social critique, including the feminist; her spirit communicators tirelessly decried injustice in inimitably vivid rhetoric, pointedly enhancing her capacity, as a woman, to make a mark in the world.

In 1920 Sir Arthur Conan Doyle, the celebrated creator of Sherlock Holmes and an avid Spiritualist, spoke to packed auditoria in the major New Zealand cities as part of a lecture tour described in his *Wanderings of a Spiritualist*.[4] He was followed a couple of years later by another English Spiritualist, Horace Leaf, whose antipodal circuit is delineated in his *Under the Southern Cross*.[5] In the 1980s, the pattern of Spiritualist renewal around public figures was perhaps continued through the work of Mary Fry, whose controversial radio programme and book, *New Zealand's Radio Clairvoyant*,[6] were accompanied by discussion and (according to census figures) an upsurge in the number of Spiritualists.

Other groups have followed in the Spiritualist tradition. The British-based White Eagle Lodge is established on the teachings of the discarnate entity White Eagle through its foundress, Grace Cooke. But the Lodge's emphasis now is on meditation, healing, and spiritual growth rather than further communications.[7]

Particularly fascinating are the spiritual currents surrounding interest in unidentified flying objects, UFOs. Virtually since the first in the current series of UFO sightings was reported in the U.S.A. in 1947, individuals have come forward claiming to be 'contactees', persons contacted by the occupants of the flying saucers. The messages they allegedly received from the otherworldly envoys frequently had a spiritual dimension, such as a warning that earthmen must improve morally or face destruction, while painting a paradisal picture of more advanced planets. Among the best known was the Polish-born Californian George Adamski, who made a well-publicised lecture tour of New Zealand in 1959; his accounts of beautiful Venusians and spaceships voyages were greeted with interest mingled with scepticism.[8]

But general interest in UFOs has tended to run high in New Zealand, the locale of some important sightings, and even as sentiment over Adamski and the 'contactee' phenomenon has divided UFO buffs, several UFO-based spiritual groups have appeared.[9] The best-known is the Aetherius Society, founded on communications from space beings through the former Londoner George King. Others have functioned more as 'circles' in which messages from UFO captains have been received successively by several members of the group; one such circle has, since 1987, been receiving words from a being called Voltra who represents the Universal Confederation.

Theosophy

Frequently the philosophical perspective of Spiritualist teachers seems heavily influenced by Theosophy. We will now return to that tradition, which has also been quite important in New Zealand. The Theosophical Society was founded in New York in 1875 by Helena P. Blavatsky, a Russian woman of aristocratic background, and the American lawyer and journalist Henry Steel Olcott. In his inaugural address as president of the new society, Olcott spoke of the 'superstition' of religion and the 'arrogance' of science, the two self-proclaimed purveyors of truth in the present age; what was called for was a third way based on the wisdom of the ancients, for whom mind and spirit were better joined.[10] This 'ancient wisdom', underlying all the great religions of the world, came to embrace belief in karma, reincarnation, cosmic evolution, and the existence of 'masters' in advance of us on that evolutionary path who are able to serve as helpers and guides. But its deepest doctrine was the pervasive interaction of consciousness and matter throughout the universe.

For many, on the other hand, Theosophy in the nineteenth century seemed no doubt like an advanced level of Spiritualism, offering its adepts as especially high and reliable communicators and their doctrine as deep insights into the workings of a spirit-matter universe. On a more mundane plane, it is worth noting that Theosophy also tended to appear socially more genteel than Spiritualism, often attracting members a cut above the Spiritualist average in the social hierarchy.

While certainly not all New Zealand Theosophists have been socially prominent, the first lodge, founded by E.T. Sturdy in Wellington in 1888, included no less a personage than the Prime Minister, Sir Harry Atkinson, several other members of the prominent Atkinson and Richmond families, and Edward Tregear, Maori scholar and later a major figure in the 1890s reform government, as well as a Jewish rabbi and a Maori tohunga.[11] For one dazzling moment, it might have seemed that in New Zealand Theosophy's fondest dream was to be realised of attracting the best minds, guiding the course of social evolution, and unifying all religions on the inner planes. But Sturdy had to return to England and the 1888 lodge fell apart. When Theosophy was re-established in New Zealand in the nineties, it was with fewer luminaries but with more persons prepared to last the long haul.

A.Y. Atkinson has studied key members of the Theosophical Society founded in Dunedin in 1893.[12] Although never reaching more than some 35 members in the 1890s, the novel group generated much controversy in that originally Scots Presbyterian settlement, which was also the seat of heated debate over Spiritualism and Rationalism in the seventies and eighties. Atkinson has shown that the 1890s Theosophists were almost all British immigrants who had attained modest but respectable niches in society as chemists, teachers, clerks, or businessmen, or were married to people in the same occupations. They often recounted a 'strict' religious upbringing in the old country. But in the course of the long progress to the antipodes that conditioning wore thin; there was often a period of indifference or atheism.

At the same time, another characteristic of this group was that they were all voracious readers, and one might say self-made intellectuals. One gets a sense of outwardly diligent but inwardly lonely and searching persons transported far from their birthplaces, and the sort who would rather alleviate these feelings at home with a demanding book - as Theosophical literature certainly was - than in the pub. They were then ripe to seize at a system of thought which would interpret both the universe and their own oft-solitary pilgrimage in it, and offer an intellectual enthusiasm to take up the long evenings. We see that, sometimes purely by chance, a Theosophical tract fell into someone's hands, and he latched on to what it taught with the characteristic single-mindedness of the Victorian convert.

However, Dunedin Theosophy did not flower without opposition. Hardly had the Society been established there than local preachers began pronouncing against it, letters began appearing in the newspapers, and articles in journals like the *Christian Observer* were wheeled into place to confront the new heresy. The *Christian Observer* was a thoughtful periodical of conservative Presbyterian outlook, but intelligently aware of the great theological issues of the day: Darwinism, 'higher criticism', religion and social reform, Christianity versus the other world religions.

Theosophy got attention, then, and Theosophists responded through letters and lectures with as good as they got. Disputed questions included the impersonal divinity of Theosophy versus the Christian personal God, Theosophists finding the latter capricious and vain, and Christians the Theosophical deity intolerably bleak and abstract; karma versus grace, Theosophists contending karma was the only just way to understand the world's inequities, while Christians saw it devoid of love or mercy; and of course the authority of the Bible versus the other scriptures and revelations of the world. In one argument, a Christian - neither for the first nor last time - pointed to the terrible poverty of India, the land Theosophists claimed to find so spiritual; a week or so later, a Theosophical letter appeared in the same paper, asking what a Hindu, first setting foot in the slums of London's East End, would think of the way a supposedly Christian nation cared for its poor.

A different and significant further arena of polemic involved the credentials and reputed scandals of Helena Blavatsky, Annie Besant, and other early Theosophical leaders. Here Christian writers, above all clergymen, were capable of reaching veritable frenzies of satire and invective in retailing accounts of Blavatsky's chicanery, forging of 'Mahatma' letters, and exposure (still debated) by the Society for Psychical Research, or Besant's long career from unhappy wife of an Anglican parson through Freethought and close association with the radical Charles Bradlaugh to Theosophy.

Yet in arguing accusations like these, Theosophists and their critics never seemed quite to engage. Critics appeared to take for granted that such *ad hominem* (more precisely, *ad feminam*) arguments, once broadcast, would devastate Theosophy and turn its adherents back to their senses. But Theosophists responded with remarkable equilibrium, mildly stating that while some such accounts were biased against their leaders, they did not claim those mentors were perfect as human beings. The important thing was the ideas they taught, and the question of whether or not those ideas were true stood apart from the character of the messengers. To judge Theosophy, they said, read the books, not the persons.[13]

One can hardly avoid detecting a strong note of class and sexist ardour in much of the criticism, especially when it comes from persons of high 'establishment' educational and ecclesiastical status, and is directed at women like Blavatsky and Besant who, though obviously highly intelligent and capable as well as spirited, could not have hoped in their day for similar attainment. Yet these women were making a mark in the world, often generating enthusiasm and a level of spiritual discussion the churches could only envy. In the same light, one can understand the remarkable adherence of women like these, and an assortment of independent seekers of both genders, to Theosophy, despite the scandals and the scorn.

There is an account in the *Christian Observer* of a Theosophical lecture given in the Wairarapa in 1895 by Countess Wachtmeister, a former intimate of Blavatsky and one of several intrepid Theosophical women who travelled the land on speaking tours in the nineties. During the question period after the lecture, she was harangued by an impassioned minister, who had written hard-hitting tracts against Spiritualism and Theosophy, until the discussion had to be terminated and the meeting apparently ended in an uproar. Shortly after, Wachtmeister put a letter in the local paper stating she felt the clergyman was 'an incarnation of one of the monks that tore the quivering flesh of Hypatia!'[14]

(Hypatia, a brilliant fourth century Alexandrian mathematician and Neoplatonist, was well known at the time, having been the subject of a popular novel by Charles Kingsley. This woman had been put to death by a mob led by monks of the newly victorious Christian church, and the novelist spared nothing to portray her vividly as a noble woman destroyed by bigotry. Given Theosophy's Neoplatonist bent, it is more than understandable that a clerically abused modern Theosophical woman would see herself in the ancient martyr's role - and her remark suggests the depth of feeling Theosophy could evoke in the New Zealand countryside.)

A.Y. Atkinson nonetheless asks, quite properly, why Theosophy, which in the period never had more than three dozen adherents out of a population of some two hundred thousand in the Dunedin area, should have provoked such vehement Christian opposition. It was, in an age of rapid change and growing secularism, hardly the church's most serious foe. Atkinson's answer is, I think, perceptive and correct: 'The Society was attacked largely because it seemed to give concrete form to undercurrents of fear and religious doubt prevalent in Dunedin.'[15]

Theosophy, in other words, though minuscule represented an egregious and visible example of many things traditional Christianity now had to contend with in an age of doubt; Darwin, social change, and incipient globalism. Often these presences were amorphous yet threatening clouds, but in Theosophy they seemed personified in their most extreme forms, so it is little wonder the Society drew lightning. It was a time of increasing uncertainty in religion, and of growing polarisation in churches between liberal and conservative wings. But on the issues at hand - evolution, the Bible, the claims of rival faiths - Theosophy took a more advanced position than even the most progressive churchmen, speaking of cosmic evolution in the most sweeping terms as embracing everything from atoms to consciousness, of the Bible as at best only a partial and distorted version of the ancient wisdom, of all religions - and especially some of those most despised by the orthodox, such as Gnosticism and Hinduism - as bearers of the occult light. On top of this, as we have seen, Theosophy challenged the Christian ecclesiastical establishment structurally, in the provision of lay and particularly female leadership.

Ken Elsmore

Theosophical Society General Secretary William Johnstone addresses local meeting (June 1990)

Today New Zealand Theosophy retains an active though undramatic life. Its lodges in the major cities offer interesting lectures, but less of the colourful pageants, musicals, and youth activities than in an earlier era. Its pleasant family camps and conventions, however, give Theosophists and their friends ample opportunity for participation in the social as well as intellectual life of the venerable Society.

Theosophy's heritage - other branches

Other groups also share in the Theosophical heritage. The Liberal Catholic Church, founded in 1916 and almost immediately brought to New Zealand, numbers many Theosophists among its members, offering them a liturgical form of worship capable of Theosophical interpretation. Its chief rite is a mass using vestments and prayers similar to a traditional Roman Catholic or Anglican Eucharist, but understood in Theosophical terms. As its priests move with the slowness and beauty of ancient ritual, they are believed to be building an invisible temple comprised of psychic energy through which spiritual light can stream into the world.

Alice A. Bailey was a former Theosophist who wrote a long series of books, reportedly under the guidance of a Theosophical master called the Tibetan. They expound and in some respects develop Theosophical doctrine, putting special emphasis on the coming of the Christ principle into the world and the importance of group meditation to prepare the way. Followers of this teaching are best known for their meetings for guided meditation every full moon. Students of the Alice Bailey teachings have formed organisations with such names as Goodwill, the Triangle Centre, the Arcane School, and Meditation Groups for the New Age.

The Anthroposophical Society was founded by Rudolf Steiner, a German former Theosophist concerned to present a more Western spiritual emphasis than he detected in Theosophy. Anthroposophy is known in New Zealand as elsewhere for its educational work (its Steiner or Waldorf schools are highly regarded), its 'bio-dynamic' agriculture, its movement art called eurythmy, and its herbal medicinals. All are based on the concept that the spiritual nature of oneself and the world can be known and opened up through harmony and insight, as taught in the rich but demanding works of Steiner. Anthroposophical meetings are generally lively discussions of these books and articles, though Anthroposophists characteristically spend much of their time putting the ideas into practice by labouring assiduously on behalf of health and education, or expressing themselves and the spiritual inner side of reality through art.

Other groups are drawn from some of the same sources as Theosophy but are not directly a part of that heritage. One thinks particularly of those based on the European esoteric tradition expressed in classical Neoplatonism and Gnosticism, or the medieval Jewish mystical system called the Kabbala, or that Renaissance mix of alchemy, astrology, kabbalism and Neoplatonism sometimes denominated Rosicrucianism. (The name comes from a 1614 German pamphlet extolling a legendary knight-initiate called Christian Rosencreutz (Rosy Cross) and calling on others to seek out his mystical order.)

The Society of Guardians in Auckland is a kabbalistic order of 'technical mystics' which traces its origins back to the twelfth century among working-class Christians who maintained close relations with Jews. After many vicissitudes the headquarters of the order found its way in 1970 to the slopes of Mt. Eden, where the brown-robed Senior Guardian, Michael Freedman, presides over libraries and ritual chambers packed with curious lore and arcane symbols. Members meet weekly for study and meditation, performing elaborate ceremonies at the solstices and other special festivals. There is a special interest in astrology and the spiritual side of alchemy.

The Builders of the Adytum, whose New Zealand headquarters is in Lower Hutt, also emphasises the Kabbala though within another tradition. Its temples, both in New Zealand and in Los Angeles where its international headquarters are located, are vivid with brightly coloured representations of the tarot cards and the 'kabbalistic tree', that series of interrelated spheres which diagrams the emanation of being from the depths of God to the human plane. Worship includes attractive chanting and ritual to align people with the energies embedded in this system. Life itself, the B.O.T.A. teaches, is ritual, for it is a continuing process of organisation and reorganisation; what frees us is to know and become parts of that great dance.

Rosicrucianism itself is represented in New Zealand, as elsewhere, in the organisation known as the Ancient and Mystical Order of the Rosy Cross (AMORC). Founded in its modern form in America in 1915 by H. Spencer Lewis, it is well known for its widespread advertising, and describes itself as not a religion but as continuous with a very archaic lineage of esoteric teachings. The key to these teachings is the concept of a dual human nature, the physical body and a 'greater inner self'. Techniques of meditation and other practices taught by the order can help one discover that inner self.

The name is also used by the Lectorium Rosicrucianum, headquartered in the Netherlands but represented in Auckland. This small but interesting group appears to have much in common with ancient Manichaeanism, believing that the two human natures, the physical and the inner divine spark, are radically different, having totally different origins. One can escape from the physical prisonhouse with its endless wheel of birth and death through the process known as 'transfiguration', or entry into the divine order, taught by Jesus Christ; the Lectorium is a school that can help one realise transfiguration in one's own life.

The Ordo Temple Orientis, Order of the Oriental Templars, though founded in Germany around the turn of the century, is associated with the celebrated (and notorious) Aleister Crowley, who was its 'outer head' during the 1920s.[16] A central teaching is Crowley's dictum, 'Do what thou wilt shall be the whole of the Law', which does not however mean living according to impulse but to development of the will so that it expresses one's true nature and the central purpose of one's life. To this end ceremonial magic, meditation, and other forms of psychic development are practised as one moves through a series of degrees. The New Zealand membership, centred in Auckland, is small but meets from time to time for study and ritual.

The Golden Dawn Order

A further fascinating and important esoteric group is the Hermetic Order of the Golden Dawn, which was in operation in Havelock North from 1912 until 1978. Its long-successful second life in New Zealand after its near-terminal decline in its homeland is one of the most extraordinary stories in the history of esoterica.

The Golden Dawn was a celebrated magical order that flourished in London in the 1890s. It has attracted the interest of literary and social historians because of the participation of people in it like the poet W.B. Yeats, the actress and friend of G.B. Shaw Florence Farr, the mother of Oscar Wilde, and other colourful figures from the lively artistic and esoteric worlds of the 'mauve decade'. The Golden Dawn, furthermore, has had much influence as a model for later magical orders, though none has approached its success; in the end it counted several hundred initiates.[17]

The fundamental assumptions of the Golden Dawn were based on the teachings of the noted nineteenth century French occultist Eliphas Levi (Benjamin Constant).[18] The first premise was that powers exist 'out there' in the universe - call them gods, angels, entities, what you will - that correspond to such qualities within us as love, strength, joy, knowledge, or energy. We can align ourselves with these cosmic counterparts, and thereby draw power to enhance that of them within ourselves, through 'magic' - which may be defined as using symbol systems related to the desired power combined with intense concentration of mind and will. To enhance our capacity to love, we might ritually evoke the goddess of love by decking an altar with all her symbols, colours, and incenses, and at the astrologically correct hour - say with Venus in the ascendant - call her down in a magical rite culminating in summoning chants propelled by fervent concentrations of will.

In its capacity as a teaching and initiatory order, however, the Golden Dawn was concerned with transmitting the elaborate symbolic apparatus, based on the Kabbala, which it found most effective for coordinating intra-psychic with supra-psychic realities, and inculcating mental attitudes conducive to concentration. Very important was the schema of grades through which students progressed. Starting with such basics as the Hebrew alphabet (necessary for kabbalism) and astrological signs, the study course ultimately gave a thorough grounding in the whole of the western occult and magical tradition. Students passed each grade through examination, and were admitted to it through impressive, theatrical initiation rituals. For a while the Golden Dawn went quite well, with some members reportedly accomplished in such practices as astral travelling.

But by 1900 the Order was in severe trouble. The head, S.L. MacGregor Mathers, showed signs of serious instability. Crisis followed crisis until the Golden Dawn had split. A few remained loyal to Mathers. Aleister Crowley, mentioned in connection with the O.T.O., after a brief but meteoric career in the Golden Dawn, went his own way. One fairly substantial segment of the Golden Dawn followed the well-known mystical writer A.E. Waite, who quickly did away with most of the ritual magic in favour of esoteric studies with a certain Christian emphasis. Another group, led by Dr

Robert Felkin, emerged as the Stella Matutina, a faction which preserved faithfully the ritual and magical tradition of the Golden Dawn.

Our interest now shifts to Robert Felkin. Born in Nottingham of a nonconformist family, as a young medical student Felkin became an Anglican, in large part because of a deep belief in the importance of ritual. He then spent some years as a medical missionary in Africa, where he had many adventures and became something of an authority on tropical medicine. After his return to Britain for reasons of health, he combined a practice in Edinburgh and later London with a growing interest in occultism, initially stimulated by Theosophy. He joined the Golden Dawn, where the events of 1900 threw him unexpectedly into a position of leadership.

We must now turn to New Zealand and Havelock North. Around 1908 there emerged in that community a movement known as the 'Havelock Work', a vigorous local effort at cultural improvement. It began, reportedly, with readings from Shakespeare and Dickens in a bare room, with only a dozen or so present. But it eventuated in regular Wednesday night entertainments plus social afternoons, classes in art and dramatics, and finally great Arthurian and Shakespearean fetes, complete with splendid processions, Morris dancers, and ample refreshments.

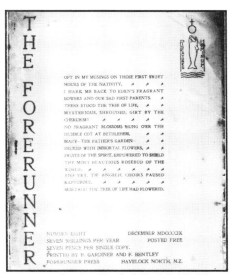

Courtesy Havelock North Public Library

'The Forerunner', journal of the Havelock Work

The 'Havelock Work' also produced a beautifully printed periodical, the *Forerunner*, featuring articles on art, philosophy, and religion, together with stories and poems. It bore the stamp of the then-fashionable 'preraphaelite' interest in traditional crafts and late-romantic moods, yet the *Forerunner* seemed also embarked on its own intriguing spiritual quest. According to a 1912 lead article, the aestheticism of the Work resulted from a conviction that 'behind the outward manifestation of things lay the ideal', and other articles, such as one by the celebrated architect Chapman-Taylor, extolled the value of ritual in revealing the inner ideal. Others wrote of the Christian mysticism of figures like Augustine and Ruysbroeck. It appears that an 'inner circle' of the Havelock Work, in which the newspaper editor Reginald Gardiner and his family were prominent, comprised a small meditation group wherein a simple form of ritual was introduced.

Then in 1910 an Anglican monastic order, the Community of the Resurrection, or 'Mirfield Fathers', sent a mission to the area. One of the visiting priests became interested in the Havelock set's spirituality and promised to send help. In 1912 that took the form of Dr Felkin, whose combination of Anglican piety and esoteric knowledge seemed what was called for; he spent three months in New Zealand organising the Havelock group into a lodge of his Stella Matutina.

The *Forerunner* was not published after the onset of World War I, but the esoteric order persevered. Its members felt a need, however, for further guidance. In 1916 they persuaded Felkin, with his wife Harriot and daughter (by a previous marriage) Ethelwyn, to move permanently to New Zealand. He established a medical practice in Havelock and resided in the impressive home called Whare Ra which the noted architect Chapman-Taylor had just built as headquarters for the New Zealand Stella Matutina (after 1930 again known just as the Golden Dawn). Robert Felkin supervised the Order until his death in 1926. He was succeeded by his wife, who died in 1959.

Before declining to the point where, in 1978, the leadership felt that it should be dissolved, the New Zealand Golden Dawn was a remarkable organisation for several decades. Although secret, it seems to have embraced many of the leading citizens of conservative and well-to-do Havelock North, as well as persons from other Hawkes Bay communities. It was in fact probably larger than the London Golden Dawn in its heyday, and certainly survived much longer without schism. It was therefore strikingly different sociologically from the factious and rather 'bohemian' London version though nearly identical in ideology and ritual. The Havelock group's success can be attributed to the special spirit engendered by the 'Havelock Work' by the capable leadership the Felkins seemed able to give it, and to their Christian emphasis - like them, many members were also pillars of local churches and saw no contradiction between the two commitments.

Whare Ra, now in private ownership, is a singular edifice. The residential portion embodies the best of Chapman-Taylor's justly famous turn-of-the-century design. In the basement is the large rectangular chamber of the hermetic order, with its imposing doors through which initiates and richly vested hierarchs could enter and leave amid flickering lamps and clouds of incense. One can see today, in the mind's eye, neophytes being led, robed and blindfolded, down the turning stone staircase to the antechamber, then into the great hall where, eyes unveiled, they would for the first time discern the walls covered with kabbalistic symbols (unfortunately now gone) and the solemn, secret rites of the Order.

Most impressive of all the features of this underground crypt is the seven-sided 'vault' with concealed entryway which comprises part of the partition between the ritual chamber and the smaller room, apparently a dressing alcove, behind it. Penetrating the vault, one can still be surrounded by the strange astrological and other symbols that embellish its walls and ceiling, and gaze at them until one feels lost in a kabbalistic universe. Here, it is said, initiates to high degree would spend an entire night in meditation.

A Golden Dawn legacy of a different sort is the Tauhara Conference Centre, beautifully situated on the slopes above Lake Taupo. Harriot Felkin was a major force in its creation in the 1940s; the centre reflects the fact that this vigorous woman had broad ecumenical spiritual interests as well as the esoteric. Tauhara now offers attractive facilities for conferences and retreats to spiritual groups of all sorts, but with a special emphasis on those in the alternative spirituality traditions. It has done much to support their presence in New Zealand.

Another esoteric group brought by Robert Felkin to New Zealand was the Order of the Table Round, a society of somewhat uncertain background based on the story of King Arthur and his knights. It survives with a small lodge building in Havelock North whose central accoutrements include a round table on which the traditional twelve knights are identified with the twelve signs of the zodiac.

Other Esoteric Movements

A few groups in New Zealand independent of the Spiritualist, Theosophical, and Golden Dawn traditions need to be mentioned. The Church of Scientology promulgates the teachings of its founder, the late L. Ron Hubbard, an American who was a prolific science fiction writer as well as the author of the best-selling *Dianetics* (1950). This work tells us there are two parts to the human mind, the analytic and the reactive. Most people are enslaved to the reactive mind, governed by 'engrams', embedded habitual responses to stimuli set early in life, or perhaps in previous lifetimes. Dianetic or Scientological 'processing' can enable one to 'go clear' and be 'at cause' in one's life rather than reactive. Further steps give one the freedom of being an O.T., 'Operating Thetan' or liberated soul. The Church of Scientology regards itself as an 'applied religious philosophy' facilitating these stages of growth through techniques of a counselling sort. It has been controversial, accused by governments and critics in several countries of financial irregularities, exaggerated or deceptive claims, and authoritarianism. But it is among the most successful of recent spiritual movements, with an enthusiastic following.[19]

Church of Scientology

Lecture on Affinity, Reality and Communication at the Auckland Scientology Church

G.G. Gurdjieff (1872? - 1949), a modern magus born in Russian Armenia, is well known to New Zealanders because of his relationship to Katherine Mansfield, who died at his famous 1920s centre in Fontainebleau, France. Gurdjieff's basic point was that most human beings are asleep, compared to what we might be, and need to wake up. He advanced many techniques to induce awakening: self-awareness, sacred dance, abruptly starting and stopping manual labour projects.[20] Several New Zealand movements today seem to be in the Gurdjieff tradition. The Gnostic Society, centred in Auckland but with meetings in other cities, is an interesting group that reflects a spiritual pilgrimage more than a single teaching. The quest was started in the early 1960s by the late Abdullah (Neil) Dougan as a Gurdjieff group. Subsequently Dougan became more interested in the Sufi antecedents of Gurdjieff, studied under Sufi masters in Asia, and formally became a Muslim. Still later he, with his followers, moderated this commitment and turned toward the Christian Gnostic writings. But Dougan's own writings remain basic texts studied by the group, and reflect, behind all these means toward awakening, a Gurdjieffian interest in self-awareness, though put in the author's own highly idiosyncratic style. For example, the group keeps the Muslim fast of Ramadan, though without following all other Islamic practices, and with emphasis on understanding how the experience of fasting makes one more aware of the way one's thoughts and feelings work.[21]

The Emin Foundation is a teaching group located mainly in Auckland, noted for dramatic performances and experiments to enhance awareness of the subtle dimensions of human nature. Gurdjieff seems to be a major though unacknowledged source of its elaborate teaching about the meaning of human life and destiny. The School of Philosophy, with imposing buildings in both Auckland and Wellington, presents eclectic teachings on practical philosophy historically first inspired by P.D. Ouspensky, a disciple of Gurdjieff, though one who differed from his master in some respects.

Centrepoint Community

A celebration day with friends at Centrepoint Community

A social and spiritual development of a different sort is the Centrepoint community in Albany north of Auckland. It is a cooperative, communal (all things in common) society growing out of the humanistic psychology movement, which stressed the extensive potential for growth in all persons and the need for a free, supportive social environment to facilitate that growth. Centrepoint was founded in 1972 by Bert Potter, a much-loved, charismatic man who - without teaching religion explicitly - lends a spiritual tone to the enterprise. The community has gone through many vicissitudes, and generated much controversy and misunderstanding, but appears to have a strong capacity for survival.[22]

Neo-Paganism

Throughout the English-speaking world, one of the most unexpected but potentially most important of new movements has been Neo-Paganism. The term embraces groups dedicated to the revival of ancient Egyptian, Greek, Celtic, Nordic and increasingly other primordial, shamanistic religions worldwide. In the United States a burgeoning interest in the practice of Native American religion by persons of European descent, and of African religion by Blacks, is appearing. (In New Zealand one can observe a comparable renewal of spiritual roots in the Maori population, and the potential for discovery and participation by Pakeha is certainly there.) Wicca or modern witchcraft is part of the movement too when it is interpreted, as it is by most practitioners, as a continuation of themes of the old, pre-Christian religions of Europe. Its stress on the Goddess and sexual equality has recently made it attractive to many spiritual feminists. Yet, although there are Wiccan and other Neo-Pagan groups in New Zealand, at the time of writing this seems to be a movement still gathering its strength.[23] It should not be confused with Satanism (also present), which is instead a deviant form of the Judeo-Christian tradition, worshipping that which the tradition regards as the source of evil.

Conclusion

Undoubtedly the special character of contemporary New Zealand as a society shaped by nineteenth-century British immigration has led to its high degree of receptivity to esoteric spiritual movements, whether of the Spiritualist, Theosophical, Golden Dawn, or other sort. This was a society of persons - typically adventurous - who had left behind an old society with its religious and other support systems. Sometimes they were willing to rebuild them in the antipodes, but some among them had undergone a 'sea change' in which old beliefs had faded. At the same time, they were not immune to the romantic and utopian dreams of the era, which often suggested that a new society in the new place might require fresh spiritual underpinnings, and which as often supported a mentality congenial to such esoteric movements. Further, frontier conditions encouraged pragmatic, 'do-it-yourself' approaches, and also the equality of men and women; movements like those we have looked at were congenial to both conditions, with their allegedly empirical, experience-centred work and their female as well as male leadership.

These esoteric movements have thus been a significant part of New Zealand life. While being a considerably secularised society in the eyes of many, New Zealand has also experimented with spiritual alternatives of great, and perhaps lasting, interest.

Notes

1. For brief descriptions and addresses of most of these groups see *Beliefs and Practices in New Zealand: A Directory,* Palmerston North: Religious Studies Department, Massey University, 2nd edition (revised and enlarged) 1985, (available in most libraries).
2. Britten, Emma Hardinge, 1881. *Nineteenth Century Miracles,* New York, Lovell.
3. Nation, W.C., 1920. *The Unseen World,* Levin, W.C. Nation. See also an earlier and briefer account of the same phenomena, Nation, W.C., 1907. *Remarkable Experiences in the Phenomena of Spiritualism in New Zealand,* Levin, W.C. Nation, and the original newspaper account, 'Alleged Spiritual Manifestations in the Wairarapa', *New Zealand Mail,* 30 May 1884, supplement.
4. Doyle, Arthur Conan, 1921. *The Wanderings of a Spiritualist,* London, Hodder & Stoughton.
5. Leaf, Horace, 1923. *Under the Southern Cross,* London, Cecil Palmer.
6. Fry, Mary, 1987. *New Zealand's Radio Clairvoyant,* Wellington, Grantham.
7. See Ingrid Lind, *The White Eagle Inheritance,* Wellingborough, Northamptonshire, Turnstone Press, 1984.
8. For Adamski's own account of his New Zealand lecture tour, see George Adamski, *Flying Saucer Farewell,* London & New York: Abelard-Schuman, 1961, pp. 121-133.
9. See Henry Quast, 'A History of the UFO Movement in New Zealand', *Xenolog,* 100 (Sept.-Oct. 1975 special issue).
10. 'Inaugural Address of the President of the Theosophical Society', facsimile centenary edition, Wheaton, IL, 1975.
11. See, for example, 'Roll of Members, 1879-1894', *Theosophy in New Zealand,* special jubilee number, VII, 2 (April-June 1946), p. 54.
12. Atkinson, A.Y. 1978. 'The Dunedin Theosophical Society, 1892-1900', unpublished thesis presented in partial fulfillment of the requirements for the degree of B.A. Hons. in History at the University of Otago.
13. *Christian Observer, Otago Daily Times, Evening Star* (Dunedin), 1893-97, passim.
14. *Christian Observer,* March 28, 1896, p. 99.
15. Atkinson, A.Y. p. 47.
16. Of the several books on Crowley, one of the most useful for information on the O.T.O. is Francis King, *The Magical World of Aleister Crowley,* London, Weidenfelt and Nicolson, 1977; Arrow Books, 1987.

17. On the Golden Dawn, see Ellic Howe, *The Magicians of the Golden Dawn: A Documentary History of a Magical Order 1887-1923*, London, Routledge & Kegan Paul, 1972, reissue with new preface by Aquarian Press, 1985; R.A. Gilbert, *The Golden Dawn: Twilight of the Magicians*, Wellingborough, Northants, Aquarian, 1983; R.A. Gilbert, *The Golden Dawn Companion*, Aquarian, 1986. A book with a chapter on the New Zealand Golden Dawn is Patrick J. Zalewski, *Secret Inner Order Rituals of the Golden Dawn*, Phoenix, Arizona, Falcon Press, 1988.

18. See Christopher McIntosh, *Eliphas Levi and the French Occult Revival*, New York, Samuel Weiser, 1972, 1974.

19. A standard independent account of Scientology is Roy Wallis, *The Road to Total Freedom*, New York, Columbia University Press, 1977.

20. There are many books about Gurdjieff. Two good introductions to the doctrines and the movement respectively are Kenneth Walker, *Gurdjieff: A Study of his Teaching*, London, Allen & Unwin, 1980, and James Webb, *The Harmonious Circle: The Lives and Work of G.I. Gurdjieff, P.D. Ouspensky, and their Followers*, New York, Putnam, 1980.

21. For an autobiographical account of Dougan's life, with emphasis on his Gurdjieff and Islamic involvement, and a forty-day fast he undertook, see Abdullah Dougan, *40 Days*, Auckland, Gnostic Press, 1978. For his teachings see Abdullah Dougan, *Probings*, Auckland: Gnostic Press, 1979.

22. See Len Oakes, *Inside Centrepoint*, Auckland, Benton Ross, 1986.

23. On Neo-paganism see chapter 17, below.

Hinduism

Jim Wilson

The hall looks like many others in Aotearoa, solid and unpretentious. But sari-clad women are flowing in, many men are wearing loose-fitting cotton trousers and tops, and the children are a kaleidoscope of colour. For this is the Christchurch Indian Association's Hall, and the occasion their annual celebration of Diwali. This 'festival of lights' links these New Zealanders to their roots in India, immersing them afresh in sights, fragrances, feelings, rituals, beliefs and stories of Hinduism.[1]

On the stage inside, enshrined on a throne, is an image of the god Ram (or Rama), bow and arrows slung across his shoulders. Around the walls are bright posters of other goddesses and gods, including Lakshmi, goddess of prosperity; Kali, awesome goddess, and Shiva, awesome god, of destruction and creation; flute-playing Krishna; and Ganesh, elephant-headed god of strength and success. There are posters also of humans: Indira Gandhi, Prime Minister of India till her assassination in 1984; Jahawarlal Nehru, Indira's father and modern India's first Prime Minister; and Surdi Sai Baba, a holy man who died early this century. Entering the hall, therefore, we are already beginning to enter the rich and varied Hindu picture of the universe in which divine, human and other animal forms mingle and merge.

Diwali for predominantly Gujarati communities such as the Christchurch one (Gujarat is a state in India) is primarily about two of the divine beings: Rama and Lakshmi. After a brief introduction by Govind Lallu, the president of the Association, Nalini Ram, followed by four other young women, retells the stories and significance of the festival. Sita, princess of Ayodhya (a city in northern India) had been kidnapped by Ravan, a fearsome demon. Her husband, Ram, after a long search and a dreadful battle, had rescued her, and the two returned to Ayodhya. Overjoyed, people cleaned and decorated their houses and city with extra care, then came out to greet Sita and Ram with lamps.

Making your house especially beautiful and decorating it with lights at Diwali also commemorates the story of a poor couple to whose humble but beautifully-kept house Lakshmi came with prosperity and generosity. This links with celebration of a new year: old things are cleaned out and gifts given to family and friends, last year's business books are closed and new ones opened, and prayers are offered to Lakshmi for an end to misfortune and a new year of prosperity and happiness.

Nalini then spoke of the importance of retaining Indian culture and Gujarati language in New Zealand. She and other women had recently started the Association's Gujarati language school, which meets fortnightly on Sundays, and to her delight it was receiving good support. Displays of

Diwali cards and decorated trays holding *dipam* for *arati* (wick lamps circled before images of deities) were the efforts of this school's pupils, and prizes were given out for those judged best.

Young women then performed Gujarati dances, depicting other stories of goddesses and gods, and a young man sang both religious and popular love songs, accompanied by *tabla* (two tuned drums).

The *arati* lamps were lit, and school pupils and teachers circled them reverently in front of Ram on his throne, and took them round all the people. The President then thanked Nalini and her helpers who had run the evening so enjoyably, and invited everyone to share a delicious Indian meal.

The Christchurch Indian Association, though mainly made up of Hindus of Gujarati origin, is not solely so. Nor does it celebrate only Hindu festivals. Indian Independence Day (January 26), for example, is one of their most important days. But this chapter concentrates on Hindu occasions. Besides Diwali (in October or November), the Association also celebrates Janmashtami and Navaratri. Janmashtami, in August, September or October, celebrates Krishna's birthday.[2] Bhajans (hymns) are sung, and offerings of flowers and food are placed before an image of baby Krishna seated on a swing. At midnight, when Krishna was born, *arati* is performed (the circling lamps) and food-offerings (*prasad*) are given to Krishna. Two dances are performed; Garbha, with rhythmic clapping, and Dandia, in which sticks are twirled and clapped together. Then everyone takes their turn at swinging baby Krishna to sleep. Using image or picture as concrete focus for devotion to the deity, treating it as honoured guest in hall or home, offering food and water, often bathing and dressing it in the morning and inviting it to sleep in the evening, is typical of Hindu worship (*puja*). It gives colour and immediacy to the otherwise abstract idea of the divine being with us, honoured by us and responsive to our needs.

In the past, a cultural subcommittee has made the swing and shrine and decorated the hall for Janmashtami. In 1989, children from the Gujarati language school did so. This is part of an on-going concern that new generations of Hindu New Zealanders become involved and familiar with their heritage; not something which can be taken for granted as it can in India, for here Hindus are a small minority island in a sea of largely European/Christian culture.

Navaratri (nine nights) is celebrated in October. As the name of the festival indicates, it continues for nine nights, with dancing and worship of Amba (also known as Kali and Durga). People dress up as if for New Year's Day, dance Garbha (the clapping dance), and worship and sing bhajans to Amba.

And Krishna and Amba - who are they? For now, we will introduce them simply as one of the gods and one of the goddesses of Hindus. Later we will discuss how these two, and many other goddesses and gods, fit into Hindu beliefs about the divine power which pervades this vast universe we live in.

Religious practices in homes

Diwali, Janmashtami and Navratri are annual highlights for the Hindu community in Christchurch. But in Aotearoa, as in India, much Hindu practice is home and family based. The holy month of Shravan, for example, is celebrated in smaller groups in homes, not by the whole community in the hall. During this month (July-August) families arrange evenings for hymns (*bhajan*) and stories (*katha*), and invite others to join them.

Telling stories about goddesses, gods and remarkable humans is an important part of Hindu practice. For Gujaratis the story of Ram and Sita, incarnations (*avatar*) of the Supreme God and Goddess, is the most popular. The 15th century Hindi poem by Tulsidas, which retells the ancient

Sanskrit epic *Ramayana*, is one of their most important books. The other is the *Bhagavadgita* (God's song), which is part of the epic *Mahabharata*, and which has Krishna as its focus. At *katha* sessions stories are told from these epics, and also from Puranas, collections of stories and teachings of deities and sages.

Sages (spiritually advanced women and men) are interesting characters. Their endurance of long and severe deprivation and pain and their intense Yogic meditation give them extraordinary powers to place curses or grant boons. Often even gods are afraid of them. Stories about them, like those about deities, evoke an awesome feeling of the power and importance of spiritual beings and practices, and most have a moral lesson as well.

In India, *katha* sessions are conducted by *Brahman* priests skilled in the rituals and stories. In Christchurch, tapes from India are used. But hymns (*bhajan*) are sung by the people present, accompanied by *tabla* (two tuned drums), *dholak* (double-ended drum), *manjeera* (small brass cymbals) and harmonium, and by clapping. *Puja* (worship which includes incense), the eating of food offered to deities, and a communal meal, form part of a katha evening, so all senses are involved - sight, smell, hearing, taste and touch - as well as feelings and thoughts evoked by *puja* and stories. This many-sided involvement is typical of Hindu celebrations.

Shravan activities, though home-based, are once-a-year occasions. The real heart-beats of Hinduism are daily rituals. In India these occur in temples and homes; in Aotearoa, so far, only in homes. Regularity and intensity of involvement varies from family to family. A common practice is for one person to perform daily *puja* on behalf of the whole family. Frequently this person is an older woman who, in the later stages of her life, is free to spend more time in spiritual pursuits. She thus provides for the family's spiritual welfare while younger women and men provide for its physical welfare.

In one Christchurch family, for example, the grandmother faithfully performed daily *puja* until her recent death. In a corner of the main room of the house, set into the wall, is a shrine with pictures of Amba, of Ram and Sita, and of Jalaram (a Gujarati saint), amongst others, and with images of Radha and Krishna, and of Ganesh, on a small silver stage. Every morning, from about 9 till about 11.30, Mrs. Ram washed, polished and refilled the little oil lamps (*dipam*) on the shrine, cleaned the images and pictures, and with special care bathed the image of Krishna. She then lit lamps and incense, circled the lamps before the deities (*arati*), and offered them water and food (usually slices of fruit and Indian sweets). The deities enjoyed the essence of this food and the physical aspect was eaten (*prasad*) by the family at their evening meal. Still before the shrine, she read a chapter of the *Bhagavadgita*, in which Krishna instructs Arjuna, one of the heroes of the *Mahabharata*. Since Mrs Ram's death her daughters-in-law, Nalini and *Gita*, continue the rituals, though more briefly as they are still in the busy stage of their lives.

This daily *puja* honours deities and invokes their blessings and protection on the whole family. In addition, the shrine is a constant reminder of the divine and a teaching aid for the youngest generation. Mrs. Ram's grandchildren used to ask her what she was doing, and who the images and pictures represent. Through her answers they have become familiar with symbols and activities of many deities and saints of Hinduism, naturally in their family rather than formally in special classes.

Hindu immigration and Indian Associations[3]

Hindus began arriving in New Zealand towards the end of last century. From then till now most came from two small but densely populated districts in Gujarat, a state in Western India. Despite discouragement from the 1899 Immigration Restriction Act, aimed at keeping out people other than of European-Christian background, a significant number of Hindus had entered the country by 1920. Almost all were men, and probably most planned to earn money here then return to India. It seems some took up labouring jobs in rural areas, and others earned money in Auckland and Wellington by trading fruit and vegetables or collecting and selling bottles. But information is sparse, even on their numbers. Available records refer to Indian arrivals, which would include Sikhs, Muslims and Christians as well as Hindus. The 1921 census records 671 Indians living in Aotearoa (49 women and 622 men, .05 per cent of the total population at that time), and probably about 80 per cent would be Hindus. Though a significant increase from the 181 Indians recorded in 1916, neither the number nor the percentage of the total population could reasonably be regarded as a threat to Pakeha dominance of the country.

In 1920, however, in response to agitation against Asian immigration by European New Zealanders, a much more restrictive immigration act was passed, giving the Minister of Customs sole discretionary power to permit or disallow the entry of persons of non-European origin. Together with economic depression in the 1930s this slowed the rate of Indian settlement in New Zealand for the following twenty-five years. Hindu New Zealanders remained a small group and suffered from considerable prejudice against them from the European-Christian majority. For example, Indian market gardeners in Pukekohe in the early 1920s found themselves ostracised by the European Growers Association; there were strong moves to make illegal the sale or lease of land to Asians; and in 1926 the White New Zealand League was founded.

In response, Indian Associations were formed to protect Indians' rights as New Zealand citizens by legal and peaceful means, and to give mutual support in preserving their cultures and religions. Gujarati Hindus formed a majority in most of these associations, but they were Indian Associations, not Hindu, and included Sikhs and Muslims as well. Prejudice against them reinforced their feeling that they were Indian New Zealanders primarily, rather than of a particular caste or profession or state or religion. This feeling remains strong today and ensures close co-operation between the two main Indian groups in Aotearoa, Gujarati Hindus and Punjabi Sikhs.

Auckland, still the area with the greatest concentration of Indians, was the first to form an association, in 1920. It included Sikhs and Gujaratis. The Wellington Association, mainly Gujarati, was formed in 1925. The Country Section Indian Association, centring on the Waikato and the King Country and composed predominantly of Sikhs, was formed in 1926. Also in 1926 a Central Indian Association was constituted, meeting first in Taumarunui, and all local associations became affiliated to it.

These associations had four main aims: to persuade Government to ease restrictions on Asian immigration; to counter European moves to prevent sale or lease of land to Asians; to help Indian immigrants (still mainly men) to bring wives and families to join them; and to preserve a sense of unity amongst the various Indian groups, Gujarati Hindus, Punjabi Sikhs, Muslims, and some Parsis and Christians. The Associations, and individual Indian New Zealanders, also actively supported India's struggle for independence from Britain, and the rights of Indians in other parts of the British Empire.

Since 1945, the number of Indians living in Aotearoa has risen steadily to reach just over 12,000 in the latest census. More importantly, between 1936 and 1956 the increase in the number of Indian women exceeded that of Indian men. From being mainly groups of men earning money here for families in India, the Indian community was evolving into stable family groups who regard New Zealand as their permanent home. Increase is now by births here as well as by immigration. White prejudice against them, though not dead, has muted considerably, so Indian Associations can now concentrate on cultural and religious activities rather than on fighting prejudice. The range of groups and occupations amongst Indian New Zealanders has also widened, with Indian doctors, university teachers and scientists immigrating from various parts of India, and from Fiji and other countries.

The number of Indian Associations has also increased: Pukekohe in 1936 (preceded by the Pukekohe Indian Grower's Association); Christchurch and Bay of Plenty also in 1936; Manawatu-Hawke's Bay and Waikato in 1945; and Taranaki in 1956. These, and the earlier associations, held their functions for many years in halls rented for each occasion, but most now have their own halls.

Auckland activities

These are Indian, not solely Hindu, associations. But they play important roles in maintaining Hindu and Gujarati customs and festivals. Christchurch examples were given earlier; here we add examples from Auckland and Wellington, the two largest associations.

At first, the Auckland Association and its individual members were absorbed in the struggle to remove discrimination and to establish themselves economically. Nonetheless, in 1921, and again in 1935, monthly issues of a Gujarati-language magazine were started, though on both occasions it was short-lived. In 1935 also a group began meeting weekly to read and discuss the *Bhagavadgita*; this continued until the outbreak of war in 1939. And in 1937 the Association bought a central city site, on Victoria Street, with a view to building a community centre for cultural, religious and social activities.

By the early 1950s, with discrimination easing and the Indian community becoming economically and socially more secure, time and energy was available for wider activities. In 1955 Gandhi Hall was completed and opened by the Mayor of Auckland on October 2, Gandhi's birthday. (This was not the first Indian Hall in Aotearoa, however; Pukekohe's Nehru Hall had been opened in 1953.) Sunday Gujarati language classes were also started in 1955, and continue still, in some years attracting up to 200 students. Then in 1964, reviving and extending the *Gita* discussions, the Sanskara Kendra (Centre for Religious Instruction) was started. Dominant themes of the *Bhagavadgita*, *Ramayana*, *Mahabharata*, Puranas, *Upanishads* and Bible are discussed, and visiting swamis (religious scholars/teachers) and other scholars are invited to give instruction whenever possible. The Qur'an will be added to the scriptures studied when a suitable text and teacher is available. The centre also fosters Indian drama, dance, painting and singing, much of which focuses on Hindu religious themes. In addition to the Sanskara Kendra activities, the Association celebrates several Hindu festivals at Gandhi Hall.

To these religious activities are added moral activities, which Hindus believe should flow from the religious. The Association regularly assists in collecting funds for CORSO, Heart Foundation, Cancer Society, Crippled Children Welfare Society and other similar organisations. And frequently money is sent to India to assist when floods or other crises occur there.

Auckland lacked a Hindu temple, however. It was felt inappropriate for the Association, which includes non-Hindus, to remedy this, so a separate Bharatiya Mandir (Indian Temple) organisation was formed in 1987. About the same time an Auckland businessman, Mohan Daya, returned from a visit to his guru in India, Pujya Morari Bapu. Morari Bapu is a remarkable Gujarati expert in Ram Katha (reciting and expounding the *Ramayana*). Mohan Daya returned fired with enthusiasm for bringing Morari Bapu to Auckland for a nine day Ram Katha.

Fundraising for Bapu's visit was tremendously successful. And the Ram Katha, in October 1988, was perhaps the most significant Hindu occasion in Aotearoa since Hindus first came here - 'the awakening of religious feeling after three generations', a participant from Christchurch

Natu and Nalini Ram

Morari Bapu teaching at Auckland Ram Katha

called it. The Logan Campbell Centre, which holds 3,500 people, was more than two-thirds full throughout the nine days and nights, and was often packed to capacity. The majority were from Auckland and Pukekohe, but people came from all over Aotearoa, and from Australia and Fiji.

Two sessions were held each day, each lasting three or four hours. With Morari Bapu were musicians skilled in accompanying *bhajan* (hymns), and part of each session was spent in singing. Morari and another sang the lead lines, and the centre resounded as all repeated their lead. Then Morari explained the significance and benefits of Ram Katha, and proceeded to sing sections of Tulsi's Hindi *Ramayana* and expound its meaning in Gujarati.

Morari Bapu proved an exceptionally gifted singer and preacher, simple, direct, with a wonderful sense of humour. Even in his short stay here, he said, he had noticed Indian New Zealanders were drifting away from Indian culture towards Western ways. He did not think all Western culture bad, but that Indians were taking up wrong aspects of it. 'You should be aware you have your own religion and should be proud of it.' A family man himself, who lives with his wife, three daughters and son in an *ashram* (spiritual community), Bapu's fundamental message was that it was not necessary to withdraw from the world in order to live out your religion. Rather, what was required was devotion (*bhakti*) to God within your everyday life and work; and, as a result of that devotion, love and help for others. 'Give 10 per cent of your income to religious or charitable causes,' he urged. 'For example, if you pay a visit to India and see a destitute family there, build them a home - and don't mention it to anyone.' He stressed family love and unity as the basis for a healthy, caring community, urging people to strive to be like Sita's and Ram's model family in the *Ramayana*. And, extending concern beyond humans, he laid strong stress on vegetarianism.

The Ram Katha was a tremendous boost to the temple project, in funds and enthusiasm. A site in Balmoral Road had already been secured, and Bapu performed the ground-breaking ceremony there. It is hoped that when the temple is completed Bapu will return for the opening ceremony.

The Wellington scene

The Indian Association in Wellington has also focused on religious activities, especially those of Gujarati Hindus. Its meetings during its first year, 1925, commenced with prayers and readings from the *Bhagavadgita*. In 1926 a regular *Gita* class was started which is still very important today. And in addition to the festivals observed in Christchurch, Wellington celebrates Ganesh Chaturthi, in August/September. An image of Ganesh, the elephant-headed remover of obstacles, is set up in their hall in Tasman Street, Bharat Bhavan, and people gather there for worship (*puja*) in the evening, then return home for a festive meal.

The festivals, and other activities, are mostly conducted in Gujarati. A Sunday Gujarati-language school has been running in Wellington since 1952, and now holds additional classes in the Hutt Valley. Classes in Indian music and dancing are also held.

The Association contributes to and collects for organisations such as CORSO, Crippled Childrens' Society, Save the Children Fund, Red Cross, Foundation for the Blind, and the Maori Education Fund. It has donated the clock at the entrance to Wellington Hospital, a projector to the Free Ambulance Society, and a premature baby's incubator to Lower Hutt Hospital. And it responds generously to crises in India. All this is seen as the practical outcome of Hindu stress on the unity of all life, and on compassion for all.

In 1972 a women's organisation, the Mahayla Samaj, was formed. The Samaj organises afternoon cooking, sewing and arts and crafts demonstrations, which conclude with afternoon tea and a chance for women to meet and socialise. It also holds monthly *bhajan* (hymn) evenings. And it is active in running the Association's festivals and cultural performances, and in fund raising with an Indian Food Fiesta and an Indian Bazaar. 'The aim of the Mahayla Samaj is to allow the women of the Indian community to take an active cultural, social and political part in the running of their community's Association.'[4] The Chairwoman of the Samaj is also a member of the Association's Executive Committee. Since the formation of this Wellington organisation, Auckland and Pukekohe women have also started Mahayla Samaj's within their Associations.

Norman Rorke

Young woman doing classical South Indian dance at Diwali celebrations, Bharat Bhavan, Wellington

A Hindu temple is well under way in Wellington. A large building, with three divisions, has been purchased. Two of the divisions will be leased and the third transformed into a temple and a hall. *Yajna* (an ancient Indian ritual) has already been performed to dedicate the building to its new and holy use.

Festivals, humanitarian works, temples: these are the public face of Hinduism. The private heart, in Wellington as elsewhere, is within families. And while on public occasions and temple committees men are usually in the most visible roles, in families the Hindu heart-beat is often sustained most faithfully by women. It is in families that daily *puja* to Krishna and Kali and Lakshmi and Ram takes place. It is from grandmothers and mothers that Hindu children most frequently hear stories about these divine beings, and about Hindu saints and devotees and heroines and heroes who are such powerful role-models of Hindu devotion and behaviour.

The Wider Tradition - Brahman, Goddesses and Gods

Lakshmi, Sita and Ram, Krishna, Kali ... who are these deities, and how do stories about them and worship to them in Aotearoa fit into the Hindu tradition as a whole?

Feelings, practices and beliefs of Hindus are in detail varied and complex. But they cluster round a few simple basic themes. Most basic is belief in One Holy Power or Being, *Brahman*. This power is manifest in immensely varied ways: in stars forming and exploding; in vibrating atoms; in growing and decaying plants and animals; in feelings and thoughts of conscious beings like ourselves; in everything there is. But it is one and the same Power in all these diverse processes.

We living beings on this earth are but a tiny part, and normally understand only a tiny part, of this great flow of energy. It also forms countless other world systems, each, like ours, with earth, heavens and hells, with goddesses and gods, earthly life-forms and demons. Our final goal is to understand this energy, but our minds have difficulty grasping its immensity.

So we need symbols - smaller, more familiar things within our experience that, by 'standing for' *Brahman* the immense, help us understand It more and prepare us for fuller realisation in future days or lives.

In India, the holy river Ganga (Ganges) is a superb symbol. Like *Brahman* through the universe, Ganga runs its silver thread through northern India, seemingly infinite in form and mood, yet one river, ever the same. And Ganga, like *Brahman*, is life as well as death. With her monsoon floods she has built up fertile plains. Each monsoon anew she brings life to her plains dried to dust by summer heat. And even in summer, though diminished in flow, she gives water for drinking and irrigation, the essential support of life.

But the monsoon floods that build the land also eat it away, undermining houses, removing fields, overflowing banks, and drowning crops and people. Villagers living on Ganga's banks understand that as they live on the river's blessings they must also accept her blows. To learn this from Ganga then apply it to life as a whole - this is one way of expressing a key aim of Hinduism. Like Ganga, life gives and takes in a way indifferent to individual human desires. Wisdom is realising it cannot be otherwise, and enjoying when it gives and enduring when it takes. But for many even the river is too great to grasp. So Ganga is personified, pictured as a goddess, human in form, easy to relate to.

At this point, often, outsiders get confused. Ganga is just one amongst numerous female images of the universal energy. There are also Kali and Durga and Amba, often fiercely horrifying and riding on lions or tigers, but also loved as mothers, hence encompassing the destructive and the creative aspects of life. There is Lakshmi on her lotus, goddess of prosperity; and Saraswati on her swan, goddess of learning and music. There is Sita, whose husband is Ram; Radha, rapt in play of love with Krishna; and Parvati, who makes Shiva her husband through the power of her penances. Images and pictures of these goddesses abound in Hindu temples and homes. There are also innumerable local goddesses in India, but as they relate to particular villages or shrines their images seldom travel with migrants to new lands.

These are just some of the female manifestations of *Brahman*. Amongst male manifestations, Shiva and Vishna are pre-eminent. Shiva, especially as Nataraj (Lord of Dance), portrays perfect poise in the midst of the furious alternation between creation and destruction. Vishnu is primarily the preserver and re-creator. Asleep on a coiled serpent in the formless ocean which follows universal destruction, he dreams the scattered elements together, ready to emit again a formed universe.

There are many other male forms. Ganesh, elephant-headed son of Parvati, is prayed to for success in hard tasks. Ram is the ideal of righteousness and family fidelity, and Hanuman, his monkey helper, of loyalty, devotion and courage. Krishna, like Ram, is one of the most important incarnations (*avatar*) of Vishnu, and from mischievous childhood through loving youth to lofty teaching in the *Bhagavadgita*, he is a fascinating and complex figure.

Significantly, animal forms other than human are regarded as manifestations of the divine.

Ganesh and Hanuman are examples already mentioned; others are incarnations of Vishnu as a boar, as a tortoise, and as a fish. Thus Hindu feeling for unity of all life, and respect for all beings, is both symbolised and inculcated.

Much Hindu literature and art is inspired by these goddesses and gods. And to them, through images and pictures, devotees bring offerings of flowers and food, with *mantra* (chants) or simple prayers. Their requests are as basic and varied as their lives: healing from sickness; rain when crops wither; business success; higher rebirth; happy marriage; strength to live a morally good life. So in *puja* to Lakshmi and Ram and Amba and Krishna, though they may adapt details to this different land, Hindus in Aotearoa are following the ancient ways of India.

Many goddesses, many gods; Hindus bring offerings, make images, tell stories, as if they are separate beings. Yet, for all Hindus, there is only One Holy Power, One Supreme Being. Amongst the innumerable manifestations of this Power are those we call goddesses and gods; and in one sense they are as separate from each other and from us as we are from each other and from mountains and rivers and trees. Nonetheless, they are just different manifestations of One Power. In deepest religious sentiment and belief they are not separate beings, and there is only One Goddess/God.

The many manifestations are signs of divine grace. We are all different and developing. One divine form appeals to one of us, another to another; one now, another later. No form can contain the whole truth of the divine being. But, moved now by one now by another, we may grow towards a more profound understanding denied if we were bound to one partial manifestation only.

Samsara and Karma

Hindus believe we have all the time we need to develop this understanding. For we live not one life only, but a beginningless and potentially endless series of lives. Indeed, the entire universe repeats a cyclic pattern over and again, evolving from formless *Brahman* into concrete diversity of form, then dissolving back in fire and flood at the end of each age. The time scale is staggering - 311,040,000,000,000 human years for each cycle according to one computation. And space is unimaginably immense:

> But the universes side by side at any given moment ... who will estimate the number of these? Beyond the farthest vision, crowding outer space, the universes come and go, an innumerable host. Like delicate boats they float on the fathomless, pure waters that form the body of Vishnu. Out of every hair-pore of that body a universe bubbles and breaks.[5]

As the universe revolves so also all things in it go through their own cycles. This cyclic wandering is called *samsara*. Many cycles are mindless repetitions. But for living beings, through rebirths, purposeful spirals are possible, up or down a scale of spiritual ability. The law which determines rebirths is called *karma*. As we live a life we think and act in certain ways. We thus create habits, which form and express our basic character, and which influence us long after their initial formation and far beyond their original sphere. For example, business people need for their jobs to build up habits of dealing with situations in economic terms. Though they formed them, these habits can take control of them, following them out of office hours and into relations with family and friends. There, where less tangible techniques and measures of success are needed, such habits can be disastrous. But their momentum is such that often it takes much time and effort to free oneself from them and forge a new character and a new life.

Hindus believe the momentum of habits is not ended by death. Habits (*karma*) cause and determine characteristics and status of our next life. It follows that our present nature and status are the result of our past deeds, over a beginningless series of causally-connected previous lives. This can give us peace of mind and calm acceptance of present limitations; after all, they were not given by unjust fate, we created them ourselves. It should not resign us to what the future may bring, however. For it follows also that our future is in our own hands; as we act now so we will be, later in this life and in our next life. Belief in *karma* gives grounds for affirming control over our destiny rather than for fatalism and resignation as is often supposed by outsiders.

Social Dharma: caste and gender

It can still seem daunting. Our future is in our hands; but past habits limit chances for change in this life, we have countless lives to come, and we are surrounded by an infinite cycling universe. But again Hindus divide the immense whole into more manageable parts, providing social and individual frameworks within which we can take one small step at a time towards the final goal of full understanding and freedom.

Hindu social frameworks have been criticised frequently by Hindus and outsiders. Most strongly attacked is the caste system. This divides Indian village societies into occupational and religious and sometimes tribal groups which are not supposed to inter-marry and which also have complex restrictions on eating together and on other social interactions. Much Hindu literature insists that these castes can be ranked as superior or inferior, pure or impure. This in turn is linked to belief in rebirth and *karma* to suggest we deserve our present place, high or low, rich or poor, because of deeds in past lives. Correlation between 'high' spiritually and 'high' socially and economically has never been as simple and close as some Brahmans (the priestly/scholarly caste, who consider themselves the highest) would like it to be. Nor has caste been solely an instrument of oppression and privilege. It enabled all tasks necessary to smooth running of a village to be performed by people who learned easily by imitating parents rather than boringly in classrooms. People believed themselves suited to their jobs, and their jobs to their current stage of spiritual development and prospects for future lives. Moreover, castes were mutual-help groups for members, giving a secure niche in complex communities. Each caste regulated its own affairs, through caste councils, and most had representatives on the village council. Nonetheless, there is no doubt that caste, and supporting religious ideas of rebirth and religious purity and impurity, have played an important part in protecting 'higher castes' privileges and in keeping 'lower' castes in a depressed condition.

Caste relates primarily to Indian villages, though it has affected Indian city life considerably. In the very different conditions of other countries to which Hindus have emigrated it is impossible to abide fully by caste occupational, food and social regulations. Probably, too, the adventurous who emigrated did not wish to establish caste rigidly in their new country; and, as noted, in minority situations being Indian or Hindu becomes more important than being of this or that caste. Consciousness of caste persisted during the early period of Hindu settlement in Aotearoa, and still today all would know what caste (*jati*) they come from. But in terms of practical effects on their lives, caste is now of significance to most Hindus here only in marriage; it remains important to parents to arrange for their children a marriage within their caste. Since numbers are still relatively small in Aotearoa, this often requires seeking a suitable bride or groom in India, or on occasions in Fiji.

More fundamental than caste, however, are divisions in role and status between women and men. The patriarchical view, dominant in recorded Hindu literature (recorded mainly by *Brahman* men), is that women are inferior to and should be dependent on men. This is explicit in the Laws of Manu, and is repeated frequently in the epics (the *Mahabharata* and the *Ramayana*). Men are instructed to 'honour and adorn' 'their' women but this also makes clear women are regarded as 'belonging' to men. Role models such as Sita, submissive wife of Ram, reinforce this feeling in women and in men. Moreover, some passages say women are inherently impure and untrustworthy. And women are told they deserve their dependent *dharma* (role) on account of deeds in past lives; only by fulfilling it can they gain a 'better' rebirth next time.

But this view does not go unchallenged, even in *Brahman* literature. In the *Ramayana*, especially early versions, Sita asserts herself against Ram - incidents stressed by some Hindu feminists today. In the *Mahabharata*, some stories paint very different pictures of roles and status of women, giving dynamic and independent role models. And in goddesses, especially Amba, Kali and Durga, the divine all-powerful energy of the universe is female.

Differences between women and men, and influence from these varied presentations of them, came to Aotearoa with Hindu migrants. But in the different family and social conditions here these differences have lessened. Women and men work together outside the home to keep a business going, for example. Younger men are beginning to take more share of work in home and family. Moreover, unlike most other New Zealanders, Hindus have goddesses prominent in worship. This can give religious backing for moves to lessen the supposed lower status of women.

The aims and stages of life

The religious purpose of these social divisions remains important for they provide manageable steps towards the final religious goal. For this same purpose Hinduism provides divisions for individual lives as well. Our many desires can be sorted into four basic aims. First are two 'lower' aims: material success and sensual enjoyment. These are legitimate aims, and guidance is given on how best to achieve them. But they are subject to morality (*sanatana dharma*), which requires us not to injure other beings. And it is expected that eventually we will learn that these aims give no lasting satisfaction; that material possessions and social position fade and decay, and relationships flow and ebb and end. Then we will willingly move on to the third aim of social, moral and religious virtue (*dharma*), placing the divine, and all other beings, before ourselves. *Dharma* brings greater happiness, to us and to others, than does pursuit of possessions, powers or pleasures. It will also move us away from narrow self-interest, which is what causes our rebirth as selfish individuals. Thus we will build up habits which fit us finally for the fourth and highest aim, *moksha*.

Our lives can also be divided into four stages. As students we learn about Hindu beliefs from grandparents and parents, and from scriptures read at family and community ceremonies. In India, if strictly orthodox or particularly religious, we might live with a priest or *sadhu* (holy person) as a disciple. Then the householder stage: we marry, raise children, look after our family or earn a living in an appropriate occupation, and take part in religious activities. Throughout this busy period we can be comforted by anticipation of the third and fourth stages when we should concentrate on spiritual matters. We may do this at home, reading scriptures and performing *puja*. Or we may leave home and wander in search of *moksha* in the fourth stage, if determined enough, with no possessions and no ties at all.

In India, a popular way into these later stages is through pilgrimage to holy places. Hindus here are distant from these places, so increased religious activity at home, like Mrs. Ram in

Christchurch, is the most viable option. But many manage a trip to India, with religious as well as social and cultural expectations.

Sanatana dharma - love, truth and tolerance

In these aims and life-stages, as in caste and gender divisions, the idea of *dharma* is basic: that each of us has our specific role to play, appropriate to spiritual and social *karma* (habits) formed in previous lives. The awesome aim of freedom from rebirth (*moksha*) is thus made manageable. If we adequately fulfil our present *dharma* - as woman or man, business person or homemaker or doctor, student or householder, in pursuit of wealth or pleasure or virtue - then by this we will be rising spiritually, and in some future life will be able to seek *moksha* directly.

But in addition to individuals' differing dharmas, there is eternal *(sanatana) dharma* which we should strive to follow at all times. The *Mahabharata* makes clear its central requirement:

> Dharma was declared for the advancement and growth of all creatures ... for restraining creatures from injuring one another. I know morality, which is eternal ... it consists of universal friendliness ... That mode of living which is founded upon total harmlessness towards all creatures, or ... upon a minimum of such harm, is highest morality.[6]

This sympathetic feeling towards all life forms, not humans only, is fostered by belief that all are manifestations of One Holy Power:

> We should visualise God in every living thing - inside that fly, that tree - therefore we should give no pain to any living thing or creature, including even vegetable life.[7]

This daunting ideal is also divided into manageable parts. Not instead of concern for all, but as an essential starting point, we should show loving respect to those in special relationships with us, particularly family. By doing so we follow the example of Sita's and Ram's ideal family portrayed in the *Ramayana*.

In *sanatana dharma* there is also strong emphasis on truthfulness, which means seeking as well as telling the truth. If we do this in our present family and social responsibilities we are also moving closer to the final goal of *moksha*, when we will fully realise the truth about ourselves and the Holy Power.

Hindus recognise, however, that prior to this final goal, truth is relative to our particular setting and spiritual aptitude. Hence they seldom insist that 'their truth' should be adopted by all. Rather they feel that by respecting and learning from each other's partial truths we can together move closer to ultimate truth. This supports tolerance of other customs and religions, another basic part of *sanatana dharma*.

Moksha: the final goal

By social divisions, by aims and stages of life, by moral ideals, and by images of goddesses and gods, Hindus break down the immensity of *Brahman* (the Holy Power) into understandable parts. At the same time, by the same means, they direct themselves to the highest goal, *moksha*: the heroic aim of fully understanding *Brahman*.

Most Hindus live in tension between the two ends of this scale. Their pressing immediate problems are those of a limited life here and now: well-being for self and family, personal and community relations, emotional adjustment to life. As students and householders, concerned with lower aims, they approach partial manifestations of *Brahman* through images, seeking help and comfort. But always come reminders that these lesser symbols and lower aims have no finality: a family member is healed, but may sicken again and eventually die; today's business or this year's crop may succeed, but there is tomorrow's and next year's to worry about. And always the aims and stages they should move through, the moral ideals they aspire to, and the goddesses and gods to whom they bring their petitions, remind them of higher concerns and an enduring goal.

There are two main ways of thinking of this goal: as a loving relationship with the Supreme Being (theism); and as realisation of unity with *Brahman* (non-dualism). To these two ways of thinking of the goal correspond two paths to the goal: devotion (*bhakti*) and knowledge (*jnana*).

The devotional path grows naturally out of *puja* to goddesses and gods. As well as hope for assistance in worldly goals, *puja* always expresses love and gratitude to the deity. Gradually, as we move to later stages of life or spiritually higher rebirths, or suddenly, as a crisis convinces us of the insignificance of all worldly goals, this love of the deity becomes the primary and then the sole aim. Then *puja*, with its images and rituals, becomes irrelevant; the inner spark of the divine in each of us, our real self, strives for direct relationship with the Supreme Self. Intense yearning for this relationship, and agony experienced when it seems blocked and the soul bound to further rebirths, form the main themes of *bhakti* hymns. Names and imagery of major manifestations of *Brahman*, especially Kali, Shiva, Krishna and Ram, make this intense love poetry vividly personal. But the outpouring is through these names and imagery to the One Supreme Being, not to a partial manifestation of Her:

> How many times, Mother, are You going
> To trundle me on this wheel like a blind-
> Folded ox grinding out oil? ...
> All these births - eighty times 100,000-
> As beast and bird and still the door
> Of the womb is not shut on me
> And I come out hurting once more!
>
> Take this blindfold off so I can see
> The feet that give comfort....
> There's only one hope
> For Ramprasad, Mother - that in the end
> He will be safe at Your feet.[8]

Linked to this devotion-path (*bhakti-marga*) is the action-path (*karma-marga*). Actions appropriate to our *dharma* (role in life) are believed to lead to spiritually higher rebirth. In the *Bhagavadgita*, Krishna promises that if we fulfil our *dharma* not for selfish reasons but solely out of devotion to him, we will come directly to him, the Supreme Self, and will no longer be reborn.

The non-dual path of knowledge is harder to explain. The sole reality of the universe, *Brahman*, is thought of not as a personal Supreme Self with whom we can have a relationship but as the creative power of consciousness. It follows that in our own consciousness, underlying layers of sensations, emotions and thoughts, we have direct access to the One Reality; or, more accurately, we all are that One Reality. So to achieve release from rebirth we must penetrate beneath these layers, which are what make us feel different from other 'individuals', and experience our pure core of consciousness, which is the same for all. This we do by meditation. Physical, emotional and mental focusing techniques, such as stable (Yogic) postures and the chanting of *mantra*, enable us to concentrate on, and experience directly, our deepest level of consciousness. At the instant, and to the extent, that we do this, we realise that our consciousness is no different from Supreme Consciousness (*Brahman*). As all individuality drops away, we are absorbed into the bliss of non-duality; as a drop of water, momentarily tossed up by wind and wave, merges again with the ocean as soon as it drops back in.

The devotional and the non-dual ways of envisaging the Supreme and the goal, and their respective paths, seem very different, even contradictory, when expressed in words. And they are hotly debated by Hindu philosophers. But by most Hindus they are not seen as rivals but as complementary, two ways of attempting to point to the same humanly indescribable goal. So non-dual meditators use *mantra* which call on the name of Shiva, for example, and even sing devotional hymns; for love imagery is accepted as an effective means of moving towards experiencing unity. And followers of the devotional path frequently use non-dual imagery, such as that of a salt doll dissolving in the ocean. Ramprasad Sen says:

> ... you end, brother,
> Where you began, a reflection
> Rising in water, mixing in water,
> Finally one with water.[9]

This should not surprise us. An intense love relationship with the divine can easily feel like complete absorption in the beloved ('To the utterly at-one with Siva' one hymn begins)[10] as it can in intense love between humans from which the moving imagery of *bhakti* is drawn.

Philosophically, however, theism and non-dualism are basic divisions of Hindu thought, together with a third view which says living selves and non-living matter are two separate aspects of reality (hence dualism, i.e. two-ism). Round and between these differing views an immense literature of complex theories and arguments evolved. This chapter cannot discuss these in detail. But it is worth noting that subtle physical theories, as well as religious, were developed. One explained how all physical processes and objects result from complex interactions of four basic types of atoms. Another, to explain why types of atoms differ, said they were composed of different numbers and combinations of sub-atomic particles infused with different sorts of motion. And some Indian Buddhist theories, in ways uncannily like some modern physical theories, did away with particles altogether, insisting that apparently stable physical objects and processes are really successive combinations of momentary flashes of energy.

Influence on non-Indian New Zealanders

New Zealanders whose forebears, or who themselves, immigrated from India comprise the majority of Hindus here. But the Hindu tradition influences other New Zealanders also. Many practise Yoga, for example, some seeking physical benefit, others concentrating on spiritual goals. And other movements of Hindu origin are active in Aotearoa.[11] We will briefly mention one, perhaps the most visible, of these movements.

Trundling through the streets of Auckland recently, as part of a big and diverse parade, was a large chariot carrying the deities of Jagannatha (Krishna as Lord of the Universe, with his brother

Balarama and sister Subhadra), pulled by devotees and members of the public. This was just the most dramatic of many obvious signs of the presence in Aotearoa of the International Society for Krishna Consciousness, popularly known as the Hare Krishna movement. Most New Zealanders have seen Krishna devotees chanting and distributing literature, many have eaten at their restaurants, and some have attended *puja* or festivals at their temples.

Folk News

Auckland Hare Krishna Jagannatha procession

This branch of Krishna *bhakti* (devotion) grew from an influential devotee known as Chaitanya, who lived in Bengal in the 16th century. Chaitanya danced and chanted Krishna's name, privately and publicly. While doing so he frequently fell into ecstatic trances in which he felt absorbed into Krishna. The group which grew round him continued after his death, and his movement is still important in Bengal. To his followers, Chaitanya came to be understood to be an incarnation of Krishna.

In 1965 a Bengali member of this movement, A.C. Bhaktivedanta Swami, known now as Srila Prabhupada, came to the USA to teach Krishna Consciousness to the western world. He founded the International Society for Krishna Consciousness the following year, and it has since attracted members in many parts of the world. Krishna Consciousness came to Aotearoa in 1972, and there are now communities of devotees in Auckland, Wellington, and Christchurch.

Full-time members live together, with daily individual and communal meditation, chanting of Krishna's and Ram's names, and *puja*. They also have frequent festival days celebrating events in Krishna's life on earth and important occasions of other *avatar* (incarnations) and of spiritual teachers. (Many of these festivals are the same as those celebrated by Indian Associations). Anybody is welcome to attend these rituals and festivals, and to share the *prasad* (meals of food offered first to Krishna).

At 'New Varshan', north of Auckland, the community has a temple under construction, and runs a farm dedicated to Krishna, concentrating on cows, for Krishna in his youth was a village cowherd. Devotees also move around in the community at large, distributing Krishna Consciousness literature, and chanting, often to the accompaniment of cymbals. In all these activities the aim is not self-gratification, but the offering of every action to Krishna, as the *Gita* teaches.

Notes

1. These opening two sections were compiled with generous assistance from Nalini and Natu Ram, and the kind cooperation of the Christchurch Indian Association.
2. As the Hindu calendar is lunar, Western (solar) calendar equivalents for Hindu months and days vary from year to year.

3. Much of the information in this and the next two sections comes from *Indians in New Zealand*, edited by Kapil N. Tiwari, ch.1 by Kapil N. Tiwari, and ch.9 by L. Kasanji; from Kasanji, Lalita Vanmali, '*The Gujaratis in Wellington*', MA thesis (unpublished), Victoria University of Wellington, 1981; and from generous additional assistance from Lalita Kasanji.

4. Communication from Lalita Kasanji, 13.3.90

5. Zimmer, H., 1966. *Myths and Symbols in Indian Art and Civilization*, New York: Harper & Row, p.6.

6. Mahabharata, Santiparva 252.5; quoted from *A Source Book in Indian Philosophy*, edited by S.Radhakrishnan and C.A. Moore, Princeton, N.J.: Princeton University Press, 1957, p.164.

7. see '*Text and Context in Fijian Hinduism*', by Jim Wilson, in *Religion*, Spring 1975, p.62.

8. Ramprasad Sen, hymn 9 in *Grace and Mercy in Her Wild Hair*, trs. Leonard Nathan and Clinton Seely, Boulder, Colorado: Great Eastern, 1982.

9. ibid, hymn 3.

10. Devara Dasimayya, hymn 98 in *Speaking of Siva*, trs. A.K. Ramanujan, Harmondsworth: Penguin Books, 1973.

11. *Beliefs and Practices in New Zealand: a Directory*, Massey University, 1985, gives information on the following movements of Hindu origin: Ananda Marga; Divine Life Yoga; Divine-Love Consciousness; International Society for Krishna Consciousness (ISKCON); International Yoga Teachers Association; Meher Baba; New Zealand School of Yoga; Radha Soami; Raja Yoga; Rajneeshism; Rebirthing; Sahaja Yoga; Siddha Yoga; Sri Chinmoy; Sri Sathya Sai Baba; Star of Asia Order; Theosophy; Transcendental Meditation; Yogadarshan Ashram. Also mentioned are Divine Light Mission, Haribol New Zealand, Krishnamurti Foundation Trust, and Laurel House Yoga School.

Further Reading

Kinsley, D.R., *Hinduism*, New Jersey: Prentice-Hall, 1982.

Tiwari, Kapil N., (ed.), *Indians in New Zealand:* Studies in a sub-culture, Wellington: Price Milburn, for the New Zealand Indian Central Association Inc., 1980.

Zimmer, H., *Myths and Symbols in Indian Art and Civilization*, Harper Torchbook, New York: Harper & Row, 1966.

Humanism

Beverley Earles

> While it is quite clear that New Zealanders are withdrawing from the traditional ecclesias-
> tical institutions and casting off the traditional religious labels, it by no means follows that
> they are becoming careless, disinterested people who cherish nothing, people who have no
> ultimate concern....
>
> Lloyd Geering[1]

Though small in numbers, the New Zealand Humanist movement provides an important, institutionalised illustration of the phenomenon Lloyd Geering is describing. Whether this phenomenon is to be referred to as 'religion' however is both a separate and highly debatable issue and one which can hardly be ignored in the present context of religions of New Zealanders. After all, even if Humanists do have ultimate concerns that does not necessarily mean they are religious; and many scholars and Humanists would object to the very existence of this chapter. New Zealand Humanists have, however, warmly supported the present chapter on their movement provided some explanation is given of the nature of 'religion' and of its relationship to the Humanist phenomenon.

First we shall identify Humanists; then deal with the problem of 'religion' and Humanism, using the Humanist Society of New Zealand (HSNZ) to illustrate some of the difficulties. Third we shall devote attention to phenomenological description.[2]

Our concern here is with organised Humanists (denoted by the capital letter) rather than with humanists. Throughout the world, Humanists have given a specific and institutionalised expression to a much more diffused humanistic attitude in which there is a this-worldly, human-centred response to existence. This response has become increasingly evident in the past three hundred years of Western culture and it reflects anything from a marginal turning away to an outright rejection of the 'other world' of trans-empirical (some would say 'supernatural' or 'transcendent') realities which dominated Western thinking up until the Renaissance and thereafter began to gradually fade from view in a process called secularisation.

Twentieth-century Humanists have mainly appeared since World War II in a further development of the traditions of Secularism, Freethought, Rationalism and Liberal Unitarianism. Although they are by no means a homogeneous group they do share a number of basic characteristics, one of these being the conviction that human beings are the only known source of meaning, value and hope. Humanists trace the origin of this position to the pre-Socratic Greek philosopher Protagoras who stated it as 'man is the measure of all things', but the modern Humanist comes to it through a commitment to scientific method. As a position of unqualified human-centredness it is one of the more important distinguishing factors between Humanists and most liberal Christians who claim the humanist title.

But the essentials of Humanist identity amount to much more than a particular idea about

reality. Intellectual convictions pertain to the cognitive mode of Humanism and this is but one of many modes (ethical, social, experiential, mythical and ritual) that make up a total Humanist way of life.[3] One of Humanism's leading North American exponents describes this way of life as one of 'joyous service for the greater good of all humanity in this natural world and advocating the methods of reason, science, and democracy.'[4]

We should point out that in speaking of the 'modes' of Humanism we are making use of structures more commonly employed in descriptions of religious traditions. Humanism has rarely been included in such descriptions, for reasons having a direct bearing on our subject. First, because scholars have assumed that 'religion' necessarily includes belief in a transcendent

The 'Happy Person' - international Humanist symbol

or trans-empirical reality and thus the Humanist rejection of such belief has made them of only marginal interest as 'nay sayers'; second, because Humanists themselves have for the most part adamantly rejected the religious label, and scholars have thought themselves unjustified in hauling them kicking and screaming into the religious arena.

But traditional theoretical assumptions have been questioned both by a number of scholars and Humanists alike. There have been discussions in both camps concerning functional common ground to be discerned between the traditionally religious and the secular. Both manifest phenomena which have been seen as fulfilling a greater or lesser number of similar needs pertaining to meaning and values for living. It is precisely at this juncture that Humanists worldwide have debated (sometimes bitterly) over the alleged 'religiosity' of Humanism.[5]

There is no unanimity among New Zealand Humanists as to whether Humanism may be properly referred to as religious. Certainly we did not find anyone using the term 'Religious Humanist' for personal reference (unlike many North American Humanists) and neither did we find any instance in which the HSNZ was referred to as a religious institution. But the matter certainly does not rest here. Solicited opinions as to whether Humanism could be regarded as functionally religious were evenly divided among the 'yes's', 'no's' and 'partly's' and each individual spoke of Humanism in functionally religious tones.[6] This committed core spoke of Humanism in terms of attitudes governing the way in which they evaluated, found purpose in and generally comprehended most matters in living. Humanism as a total way of life and commitment was expressed in statements such as: 'I'd be ashamed not to live up to the things I believe in', 'Humanism takes up all my time really because my whole life is lived as a Humanist', and 'It's the way I am.'

The functional common ground that New Zealand Humanists find with religionists has also been evident in their dealings with a number of public authorities. We shall instance but two of these.

First, the HSNZ made a submission to the Royal Commission on Broadcasting in June 1985, urging the Corporation to adopt a wider definition of the word 'religion' in its rules and standards.

They wrote:

> [Some experts define religion as] 'concern for the ultimate values of life as a whole'.... We feel that the Broadcasting Corporation has a duty to cater for people's concerns with ultimate values.... To promote only those viewpoints that conform to the narrow theistic definition of religion is to exclude a whole series of beliefs, attitudes and practices that are non-theistic, yet have religious characteristics and functions.[7]

This submission followed a number of similarly motivated activities: for instance, the Society lobbied for some years to gain access to public radio's 'Faith for Today' program which had an exclusively Christian perspective. While these efforts were unsuccessful, Humanist materials have been solicited and used on 'Soundings' which is a programme that has replaced 'Faith for Today' and which gives air time to a great number of traditions besides the Christian.[8] Furthermore, Humanists can now fulfil their wish to submit scripts for public radio's 'Morning Comment' for that programme no longer requires the measurement of current events in New Zealand against the Christian ethic.

Second, the majority of Humanists evidently did not want to describe themselves as religious in the last census[9] but they were most distressed at being unable to actually identify their position by name. They wrote a letter of complaint to the Government Statistician asserting the unfairness of allowing only religious people to name their particular allegiances and suggesting that the problem could be resolved by using 'religion' and 'belief' as functional alternatives in future censuses.[10] (They suggested 'belief' here on the grounds that it would be more widely understood than 'life-stance' or similar terms used by Humanists).

The brief discussion above suggests that New Zealand Humanists have a rather sophisticated knowledge of the complexities of 'religiosity' and that their use of the term is ambivalent - traditionally exclusive as well as functional and inclusive. But however they choose to describe themselves New Zealand Humanists do manifest commitments of a primary kind. They represent one instance of the kind of serious moral concern and sensitivity which Lloyd Geering is suggesting is alive and well today in New Zealand in spite of the overall decline in church allegiance. It is this attitude of concern that gives Humanists a place in the present book, but because description of it as religious is fraught with problems we have deliberately chosen to refer to Humanist commitment instead.

We shall now discuss the various ways (modes) by which New Zealand Humanists express their commitments. Because of limitations of space we can only deal with two of these in any detail (the Social and the Ritual) and it should be understood at the outset that New Zealand Humanists share in the general characteristics of the worldwide Humanist community with respect to all of the modes described.

Modes of commitment - the cognitive mode

As do its counterparts in other traditions, the cognitive mode functions to articulate ideas and to give the community of Humanists an identity. The HSNZ uses two formulations of the (international Humanist) Amsterdam Declaration to state its position, a position which we have already seen to be based on human-centredness. Briefly stated, Humanists believe that:

1) factual claims must be verifiable according to scientific standards and all conclusions are

therefore provisional (there are no Humanist creeds in the sense of lists of tenets held to be eternally valid);

2) humans are an evolutionary product of nature and live and die in the natural course of things (there is no life-hereafter);

3) humans are without any known 'outside assistance' in this world but can use their powers of reason and sympathy to build an environment in which not only the basic needs for food and shelter are met but where the individual can experience 'the greatest possible freedom of development compatible with the rights of others'.

The ethical mode

If 'man is the measure' in knowledge it is also the case in values, and the time of eternal guarantees is therefore over. This absence of absolutes means that rational deliberation with reference to both the situation and one's fundamental principles is the modus operandi of the Humanist ethical mode.[11] It also means that rules must serve us, not we the rules, and it is assumed that people should be treated as ends and not as means.

General rules may need to be broken in cases where, for instance, an ethical imperative to preserve life is overridden in the interests of quality of human life. For this reason some Wellington Humanists founded the Society for Voluntary Euthanasia to advocate legalised euthanasia. Humanists in other countries have also done this, with notable success having been achieved in the Netherlands where both active and passive euthanasia are now practised.

Humanists maintain that basic ethical principles are suggested by the human condition itself. For instance, all cultures have had standards of right and wrong because human survival has been a social affair depending on co-operation; and humans are born with the greater part of their personalities as yet undeveloped and dependent upon the community for ensuring that development occurs. Humanists worldwide treat these as imperatives for their everyday personal lives as well as for special acts of social service and promotion of self-development. Education is given special attention because it is, as it were, 'the path' to fulfilling the basic aspirations of self-determination and social advancement. Among other things, New Zealand Humanists agitate for a higher proportion of national resources to be spent on education, for schools to be modelled on the open society, for a minimum of reliance on authoritarian methods and for the teaching of comparative religion.

In the pursuit of humanitarian causes Humanists often find themselves rubbing shoulders with Christians and likewise have produced their own 'saints' or heroes. These persons (such as Margaret Sanger, Bertrand and Dora Russell) are not venerated but they do serve as mentors within the movement. The HSNZ has rewarded persons whom it believes have made significant ethical contributions to society, including Fran Wilde M.P. for introducing legislation to repeal the law against homosexual activity, and Sandra Coney with Phillida Bunkle for their 'outstanding achievement in investigating and bringing to public attention unethical medical research practices and the disregard of patients' rights.'

The social mode

The social mode refers to the history, style and activities of an organisation, in this case that of the HSNZ. The social mode of traditional religious institutions is to greater or lesser degrees otherworldly oriented whereas Humanist institutions are entirely this-worldly; the welfare of mortal human beings has altogether replaced institutional concern for the soul.

The predecessors of the HSNZ were the Freethinkers and the Secular and Rationalist Societies. The Freethinkers and Secularists had their heyday during the 1880s when Societies owned their own buildings in Dunedin and Canterbury and numbered more than thirty groups throughout the country. Many functioned as 'surrogate churches' with their musical selections and choirs, poetry readings, Sunday Schools and lectures.[12] Among the leading Freethinkers of New Zealand were two Prime Ministers, Robert Stout and John Ballance.

A Rationalist society first appeared in Auckland in 1883 but did not maintain a constant existence until after revival initiatives in 1927. For about the next twenty years this was a vigorous organisation that gave lectures to large audiences and agitated with some success against various restrictions on Sunday leisure activities. In 1954 it took over the title New Zealand Rationalist Association (NZRA) from the Christchurch Freethought organisation which had assumed that name in 1907. Leading Rationalists earlier this century have included Professors James Shelley of Canterbury University and Thomas Hunter of Victoria University and the politicians John A. Lee, E.J. Howard and Michael Joseph Savage (for a time).[13] Branches of the NZRA have tended to come and go but the Auckland group survives and continues to publish the journal and hold meetings. The NZRA owns Rationalist House in central Auckland.

A small group of freethinking students formed the Auckland University Humanist Society in 1965 and affiliated with the NZRA. The group was apparently short-lived but two years later the HSNZ was founded, again in Auckland and again with a Rationalist connection. The founders of the HSNZ were mainly former members of the NZRA who felt that the latter had an authoritarian president and was in need of taking the initiative in promoting positive social reforms.[14] At about the same time, and unbeknown to the Aucklanders, Bryon Mann was forming a group in Christchurch. Mann had recently moved from the United Kingdom where he had been a member of the British Humanist Association. The Christchurch group became a branch of the HSNZ and in 1971 they were joined by a group in Wellington.

Unlike some other Humanist organisations (particularly the American Humanist Association), the HSNZ had virtually no connection with its natural ally the Unitarian Church. The Humanists had just agreed to contribute to the Unitarian journal *Motive* when the latter folded, along with the New Zealand Society of Unitarians. Currently some Humanists do however attend the Unitarian Church in Auckland on an irregular basis.

The HSNZ developed an institutional model with both a communal aspect for a minority of members and an associational aspect for the remainder. This means that a few members regularly come together for lectures, discussions, companionship, social action and celebration, and other members may never attend a meeting in a lifetime, preferring to financially support the efforts of the active core. By Humanist standards the financial-only members are not necessarily nominal and may well be actively involved in a humanistic one-issue movement. The institutional model of the HSNZ is common for those Humanist organisations worldwide in which there is a significant Rationalist influence, whereas there are other organisations such as the Society for Ethical Culture and the Society for Humanistic Judaism, which use the church and temple model respectively and are much more congregational.

For reasons beyond the scope of this chapter, the vast majority of those referring to themselves as Humanists in New Zealand censuses have not belonged to the organisation. In 1989 the HSNZ had approximately 180 members, most belonging to the Wellington and Auckland branches and some being former members of the Christchurch branch which folded in 1988.

The Society has a National Council which functions to formulate policy and make recommendations to the membership as to appropriate activities. It is responsible for the magazine and the archives and holds an annual membership meeting. In recent years the annual meeting has been held in conjunction with a series of one-day public seminars on subjects of Humanist concern including 'Evolution updated', 'New Birth Technologies', 'Non-Religious New Zealanders' and 'Focus on Humanism'. These seminars usually engage several speakers with expertise in the area and have regularly attracted about a hundred non-members. The annual seminar gives Humanists throughout New Zealand the opportunity to get together, although they can also do this by participating in the Humanist holiday camps run on an irregular basis in the summer.

The principal activities of the HSNZ are conducted within the branches. The main activity is a monthly lecture/discussion that is usually led by an outside speaker and to which the public is invited. This meeting may be preceded by a shared meal and includes time for questions, discussion and socialising. Topics covered by the Wellington branch in recent years have included freedom from religion, women against pornography, Humanists as parents and teachers, immortality, critical thinking, Humanist ethics and Project Waitangi.

Beyond the habitual pattern that these meetings take there is nothing commonly recognisable as ritual although the Wellington branch recently sang the International Humanist Song *Die Gedanken sind frei*, 'Thoughts are free', at one of its branch meetings and at two celebrations. Most of the regular Wellington members seem to be in favour of regularly singing this song and do so with gusto, but there are a few who regard such activity as objectionably churchlike. Dating from the German Peasant's Revolt, the English text of the song expresses the ongoing Humanist commitment to freethought:

I think as I please,
And this gives me pleasure,
My conscience decrees,
This right I must treasure;
My thoughts will not cater
To duke or dictator,
No one can deny -
Die Gedanken sind frei.

And should tyrants take me
And throw me in prison,
My thoughts will burst free,
Like blossoms in season.
Foundations will crumble,
And structures will tumble,
Free people will cry -
Die Gedanken sind frei.

Additional branch activities include running study groups of various kinds and forming ad hoc committees for the formulation of submissions to parliament on matters of Humanistic concern. Members of the Wellington branch have been particularly active in drawing up submissions not only for the branch but for the national body also.

A major activity of the Wellington branch has been participation in the refugee resettlement programme principally run by the Inter-church Commission on Immigration. Wellington has settled six families in six years. The programme has involved a great deal of time and money on the part of a small group lacking the resources available to most churches. They have recently received a donation from the Todd Foundation making this the first charity to give the branch funds for its welfare activities. Wellington has also been running a bi-monthly (now monthly) Access Radio show 'Humanist Outlook' as part of its 'out-reach' program.

Christchurch had responsibility for the *New Zealand Humanist* magazine up until 1990 and one former member started a distribution service for Humanist books published mainly by Prometheus and Pemberton. This service is now in the hands of a National Council official and continues to be the only source in New Zealand for many Humanist publications.

Auckland provides regular volunteer help at a local psychiatric hospital but has been particularly concerned with the performing of rites of passage. While secular marriages are nowadays performed by a great number of non-humanists it is important to note that the Humanist

Society played a key role in getting the Marriage Act changed to provide for non-religious celebrants.[15] The HSNZ was the first to take advantage of the Marriage Amendment Act of 1976 with the first celebrant, Aucklander Barbara Shaw, receiving considerable newspaper publicity over her appointment. When demand intensified for her services, Ray Carr became a celebrant in 1980 followed by several others both in Auckland and elsewhere. To date approximately 500 Humanist weddings have been performed in the Auckland area and Humanists applaud the large numbers of other non-religious marriages that are taking place. Auckland members have also performed by far the most funerals of the HSNZ with Ray Carr recently having conducted his hundredth.

Apart from the activities listed above, the Society supports a wide variety of humanitarian organisations and some members have active involvement in at least one if not more of these. Some of the more commonly supported organisations are the Workers Educational Association, the Civil Liberties Union, the Society for the Protection of Public Education, the Society for Voluntary Euthanasia, Amnesty International and a number of peace and environmental groups.

The experiential mode

Religious experience typically refers to something having an other-worldly dimension, but insofar as it includes experience pertaining to fundamental concerns we would have to say that Humanists also have such experiences. The difference is that Humanist experience occurs within an entirely this-worldly or naturalistic context. Unlike religionists, Humanists rarely speak or write about 'Humanist experience' per se. But if you ask them about it, whether in New Zealand, Holland, the United States or India you will find that they speak of it in terms of fulfilling human relationships, self-cultivation, actions of social responsibility and feelings of at-homeness in this world. All of these can be a source of fundamental existential satisfaction for Humanists despite the absence of an 'other-worldly' content. Many experiences are of the everyday type but others seem to be more like the 'peak experiences' that religionists speak of.

One of the Wellington Humanists has said that contemplating the awesomeness of space and the place of the earth and humans in it is for her a never-ending and indeed fundamental source of wonderment and joy. It is the kind of experience that 'moves' her. A couple described attendance at an International Humanist Conference as an inspiring Humanist experience and another spoke in similar tones of her participation in a demonstration for homosexual law reform. One described her 'conversion' to Humanism as a moment of release and illumination: when she came across the Humanist society and found out what it stood for, she suddenly realised that she had been a Humanist for years - she discovered her identity.

The mythical and ritual modes

Many Humanists respond negatively to the terms 'myth' and 'ritual'. They think that 'myth' refers to tales having no truth value, and that 'ritual' denotes superstitious behaviour expressing a diminished appreciation of the human ability to fend for itself. Even Religious Humanists in the United States seem to prefer the term 'aesthetics' to 'ritual'.

But the fact is that Humanists do have myths. Myths are not false stories but the means by which peoples explain, validate and justify their place in the universe. Mythical truths function as presuppositions for living and carry an authority beyond that of mundane belief. The foundations of Humanist living would be seriously shaken if the validity of scientific method and of basic Humanist ethical imperatives were seriously brought into question.

The Humanists not only have myths but they express them ritually. Rituals reflect, reinforce and to a greater or lesser extent create the fundamental commitments of a group, and Humanists do this by celebrating significant natural and historical events (particularly the winter solstice and the birthdays of famous Humanists and Freethinkers), but most obviously through rites of passage. Humanists are no different from other members of the human community in wanting to move people through recognised points in the life cycle, thus integrating 'human and cultural experiences with biological destiny'.[16] But all Humanist rituals are naturalistic and person-centred and they draw their music and readings from that context.

Whilst not as dominant as in other Humanist organisations (such as the Society for Humanistic Judaism and Ethical Culture) rites of passage are becoming an increasingly important part of advocacy and community service for the HSNZ, particularly in Auckland.

Child welcoming/naming ceremonies

This ceremony replaces traditional infant baptism and celebrates the child as a biological and cultural continuation of the species. For Humanists, people are not born in sin but with the potential for both good and bad. There is therefore no need for a ritual cleansing but for the child to be entrusted entirely to the guidance and care of the community. It is hoped that in this way the potential for good might reach optimum levels of development and that the child will eventually contribute to the advancement of human welfare for the duration of its (one and only) life.

Here is a brief excerpt from a Humanist naming ceremony recently performed in Auckland by Humanist celebrant Ray Carr.

> *Celebrant:* Greetings everyone. We have been invited here because Caroline and Paul wish to share their joy with you and to formally introduce Kelly Marie to each of you. Paul and Caroline are delighted that Kelly has arrived safely in this world and ... wish to enlist your cooperation in welcoming her into the family unit and the wider community of their friends.... Just as they wish to share their happiness with you all, on their behalf I ask you to share in their responsibilities. Will you all affirm your continuing support for Kelly Marie in the years ahead?

> *Those gathered:* Yes we will.

> *Reader:*
> Your children are the sons and daughters of life,
> They come through you but are not from you,
> And though they are with you, they belong not to you.
> You may give them love, but not your thoughts,
> For they have their own thoughts....
> from Kahlil Gibran

> *Celebrant:* Would everyone please repeat after me ...

> *All:* We all agree to call you Kelly Marie
> So we therefore name you Kelly Marie.

Celebrant (takes baby in arms for pronouncement or 'blessing'): We wish you a long life of happiness in a loving and peaceful world. May you bring joy to your parents, to all of us, your family and friends. May you contribute to making this world a better and happier place. On behalf of everyone present, I congratulate Paul and Caroline and baby Kelly, too. I have pleasure in signing Kelly's certificate.

Wedding ceremonies

Many Humanists feel that a civil ceremony does not do justice to the significance of marrying and can be insufficiently human-centred. They claim that it is the couple that does the marrying and that institutions can only recognise the relationship that has already been developing. This attitude has given rise to a number of common approaches to both the ceremonial style and content of Humanist weddings and foremost amongst these is the creative role taken by the couple - it is their wedding and they decide upon its entire format although the celebrant is expected to assist with suggestions when asked. (This approach is also increasingly common in other non-religious weddings.) The result is a unique and personal ceremony.

Another common feature is the central place given to the couple in relation to the guests and celebrant. In traditional weddings the official is usually raised above the couple facing the guests; in a Humanist wedding it is the couple that usually face the guests. In smaller weddings, all present may stand in a circle to demonstrate the support for the couple that comes from humankind rather than from some 'otherkind'.

Humanist weddings rarely, if ever, include the patriarchal practice of giving the bride away and there is very often a strong emphasis upon retaining individuality after marriage. It was in the latter spirit that Wellington Humanist celebrant Jean van Gorkem began a recent wedding thus:

> We are here today to celebrate the marriage of Tony and Elizabeth. Marriage is the promise between a man and a woman who love one another, who trust that love and wish to share the future with each other. It is not the submission of one partner in the other, but the recognition of the uniqueness of each individual.
>
> Marriage enables two separate people to share their hopes and dreams, and to help each other through their adversities....

Funerals

These have become an important part of Humanist services to the community because of a lack of readily available alternatives to traditional rites. This is particularly true for the Humanist Societies in Britain and the Netherlands as well as in Auckland, New Zealand. The HSNZ Auckland branch has in fact produced a booklet *It's Your Funeral - Before, When, and After You Die* (1982) which gives practical advice on how to deal with financial, medical and ceremonial matters relating to death.

Humanist funerals are like child welcome ceremonies in that they typically direct attention to the transiency of life as the symbol of its meaningfulness and hope. Birth and death are

Booklet published by Auckland branch, Humanist Society of New Zealand

placed in an evolutionary context and the naturalness of the whole process is stressed. The finality of death as the end of an individual's existence is often baldly stated but the sense of purpose, hope and immortality to be achieved through service to human welfare and the continuation of the species are emphasised.

The following is an excerpt from a funeral service performed by Ray Carr for a former New Zealand member of parliament. The ceremony included readings from Robert Burns and from Humanist heroes John Stuart Mill and Bertrand Russell. There were several eulogies given by friends and colleagues.

Celebrant: Good afternoon everyone. On behalf of the family of ------ I thank you all for coming here today to show your support. First to introduce myself: I am Ray Carr and I'm proud to share the philosophy of the man, whose life, love, labours and death we are to commemorate. Although the commemoration will take a non-religious form, your own personal memories of, and respect for, our friend will enhance my own very inadequate words on an occasion like this. Let us stand in silent meditation ... in living memory of one who was loved and respected in the community....

Celebrant: Please sit.
We are all part of nature's cycle. We are born the fruits of our parents' love. We are nurtured by them. We grow physically, mentally and emotionally. We follow our elders or peers. We learn through play and work and from our mistakes, too, until the stage when we can fend for ourselves. We enjoy, or suffer, a formal education but continue to learn in the school of life. The adult emerges. As adults we work and learn our jobs, and we develop other skills. Eventually we marry and look forward to a new adventure in an expanded family. As the world watches our progress it hopes we may make some special contribution to the society which has nurtured us over these years. Some can, some can't, some will and some won't. Those who do, give more than they have received, usually. They enrich human experience. The world is a better place and we are better people for having known them. Although I had met our friend only once or twice, I know he has helped make the world a better place for us all to live in....

------'s one wish, I'm sure, would be that we all think lovingly of him without grieving.... To all you grandchildren, your grandad leaves you with a priceless legacy worth much more than mere worldly goods. He leaves you with the bond of a happy, loving, united family, which will remain thus as long as you continue to love one another as he loved you.

Please stand. With fond memories we rejoice that ------ was and still is part of our lives. His influences endure in the unending consequences flowing from his lifetime devotion to worthy causes. They endure in our thoughts and acts. I believe immortality is living on in the thoughts of we who remain. As we dedicate ourselves to those great ethical aims and ideals that have long been part of our cultural heritage, let us reaffirm our friendliness and sympathy toward our fellow humans which now as ever remain the foundation stone of the good society. We leave our friend in peace. With respect we bid him farewell. And thus thinking of him, let us go in quietness of spirit and live in charity one with the other.

Conclusion

Our brief excursion into the world of New Zealand Humanists demonstrates how the concerns and commitments of this movement would easily qualify it as a religion on the part of those employing an inclusive, functional definition. For those maintaining a stricter definition the common ground between the religious and the secular is shown to be far from negligible.

Either way the Humanists do present a challenge to some of the conclusions reached by Alan Webster and Paul Perry in their recent survey *The Religious Factor in New Zealand Society.* In this research, the Humanists have suffered their usual fate of being lost among the 'nones'.[17] Apart from the fact that in some significant ways Humanists do not fit the profile of the religious 'nones' here,[18] they particularly provide clear evidence against the (albeit qualified) conclusion that 'There seems some ground for holding that the religious lifestyle is happier, more fulfilling in itself and more capable of sustaining meaning in life than are its alternatives' (ie. non-religious lifestyles).[19]

Our point is that on the questions concerned with happiness, fulfilment and meaning, Humanists would probably score on or near the top end of a positive scale provided that the measuring factors were not ecclesiastically biased.

Statistics using traditional criteria show that religious 'nones' are the second largest 'religious' category in New Zealand (indeed the largest group of all if regular church attendance is the measuring factor of religiosity)[20] and, given these facts, Webster and Perry are to be applauded for elevating 'nones' above their usual residual status. Our discussion of the HSNZ takes the matter further by demonstrating that there can be much more to being a 'none' than may at first meet the eye.[21] The HSNZ is much more than a club; like readily recognisable religious institutions it is founded on meanings and values that are fundamental rather than incidental to life itself. The Society currently has counterparts in many Western countries, with numerically strong organisations being found in Norway, where there are 37,000 Humanists in a population of approximately 4 million, and in the Netherlands, where Humanists number some 100,000. In the Netherlands, Humanists are seen as providing a functional, non-religious alternative to the churches and are given the same constitutional status and financial benefits. There is also a group in India which has instituted many programmes of social welfare and education.

These factors all suggest that a great deal more research could be done in identifying persons having a range of non-religious primary concerns, not only within New Zealand but wherever a secularising process has been evident.

Notes

1. L.G. Geering, 'New Zealand Enters the Secular Age', in *Religion in New Zealand,* edited by Christopher Nichol and James Veitch, Wellington: Tertiary Christian Studies Programme, Victoria University, 1983, p. 174.
2. All of these are discussed in considerable detail and with reference to Humanist individuals and institutions worldwide in Beverley M. Earles, 'The Faith Dimension of Humanism', Ph D. Dissertation (unpublished), Victoria University of Wellington, 1989.
3. The modes we have identified here are loosely based upon Ninian Smart's six-dimensional structure for analysing world views. He describes these in *Worldviews, Crosscultural Explorations of Human Beliefs,* New York: Scribner's, 1983, and in *The Religious Experience of Mankind,* 3rd edition, New York: Scribner's, 1984.

4. Corliss Lamont, *The Philosophy of Humanism,* 6th edition, revised and enlarged, New York: Frederick Ungar Publishing Co., 1982, p.12.

5. In the Humanist world these discussions were going on among North American liberal Unitarians at least as early as the second decade of this century. A consensus of opinion was later stated in *Humanist Manifesto I* (1933) which reads in part:

   'Religions have always been means for realising the highest values of life. Their end has been accomplished through the interpretation of the total environing situation (theology or world view), the sense of values resulting therefrom (goal or ideal), and the technique (cult) established for realising the satisfactory life ... through all changes religion itself remains constant in its quest for abiding values, an inseparable feature of human life.'

   In *Humanist Manifestos I and II,* Paul Kurtz ed., Buffalo, New York: Prometheus Books, 1973, p.7.

6. These were the opinions of fourteen members of the HSNZ, all of whom had demonstrated a consistently high level of involvement at a committee level and in other activities. Ten had been active for ten years or more, two of these from the inception of the society twenty-three years earlier. The minimum number of years of active involvement was six. One of these individuals had served as President on both the branch and national levels and helped to run the Humanist Radio Access programme. A survey of (past and present) members of the Board of Directors of the American Humanist Association produced similar results.

7. HSNZ submission to the Royal Commission on Broadcasting, June 1985 p.1.

8. This is not to say that 'religion' has been redefined across the board in New Zealand broadcasting however. As recently as 1987 the HSNZ were informed by the general manager, Special Broadcast Services, that '"Religion" is taken to mean the recognition of a god (or gods)....' Letter to Wellington branch, HSNZ, dated 16 February, 1987.

9. Humanists, atheists and agnostics could previously name their allegiances as alternatives to 'Religious Denomination', but in the 1986 Census they could state their position only under the category of 'Other Religion'. Rather than do this, most opted for the 'No Religion' category. This is evidenced in the drop in Humanist numbers from 939 in 1981 to 336 (a peak of 1,050 had been reached in 1976), together with an even greater fall in numbers of atheists and agnostics and a simultaneous increase in the 'No Religion' category from 5.3 per cent of population to 16.4 per cent - an increase of some 368,000 people. *1986 New Zealand Census of Population and Dwellings,* Series C. Report 14, tables 1 and 2. Also see Michael Hill and Wiebe Zwaga, 'The "Nones" Story: A Comparative Analysis of Religious Nonalignment', *New Zealand Sociology* 4(2), November 1989, pp.164-185.

10. Letter to the Government Statistician from the HSNZ dated 7 May, 1989.

11. This approach is commonly referred to as 'Situation Ethics' and was developed by former North American theologian Joseph Fletcher. It is noteworthy that Fletcher now considers himself to be a Secular Humanist and has simply changed the content rather than the method of his ethical decision making.

12. P.J. Lineham, 'Freethinkers in Nineteenth-Century New Zealand', *New Zealand Journal of History,* vol. 19 no. 1 (April 1985), p.77; J.C. Dakin 'A Chronicle of Freethought in New Zealand', unpublished (1985/86), pp.18, 23-4. J.C. Dakin is a former Director of the Department of University Extension (now Continuing Education), Victoria University of Wellington, and a longtime member of the HSNZ.

13. J.C. Dakin, 'Freethought Movements in New Zealand', (September 1987, publication forth-coming), p. 9 in reference to J.A. Lee, *Rhetoric and Red Dawn,* Auckland: Collins, 1965 and *Simple On a Soap-box,* Auckland: Collins, 1963.

14. Letter from Ray Carr, vice-president to president of NZRA dated August 8th 1967, and J.C. Dakin (1985/86), part 2, p.7.

15. We note here that the Quakers had been exempted from having an 'Officiating Minister' in a special section of the 1955 Act.

16. Barbara Myerhoff, Linda Camino and Edith Turner, 'Rites of Passage. An Overview', in *The Encyclopedia of Religion,* editor-in-chief Mircea Eliade, New York: Macmillan, 1987, vol. 12 p.380.

17. i.e., persons registering a 'no' on the following indicators of belief and practice:
Attendance [at a religious institution]
Personal belief in God
Belief in a personal God
Importance of God in own life
Frequency of prayer
Frequency of awareness of or influence by a presence, or power, or God
Acceptance of 1st Commandment as applying to self.
Alan C. Webster and Paul E. Perry, *The Religious Factor in New Zealand Society* - a report of the *New Zealand Study of Values,* Palmerston North: Alpha Publications, 1989, p.25.
Webster and Perry use the term 'No Religion'. The term 'none' was apparently first used by Glenn M. Vernon in 'The Religious "Nones": A Neglected Category', *Journal for the Scientific Study of Religion,* vol. vii no. 2, (Fall 1968). I owe this point to Hill and Zwaga.

18. For instance they are neither mainly young nor predominantly male. See B. Earles, PhD dissertation, 1989.

19. Webster and Perry, p.72.

20. Webster and Perry, p.26.

21. Hill and Zwaga make the point that the 'no religion' category needs to be treated as one of 'intrinsic interest rather than a residual category in a question on denominational affiliation.... Having accepted "no" for an answer, we must be sensitive to the variety of meanings contained in that response.' Hill and Zwaga, pp.182-3.

Further reading

Ericson, Edward L., *The Humanist Way - An Introduction to Ethical Humanist Religion,* (foreword by Isaac Asimov), New York: The Continuum Publishing Co, 1988.

Kurtz, Paul, *Exuberance - A Philosophy of Happiness,* Buffalo, New York: Prometheus Books, 1980.

Kurtz, Paul, (ed.), *The Humanist Alternative - Some Definitions of Humanism,* London/Buffalo, New York: Pemberton, 1973.

Russell, Dora, *The Tamarisk Tree*, vol.2 (My School and the Years of the War), London: Virago, 1981.

Stein, Gordon, (ed.), *The Encyclopedia of Unbelief,* in 2 vols., Buffalo, New York: Prometheus Books, 1985.

Islam

Christopher van der Krogt

Every year, in the lunar month of *Dhu al-Hijjah*, up to two million Muslims from all over the world gather in the sacred city of Mecca to perform the rituals of the great pilgrimage or *hajj*. One of the central rites is the circumambulation of an ancient shrine known for its shape as the *Ka'bah* or 'cube'. For many of the faithful, the journey to Mecca will be the reward of a lifetime of putting aside small sums of money to pay for this great act of devotion. All through their lives, and in whatever part of the world they live, they have faced the *Ka'bah* in their daily worship, for every mosque has a niche (*mihrab*) in the wall to indicate its direction.

In some years, there are pilgrims from the furthest mosque in the world from Mecca: the *Masjid al-Nur* or 'Mosque of Light' in Christchurch, New Zealand. While including all the traditional features of a mosque, the interior of the Masjid al-Nur is panelled with rimu. Designed by a convert to Islam, the mosque is a fitting symbol of a community which seeks to retain all the beliefs and practices of Islam while at the same time identifying with the wider society of which it forms a part. There are two mosques in this country and a third is currently being planned: clearly Islam is now an integral part of the New Zealand religious scene.

A.C. Moore

Masjid (mosque) al-Nur, Christchurch

By comparison with those of other religions, the essential beliefs and rituals of Islam are uncomplicated. What Muslims believe is summarised in the words of the *shahadah* or formula of witness: *La ilaha illa Allah; Muhammadun rasul Allah* ('There is no god but God; Muhammad is God's Messenger.') The message of Muhammad is enshrined in the *Qur'an*, the Islamic scripture, which Muslims believe to be the very words of Allah, the one God. Although Muhammad, the last

186

of the prophets, was clearly an exceptional man, Muslims do not worship him or regard him as in any sense divine. For this reason, to refer to their religion as 'Mohammedanism', by analogy with 'Christianity', is considered offensive.

The Arabic word *islam* means 'submission' or 'surrender' to Allah. In this broad sense, Islam can be said to be the oldest religion in the world, for it is the religion of Adam, the first human being and the first Muslim. It can even be said that Islam dates from the creation of the universe which submits to Allah by following the natural laws He has laid down for it. More specifically, the word *islam* refers to the religion which was founded, or re-established, in seventh-century Arabia. According to this sense of the word, Islam is the youngest of the great universal religions. The Arabic root *s-l-m*, from which the word *islam* derives, also gives several words meaning 'peace' so the name of the religion is sometimes said to mean 'peace' as well as 'surrender'. Both inner peace and peace among people are the reward of conformity to the will of Allah and peace comes to those who place all their cares before Him. The traditional Islamic greeting is *al-salamu 'alaykum* (Peace be with you), to which the reply is *wa 'alaykum al-salam* (And peace be with you).

A Muslim is one who performs the action of *islam* - one who lives according to the will of God. In the broad sense, not only Adam, but also Moses, Jesus and numerous other prophets, as well as their faithful followers, were Muslims. More commonly though, the word refers to those who obey Allah by following the teachings He revealed through Muhammad.[1]

Ummah: the Islamic Community

All Muslims belong to a single world community, the *ummah*. Ideally, the *ummah* (often translated as 'nation') transcends all class and ethnic distinctions and its members share common institutions and attitudes. During the lifetime of the Prophet Muhammad (571-632 CE), Muslims came to form a single political community under his leadership. After the Prophet's death, while the Arabs were establishing a vast empire from the Atlantic to Asia, there emerged an enduring division within the *ummah*: the distinction between *Sunni* and *Shi'i* Muslims. Shi'is belong to the party of 'Ali (*shi'at 'Ali*), which holds that the legitimate rulers of the *ummah* after the time of Muhammad were the Prophet's cousin and son-in-law, 'Ali, and then the latter's male descendants. These leaders are called the *imams*.[2] Most Shi'is recognise twelve *imams*, including 'Ali himself, and are referred to as 'Twelver' Shi'is or *Imami* Shi'is. They believe that the twelfth *imam*, Muhammad al-Muntazar (the 'awaited one'), went into hiding in 874 CE and is not dead, but will someday return as the *mahdi*, a messianic figure who will restore justice and righteousness in the world. Twelver Shi'ism has been predominant in Persia (Iran) since the sixteenth century CE and is widespread in the surrounding regions.[3]

Shi'is comprise about 15 per cent of the 900 million or so Muslims in the world: almost all the rest are Sunnis, that is, followers of the *sunnah* or 'tradition' of the Prophet. Of course Shi'is too claim to follow the *sunnah* of Muhammad and Sunnis have great respect for 'Ali whom they regard as the fourth caliph. ('Caliph' comes from the Arabic *khalifah* meaning a 'successor' of the Prophet in his capacity as leader of the Muslim community.)[4] Rejecting the view that anyone had a divinely appointed right to the caliphate, Sunnis believe that the four 'rightly-guided' caliphs - Abu Bakr, 'Umar, 'Uthman and 'Ali - held their positions on the basis of popular support. After the assassination of 'Ali by one of his own former supporters in 661 CE, the caliphate was held by the Umayyad dynasty until 750 CE when the Umayyads were overthrown and replaced by the 'Abbasid dynasty. Before long, the *ummah* was divided by war-lords who established their independent rule over various parts of the Islamic Empire, often taking the title *sultan* - an Arabic word meaning 'power'. By the time the Mongol invaders executed the last of the 'Abbasid caliphs of Baghdad in 1258 CE, Sunni theorists had already resigned themselves to accepting the rule of military adventurers and the authority of the caliphate had become largely nominal.[5]

After the time of the Prophet there would never again be universal agreement among Muslims about how their community should be organised and run. In the years since the withdrawal of the European colonial powers from Islamic countries after World War II, thirty-six independent states have emerged whose population is at least 50 per cent Muslim.[6] In most of these countries, there is a mixture of western-style institutions (such as presidents, parliaments and popular elections) and traditional institutions based on local custom and Islamic law. There is often conflict about whether 'Islamic' or 'western' forms of government should prevail. This debate is at least as important in practice as the ancient division between Sunnis and Shiʻis. Militant Islamic groups in Egypt, for example, derive inspiration from the Iranian revolution of 1978-9 CE, even though they reject many details of Shiʻi belief and practice. Well before the revolution, there was a significant rapprochement between Sunnis and Shiʻis - a development which has been complicated by the concern of governments in many Islamic countries over events in Iran.

Despite political and sectarian differences, Muslims retain a profound sense of belonging to a world community. Political boundaries are widely regarded as having only transitory significance and the distinctions between sects are not institutionalised as they are in Christianity. While there are some theological and legal differences between Sunnis and Shiʻis, they share the same faith and practices; their disputes over the caliphate or imamate have limited significance in contemporary practice. To the outsider it is remarkable that even though Arabs constitute less than one quarter of the world Muslim population, their language, the language of the Qur'an, is used for worship and religious learning throughout the Islamic community.

Unity within the *ummah* is particularly evident in a country like New Zealand. The few Shiʻi Muslims here (almost all of whom are temporary visitors) enjoy cordial relations with the Sunni majority - though there are some Sunnis who have misgivings about Shiʻism. At any one time, Muslims in this country represent as many as thirty distinct nationalities. Because of its small size, the New Zealand community's ethnic differences are less evident than in Muslim communities in other western countries where different nationalities manage their own mosques. According to the 1986 census, there were 2,544 Muslims in New Zealand on the fourth of March that year.[7] Muslims themselves estimate their numbers at about double that figure, pointing out, for example, that the recent political troubles in Fiji have led to large numbers of Fijian Indians coming to New Zealand.[8] Of the census population, 36 per cent were born in Asia and 21 per cent in the Pacific Islands.[9] In fact, Fijian Indians already constituted the largest ethnic group in the New Zealand Muslim population. Over the last few years, the community has come to include a greater proportion of families with children.

The figure of 2,544 Muslims in New Zealand represents an increase of nearly 50 per cent over the 1981 census figure of 1,701 and in recent decades the Muslim population has grown rapidly.[10] There have been Muslims in this country for over a century, although very few settled permanently before the 1950s. Even now, to judge from the 1986 census, only 26 per cent of the Muslim population were born in this country.[11] The character of the community is therefore very dependent upon foreign-born Muslims, whether temporary visitors or permanent residents. Outside of Auckland, which has by far the largest Muslim population, the active membership of local communities tends to have high proportions of students and professional people drawn from many parts of the world. There are few Muslims in rural New Zealand, most of them being slaughtermen on temporary contracts.

A growing number of New Zealanders are attracted to Islam as converts, or as they prefer to be called, 'reverts' (since it is believed that Islam is everyone's religion at birth). They include both women and men and their ages vary greatly. Some of them have learned about Islam overseas and returned home as Muslims. Others have adopted the faith as a prelude to marrying a Muslim, either in New Zealand or elsewhere. Yet others have been attracted to the religion through study or through the example of Muslims whom they have met.

Having made the decision to embrace Islam, the process of becoming a Muslim is very simple. When I visited the Masjid al-Nur at the time of the Friday prayer on a recent occasion, there was a young man present who had decided to become a Muslim. After the service he was introduced to the other worshippers and asked to repeat an Islamic creed. Having done this, he shook hands with the other men present and they were reminded that he was now one of their brothers in Islam. It is customary for converts to adopt an Islamic name, usually based on one of the attributes of Allah or a name of one of the Companions of the Prophet.

Since 1979, Muslims in New Zealand have had a national organisation: the Federation of Islamic Associations in New Zealand (FIANZ).[12] As its name suggests, FIANZ is made up of regional associations. The first of these to be established was the New Zealand Muslim Association, set up in Auckland in 1950 but reorganised in 1976. In 1989 a separate South Auckland Muslim Association was created. Wellington's International Muslim Association of New Zealand was formed by stages in the 1960s. (The acronym IMAN spells the Arabic word for 'faith' and the 'international' designation is perhaps justified by the ethnic diversity of the Muslim community in Wellington.) The Muslim Association of Canterbury was incorporated in 1977, the Waikato-Bay of Plenty Muslim Association in 1980 and the Manawatu Muslim Association in 1982. Official 'paid-up' membership of these associations is not large - there are many more practising Muslims in the country than FIANZ members - but the regional and national associations provide a means of taking action on matters of concern to the Muslim community.

The FIANZ council, a small policy-making body made up of representatives of the regional associations, leaves the running of day-to-day matters to its executive members. Until 1988, it had a number of subcommittees to deal with specific matters but in that year it was decided to devolve responsibility for these issues onto the wider community and a number of 'divisions' were established by co-opting interested personnel from around the country. These divisions are concerned with a wide range of matters, including, for example, the timing of religious festivals, the provision of religious education, women's affairs, international trade and disseminating literature.

Tawhid: affirming the oneness of God

Islam belongs to the same family of religions as Judaism and Christianity. Like them it affirms that there is only one God and the name 'Allah' is usually taken to mean 'the God'. Arabic speaking Jews and Christians refer to their God as 'Allah' and the Qur'an itself identifies Allah with the God of the Bible. From an Islamic perspective, however, Christians in particular have compromised their claim to be monotheists, since they regard the prophet Jesus as divine and believe that God is a trinity. For Muslims, the greatest sin is *shirk*, the ascribing to Allah of partners or equals in divinity and the Qur'an frequently admonishes those *mushrikun* ('associaters' or 'polytheists') who are guilty of it. The opposite of *shirk* is *tawhid*: to declare that God is one. Since this is the central doctrine of Islam, the expression *'ilm al-tawhid* ('science of unity') is sometimes used to refer to Islamic theology in general.

Some Muslims object to using the term 'God' as a translation for 'Allah' because the English word is overlaid with un-Islamic connotations such as the Christian concept of the trinity. The name 'Allah', they point out, has no plural or gender and is not associated with any visual image.

However, since most Muslims accept and use the word 'God', this usage is being maintained in the present context. The task before Muslims who want other people to understand the implications of *tawhid* is comparable with that which faced Muhammad. Just as the Prophet's contemporaries associated other deities with Allah, many New Zealanders today think of God as having a Son - a notion abhorrent to Muslims. To the adherents of revealed religions, then, the Qur'an is offered as a corrective. Muhammad's mission involved both affirming the truth about God to his hearers as well as setting right their errors. Consequently, much of what the Qur'an says about Allah is familiar to readers of the Bible.

Allah is described in the opening lines of the Qur'an as the 'Lord of the Worlds' or the 'Lord of all Being', for the entire universe lies under His dominion. He created all things in six days by simply calling them into existence and it is He who continues to sustain them. Nothing escapes His attention, not even a falling leaf. The Qur'an's emphasis on the overwhelming power and sovereignty of God, however, is balanced by a comparable stress upon His graciousness and mercy. Although Islam is not as fatalistic as some of its critics claim, acceptance of God's overriding power does help to reconcile Muslims to life's set-backs while giving cause to be grateful for life's blessings. When Muslims speak of future plans or hopes, they frequently use the phrase *insha' Allah*, 'if God wills', and the words *al-hamdu lillah*, 'praise be to God', are often spoken in connection with present or past events (whether favourable or not).[13]

To Allah belong the 'most beautiful names', of which, according to tradition, there are ninety-nine. Muslims often carry a rosary (*tasbih* or *subhah*) of thirty-three or ninety-nine beads with which to recall these names. About seventy of them are found in the Qur'an, the two most frequently invoked being *al-Rahman* (the Merciful) and *al-Rahim* (the Compassionate). Each chapter (*surah*) of the Qur'an, except the ninth, is prefaced with the *basmalah: Bism Allah al-Rahman al-Rahim* ('In the name of Allah, the Compassionate, the Merciful'). Everything a Muslim does should begin with this formula or at least the intention which it conveys. The titles of Allah are frequently used to form personal names, usually in conjunction with the word *'abd*, meaning 'servant' or 'slave'. Popular names include *'Abd al-Razzaq* (Servant of the Provider), *'Abd al-'Aziz* (Servant of the Mighty One), *'Abd al-Karim* (Servant of the Generous One) and *'Abd al-Qadir* (Servant of the Powerful One). Similar in form is *'Abd Allah* (or *'Abdallah* - Servant of God).

In the Islamic world view, there are two kinds of spirit creatures: angels and *jinn*. Angels, of whom the most important is Gabriel (*Jibril*), who communicated the Qur'an to Muhammad, are winged servants of Allah. According to Islamic tradition, they are made of light and are neither male nor female. In eschatological doctrines they are especially prominent; for example, on the Day of Judgment God's throne will be borne up by eight angels. The Qur'an also speaks of guardian angels and of angels who record each individual's good and evil deeds in anticipation of the Judgment. *Jinn* (the genii of the *Arabian Nights*) are made of fire; they are either male or female and can take physical form. While some of them have embraced Islam, they tend to be even more disposed to waywardness than are human beings and sometimes exercise strange powers.

When Allah created Adam, he told the angels to bow down before him and they obeyed. (From this story it is inferred that the angels are inferior to prophets or even to all human beings.) However, the Devil or Satan (*Iblis* or *Shaytan*), refused to prostrate himself before a creature made of clay since he himself was made of fire. For this disobedience, he was condemned to Hell but has been granted a reprieve until the Judgment. In the meantime he seeks to tempt other creatures into disobeying God.[14]

Adam was created from water and dust or clay. He and his wife were placed in a paradisaical garden but, prompted by Satan, they ate of the forbidden tree and henceforth they and their descendants had to live on the earth. Nevertheless (despite the misgivings of the angels) mankind holds the position of vicegerent (*khalifah*) of God on Earth and has been promised divine guidance. There is no doctrine of original sin in Islam and Adam and Eve were brought to Earth as a part of God's plan, not simply as a punishment. The Qur'an teaches that everything on the Earth was created for the benefit of mankind, including gardens yielding fruit and vegetables and animals to carry burdens and to produce meat and milk.

Despite the blessings they have received, however, people tend to respond to God with ingratitude. Those who refuse to acknowledge Him are said to be 'ingrates' (*kafirun*). Unbelief is really ingratitude towards Allah in the face of His blessings and the wonders of creation which are offered as a sign of His existence and nature. It is because people are so prone to overlooking their obligations towards God, that He has sent prophets to remind them.

According to the Qur'an, there have been numerous prophets but only about twenty-five are actually named in the text.[15] The prophets were sent to preach good news and to give warning of God's judgment, to which their hearers often responded with disbelief, opposition and even persecution. Like the Bible, the Qur'an tells of people who were punished after failing to heed God's messengers. Noah's contemporaries, for example, were drowned in the flood and the cities of Sodom and Gomorrah were destroyed. Punishments inflicted on people in this life should warn them of the greater penalty which awaits the unrepentant in the next life.

All the prophets taught similar messages, although some are higher in rank than others. Abraham (*Ibrahim*) is particularly prominent in the Qur'an, for it was he who built the Ka'bah, with the assistance of his first son Ishmael (*Isma'il*). Muhammad's mission was to restore the true monotheistic religion of Abraham which anteceded the errors of the Jews and the Christians. Jesus (*'Isa*) is also an important prophet in the Qur'an, where the story of the Annunciation and Virgin Birth is recounted at length. The Qur'an refers to Jesus as the 'Word of God', 'the Messiah' and even the 'Spirit of God', but there is no indication that these titles imply divinity as they do for Christians and the title 'Son of God' is firmly rejected. Jesus' mission as a messenger to the Children of Israel was attested by miracles (including the cure of the blind, healing lepers and raising the dead to life) which were performed by the authority of God. When the Jews sought to have him killed, God prevented them by taking Jesus up to Himself so that the prophet Jesus only appeared to be crucified. How Allah accomplished this is a matter of conjecture; a widespread view holds that someone else was made to look like Jesus and crucified in his place. Muslims believe that someday Jesus will return to earth and die like other mortals.

Allah's revelations through prophets were frequently given in the form of a book and the Torah of Moses, the Psalms of David and the Gospel of Jesus are the most important examples before the Qur'an. The possessors of these earlier scriptures, the People of the Book (*ahl al-kitab*), are accused in the Qur'an of failing to live up to the revelations they had received. Instead of passing them on, they have corrupted and misinterpreted their scriptures, failing to recognise that both the Torah and the Gospel foretold the coming of Muhammad.[16]

As the last of the prophets, Muhammad confirmed the message of his predecessors and brought a new scripture, the Qur'an ('recitation'), which supersedes the corrupted texts of all earlier revelations. Muslims believe that Muhammad's mission is of universal importance. He is the 'Seal of the Prophets':[17] there will be no more messengers and all that is of permanent value in the teachings of Muhammad's predecessors is reaffirmed in the Qur'an and *sunnah*. In the past every people had its own prophet, but now there has come a prophet whose teaching is for all humankind.

Muhammad was born in the Arabian town of Mecca around 571 CE. When he was about forty years old, he began to receive messages which Muslims believe were brought to him from Allah by the angel Gabriel. He would continue to receive revelations for the rest of his life and it is these which make up the Qur'an. After overcoming his own initial doubts, Muhammad spoke openly of his revelations. He denounced the injustices of Meccan society and the polytheism of the pagan Arabs. In the spirit of his ancient Hebrew predecessors, the Prophet gave warning of God's impending judgment upon idolators and oppressors of the poor. He declared that the dead would be raised to life and punished or rewarded according to their deeds. Such preaching was unacceptable to the leaders of Meccan society and the Prophet attracted only a small following, mostly from among the humbler inhabitants of the town. The Muslims were subjected to insults, persecution and the threat of assassination. In 622 CE, therefore, Muhammad and most of his followers left Mecca for the safety of Yathrib, later called Medina, an oasis settlement some 600 kilometers to the north of Mecca.

This emigration, the *hijrah* (or 'hegira' in older books), marked the establishment of the *ummah*. The Muslims had seceded from their own people and now formed a new political unit by allying with Yathrib's three main Arab tribes and the three Jewish tribes living there. In Medina, the beliefs and practices of Islam were able to develop without hindrance and fresh revelations offered guidance as new issues arose. Meanwhile, having accepted Mecca's rejected Prophet, Medina's future relations with that city were inevitably hostile. Muhammad and his allies were well situated to conduct raids on Meccan caravans in the time-honoured manner of the Arabs - an activity which was justified by Mecca's ill-treatment of the Muslims. The conflict soon escalated and, on the Muslim side, came to be seen as a struggle (*jihad*) for God's cause. After eight years of raids, battles and negotiations, Mecca finally capitulated to Muhammad and the tribal confederation based in Medina. Soon afterwards, delegations from different parts of the Arabian Peninsula came to parley with Muhammad but after his death in Medina in 632 CE, it took decisive military action on the part of Abu Bakr to assert the political dominance of Medina over the rest of Arabia, thus laying the basis for the Muslim conquests.

To Muslims, Muhammad is the supreme exemplar of what it means to live the life of *islam* or surrender to God and in the Qur'an Muslims are exhorted to obey not only Allah but also His Messenger. Some Muslims even concern themselves with reports of what the Prophet ate or how he wore his beard in order to follow his example. In receiving and passing on the Qur'an, Muhammad is believed to have been protected from making any errors. Indeed, it is believed that he was also protected from committing any sin. The veneration of Muslims for their Prophet is reflected in the phrase *salla Allahu 'alayhi wa sallim* ('May God bless him and grant him peace') uttered almost whenever the name of the Prophet is mentioned.[18]

The Prophet's closeness to God is illustrated by the story of his Night Journey (*isra'*) and Ascension (*mi'raj*). These events are said to be alluded to in the Qur'an and have been elaborated in various traditional accounts. One night Muhammad was taken from the 'Sacred Mosque' (the Ka'bah) to the 'Farthest Mosque' (evidently the site of Solomon's Temple in Jerusalem). From there he was transported up to the very presence of God in Paradise. Opinions differ as to whether the journey was a spiritual one, or a physical one in which the Prophet is said to have travelled on the steed Buraq. Muhammad's association with Jerusalem is one of the reasons why Muslims regard that city as holy, taking third place after Mecca and Medina.[19]

Muhammad's most enduring legacy is the Qur'an. Although there are traditional accounts of miracles attributed to him, it is often said that the Qur'an is the real miracle of Muhammad. The miraculous nature of the revelation is emphasised by the Muslim belief that the Prophet was illiterate and therefore could not have produced the Scripture himself. When Muhammad died, the period of revelation came to an end and in due course a definitive version of the text was compiled under the authority of 'Uthman. Despite the uncertainties of human history, Muslims hold that the Qur'an, unlike other scriptures, will always be preserved from corruption. They believe that the text was accurately recorded and passed on unaltered by Muhammad's followers (in both oral and written form) to the present day.

Since Muslims believe the Qur'an to be literally the speech of Allah (*kalam Allah*), they find blasphemous any attribution of its content to Muhammad. The Prophet was privileged to receive and pass on the very words of God Himself, without, according to the orthodox view, having any part in their formulation. When quoting from the Qur'an, Muslims often say, 'Allah says ...' or 'The Qur'an says ...' and the latter usage is an appropriate one for non-Muslims to adopt.

Only the original Arabic is *kalam Allah* and no translation is considered to be the Qur'an. When translations are authorised, they are usually printed alongside the Arabic text.[20] The Qur'an is regarded as the supreme aesthetic work of the Arabic language: indeed, the inimitability of the Qur'an is an important Islamic doctrine. To the faithful it is not necessary, however, to understand Arabic in order to appreciate the numinous quality of God's speech. This quality is enhanced by traditional methods of reciting the text and the more accomplished Qur'an reciters attract large followings in Islamic societies.

Considerable honour attaches to any individual Muslims who memorise the entire text of the Qur'an and it is believed that such a person (a *hafiz* or 'guardian' of the Qur'an) is assured of reaching Paradise. Even those who do not understand much Arabic endeavour to commit portions of the Book to memory. In mosques and Islamic centres around New Zealand there are evening and week-end classes in which young boys and girls for whom Arabic is a foreign language repeat aloud the sacred text in order to fix it in their minds. The best-known passage is the *Fatihah* or 'opening' chapter, since this is recited often in Islamic worship and is regarded as a summary of the message of the Qur'an:

> In the name of God, the Merciful, the Compassionate
>
> Praise belongs to God, the Lord of all Being,
> the All-merciful, the All-compassionate,
> the Master of the Day of Doom.
> Thee only we serve; to Thee alone we pray for succour.
> Guide us in the straight path,
> the path of those whom Thou hast blessed,
> not of those against whom Thou art wrathful,
> nor of those who are astray.[21]

The 'Day of Doom' is a theme which recurs frequently in the Qur'an and Islamic eschatology is very similar to the traditional Christian view of the last things. In describing the final destiny of human beings, the primary concern of the Qur'an and subsequent Muslim reflection has not been to satisfy mere curiosity, but to encourage righteous living by engendering fear of punishment and hope for reward. Allah alone knows when the day of judgment will be, but its arrival will be heralded by cosmic disturbances:

> When the sun shall be darkened,
> when the stars shall be thrown down,
> when the mountains shall be set moving ...
> then shall a soul know what it has produced.[22]

Islamic accounts of the end of the world sometimes describe the coming of the *mahdi* or divinely-guided one, a pious Muslim who will restore true Islam. According to a minority view, the *mahdi* is in fact Jesus, while Twelver Shi'is believe him to be the twelfth *imam*. After the sounding of the trumpet by the angel Israfil, all created beings will be temporarily extinguished and then restored to life for the judgment. For everyone who has lived, there is a book recording good and bad deeds. Those destined for salvation will receive the book in their right hand while those heading for damnation will receive it in the left hand. According to the Qur'an, each individual is responsible for her or his own deeds and there will be no intercession at the final judgment. This view has been softened, however, by the widely accepted popular belief in the intercessory role of Muhammad and even of lesser saints.

Once judged, people will be sent to Heaven ('the Garden') or Hell ('the Fire'). In the Garden, there are rivers of milk, honey and wine which has no intoxicating effects. The righteous will eat abundant fruit while reclining on luxurious couches and being served by handsome youths. Men will enjoy the company of the *houris*, chaste but seductive virgins who are a special creation. Despite the sensual imagery of the Qur'an - which most Muslims take quite literally - tradition has tended to sanction the idea that the greatest joy of Paradise will be the vision of God.

Meanwhile in Hell, which is guarded over by nineteen angels, the wicked will be tormented by fire and forced to eat horrid food. The Qur'an lays great stress on the terrible sufferings of Hell but it is widely believed among Muslims that even the wicked will eventually be purged of their sins and conveyed to the Garden - at least if they believed in God during their earthly lives.

Shari'ah: the divine law

Islam is the religion of obedience towards God, and in the *Fatihah* Muslims pray for divine guidance to keep them on the straight path. What, then, does Allah require? To answer this question in detail, Muslims have developed a complex science of jurisprudence called *fiqh*, or 'understanding'. What they seek to understand is the *shari'ah*, the law of God, which is known in its fullness only to Him. The *shari'ah* includes rules for worship, personal hygiene, etiquette, family law, taxation, commerce, government, the conduct of international relations, and more besides.

The *shari'ah*, a word originally applied to the path to a water hole, is a path or guide for human behaviour, both individual and collective. It prescribes limits within which people may act and lays down punishments for those who violate its provisions. A characteristic feature of the *shari'ah* is the classification of actions according to five categories on a scale from duties which must be performed to sins which must not be committed. Mandatory actions include, for example, worship at the prescribed times and fasting in the month of *Ramadan*. Actions in the next three categories are all permitted (*halal*) but range from the recommended (such as performing supererogatory acts of piety), through actions which are legally and morally neutral (which includes most everyday activities) to the reprehensible (such as smoking which damages one's health). Prohibited actions (*haram*) include sexual transgressions, theft, murder, idolatry, or eating forbidden foods. Different rules apply to different people or in special circumstances; for example, during menstruation women are not required to carry out the ritual obligations incumbent on them at other times and prayers and fasting may be postponed in cases of necessity, such as travel or illness. Moreover, there is often disagreement among Muslim scholars concerning the precise classification of particular actions.

Throughout Islamic history, the *shari'ah* has been honoured as the ideal to which society should aspire but in practice the requirements of the law have often been ignored. One of the great themes of Islamic history - and one which is much in evidence in our own time - is the emergence of reform movements which seek to apply the *shari'ah* more fully in all spheres of life. Certain aspects of Islamic law, notably those concerning family matters and religious ritual, have traditionally been more fully applied than others, not least because they do not impinge upon the freedom of rulers.

Much of the divine law is stated explicitly in the Qur'an, although its requirements are subject to differing interpretations. In a context making provision for orphans, for example, the Qur'an indicates that a man may have up to four wives on condition that he treat them all equally. It is often argued by modern Muslims that this text must be interpreted in the light of a later one which declares the impossibility of treating several wives equally and that the two passages together amount to a prohibition of polygamy in most circumstances.[23]

To answer questions not dealt with directly in the Qur'an, Muslims have recourse to the *sunnah* or 'exemplary tradition' of the Prophet. Since Muhammad lived in accordance with the will of God, his example can be followed in all matters of religious belief and practice. The sunnah is known through reports (hadiths) of Muhammad's words and deeds. For a *hadith* to be accepted as 'sound' (*sahih*), it requires an *isnad* or list of reliable and trustworthy Muslims who passed on the report from the original eye-witness. Various collections of hadiths were made and the two most authoritative compilations are those of the ninth century scholars al-Bukhari and Muslim, both of which are available in English translation.[24]

Not all legal or doctrinal issues can be resolved by citing appropriate passages from the Qur'an or hadiths, so Sunni scholars appeal to the consensus (*ijma'*) of their predecessors and to analogy (*qiyas*) in further elucidating the *shari'ah*. Together, the Qur'an, the *sunnah*, *ijma'* and *qiyas* constitute the four 'roots of jurisprudence' (*usul al-fiqh*).

Most Muslims do not have a detailed knowledge of *fiqh*, for it requires many years of study to master the disciplines involved. When Muslims need specialist information about law, for example on matters like fasting, inheritance, divorce, contraception or finance, they consult an *'alim* or 'scholar' who has undertaken the necessary training. Strictly speaking, there are no clergy in Islam but only *'ulama'* (plural of *'alim*), experts in the sciences of religion, of which *fiqh* is the most important. In this respect, Islam is like Judaism whose rabbis are essentially teachers of the law rather than priests or ministers.[25] When no *'ulama'* are available to conduct worship or to preach, these functions can be taken over by suitably pious and informed laymen. In New Zealand, where there are few *'ulama'*, this is the rule rather than the exception, although Auckland and Wellington each have qualified Islamic teachers.

One aspect of the *shari'ah* is not only relevant to the daily lives of Muslims but is also particularly important for New Zealand. Muslims, like other religious groups, are distinguished by their food laws. According to the Qur'an, the dietary regulations of the Jews are a punishment from God for their transgressions. Jesus and Muhammad released their followers from some of these restrictions and the Qur'an allowed Muslims to eat the food of the People of the Book. Muslims may eat any unfermented grains or vegetables but the Qur'an forbids the consumption of pork, blood, carrion or food which has been sacrificed to idols. These prohibitions, however, can be suspended in cases of necessity, such as the threat of starvation. On the basis of the Prophet's *sunnah*, this list of foods classified as *haram* ('forbidden') has been much extended. The various schools of *fiqh* disagree about the status of some foods not forbidden by the Qur'an, but most regard donkeys, reptiles and carnivorous animals as *haram*. Sea creatures are generally accepted as *halal* but crustaceans and shellfish are considered *haram* by some jurists.

To be *halal* ('permitted'), meat must not only come from certain animals, but it must also have been slaughtered with a clean, sharp knife according to the correct procedure and preferably by a Muslim. As it is being killed, the animal is faced towards Mecca and the words *Bism Allah... Allahu akbar* ('In the name of God ... God is most great') are pronounced over it.[26] God has permitted the taking of animal life in order to sustain human life and His authority must be acknowledged. No cruelty is permitted - for example, the animal should not be held down while the knife is being sharpened. The gullet, the windpipe and the two jugular veins must be severed from ear to ear to ensure a quick death. In New Zealand freezing works where *halal* killing takes place, animals are first stunned with an electric shock and this is acceptable as long as it does not cause death before the throat is cut. A further requirement for *halal* meat is that it must not come into contact with non-*halal* meat, such as pork, in the course of processing.

In New Zealand, *halal* meat is certified by three agencies. The Iranian government employs its own inspectors to ensure that meat sent to that country is *halal*, although the slaughterers need not be Iranians or even Shi'i Muslims. Meat destined for other markets is certified by Islamic-New Zealand Meat Management Limited (a Wellington-based company established in 1982) or by FIANZ. Both organisations have taken a prominent role in the securing of overseas markets for New Zealand meat. The development of *halal* meat exporting has created employment opportunities in this country for Muslims who are either permanent residents or temporary visitors. It has also ensured the ready availability of *halal* meat for New Zealand Muslims.

Arkan: the pillars of Islam

Muslims speak of their religion as being supported by five pillars (*arkan*, singular *rukn*) of which the first is the *shahadah*, which is pronounced frequently, especially in daily worship. The other four pillars are the daily ritual prayers (*salat*), paying the *zakat* tax, fasting (*sawm* or *siyam*) during the month of Ramadan and going on pilgrimage (*hajj*) to Mecca.

Salat is performed five times each day: *salat al-fajr* (just before sunrise), *salat al-zuhr* (shortly after noon), *salat al-'asr* (middle to late afternoon), *salat al-maghrib* (immediately after sunset) and *salat al-'isha'* (during the evening or night). These times are determined by the length of time between sunrise and sunset and therefore vary according to the season. In each mosque or Islamic centre there is a chart or set of clock faces indicating the current times of worship. It is not usually practicable in a country where Muslims are such a small minority to worship at all the correct times so many Muslims perform at the end of the day those prayers which have been missed. Muslims may worship in any clean place and in New Zealand most would find it impossible to go to a mosque regularly each day (although in every mosque the five daily prayers must be performed).

The Auckland mosque, located in Ponsonby, has been functioning since 1980 and the Christchurch mosque since 1985. Before these facilities became available, the Muslim communities of Auckland and Christchurch used converted houses for *salat* and other activities. Muslims in other areas, notably South Auckland, Hamilton, Palmerston North and Wellington, still use houses adapted for the purpose and refer to them as 'Islamic centres' rather than mosques. At the time of writing there are efforts being made to build a mosque in Wellington and to establish further centres in Auckland and Dunedin. A mosque (Arabic *masjid* or 'place of prostration') is more than simply a building for worship: it is also a place where meetings and classes can be held. The two mosques and, in a more modest way, the various Islamic centres, have libraries, facilities for holding seminars and accommodation for visitors and staff employed by the Muslim community.

To perform validly an act of worship, the believer must be in a state of ritual purity. Impurity can be caused by contact with anything unclean or by bodily emissions. Before entering a mosque, it is customary to remove one's shoes. Inside there are washing facilities, since in preparation for *salat* a Muslim must perform *wudu'* or ritual ablutions. While saying certain prayers, water is used to wash the hands, mouth, nose, face, arms, head, ears and feet (in that order). The transition from impurity to purity symbolises a movement from the ordinary world to a sacred context.

Shortly before the *salat* is due to begin, a *mu'adhdhin* ('muezzin') gives the call to prayer (*adhan*). In an Islamic country this call would be chanted from a minaret either in person or by playing a recording over a loudspeaker, but in New Zealand the *mu'adhdhin* simply stands up inside the mosque. With few variations, the *adhan* consists of these seven phrases (in Arabic):

> God is most great. (four times)
> I bear witness that there is no god but God. (twice)
> I bear witness that Muhammad is the Messenger of God. (twice)
> Come to *salat*. (twice)
> Come to salvation. (twice)
> God is most great. (twice)
> There is no god but God.

When they assemble for *salat*, the worshippers stand in neat rows facing the Ka'bah in Mecca. The *mihrab*, which indicates the direction (*qiblah*) of the holy city, is usually a niche in the wall of the mosque often decorated with calligraphy employing the words of the *shahadah*. Following the lead of the *imam*, who stands in front of them, the worshippers perform a series of actions called a *rak'ah*. This involves reciting the *Fatihah* and usually another passage from the Qur'an, bowing, prostrating oneself so that the toes, knees, palms and forehead touch the floor, sitting and then making a second prostration. These actions are accompanied by brief prayers and familiar phrases like the *shahadah* and the *takbir* (*Allahu akbar*: 'God is most great'). The number of rak'ahs varies according to which *salat* is being performed: it is usually two, three or four. At the end of the *salat*, the worshippers turn to their right and then to their left while wishing God's peace and mercy upon their guardian or recording angels and upon their fellow worshippers. It is a common practice to perform additional rak'ahs when the *salat* is completed.

FIANZ

Friday prayers at Masjid al-Nur

Islamic worship clearly symbolises the main features of the religion. The tight ranks of worshippers, moving in unison and all facing the direction of the Ka'bah, constitute a fellowship of equals making public obeisance to their Lord. It is, indeed, a universal fellowship, for the same form of worship is carried out by other Muslims throughout the world, all using Arabic and all facing Mecca. Moreover, since the time for prayer varies according to the season, *salat* is probably being performed somewhere in the world at all times.

There is no sabbath in Islam, but Friday is known in Arabic as *yawm al-jum'ah* ('day of the community' or 'congregation') for all men are expected to attend the Friday midday worship, which is called *salat al-jum'ah*, 'congregational worship'. It is customary to precede this *salat* with a sermon or *khutbah*. Even in New Zealand, this usually begins in Arabic but is mostly in English. Typically, the *khutbah* consists of an exhortation to righteous living and draws heavily upon the

Qur'an and the *sunnah* of the Prophet as expressed in the *hadith* literature. Sometimes it is read from a book but if the preacher (*khatib*) has some religious training, he may compose his own. The sermon is preached from a *minbar*, a pulpit consisting of a raised platform reached by a series of steps.

Men and women worship separately in a mosque and women are not required to attend, even for *salat al-jum'ah*. If women are present during worship, their part of the mosque is separated from the men's by a curtain or screen. Given the nature of the *salat* ritual, it would be considered immodest for women to pray alongside or in front of men.[27] The Auckland mosque was built without ablution facilities or an adequate place where women can worship, although in Christ-church full provision has been made for them in the Masjid al-Nur. Even there, however, not many women regularly attend *salat*. It is assumed that married women particularly are too involved in domestic responsibilities, especially child rearing, to be free to attend a mosque. Attendance by women varies according to local custom, and the lack of facilities in the Auckland mosque reflects the cultural background of those who built and manage it. The roles of *mu'adhdhin, khatib* and *imam* are invariably performed by a man (unless there are only women present). Although some knowledge of Arabic is needed, little religious training is required and one person often fulfills several roles.

Zakat, the religious obligation to give alms, is not a ritual in the narrow sense of the word, but is regarded, along with the other pillars of Islam, as a form of worship or *'ibadat*. It is also an expression of Islam's concern for the poor and of the sense of fellowship which ought to prevail within the *ummah*. In modern times the payment of *zakat* has become, even in most Islamic countries, a voluntary act of piety which individuals carry out in the manner they think most appropriate. Traditionally the amount is assessed at the rate of two and a half percent of any surplus wealth (that is, wealth which is not required for immediate day to day needs) which has been owned for one year. The money (or goods) can be distributed privately or through a charitable agency to those in need. The word *zakat* conveys the idea of purification, with the implication that one is not entitled to keep wealth unless the poor have been given a share. At the end of the month of Ramadan, a modest additional alms-tax, the *zakat al-fitr*, is collected for the poor, so that they will be able to celebrate the end of the fast.

Ramadan is an especially sacred and joyful time. Muslims are enjoined to observe a strict fast from dawn until sunset for the entire twenty-nine or thirty days, eating and drinking only during the hours of darkness. (Not until the new moon has actually been sighted is the month considered to be over.) Fasting is seen as a means of practising self-discipline, of purifying the body and soul, of experiencing the sufferings of the poor and so engendering greater compassion towards them and, by these means, of drawing closer to God.

The Islamic lunar calendar, which dates from 622 CE, the year of the *hijrah*, is eleven days shorter than the solar calendar, so the fast of Ramadan progresses through the seasons. This is seen as a blessing from Allah which eases the rigours of fasting in hot climates. During Ramadan, Muslims are expected to take particular care in the fulfilment of their religious duties and any good deeds performed in this month receive an extra reward from God. One of the most important practices associated with Ramadan is the recitation of the whole Qur'an over the course of the month. Where a *hafiz* is available, the evening worship is followed by the recitation of consecutive segments of the Qur'an, interspersed with rak'ahs and appropriate prayers.

On the first day of *Shawwal*, the month following Ramadan, there is a festival (*'Id al-Fitr*)[28] to celebrate the breaking of the fast. On this day, Muslims gather at their local mosque or Islamic centre for a special *salat* in the morning. After the prayers, the occasion is celebrated with food and presents for the children. There are many more people at the mosque than usual (including some who are but rare attenders at *salat al-jum'ah*). Men and women are segregated (if there are women present) but young children run freely between the men's and women's areas. The afternoon is spent in visiting friends and relatives.

Two months later, during the final month of the Islamic year, the annual pilgrimage to Mecca takes place. All adult Muslims are required to perform the *hajj* once in their lives, if they are physically and financially able. Before departing, they must be free of debt and make a will - conditions which reflect the dangers of travel in former times and even now. The pilgrimage is undertaken in a state of ritual purity or *ihram*, which is symbolised by the wearing of identical white garments. Differences of nationality or social status are thus temporarily dissolved in a community of equals.

While the rituals of the *hajj* can only be carried out on certain days of the month of Dhu al-Hijjah, there is also a 'lesser pilgrimage', the *'umrah*, which may be performed at any time of the year. Its ceremonies all take place in the immediate vicinity of the Sacred Mosque, in which stands the Ka'bah, and some of them are also part of the *hajj*. Most pilgrims perform both sets of rituals during their visit to the holy city. When they arrive at Mecca, they enter the Sacred Mosque and walk around the Ka'bah seven times in an anticlockwise direction. The distinctive rite of the *'umrah*, which may be performed at this time, consists of running seven times along the corridor which connects the hills of Safa and Marwa. This action recalls Hagar's frantic search for water after she and her son Ishmael had been abandoned by Abraham. Near the Ka'bah is the sacred well of Zamzam, which miraculously began to flow when Ishmael kicked the ground where he had been laid down by his mother.

Most of the rituals associated with the *hajj* recall the story of Abraham, Hagar and their son Ishmael. One of the most important ceremonies occurs on the ninth of Dhu al-Hijjah on the plain of 'Arafat, twenty-three kilometers east of Mecca. From just after noon until sunset, the pilgrims, after listening to a sermon, spend time in prayer and reflection, recalling Abraham's decision to sacrifice Ishmael at God's command.[29] Next day at Mina, on the way back to Mecca, they throw seven pebbles at three stone pillars representing Satan - an action which recalls Abraham's refusal to succumb to the Devil's temptation to disobey the command to sacrifice Ishmael. Having proved his obedience, Abraham was told to spare his son and sacrificed instead a ram. This sacrifice is recalled by the pilgrims who slaughter sheep, goats, cows or camels.

At the same time, Muslims throughout the world also celebrate the festival of sacrifice or *'Id al-Adha*, which is the greatest festival of the Islamic year. Those who can afford to kill an animal should give one third of the meat to their neighbours, one third to the poor and keep one third for themselves. In New Zealand the festival is celebrated much like the *'Id al-Fitr*, with a special *salat* in the morning followed by food and the visiting of friends and relatives. Since Islamic festivals do not usually fall on weekends or public holidays, many Muslims have to work and the festivities are muted by comparison with those held in Islamic countries. Nor is it possible to bring home a sheep for slaughter. Some Muslims make arrangements to have an animal killed on their behalf, while others may go to a farm to perform the sacrifice themselves. The slaughter of animals for *'Id al-Adha* follows the usual requirements for *halal* killing. In Mecca itself, the *hajj* ceremonies continue for another three days and many pilgrims take the opportunity to visit the tomb of the Prophet in Medina before returning home.

By means of the festival of sacrifice, the whole Islamic world participates in the *hajj* and calls to mind the significance of its rituals. The unity of the *ummah* is reaffirmed and the duty of complete obedience to Allah, as demonstrated by Abraham, is reenacted. In some cultures, Muslims who have undertaken the pilgrimage are especially honoured and bear the title *hajji*, or *hajjiyah* in its feminine form.

There are other Islamic festivals, but they do not have the same importance as the two 'Ids. Some Muslims celebrate the birthday of the Prophet, but others regard this as an innovation and not a part of genuine Islam. Recently, for example, there was disagreement in the Wellington community over whether this occasion should be observed. Some regarded it as an opportunity to express love for God's Messenger and to recall his deeds in the service of the faith, while others argued that the date of Muhammad's birth was not known with any certainty and its celebration was not sanctioned by the Qur'an or the *sunnah*.

Another potential source of disagreement among Muslims is sufism (Arabic *tasawwuf*). The earliest sufis were ascetics who apparently wore uncomfortable woollen clothing which gave them their name deriving from the Arabic word *suf* (wool). They were concerned to experience their religion personally rather than simply follow external observances. To this end they avoided worldliness and cultivated a deep sense of the presence of Allah - often by means of practices which were frowned upon by the rest of the community. Sufi *dhikr* (literally the 'remembrance' of Allah), as such practices are called, includes, for example, rhythmic repetition of the name 'Allah' and dancing as in the case of the whirling dervishes.

From the twelfth century CE, the sufis began to form brotherhoods under the leadership of recognised masters called shaykhs. These brotherhoods are called tariqahs or 'pathways', although the word *tariqah* applies primarily to the distinctive religious teaching and practices laid down by the first shaykh, rather than to the group made up of his followers. Among the Muslims of New Zealand there are no sufi tariqahs but a few overseas visitors belong to such groups in their home countries. While some Muslims here speak of the excesses of popular sufism, others regard the *sufi* way as an ideal to be emulated and the repetition of pious words or phrases is probably quite common as a private meditative practice. Muslims who follow the *sufi* path, however, are too modest to accept for themselves the appellation *sufi*, which they reserve for their teachers and mentors.[30]

Da'wah: the Islamic mission in a non-Muslim society

According to Islamic belief, all people ought to surrender themselves to God. The call (*da'wah*) to Islam is addressed not only to non-Muslims, however, but also to Muslims themselves, especially to those who neglect their religious duties. Any activity which encourages or enables believers to live more fully the life of Islam, or which attracts non-Muslims to the faith, can be called *da'wah*. Since Muslims constitute but a tiny proportion of New Zealand's population and since most of them have not been here long, the energies of the community in recent years have been focused on the tasks of organisation and the development of facilities. To put *da'wah* in its context, it must be asked whether living in a non-Islamic society raises special concerns for New Zealand Muslims.

It is not difficult to live as a Muslim in this country and Muslims regard their religion as fully compatible with the responsibilities of good citizenship. The essential requirements of Islam, such as regular worship and almsgiving, can be carried out in any country which permits freedom of religion. With the establishment of mosques and Islamic centres, the employment of Islamic teachers and the large-scale production of *halal* meat, it is, indeed, becoming easier for Muslims to carry out their religious duties.

Living in New Zealand can even have a salutary effect. Quite commonly, Muslims arriving here rediscover their Islamic identity, for the religious practices they could take for granted in their home country must now be done consciously or neglected entirely. Since foreign students and refugees, in particular, may meet very few fellow nationals in New Zealand, religious rather than ethnic groups can provide them with the support they need in an unfamiliar country.

Muslims in New Zealand have strong ties with fellow believers in other countries, not only because such a high proportion of them are temporary visitors to this country. The community regularly hosts visiting speakers and accepts aid from the wealthier Muslim countries for building mosques. International Islamic organisations provide religious literature and the Australasian representatives of the Saudi Arabian-based World Assembly of Muslim Youth (WAMY) and the Malaysian-based Regional Islamic Da'wah Council of Southeast Asia and the Pacific (RISEAP) are both located in New Zealand. Muslims from this country often travel overseas for conferences and religious training. In the summer of 1988-9 seventeen 'reverts' were given a sponsored study tour to Saudi Arabia where they undertook the *'umrah* and visited Medina. For some it was their first exposure to an Islamic culture and a unique opportunity to learn more about Islam.

FIANZ

Children at 'Mosque and books exhibition', Wellington Islamic Centre

The strong sense of community among Muslims of diverse origin is reflected in their practice of referring to each other as 'brothers' and 'sisters'. At the core of each community is the mosque or Islamic centre which is often used for meetings concerned with non-religious matters, ranging from exotic cooking to promotion of the Palestinian cause. A noteworthy feature of all such meetings is the segregation of men and women; it is not considered proper for the two sexes to mix indiscriminately. If women and men are in the same room, they tend to sit apart. Just how the relations between the sexes should be conducted is a matter for some debate and in certain quarters it is felt that there is a need for education on the role of women in Islam.

There is no disagreement, however, about rejecting prevalent western sexual mores. Prospective marital partners do not date or spend time together unchaperoned. They may seek information about each other through mutual acquaintances but are unlikely to get to know one another very well before marrying. Romantic love is not thought to be a reliable basis for a successful marriage. It is considered a religious duty to marry and raise children, for Islam has no place for monasticism. Marriage (*nikah*) is a legal contract between two families, a contract which is signed by the groom and the bride's 'guardian' (*wali*), who is usually a close male relative. For a marriage to take place, the bride must give her consent before two witnesses who report this to the *imam* and the groom. If the bride is present in the hall or mosque where the wedding takes place, she will be sitting with the other women. No marriage can take place without the groom's giving a suitable gift (*mahr*) to the bride; this may be anything agreed upon, from jewellery to a mortgage payment, its value depending on the means of the groom. Any reputable Muslim man can conduct a wedding ceremony but in practice the Islamic community has its own officially recognised marriage celebrants so that weddings can be performed in accordance with both the civil law and the *shari'ah*. As long as the legal requirements are met, the wedding may be celebrated according to the national customs of those involved. If the partners are New Zealanders, for example, a wedding cake might be considered appropriate.

The birth of a child may be celebrated among friends and there are also customary religious requirements. After the newly-born baby has been washed and clothed, the *adhan* is pronounced in its right ear and the *iqamah* (the instruction to begin *salat*) is spoken into the left ear by a male relative. One week later the *'aqiqah* sacrifice is offered: two sheep for a boy or one for a girl. New Zealand Muslims either make arrangements to have the animals killed locally or send money overseas for an animal to be killed on their behalf. The meat is distributed according to the wishes of the baby's parents. Circumcision (*khitan*) of boys is considered an important Islamic practice by most Muslims, although it is not a strict requirement of the *shari'ah*. In many countries, it is the occasion for a public celebration at some time during childhood but in New Zealand the operation is performed without religious ceremony by the family doctor while the boy is still a baby.

Where there are large enough Muslim populations, certain sections of local cemeteries are allocated to them, as for other religious communities. Before burial, the body is thoroughly washed according to a set procedure and to the accompaniment of certain prayers. It is then perfumed and wrapped in a simple white cotton shroud. The funeral prayer, (*salat al-janazah*), is usually led by a relative of the deceased and performed either at the mosque or in the funeral parlour. A grave is dug facing Mecca and the body is lain on its right side, without a coffin, although planks may be placed over it before the hole is filled in. Care must be taken in preparing a body for burial, for the dead are very sensitive to rough handling and to disrespectful comments. In the intermediate state (*barzakh*) between death and resurrection, the dead are interrogated by the angels Munkar and Nakir. (To prepare for this questioning, the deceased has been reminded of the *shahadah* before burial.) Then the righteous may be temporarily rewarded with a foretaste of the joys of the Garden, while the damned suffer the 'punishment of the grave' before lapsing into unconsciousness until the resurrection.

Although rites of passage and other requirements of Islamic life present no difficulties in New Zealand - despite some significant differences from the dominant culture - there are certain aspects of New Zealand society which offer a challenge to Muslims. Unless one is surrounded by very understanding people, it can be difficult to find a suitable place to perform *salat* at the correct times. Observance of the Islamic dress code, which demands that women be covered entirely except for the face and hands (and that men be covered from the navel to the knees) requires a willingness to stand out for one's convictions.[31] Conscientious Muslims need to be wary of what they eat, since even non-meat dishes sometimes contain non-*halal* animal fat. A safe option in cases of doubt can be to eat vegetarian food. Like the avoidance of alcohol, this has become an increasingly respected choice in New Zealand. Another area of difficulty is the strict prohibition of usury (*riba*) by the *shari'ah*. It is almost impossible to avoid completely the taking of interest and Muslims with bank accounts usually give it away to a charitable cause. Money not needed for immediate use can be invested in shares, business or property: the difference is that whereas taking interest can lead to exploitation, profits derived from risk-taking are seen as earned.

The secular and materialistic tone of New Zealand society is of particular concern to parents, who fear that even the education system endorses values incompatible with Islam. Some professional people do not intend to reside permanently in New Zealand and can afford to return home periodically. A more long-term approach will be the establishment of Islamic schools, which is being discussed. Some parents already take charge of the education of their own young children with the approval of the education authorities. By means of regional and national youth camps, the isolation of being a small minority group is reduced and Muslim children can reinforce their Islamic identity. FIANZ has set itself the task of preparing a national syllabus for the religion classes held in the mosques and Islamic centres and there are competitions for the best Qur'an reciters in the country. These are held during national gatherings of New Zealand Muslims on holiday weekends, particularly Easter. For adults, too, most of the regional associations organise discussion groups and classes in Arabic language or Qur'an recitation.

Efforts are being made to encourage non-practising Muslims to participate in the activities of the community, for example by giving them prayer timetables and Islamic calendars indicating the dates of festivals. The most concentrated action to recall the indifferent to a fuller practice of Islam is the *Tabligh* movement which is particularly strong in Auckland.[32] Founded in the 1920s by Muhammad Ilyas, the Tabligh is very much an Indian phenomenon - for example its meetings are often conducted partly in Urdu - and is not viewed in an entirely favourable light by some other Muslims. The Tabligh brethren visit their fellow Muslims, encouraging them to practise their religion more vigorously, setting high standards for themselves and others. Some argue that the rules endorsed by the Tabligh are not all sanctioned by the *sunnah*. Regular meetings are held for worship and study, as well as large-scale gatherings lasting several days. Even critics of the movement acknowledge its effectiveness, but the level of teaching on Islam offered at the Tabligh meetings is quite basic.

Although not actively seeking converts to Islam through a regular programme of proselytising, Muslims do find that many opportunities for *da'wah* arise in daily life and they welcome enquiries about their religion. As an organisation, FIANZ is active in promoting greater understanding of Islam among New Zealanders, notably by distributing literature, visiting schools and other community organisations and inviting interested groups to visit the mosques. An important recent development has been the establishment in Christchurch of an information centre able to supply literature, videos and cassette tapes on Islamic topics. It is considered important to respond to the mis-information and prejudice sometimes encountered.

Overall, Muslims with whom I have spoken express satisfaction with the higher profile of Islam in New Zealand during recent years. Locally-produced radio and television programmes have offered a more positive view of Islam and it is commonly felt among Muslims that in society at large there is an increasing appreciation of their religion. The Islamic community in this country is growing in size and its organisational base is now firmly established. Current projects include the provision of further Islamic centres, educational facilities, student accommodation and the building of a mosque in Wellington. Although the community will continue to be highly cosmopolitan in the foreseeable future, local converts are taking an increasingly prominent role in its affairs.

Notes

I should like to thank the many people who contributed to the writing of this chapter, especially those Muslims whom I interviewed at length or who made helpful comments on the complete draft.

1. Some variant spellings such as 'Moslem', 'Mohammed' and 'Koran', are sanctioned by long use, but are less accurate renderings of the original Arabic.
2. The word *imam* initially referred to one who led other Muslims in worship, and was then applied to the man who led the community in other matters also. Another use of the word is as an honorific title for a religious scholar.

3. As well as Twelver Shi'is, there are also Seveners (Isma'ilis) and Fivers (Zaydis) who recognise fewer direct descendants of 'Ali as imams and have their own distinctive views on how the *ummah* should be governed.

4. While Shi'is use the word *imam* to refer to the rightful leader of the Islamic *ummah*, Sunnis have traditionally tended to use the word *khalifah* or 'caliph', although they also often use the word *imam*.

5. In modern times the Ottoman (Turkish) Sultans claimed that the caliphate had been passed on to them by descendants of the 'Abbasids but the Ottoman sultanate and caliphate were abolished by the revolutionary government of Mustafa Kemal Ataturk in the 1920s.

6. For a list of countries with high proportions of Muslim inhabitants, see *A Handbook of Living Religions*, edited by John R. Hinnells, Harmondsworth: Penguin Books, 1984, pp. 164-5.

7. *New Zealand Census of Population and Dwellings, 1986, Series C, Report 14: Religious Professions*, Wellington: Department of Statistics, 1988, p. 13.

8. The discrepancy between census figures and Muslim estimates of the size of New Zealand's Muslim population antedates the Fiji coups of 1987. It is certainly true that the census figures were out of date by the time they were published, but there is no other reliable source of demographic information. See further W.E. Shepard, 'The Islamic Contribution' in *Religion in New Zealand Society*, edited by Brian Colless and Peter Donovan, Palmerston North: The Dunmore Press, 2nd edn, 1985, pp. 201-2.

9. Asia: 507 males and 408 females; Pacific Islands: 333 males and 213 females. *Census*, p. 24.

10. *Census*, p. 13.

11. 357 males and 303 females. *Census*, p. 24.

12. For the following, see Shepard, pp. 183-188.

13. Another pious phrase in common use after mention of the name 'Allah' is *Subhanahu wa ta'ala* ('May He be praised and exalted'). This is often abbreviated in written texts to 'S.W.T.'

14. It would appear from this account that Iblis is an angel, but the Qur'an explicitly states that he is one of the *jinn* and this is consistent with his claim to be made of fire. The apparent contradiction is explained by the view that Iblis, though a *jinn*, was so pious that he was ranked among the angels.

15. These include many biblical figures, namely Adam, Noah, Enoch, Abraham, Lot, Ishmael, Isaac, Jacob, Joseph, Moses, Aaron, Elijah, Elisha, David, Solomon, Ezekiel, Jonah, Job, John the Baptist, his father Zechariah, and Jesus Christ - not all of whom are usually thought of as prophets by Jews or Christians. Some of the most important biblical prophets, for example Isaiah, Jeremiah, Hosea and Amos, are not mentioned by name but the Qur'an does describe the careers of four Arabian prophets: Hud, Salih, Shu'ayb and Muhammad himself.

16. See especially Deuteronomy 18:18 and John 14:16.

17. Qur'an 33:40.

18. In English this is often translated as 'Peace be upon him' (or abbreviated to 'Pbuh' in a written text). The latter expression (*'alayhi al-salam* in Arabic) is also used after mentioning the name of any of the other prophets.

19. The city is also hallowed by its religious significance in pre-Islamic times and by its association with Jesus and other prophets.

20. The text and translation most used by English-speaking Muslims is *The Holy Qur'an*, translated by A. Yusuf Ali (first published in Lahore between 1934 and 1937 but subsequently republished in various editions, including Brentwood, Maryland, Amana Corporation, revd edn, 1989).

21. *The Koran Interpreted*, translated by Arthur J. Arberry, London: Allen and Unwin, 1955; reprinted by Oxford University Press, 1964, p. 1. Arberry's version is the most successful attempt to convey in English something of the literary quality of the Qur'an.

22. Qur'an 81:1-3,14 (Arberry's translation, p. 632).

23. Qur'an 4:3 and 4:129.

24. M.M. Khan, *The translation of the meanings of Sahih al-Bukhari*, Chicago: Kazi Publications, 3rd edn, 1979, (Arabic and English text in 9 vols); and A.H. Siddiqi, *Sahih Muslim*, Lahore: Sh. Muhammad Ashraf, 1973, (English text only in 4 vols). Unfortunately only an abbreviated form of the *isnad* is given in these translations.

25. Twelver Shi'is, whose methods of interpreting the *shari'ah* differ in certain respects from Sunni methodology, place greater emphasis on the authority of individual scholars. The highest ranking Shi'i *'ulama'* are given the honorific title 'Ayatollah' (*'Ayat Allah*), meaning 'miraculous sign of God'. Sunni *'ulama'* in New Zealand are usually referred to by the titles *Shaykh* or *Mawlana*.

26. These words are an abbreviated version of a longer formula which would be impracticable to recite in full where large numbers of animals are being killed, such as in a freezing works.

27. In fact, Islam generally discourages the mingling of the sexes, but it is perhaps all the more imperative in the case of *salat*.

28. *'Id* is often spelt *Eid*.

29. The Qur'an does not name the son Abraham was commanded to sacrifice, but the context implies that it was his first-born, Ishmael, and not the latter's half-brother Isaac - an interpretation upheld by Islamic tradition. (See Qur'an 37:99-113).

30. Sufism, with its emphasis on religious experience and esoteric knowledge, has held considerable appeal for westerners and there are several sufi-type groups in New Zealand. Members of these groups are not really Muslims but seekers after religious knowledge and experience who draw upon a variety of religious traditions. See *Beliefs and Practices in New Zealand: a Directory*, Palmerston North, Massey University, revised edn. 1985, pp. 101, 117-19.

31. The small number of women in New Zealand who cover even their faces belong to a Malaysian religious organisation - the *Darul Arqam* - which endorses a very strict interpretation of the *shari'ah*.

32. See further Shepard, pp. 195-197.

Further reading

Denny, Frederick Mathewson, *An Introduction to Islam*, New York/London: Macmillan/Collier Macmillan, 1986.

Martin, Richard C., *Islam: a Cultural Perspective*, Englewood Cliffs, New Jersey: Prentice-Hall, 1982.

Maududi, Sayyid Abul A'la., *Towards Understanding Islam*, translated and edited by Khurshid Ahmad (various publishers since 1960, including Leicester: Islamic Foundation, 1980).

Macintyre, Ron, (ed.), *New Zealand and the Middle East*, Christchurch: Australasian Middle East Studies Association, 1987.

Qaradawi, Yusuf al-, *The Lawful and the Prohibited in Islam*, translated by Kamal El-Helbawy *et al.*, Indianapolis: American Trust, c.1960.

Ruthven, Malise, *Islam in the World*, Harmondsworth: Penguin Books, 1984.

Shepard, William, 'The Islamic Contribution' in *Religion in New Zealand Society*, edited by Brian Colless and Peter Donovan, Palmerston North: Dunmore Press, 2nd edn, 1985.

Judaism

Norman Simms

Almost all New Zealand's different religions began long ago in other parts of the world. For Jews, their origins are in the lands of the Near and Middle East; in the ancient and even archaic legends of the early books of the Bible set in Israel, Babylonia, Egypt and Iran during periods of time estimated to be some four to six thousand years ago. Jews share that aspect of their history with Christians and Muslims and other peoples who look to the stories of Abraham and Sarah, Isaac, Jacob, Moses and Miriam, Saul, David, Isaiah, Esther, and so on.

For Jews the story of their own national history is vital to their own religion. Whereas for Christians the central story of the foundation of their faith and the opening up of a scheme of salvation centres on the miraculous birth, life, death and resurrection of Jesus Christ, for Jews there is no one special person and no archetypical biography which is focused on. Instead it is the long and complicated history of their own development as a people - a nation, a culture, a civilisation - that Jews meditate upon and, by so doing, seek to enter into and extend by their own efforts.

History

The history of the Jews is a sacred history, and all the men and women who have belonged to the Jewish people belong to the ongoing process of that sacralisation. For the story of Judaism does not confine itself to those pages of Holy Scriptures known to Christians as the Old Testament and to Jews (in a slightly different format) as *Tanakh*. The history exists, first of all, in a parallel tradition of oral traditions: a whole treasury of myths and legends, anecdotes and memories of people, images, arguments and themes that amplify, refine and alternate with the familiar materials of the written Hebrew Bible.

The sacred history of the Jews also exists in the persons and events which follow the Old Testament in what has been called 'the ocean of Oral Torah'. The ancient period of Jewish history is marked by a pattern of exiles and returns, dispersions and in-gatherings, forgettings and rememberings, losings and findings. Similarly the epic of modern post-biblical Jewish history begins with the Destruction of the Temple and the razing of Jerusalem in 70 CE. This epic forms the narrative of widespread dispersion, exile and suffering. The prose of rabbinical conversation and debate recounts the spread of Jews outwards from Israel to Babylonia, North Africa, Central Asia, Western and Eastern Europe, the Americas, and eventually the new worlds of the Pacific, Australia and New Zealand.

The Jews who came to New Zealand early in the nineteenth century were more than a mixed lot of British, West European and East European migrants bound together by a belief system called Judaism. They were also a self-consciously historical people aware and proud of their diverse history and linked by a shared faith, nurtured through a thousand forms of adversity, in the eventual restoration of a Jewish homeland in the Land of Israel. As Jews they felt the deeper inner calling for a sanctification of this world, not an otherworldly gaze on abstract salvation. This becomes clear in their notebooks, their building of synagogues, and their contribution to the emerging public life of New Zealand from the very earliest days of European settlement.

Like their fellow Jews for nearly two thousand years, these pioneers in New Zealand were aware that wherever in the world they happened to live was not a permanent home and that as much as possible they must try to respect the original inhabitants and their cultures. Those first generations of Jews, though very small in numbers, seem to have succeeded very well both in establishing themselves as prosperous and responsible members of the European or Pakeha community and in treating fairly the Maori people into whose midst they found themselves settling. Much more widespread than today, those nineteenth-century Jews built synagogues, opened shops, and took part in public life as mayors, city councillors, doctors, lawyers and teachers in almost every town and city of New Zealand. One, Sir Julius Vogel, even became Prime Minister.

Lynda Young

Rabbi blowing the 'shofar' or ram's horn during Rosh Hashanah, the New Year's celebration. (Temple Sinai, Wellington, 1960)

Today the Jews of New Zealand still remain small in numbers, perhaps no more than one quarter of one per cent of the total population. They seem to be concentrated in Auckland and Wellington, with smaller communities in Christchurch, Dunedin, Hamilton and Palmerston North. Yet some things have changed in the twentieth century that distinguish the Jews from their co-religionists in the last century, things that include those same forces of modernity that have affected all New Zealanders during the same period.

While there have not been major waves of migration to New Zealand, the constituency of the Jewish population has gradually changed over the last hundred years. These changes signal the traumatic events in Jewish experience of history in our age, a history which, alas, has been for the most part a succession of persecutions, disasters and expulsions, the most horrendous of all being the Nazi Holocaust during World War II. Of the sixteen million Jews alive on the eve of the War more than one third were murdered by Hitler's Death Machine. No Jew today, no matter where in the world he or she lives, remains untouched by the terrible events in Europe during those early years of the 1940s. The Holocaust is an event of such proportions that it necessarily shapes the way all Jews must perceive themselves and act in their daily lives, just as it tests to the extreme all received ideas about the past and the future of the people known as Israel.

The State of Israel

And yet within just a few years after the full extent of the disaster in Europe was becoming part of the living consciousness of Jewish experience, another event occurred which in its own way had and continues to have a mythic dimension. This is the founding of the State of Israel in 1949. New Zealand Jews, like all others, have always hoped and prayed for an eventual end to the Diaspora (or Dispersion) and wished each other on ritual occasions 'Next year in Jerusalem!' But almost from its inception in the 1890s, modern political Zionism has been especially influential in New Zealand. New Zealand Jews contributed large amounts of money to the Jewish National Fund (*Keren Kayemet*) to purchase land, plant trees, and help settle refugees in the State of Israel, and they have supported Israel in more practical and personal ways. For its size, New Zealand sends a very high number of young Jews to work on *kibbutzim* (cooperative or communal agricultural communities) or to go on *aliyah* (migration) to Israel each year. Many older New Zealand Jews choose to retire to the Holy Land as well.

But even those New Zealand Jews who do not make *aliyah* or who do not have near relations in Israel feel the pain of the contemporary crisis in that troubled Holy Land. They also experience the hurt and humiliation that comes from Anti-Zionist propaganda in New Zealand, particularly slurs which accuse Zionism of being racism; for these are slanders and lies against the State of Israel and the idealistic movements which dream of an end to exile and the in-gathering of all Jews to their own homeland from all the nations of the earth. In Israel today Jews not only come from all nationalities but all races: Bene Israel Jews from India and Ethiopia, North African Jews from Morocco and Libya, Iranian and Iraqi Jews from the Middle East, Italian and Bulgarian Jews from Europe, Argentinian and Brazilian Jews from South America, to name but a fraction of the mixture. Many of these same Jews come to New Zealand, along with *sabras* (citizens born in the Land of Israel) for shorter or longer periods. This country, far as it is from the great centres of Jewish settlement, does not remain immune from the joys and woes of all Jews.

It is hard to tease apart, when talking about Jews, the questions of religious belief from national identity, or ethnicity from culture. Perhaps this is because Jews are at once neither a people with a fixed set of beliefs, a nation, a race or a culture and yet all these things and more. That more is something which most Christian New Zealanders may find hardest to understand. For that more is history.

In New Zealand when we use the word 'history' we usually mean something in the past, something over and done with. 'You're history, mate,' is a Kiwi threat. But for Jews 'history' is something alive and powerfully present, and more than that: history is the tradition in which we live and by which we are shaped. In history we have an influence, though from moment to moment, as we experience the particular forces of politics and social ostracism, as Jews we often feel hopeless and alone. Jews, through their constant reading and interpretation of holy books, engage the past in arguments, so that the history of the past is never a 'closed book'. The issues of ancient and medieval times are still ours to think passionately about, and at the same time we force the persons of the past to engage with the concerns which press in on us today. Moreover, history is also the future, the people and the activities yet to come but in which we as Jews have a portion, a share of interest and an active part to play.

Through reading and practical application of the Law of Moses, Jews also help to shape the future. This future is not only the hoped-for coming of a messiah, a great human leader who will help restore Israel to its ancient glory as a nation and welcome all peoples, of whatever creed or race or nationality, to a new history of peace and harmony, but the more immediate future of our children and our children's children for whom we must feel a deep sense of moral responsibility.

Instead of worrying about heaven and hell, the prospects for immortality and such matters as sin and repentance, Jews tend to worry about this world and its all-too-real dangers and challenges.

In order to look more closely at who and what the Jews of New Zealand are and believe, in the following pages I am going to tell you some stories. The first story is the elaboration of a rabbinical anecdote, an imaginary conversation between seven students in a *yeshiva* (academy) somewhere in the Pale of Settlement in Poland about two hundred years ago. The second tale is of seven modern New Zealand Jews, young people who hold an analogous conversation in a Jewish community centre in one of the cities of this country. This procedure seems most appropriate since so much Jewish discourse is made up of conversations we have with each other, with those of us in the past and the future, as well as our arguments and debates with God. Yes, debates and arguments with God are a powerful component of Jewish sacred speech and action. For God is not only the all-powerful and all-knowing ruler of the universe; as the *Shekhinah* (Wisdom, Sabbath Bride, Face), she is the immediate knowable and even intimate presence of creative and historical wisdom. That debate and argument is what Jews hear happening in the Bible and what they understand as the Holy Scriptures themselves and what they believe the great rabbis are doing all the time. All the time!

The legend of the Seven Rabbinical Students

There is an old story that goes like this. About two hundred years ago, in a small *yeshiva* (rabbinical school) deep inside the Pale of Jewish Settlement of Czarist Russia, there were seven students sitting around a book-piled wooden table. They were arguing loudly, gesticulating broadly, as such students were wont to do. What is the true essence of Judaism? Each one had his own answer.

The first student said: 'The true essence? It is our absolute faith in the oneness, the supreme unity and simplicity of God, the God of our fathers Abraham, Isaac and Jacob, a God without name or attributes, without form or limitations. On Him, Blessed be His name forever, is all our faith, our hope, and our strength.'

'Amen,' said the second student. 'All that you have said is true, and our fundamental monotheism is central to our faith, but faith is not the essence of Judaism. The most characteristic and defining thing about us as Jews is that we have the Torah, the Five Books of Moses handed down by the Lord God blessed be He on Mount Sinai. These Scriptures were given to us, and we are at one with them. We live in and by Torah, every word, every letter of it the source of all wisdom and truth. Torah is our breath, our existence.'

'No!' said the third student banging his hand on the table. 'The revelation of Sinai to Moses our Teacher was not merely of Holy Scriptures. Torah is two-fold, a Written and an Oral Torah. The Scroll of the Five Books, the Pentateuch, we indeed learn and preserve and is a firm rock to our existence. But, my dear fellow students, the essence of Judaism is the way we relate to these written words through the Oral Torah. There is a great chain of authority from Moses through Joshua to the prophets and to men of the Great Synagogue, and from them to the rabbis and teachers of the academies in Israel and Babylonia, the writers of *Midrash* and *Talmud*, and from them to the schools and *yeshivot* of our own day; so that we, even the seven of us and our great rabbi, the principal of this school, stand in that line of tradition. Each of us, as those who will come after us, share in and are part of the revelation of Sinai. This is the essence of Judaism.'

Then the fourth student spoke, saying: 'I agree with what you, my three fellows, have said thus far, that these are crucial and beautiful parts of our identity, but the essence of Judaism is neither in belief nor in knowledge, nor even in study of the tractates of the great rabbinical books. The secure rock that distinguishes us, separates us from all other peoples, is our covenant with the Holy

Name. We are entered into that covenant, all of us, being all mystically present at Sinai, each of us having the seal of the circumcision on our bodies; and we are thus duty-bound to fulfil all the terms of that contract, all six hundred and thirteen of the *mitzvot*, which are obligations and blessings. Thus we are given the Sabbath, a token experience in this world of the eternal world to come.'

'True enough,' said the fifth young man, 'we perform the ritual obligations of Torah with awe and joy. But it is not the ritual acts that define us as Jews. Even the laws of the Sabbath and of pure foods may be suspended for the sake of life. And of the 613 *mitzvot*, why most of them cannot be fulfilled until the Messiah returns to Jerusalem to rebuild the Temple and restore the cult of the priests and of sacrifice. How can we be identified with ritual laws we only know in books and that we dream of? No, what distinguishes us, what is the essence of Judaism is the way we have transformed the cult of the priests and of sacrifice into a system of "as if" worship of God. We study as if it were the equivalent of killing clean beasts in the Temple. We learn the laws of purity as if all were still operative and we were all living in the Land of Israel. The table in our homes has even more become the altar of the Temple. The father and mother who preside over the family are the high priests. We gather to pray in the synagogue each week and through the calendar of the liturgical year according to the schedule of sacrifices at the Temple and in the seasons of the great pilgrimage festivals. In the intimacies of our family life, in the social and economic structures of our communities, and in our identity as Jews we sanctify the world in the Holy Name of the Eternal, blessed be He.'

'Not enough!' exclaimed the sixth rabbinical student, pointing his finger into the air. 'The true essence of Judaism cannot be found only in such parochialism, such "as if" gestures. In the great universal vision of the prophets, as expounded by the great sages of blessed memory, there is a special mission for us as Jews. Our gift to the world and our duty to God is to spread the message of this universal justice through acts of loving kindness, service to all humanity. And we do this, not through vague sentimental appeals to love, but through the practice of righteous behaviour, specific acts of charity, and an assertive programme of ethics. We are, in this way, participating in *tikkun*, the repair and restoration of the world, so that the Messiah may come, speedily, in our day. We are gathering up the lost sparks of light and truth dissipated from the beginning. This is our special privilege and awesome responsibility, this sanctification of the world. And we recall that we were slaves to Pharaoh in Egypt, and that we cannot rest from our wanderings until all men and women are free.'

Then spoke the seventh student, quietly, almost unheard by his fellows. 'Alas,' he said, 'were it only as easy as you all have said! If it were only that we had to believe unyieldingly in the oneness of the Lord, or to know every jot and tittle of the Five Books of Moses, or to study and be part of the rabbinical tradition, or to perform this and that mitzvah with precision, understanding and joy. If it were only that we should live our ordinary lives in the sanctity of divine direction, or that we went forth as a beacon of righteousness and justice amongst the nations. If only it were so! But we are a nation that suffers, a people in exile and wretchedness; we are the victims of a thousand persecutions. Cast forth from our land, our Temple in ruins, we wander amongst hostile strangers. When have the heathen not risen up against us? No, my fellow students, I can assure you, the essence of Judaism is in none of things you have said, marvellous as they all are. The essence is in our awareness that this world is disordered, unjust and meaningless until the coming of the Messiah. As Jews we must not just wait patiently, but complain aloud, call God to account, and urge that the time of His coming be soon in our day!'

At that very moment, the door to the little darkened room where the seven students argued opened, and in walked the *rosh yeshiva*, the head of the rabbinical academy. He saw the students and he said, 'Nu, so what is going on here?'

All at once, the seven students told him of their disagreements, and of their wish to know the true essence of Judaism. Then each one rehearsed his own point of view, and the old rabbi listened quietly, leaning back in his chair, stroking his long white beard.

'My dear young friends, my beloved students,' the old rabbi said, 'you want me to decide amongst you, tell you what the essence of Judaism is? You want me to make such a decision?'

The seven students all nodded their agreement. The wise old sage leaned forward and whispered, 'Well, this is my judgement. The essence of Judaism is the discussion you have just had.'

New conditions in New Zealand

Conditions and situations have changed in two hundred years, and New Zealand in the 1990s is not the Pale of Settlement in the 1780s. While the essence of Judaism, as the wise old rabbi says in the story, is in the diversity of opinions it can generate from within itself, the story, if told about New Zealand Jews, would be different is several ways. How so forms the rest of this chapter.

First of all, there is as yet no *yeshiva* in New Zealand. The Jewish community is too small and too diverse, and the nature of its commitment to the traditions of Judaism has been transformed by the events which have taken place since our imaginary argument in Eastern Europe on the eve of the nineteenth century.

Second, if we were to visualise such a group of young people sitting around a table and discussing the essence of Judaism, we would have to see that they were in appearance like any other young Kiwis, and they would be young women as well as young men. They would speak in English, not in Yiddish, and perhaps not even know the holy languages of Hebrew and Aramaic that the Torah and Talmud are written in.

Third, these young people would know, as their imaginary counterparts in the small academy in that Polish or Ukrainian *shtetl* (small rural town) could not, that they were free to move out of, not just a 'pale' or restricted area of Jewish settlement but out of Judaism altogether; they could assimilate to an essentially secular New Zealand society without anyone knowing or caring about their origins. Indeed, aside from some rather old and very flat sayings about someone 'jewing' you out of money, there is no public sense of Jewishness in New Zealand, positive or negative, and the person who wants to live fully as a Jew can do so virtually invisibly. This is a very new and strange phenomenon in the world.

Let us now look at these three general changes in the conditions of Jews as they live in New Zealand, and then we can go back to the arguments put forward by our seven imaginary rabbinical students to see how they would appear today if seven young New Zealand Jews were having a similar discussion.

(1) Our New Zealand students would most likely find themselves in a youth group connected to one of the several synagogues in Auckland, Wellington, Christchurch and Dunedin. In the past hundred years, there were also synagogues in other towns and cities of New Zealand, but gradually as Jews have tended to concentrate in the traditional four main centres so the formal community life has focused on those same four areas. From time to time, however, informal groups form themselves in provincial towns, such as Nelson, Palmerston North and Hamilton.

Today there are only six synagogues, four of them belonging more or less to what is known

Lynda Young

Chanukah, the Festival of Lights (at Temple Sinai, Wellington in 1961)

as Orthodox Judaism and two as well in Auckland and Wellington to the Liberal movement. This division of Judaism follows the British model. In America and Canada, and even in Israel itself, another model is used in which Judaism groups into three main categories: Orthodoxy, Conservatism and Reformed. There are also other movements within Judaism, ranging from the eighteenth-century mystical sects known as Hasidism through to the late nineteenth-century rationalising Reconstructionists. Because in many ways the range of possible permutations and combinations of the seven 'essences' allows for many movements within Judaism, the two-fold British model in New Zealand only roughly reflects the actual differences in opinion. It is important to remember, though, that these movements are all within one rabbinical Judaism, and not separate 'churches' or 'denominations'. Though there is some rivalry, there is also a great cooperation between the movements in this country. Because congregations are small and often shifting about, where there are not two separate buildings, the actual affiliations to British organisations can change from time to time.

(2) The different movements in modern Judaism began in Europe about three hundred years ago, and until the mid-nineteenth century were not formalised into separate organisations with institutionalised names. Each of the groups can claim that it is part - or even the most important part - of the mainstream traditions of what is called 'normative Judaism', at the same time that they each also assert a purer or better rearrangement of the seven essences. In general, Orthodox Judaism sees itself as continuing Talmudic Judaism focused on the rabbinical writings of the first few hundred years after the destruction of the Temple (70 CE) and Liberal Judaism defines itself by its claims to both a return to prophetic justice of the Bible and a moral adaptation of the rabbinical code to modernity.

In particular matters, where Orthodoxy believes, for instance, that the period of dynamic revelation is completed and the time allows for codification, study and practice of the *mitzvot* - religious obligations, duties and responsibilities - the Liberals believe that the oral revelation continues and thus more emphasis should be placed on the study and interpretation of the

Written Torah. In another example, Orthodox Jews stress their hope for the coming of the Messiah and the restoration of the Temple in Jerusalem and reformed Jews stress the need for sanctification of the world by ethical deeds. However, these are matters of emphasis and stress, not of dogma or creed, and they form part of the essential argument of Judaism.

The more visible and practical differences between these groups in New Zealand may be seen in the architecture and conduct of the synagogues. Whereas men and women sit together in Liberalism, in Orthodoxy they continue the medieval practice of sitting apart. Women have from time to time been rabbis in Liberal synagogues, but this is forbidden in Orthodoxy. Liberal worship services on the sabbath (Friday evening to Saturday sundown) are generally shorter and more structured on responsive rabbi-congregation interaction, while Orthodox worship is longer and focused on the reading out of the weekly passages of the Pentateuch and its *haftorah* in Prophets or Writings by selected male members of the congregation. During the services, Orthodox men will not only keep their heads covered with a skullcap (*kippa* or *yarmulka*), but wear a praying shawl (*tallis*). They will also, at appropriate times, wear phylacteries (*tfillin*), small leather boxes containing selected prayers wrapped ritually round their left arm and on their forehead. Liberal men and women will not necessarily observe any of these sartorial or sumptuary rules.

(3) Outside of the synagogue there are other differences to be seen. The more observant members of the Orthodox community will dress and eat in strict accordance with the rabbinical codes, men wearing hats at all times, married women wearing wigs to cover their shaved heads, all avoiding proscribed foods and mixtures of meat and dairy products. Liberal Jews will tend, in general, to conform to the dress codes of their nationality and adapt their diets to social custom, though conformity and adaptation are usually based on a desire to follow Jewish tradition as well. As there are as yet no Hasidim, who wear distinctive black garb, in New Zealand (although there are growing numbers in Australia), New Zealand Jews remain virtually indistinguishable in appearance and everyday life from other Kiwis.

(4) Most Jewish homes will be marked out from the ordinary New Zealander's abode only by a *mizzuzah* on the doorpost. This is a small metal or clay tube holding ritual prayers. An eight-branched lampstand or *hannukiah* (sometimes called a *menorah*) will often be found on display in the lounge, although it is only lit during the celebration of Hannukah or The Festival of Lights. There will almost certainly be a pair or more of Sabbath candlestick holders for lighting on Friday evening. But probably one of the most distinguishing features of the Jewish household will be books: volumes of the *Tanakh*, histories of Judaism, accounts of the Holocaust, pictures from Israel, and a wide range of other titles. For Jews of all persuasions remain a people of the book, a people who study, think, and argue.

Michael Clements

Family celebrates Erev Shabbat, the beginning of the Sabbath

In families where the laws of *kashrut* or ritual purity are observed, the kitchen will contain at least two sets of cooking utensils, dishes and cutlery, one set for meat meals and one for dairy. The family table remains the centre of Jewish life and thus the choice of foods and the presentation of meals remains a primary aspect of Judaism. Even where the family is not strictly kosher (as laid out in the laws of Leviticus and the discussions of the Mishnah), it will tend not to eat forbidden foods (such as pork products and shellfish) and to avoid forbidden mixtures (such as milk and meat). In addition, because of the importance of the long tradition of Jewish life in many lands of the Diaspora, Jewish cuisine tends to be highly eclectic and exotic. Meals may consist of anything from the pickled and salted delicacies of Eastern Europe, such as smoked salmon (*lox*), salami, or schmalz-herring to the Mediterranean foods of Israel, such as falafle, humus, pita and olives. Eating thus not only is a way of sanctifying the body and honouring the maker of the foods but it is also a way of maintaining bodily contact with ancestors and co-religionists around the world.

(5) Our seven imaginary Jewish students, whether Orthodox, Liberal or secular, would all probably be aware of themselves as Jews, and thus as at once ordinary New Zealanders and different. How they worship in synagogue would, of course, be different to services in a Christian church. How they live at home would be more or less the same as their Kiwi mates. The family customs would be somewhat different in terms of food and conduct at the table. It would probably be even a little different in terms of what was talked about. Since the centre of all Judaisms is study and practice of the Law in one way or another, Jews have always had to be an extremely articulate and intellectual people: reading and debate are stressed in education, and it follows that in the home Jews like to talk and argue. As Jewish history is also punctuated by disaster and exile, families stress their continuity with the past and the diversity of Jewish experience 'among the nations'.

For most New Zealand Jews, family history will go back through England and Western Europe to Eastern Europe, that is, the Ashkenazi tradition; although there are some families who trace their heritage through Sephardic tradition, which includes those Spanish and Portuguese Jews expelled from the Iberian peninsula in the 1490s and who then settled variously in Holland, Greece, Bulgaria and elsewhere in the Ottoman Empire. In more recent times, almost every Jewish family in New Zealand can recall tragic experiences in the pogroms in Czarist Russia and Poland in the late nineteenth century and in the Nazi campaign to exterminate the Jews. Today they also share a concern for the security and welfare of Israel.

(6) Our seven imaginary students would then probably seem to be a very noisy and emotive group of educated young men and women, gesturing far more than a comparable group of ordinary Kiwis. They would not only be thinking very hard about their future vocations and personal commitments, as other young New Zealanders do, but they would also have to think intently on the question of whether or not to go to Israel, and how they have to evaluate, from a deeply moral and ethical perspective, the political events there and in many parts of the world. For as Jews, no matter how secular or pious they might be, they would all know that they could not be indifferent to what happens in Israel or Russia or America or Africa. Troubles in any one area often have ramifications elsewhere. Persecution of any minority is felt by Jews as a threat to their own place in the world. Too often in history Jews have had to flee the lands of their birth.

(7) Thus to be a Jew means being ready at all times to confront such historical questions, at the same time as it means a thorough commitment to the intellectual, cultural and moral enhancement of the land in which you are a citizen. Wherever they have been allowed by law to do so, Jews have played important roles in the scientific, artistic, political, commercial and social life of their society. This forms part of the essential concept of *tikkun*, the active

participation by Jews as individuals and as a group in the sanctification and improvement of the world.

Seven New Zealand Jewish students

As we said earlier, this group of Kiwi young people, unlike the *yeshiva* students in eighteenth-century Poland, would probably consist of women as well as men and include secular Jews as well as pious believers. Aware that they live in a relatively free, tolerant and peaceful society these Jews would know they have options not available to the earlier group. These Kiwis can choose to assimilate wholly to New Zealand life (or migrate to Australia or some other English-speaking country) or make *aliyah* to Israel and so commit themselves to a politically charged Jewish existence, although not necessarily a religious one. They can choose to stay in New Zealand as Jews and work and live in association with one of the synagogue communities, identifying more or less as Jews to the general public, knowing there would be no stigma attached to that decision.

But by staying in New Zealand, these young people would also be aware that they remain away from the dynamic of Jewish cultural and spiritual life of overseas countries, especially America and Israel. Therefore, if they choose to stay, they cannot participate in or experience the full range of Jewish activities the modern world affords. In parts of America (neighbourhoods in New York City or Los Angeles, for example) as well as in Israel, to be a Jew is to be in the majority and thus to be 'normal'; to remain in New Zealand is always to be 'different'. If you live in London or Tel-Aviv, Jewish foods are always available; if you live in Hamilton or Invercargill, you may have to wait until your next overseas trip before eating a bagle or smelling a real kosher dill pickle. But wherever you are, if you choose to be Jewish - and in New Zealand there is a choice; in some countries the choice is made for you and stamped in your passport - then there always remains a deep religious obligation to be involved in the ethical status of the human community, a covenant with God to act and speak in the Jewish way.

Now let us look at what the seven essences of Judaism might look like from a New Zealand perspective by imagining what seven young people would say as they sat around the table in a community centre building somewhere in one of our larger cities.

The first modern young woman is a feminist and a Jew. 'For me', she said, 'the essence of Judaism is in its special form of monotheism. This means that our God has no gender, as well as no human form in general, and we can imagine her or him as female or male, mother or father, old or young and so on. There is a richness in the Written Torah, a diversity in the Oral Torah, and a great wealth of figurative images to choose from in our liturgies, our commentaries, and our other secular and sacred texts. Because of this, not only do I feel comfortable in my Judaism as a woman and as a feminist but I recognise that I can participate in the exciting revaluation of our traditions and customs to make my own integrity as a person resonate with all that we have experienced and created as a Jewish people.'

The second student, an environmentalist, then said, 'I can understand partly what you are saying, but think the real essence is not in that always-evolving capacity of Judaism to image its deity in ways that don't fix him or her into mythological form. Rather, the essence rests in our ability to be at once a unique people and a people who contribute deeply and widely to all of human society. We are not concerned, as Jews, with either the salvation of our own souls or of the rest of humanity, but with sanctification of the world. We don't turn away from this world at all. It is our special obligation, coded into the language of the Covenant at Sinai, to make this world a better place to live in, to work with the eternally creative forces of the universe we name God, and to help the very material stuff of nature and history achieve its full potential as holy. We do this by remaining a specific, clearly identifiable people, thus stressing the real, the material and the human as part of the divine.'

'If you two speak like that,' said the third young man, a student of history at the university, 'your words could be misconstrued. One of you makes Judaism slide towards an easy accommodation with modern liberalism, admirable and desirable as its principles may be; and the other starts to slide towards a form of pantheism or deism, modes of thought that have no real justifying power for moral and ethical behaviour. I think your views are compatible with Judaism only if you stress the historical continuity of our people and our beliefs, a continuity that is in itself dynamic and creative. The essence is thus the dual revelation of the Written and the Oral Torah, the dialectic of stability and growth, of historical specificity and universal development. Our view of the past is not of a backwards glance, a nostalgia or a reactionary urge: the past is the central point of our being, defining our present and, at the same time, always reshaped by our engagement with the here and now.'

The fourth student, a social worker, leaned across the table and pointed her finger at the one who just spoke. 'You are almost right,' she said. 'Just as we Jews don't make a big fuss about heaven or hell, and even have hardly any concepts about such afterlife dispensations, we don't see the past and the present in contention with each other. My argument with most New Zealanders is that they tend to dismiss the past too easily, maybe because the whole reason for coming to this country was to break with the pretensions of class and privilege in England. As Jews we know intimately, through very recent history, that the real problems of the world cannot be escaped by distance or ignorance of history. In a way they are too idealistic and too naive, even though I greatly admire their belief in an equitable classless society. But we know that if we engage too much with the here and now, and glide too easily on the currents of fashionable ideas, no matter how good they may actually be, we lose touch with what it really means to be human - in fact, to really be a part of the world.'

The fourth student went on, 'By not thinking of our God as a person, of whatever sex, and by not forgetting the real differences that language, custom and history make, we don't ask more of the world than it can give: but we do, because of our thousands of years of exile and suffering and struggle, keep asking more of ourselves than other people do. That dialectical reading and interpretation of Torah you speak of has to be understood as more than just some exercise in intellectual gymnastics: it is a way of understanding the complicated place we have in the world. That understanding, that process is what creates and sustains justice in a universe that otherwise is meaningless and chaotic, if not downright hostile to human needs. The essence of Judaism is thus our belief that, without our active engagement in the creation of justice, there is no sanctification of the world.'

'Wait a second,' said the fifth student, a young woman thinking seriously about becoming a Liberal rabbi, 'all this is becoming too abstract again. I don't believe each of us has to spend all of his or her time thinking about and studying the six hundred and thirteen *mitzvot* in the Talmud; but we do need to know what they are and why, when we choose here in New Zealand to make compromises, we make substitutions and alternations to suit the climate and the society we live in. There are some ritual acts we ought to perform. I include here such things as observing the laws of *kashrut*, not eating pork, not mixing meat and milk, and so on. Why? Because these laws of purity force us to think through to the sanctifying quality of our everyday actions. You cannot philosophise about the nature of the universe without taking very practical, specific steps. Every day in all the ordinary performances and relationships we ought to be aware that we are Jews, that we live under special obligations, that our actions have meaning. The meanings are various, of course. They maintain continuity with the past and project our concerns into the future. They focus our attention on the inter-relatedness of all things and at the same time they enact the processes of distinction and integrity. They make us self-consciously aware how the very experience of being human is also an insight into the creative moral reality of God. I could go on, but my point is that the essence of Judaism is its tangible day-by-day ritualisation of life, and this manifests itself in many appearances and actions that in many ways set us apart from the rest of our fellow New Zealanders.' The fifth student paused, and then she spoke again, this time more forcefully but with controlled intensity. 'I have been listening patiently to all of you and as each of you speak I tend to agree. But I am troubled by what was just said. If we choose to live in New Zealand, then surely we are making many compromises with our Judaism, and I wonder if we can hold on to the essence once we admit compromises. Many of our friends have gone to Israel, made *aliya*, in order to get away from such compromises. Not, of course, that they all become religious because we all know that in Israel "religious" means being like the *haredim*, the ultra-orthodox, a view of Judaism which also tends to mean a certain rightwing political involvement with current events. In fact, as many Israelis say, if you are Jew in Israel you don't really have to be Jewish, just Israeli. The fact of living there and accepting the dangers and the inconveniences is enough.

'But if we are talking about Judaism in New Zealand,' she continued, 'then paradoxically you really do have to leave New Zealand. That is because you can't be a real Jew alone, or in a very tiny and isolated group. To pray you have to have a *minyan*, a group of ten. To eat kosher food, you need the ritual butcher and other rabbinical officials who can oversee the preparation of meat and other food products. To study the Torah and the Talmud properly you don't sit all alone in silence and contemplate the page; you engage in dialogue and debate. To preserve the languages of Judaism - Hebrew, Yiddish and Ladino - you need a community of speakers. In fact, it's more than the need for a legal and intellectual sense of Judaism that you need a community, even a network of communities. It's for that emotional, close-to-the-gut sense of *hamishkeit*, the warm mutual support of other Jews.'

The sixth student, a philosophical dreamer, drummed on the table with his fingers a few minutes after the fifth sat back in her seat. He nodded his head. 'Like all of you,' he began, 'I agree with everybody, and especially with my would-be rabbi friend who has just spoken. It's very hard to get Jewish food in New Zealand. I feel so alone when I see a Woody Allen film and am the only one in the theatre to laugh at the Jewish jokes. But somehow I think there is something else, and that it is not impossible to be a Jew in New Zealand, and to be a Jew who somehow grasps the essence of our civilisation or our nationality or our peoplehood or whatever you want to call it.

'Yes, we can talk about our God in such ways as not to offend feminists and to think of universal trans-national morality that respects and is sensitive to other people's beliefs and customs. Yes, we can take seriously the obligations of the Covenant and at the same time as we wear skullcaps and decline to eat shrimp salad. We can continue the Jewish tradition in New Zealand of taking a full, perhaps even an inordinate part in the running of charities and social-welfare organisations. We have played and will continue to play our part in public life by being mayors and town councillors. In a strange way, in New Zealand, as Jews we remain at once invisible to most of the community and yet, to ourselves, distinct and unique. After all, the highest ideal of charity according to the Talmud is to help others without them being aware that they are receiving such help or even that they need help.

'But I am thinking of something else,' he continued, 'which is far more essential to our Judaism, though all these other things certainly are part and parcel of our self-definition as Jews. It is something which, ironically, may be clearer to us here in New Zealand than to Jews elsewhere, whether in the Land of Israel itself or in those deeply Jewish centres in America, Canada, Britain and Australia.

'I know you are looking at me in a funny way when I say that. What I am talking about, though, is an awareness of the essence, not that we have it in New Zealand and the Jews in New York, Tel-Aviv or Melbourne don't. It is exactly because we do not live immersed in a Jewish culture and cannot, even if we wanted, live our lives according to the strict laws of rabbinical authority. It is precisely because we do not have to make political or social choices within Judaism that perhaps we can see the essence.'

'Well, nu?' the other five students asked. 'What is it?' But before the answer came, the seventh student coughed. She had been listening so quietly in the corner that everyone had seemed to forget she was there. Yet they all knew and liked her. She had grown with them, gone to summer camps, sometimes with the more religious *B' nei Akiba* group and sometimes the more secular and Zionist *Habonim* club, and was in her last year of medical school.

'Please, before you answer - please listen to me,' she said, a little haltingly, 'so that maybe you won't answer at all. I know what you're going to say. Something like: we have a unique epistemological distance from which to view Judaism, we Jews who live as much out of the Diaspora as away from the land of Israel. I've heard that kind of argument before. It's all too Kiwi, if you know what I mean.'

The other students sat back in their chairs, silenced by the intensity of her voice. She went on: 'Some people like to say that New Zealand can see the world better than any other country, from its vantage point at the bottom of the world, separated by vast distances from everywhere else, even from Australia. We Kiwis are supposed to view the world with a dispassionate gaze and we can consequently pick and choose amongst the world's options, as well as creating our indigenous cultural choices. The people who say this even tend to be quite smug about our race relations and our health care and our educational system. More than that, there are Kiwis who actually believe we are as good in just about everything that matters to human relations as we are in rugby.'

The six students looked at each other and laughed nervously. 'Epis,' they asked, their intonations slipping away from Kiwi speech towards their parents or grandparents' Yiddish singsong patterns, 'so what is it you are trying to tell us?'

'Simply this,' she said. 'Or not simply this: something more complicated. First, I don't believe we can reduce Judaism to any essence, even this last epistemological perspective, in which somehow you are going to twist being in New Zealand to a refined image of being a Jew vis-a-vis the rest of the world. New Zealand is not all that separated, as we all know from movies to television to MacDonalds and Pizza Hut. And Jews are certainly not separated, as much as we may feel in exile from Exile. The baggage in our minds and in our tastebuds links us to all that our parents and their parents and back a thousand or more generations have known and experienced. But it's not just that either.

'Jews have experienced history, like geography, differently from other peoples. The limits of Christendom and Islam, for instance, were not ours: our ancestors moved back and forth, spoke in other languages, and dressed in a mixture of costumes. And still that isn't the essence.

'More than customs and costumes, which have always tended to follow the external communities like a chameleon's skin, we have assimilated, transformed and recreated all those philosophical systems and modes of belief we have encountered, taken what we wanted and rejected the rest, and by and large outlasted them all.

'If you try to pin down any belief or practice or aspect of our history, then you do what our enemies have always tried to do: make clear and fixed what is necessarily various and dynamic. Why, even in the Talmud our sages allow arguments to be valid on such topics as whether or not there is an afterlife.'

Then the first student said, 'Are you trying to tell me that Judaism is an eclectic muddle?'

'No, I am trying to tell you it is a continuing argument with many competing ideas, united by the concern to understand the Written and the Oral Torah, the revelation at Sinai that continues to our day and beyond.'

The second student said, 'I don't believe you can really deny that Judaism has, despite later practice, a core of admirable feminist theology as well as sound arguments for environmentalism.'

'Who would want to?' answered the seventh student. 'But I hope you are not going to be reductive, suppress our own Jewish history, embarrassing and contradictory as it often is, to make it all focus on a few modern issues, however pressing and worthy they might be right now.'

'I smell a rat,' said the third student. 'You are using history as what is called an amoeba word, a kind of catch-all, so that it comes to mean anything you want it to; whereas for me history is the dynamic, living presence of God's rationality working itself out in the world.'

'Smell all you want,' answered the seventh student, 'but let me tell you that history is no one thing, no line, circle, curlicue, or series of punctuation marks - exile and return, suffering and recompense, despair and illumination. We are history and only when you can respect the very complexity and indeterminacy of yourself can you begin to respect and understand the sacredness of the history we Jews embody.'

The fourth student then objected. 'Surely you are dismissive of the need for long disciplined study of the sacred books before reaching any kind of generalisations about anything. That discipline is itself a way of bringing ourselves into alignment with the men and women who constitute our sacred history, so that in the end when we read the Scriptures properly we are reading ourselves properly, reading in a harmonious dialogue with God, making oral (by which we mean more than audible, but also visible and active in ethical life) what is inscribed forever on the scrolls of the Torah.'

'Why do you keep misunderstanding me?' asked the seventh student. 'I don't want to deny anything any of you have said, except to argue with your reductionism, your effort to specify a single essence. The life of Torah, of course, is important, but only because we know that Torah means the Ten Commandments, the Five Books of Moses, the whole *Tanakh*, the Written and the Oral Torah, the commentaries and codifications of the Law in general, and the exemplary and ordinary behaviour of all Jews who accept the premises of this debate we are having.'

'But what about us here in New Zealand?' asked the sixth student. 'We have to make not just the choice between *Galut* (Exile) and Israel, but also between joining the rich diversity of the Diaspora, exemplified best in places like New York and Montreal or Melbourne, and staying away on the very margins of European civilisation. I would like to think we could make a virtue of necessity, and thus find that when we are on the fringes, we are like the fringes on a *tallit*, the sacred praying shawl. Our marginal status permits us to be at once inside and outside both of Israel and the Diaspora.'

'Even if most Jews everywhere usually forget we exist?' asked the seventh student, somewhat mockingly. 'You even forget the Jews in other parts of New Zealand, like Hamilton', she added. 'How are you going to make your role as sacred fringe work, if for the most part being in New Zealand means compromising away our emphasis on study, our need to live by the laws of *kashrut*, and our requirement to be part of a functioning Jewish community?' The other six looked hurt and mystified.

'No, don't answer,' said the seventh student. 'I don't mean to insult you. My point is not to disparage the really good efforts that go on here, especially in Wellington and Auckland. There are synagogues, ritual baths and properly slaughtered meat for those who want them, and an increasing number of formal and informal learning situations, from day schools to evening and weekend classes for teenagers and adults. I just don't want you to get a swelled head.'

She leaned across and kissed the sixth student on the forehead. 'There,' she said, 'let's be friends again.'

Just then, who should open the door and walk in, than the rabbi. 'What's going on in here,' he said, 'kissing games?'

'No,' they all said, and one by one they recounted to him the argument they had been having, and finally said in unison: 'Please, rabbi, can you please tell us, is there or is there not an essence to Judaism? If there is, what is it?'

The rabbi leaned back against the wall, stroked his beard with his left hand, and then, pointing with the index finger of his right hand, he said:

'Listen to me, my dear children: Once, about two hundred years ago, in Poland, there was a *yeshiva*, and in the *yeshiva* were seven students...'

Further reading

On Jews in New Zealand:

Gluckman, Ann, (ed.), *Identity and Involvement: Auckland Jewry, Past and Present,* Palmerston North: The Dunmore Press, 1990.

Goldmann, Lazarus, M., *The History of the Jews in New Zealand,* Wellington: A.H. & A.W. Reed, 1958.

Rosenthal, Odeda, *Not Strictly Kosher: Pioneer Jews in New Zealand,* Wainscott, N.Y.: Starchand Press, 1988.

On British background to New Zealand Jewry:

Roth, Cecil, *A History of the Jews in England, 3rd. edition,* Oxford: Clarendon Press, 1964.

Representative general works on Jewish civilisation:

de Lange, Nicholas, *Judaism,* Oxford: Oxford University Press, 1986; Opus series 1987.

Epstein, Isadore, *Judaism,* Harmondsworth: Penguin Books, 1959, various reprints.

Mendes-Flohr, Paul A. and Jehuda Reinharz, (eds.), *The Jew in the Modern World: A Documentary History,* New York: Oxford University Press, 1980.

Sikhism

Pritam Singh*

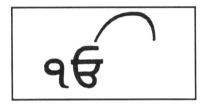

Ik Onkaar - There Is Only One God

Sikhism is one of the younger faiths of the world, compared with religions like Hinduism, Buddhism, Judaism, Christianity or Islam. It is a monotheistic faith, preaching the existence of only one God, and teaching ideals that may be universally accepted today and in the future: honesty, compassion, humility, piety, social commitment, and most of all tolerance for other religions.

The word 'Sikh', derived from the Sanskrit word *shishya*, means a disciple, a learner, a seeker of truth. A Sikh believes in One God and the teachings of the ten Gurus, embodied in the Sikh Holy Scripture, the *Guru Granth Sahib*.[1] Additionally, he or she should take *amrit*,[2] the Sikh baptism.

Sikhism was founded by Guru Nanak Dev Ji at the beginning of the sixteenth century. The succeeding nine Gurus nurtured and developed his ideas and teachings. Guru Gobind Singh Ji, the tenth Guru, brought to an end the line of human Gurus and in 1708 installed the *Guru Granth Sahib* as the permanent Guru of the Sikhs.

The Sikh Gurus provided guidance for about 240 years. They taught the basic values of freedom, brotherhood, charity, obedience, understanding, sympathy, patience, humility, simplicity and piety, and outlined the path to spirituality in life. The Gurus themselves said that they were human and were not to be worshipped as God but were mere servants of God. Guru Gobind Singh said: 'See me only as the slave of God. Let this be known beyond the shadow of doubt.'

* This chapter is dedicated to my parents, Sardar Partap Singh and Sardarni Kartar Kaur. It also gives me great pleasure to acknowledge the stimulation provided by my son Gurpaul Singh and daughter Seema Kaur, who assisted me with many discussions, editing and formatting. Without their assistance it would not have been possible to complete the chapter. I am grateful to my wife, Harminder Kaur, for critically reading the manuscript.

The basic belief of Sikhs

The *Mool Mantar* (literally, the root verse; the first hymn composed by Guru Nanak) sums up the basic belief of the Sikhs. The *Guru Granth Sahib* begins with the *Mool Mantar*. Every Sikh is expected to recite it daily. The English translation is given below:

Mool Mantar

Ik Onkaar	There is only one God
Sat Naam	His Name is Truth
Karta Purkh	He is the Creator
Nir Bhau	He is without fear
Nir Vair	He is without hate
Akaal Moorat	He is beyond time immortal
Ajooni	He is beyond birth and death
Saibhang	He is self-existent
Gur Parsaad	He is realised by the Guru's grace.

The ten Gurus of the Sikhs

The *Guru*[3] in Sikhism is an enlightener and messenger. He is not necessarily a human being. The Guru's word or hymn is also *Guru*. 'The universe is the temple of God but without the Guru darkness reigns supreme.'

The Gurus have raised the conscience of the Sikhs to such a level where they can be one with God. They are the light-bearers for humanity. They are the messengers of the timeless. They renew the eternal wisdom. They are universal men who free our minds from bigotry and superstition, dogmas and rituals, and emphasise the simplicities of religion. They appear outside in human form to those who crave for visible and physical guides. The enlighteners are the inner selves.

The first of the Gurus and the founder of the Sikh religion was Guru Nanak. He was born in Talwandi, now known as Nankana Sahib (near Lahore in Pakistan) in 1469 CE. Guru Nanak married and had two sons. This was the darkest period of India's history when the people were absolutely divided and demoralised. Guru Nanak himself describes the scene in the following words:

> The age is a knife. Kings are butchers. They dispense justice when their palms are filled. Decency and laws have vanished, falsehood stalks abroad. Then came Babar to Hindustan. Death disguised as a Moghul made war on us. There was slaughter and lamentation. Did not Thou, O Lord, feel the pain?

In addition, the priests had reduced religion to a mockery. The public was blind in its faith, and governed by superstitions. Seeing all this, Guru Nanak started building a nation of self-respecting men and women, devoted to God and their leaders, filled with a sense of equality and brotherhood for all. He pronounced, for the benefit of all:

To worship an image, to make pilgrimage to a shrine, to remain in a desert, and yet have the mind impure is all in vain; to be saved worship only the TRUTH....
Keeping no feeling of enmity for anyone. God is contained in every bosom.
FORGIVENESS is love at its highest power....
Where there is forgiveness there is God Himself.
Do not wish evil for anyone.
Do not speak harsh of anyone.
Do not obstruct anyone's work.
If a man speaks ill of you, forgive him.
Practise physical, mental and spiritual endurance.
Help the suffering even at the cost of your own life.

Against social inequality Guru Nanak preached:

There is only One Father of us all,
And we are all His children.
Recognise all the human race as one.

Giving women their proper place in society, he said,

Born of women, nourished by women, wedded to women,
why do they revile women? How can women be called inferior
when they give birth to kings and prophets?

Guru Nanak was a friend of the down-trodden.

There are low castes, lowliest of the low.
I, Nanak, have my place with them; what have
I to do with the high born? God's grace is
there where the down-trodden are taken care of.

He also preached the concept of 'honest-productive-labour', *kirat kamai*.

Only such a person can realise the spiritual
path who earns by the sweat of his brow and
shares his earnings with the needy.

There was not a single aspect of earthly or spiritual life which was not enlightened by Guru Nanak. He passed away on 7 September 1539.

The second Guru, Siri Guru Angad Dev Ji was born in 1504, and first met Guru Nanak in 1532. Guru Angad invented and introduced the *Gurmukhi* (written form of Punjabi) script and made it known to all Sikhs. The scripture of the *Guru Granth Sahib Ji* is written in *Gurmukhi*. This scripture is also the basis of Punjabi language. Guru Angad was a model of selfless service to his Sikhs and showed them the way to devotional prayers.

The third Guru, Siri Guru Amar Das Ji was born in 1479. He met Guru Angad in 1541 who transmitted the same light to Guru Amardas in 1552. Guru Amardas took up cudgels of spirituality to fight against cast restrictions, cast prejudices and the curse of untouchability. He started the tradition of the free kitchen, *Guru ka langar*, and made his disciples, whether rich or poor, whether high-born or low-born (according to the Hindu caste system), have their meals together sitting in one place. He thus established practical equality amongst the people. Guru Amardas introduced the *anand karaj* marriage ceremony for the Sikhs, replacing the Hindu form. He also completely abolished amongst the Sikhs the custom of *sati*, in which a married women was forced to burn herself at the funeral of her husband. The custom of *paradah*, in which a woman covers her face with a veil, was also done away with.

The fourth Guru, Siri Guru Ram Das Ji was born in 1534 and became Guru in 1574. He started the construction of the famous Golden Temple at Amritsar, the holy city of the Sikhs. The temple remains open on all sides and at all times for everyone. This indicates that the Sikhs believe in One God who has no partiality for any particular place, direction or time.

The fifth Guru, Siri Guru Arjan Dev Ji was bestowed the 'Divine Light' by Guru Ram Das Ji in 1581. He was born in 1563. Guru Arjan was a saint and scholar of the highest quality and repute. He compiled the hymns and compositions of Guru Nanak and his other predecessors, selected the sacred songs of some Hindu and Muslim saints, composed his own hymns and thus compiled the *Adi Granth*.[4] He proved that holy beings of whatever caste or creed are equally worthy of respect and reverence. The achievements and the works of Guru Arjan upset the reigning Emperor, Jahangir, who implicated him and tortured him in a most inhuman way. The Guru suffered quietly and bravely, setting the world an unequalled example of self-sacrifice and peaceful sufferings. Despite being made to sit in boiling water, and on a red hot iron plate while burning sand was poured over his body, he chanted cheerfully and softly 'Sweet is Thy Will, my Lord; Thy grace alone I beseech'. He breathed his last in 1606.

The sixth Guru, Siri Guru Hargobind Sahib Ji was born in 1595. He became Guru in 1606. He built many religious shrines and felt the necessity of imparting the spirit of soldiership to the Sikhs. He urged them to be well versed in the art of using swords and other arms for self-defence and self-preservation. He himself wore two swords, *Miri* representing political sovereignty and *Piri* signifying spiritual sovereignty; a balance of material and spiritual life in the world.

The seventh Guru, Siri Guru Har Rai Ji, born in 1630, spent most of his life in devotional meditation and preaching the Gospel of Guru Nanak. He also continued the grand task of nation-building initiated by Guru Har Gobind.

The eighth Guru, Siri Guru Har Krishan Ji was born in 1656. The 'Divine Light' was bestowed upon him in 1661. To the Sikhs he proved to be the symbol of service, purity and truth. The Guru gave his life while serving and healing the epidemic-stricken people in Delhi. Anyone who invokes him with a pure heart has no difficulties whatsoever in their life.

The ninth Guru, Siri Guru Tegh Bahadur Ji, was born in 1621 in Amritsar and became Guru in 1664. He established the town of Anandpur. The Guru laid down his life for the protection of Hindus and their *tilak* (devotional mark painted on the forehead), and sacred thread. He was a firm believer in the right of the people to freedom of worship. It was for this cause that he faced martyrdom for the defence of the down-trodden Hindus. So pathetic was the torture of Guru Tegh Bahadur that his body had to be cremated clandestinely at Delhi while his head was taken four hundred kilometers away to Anandpur Sahib for cremation.

The tenth Guru, Siri Guru Gobind Singh Ji was born in 1666 and became Guru after the martyrdom of his father Guru Tegh Bahadur. He created the *Khalsa* (Pure Ones) in 1699, changing the Sikhs into a saint-soldier order with special symbols and sacraments for protecting themselves. He fought many wars against oppression. His four sons also gave their lives in defence of their faith. He died in 1708.

Thus the tree whose seed was planted by Guru Nanak came to fruition when Guru Gobind Singh created the *Khalsa* and on 3 October 1708 appointed *Guru Granth Sahib* as the Guru of the Sikhs. He commanded: 'Let all bow before my successor, the Guru Granth. The Word is Guru now.'

Guru Granth Sahib Ji

The *Guru Granth Sahib*[5] contains the scriptures of the Sikhs. No Sikh ceremony is regarded as complete unless it is performed in the presence of the *Guru Granth Sahib*. The Granth was written in *Gurmukhi* script and contains the actual words and verses as uttered by the Sikh Gurus. Initially known as the *Adi Granth*, it was compiled by the fifth Guru Arjan and installed in 1604, in the Harimander Sahib (known as Golden Temple), Amritsar. The tenth Guru Gobind Singh added to the *Adi Granth* the composition of his father, Guru Tegh Bahadur. It is believed that four copies of the Granth Sahib were prepared; the first one was sent to the Harimander Sahib at Amritsar, the second to Anandpur, the third to Patna and the fourth was kept by him at Nander. Guru Gobind Singh did not include his own verses in the Granth, owing to his modesty and humility.

When Guru Gobind Singh ended the line of living Sikh Gurus by raising the *Adi Granth* to the status of a permanent Guru he renamed it *Guru Granth Sahib*. He then commanded the Sikhs that it was to be revered as the body and spirit of the ten Gurus.

Every copy of the *Guru Granth Sahib* consists of 1430 pages. It contains the *banis* (sacred compositions) of the first five Gurus and the ninth Guru as well as a number of passages of verses written by several non-Sikh saints from Muslims, Hindus and even so-called 'untouchables'. This was done to demonstrate the Sikh's respect for other saints and tolerance for all faiths. Altogether the *Guru Granth Sahib* includes 5894 *shabads* (hymns or holy verses) which are arranged in thirty-one *ragas* (musical measures). The first verse is *Mool Mantar* (or *Mantra*), the Root Verse, followed by daily prayer or *nitnem* namely, *Japji*, *Sodar* and *Kirtan Sohila*. The remaining verses have been arranged according to their individual musical patterns or *ragas*.

The *Guru Granth Sahib* is an anthology of prayers and hymns. Most of the hymns are addressed to God and often describe the devotee's condition: his aspirations and yearning, his agony in separation and his longing to be with the Lord. The subject of *Guru Granth Sahib* is truth: how to become 'a person of truth', that is, an ideal person. As Guru Nanak states in the *Mool Mantra*, God is the Ultimate Truth and one has to cultivate those qualities which are associated with Him, in order to be like Him. The basic concept behind the hymns is that sacred music, when sung or listened to with devotion and undivided attention, can link the individual's consciousness with God. A mind may become stable and enjoy the peace of His divine presence, as listening to the hymns can exert a powerful influence on the mind and help to establish its communion with God.

In the *Guru Granth Sahib*, revelation and *raga* go hand in hand. The Gurus were emphatic about the religious

Pritam Singh

Congregation singing sacred hymns inside the Sikh Temple in Otahuhu

value of sacred music or *kirtan* and stressed its continuous use, as a source of divine joy and bliss. Sacred music is fine art wedded closely to the spiritual theme. It is devotional music in praise of the Glory of God conveyed by melody and rhythm. The goal or objective of *kirtan* is to put the individual soul in tune with God.

The *Guru Granth Sahib* is a book of revelation. It conveys the Word of the Master through His messengers on earth. It is universal in its scope. For Sikhs the greatness of *Guru Granth Sahib* lies not only in its being their holy book but also in it being a general scripture intended for everybody, everywhere.

The Granth also explains what Guru Nanak meant by a 'perfect individual' or a *gurmukh*. It is a remarkable storehouse of spiritual knowledge and teachings which does not preach any rites or rituals but stresses meditation on the Name of God. Through its teachings, it can enable men and women to lead a purposeful and rewarding life while being members of a society. It seeks universal peace and the good of all mankind. The *Guru Granth Sahib* also stresses the democratic way of life and the equality of all people. It teaches that we are *karam yogis*, that is we reap what we sow. The emphasis is on moral actions, noble living and working for the welfare of all people. Respect and veneration for the *Guru Granth Sahib* does not imply idol worship, but rather respect for a divine message, the ideas and ideals contained in the Sikh scripture. Meditation on the True Word, *Satnam* or the Wonderful Enlightener, *Waheguru*, or on any line of a verse in the *Guru Granth Sahib*, may bring the true devotee or disciple to be in tune with God.

The birth of the Khalsa

Guru Gobind Singh invited his followers from all over India to a special congregation at Anandpur on *Baisakhi* Day, 30 March 1699. He asked, with a naked sword in his hand, 'Is there any one among you who is prepared to die for the Sikh faith?' When people heard his call, they were taken aback. Some of the wavering followers left the congregation, while others began to look at one another in amazement. After a few minutes, a Sikh from Lahore named Daya Ram stood up and offered his life to the Guru. The Guru took him to a tent pitched close by, and after some time came out with a sword dripping blood. The Sikhs thought Daya Ram had been slain. The Guru repeated his demand calling for another Sikh who was prepared to die at his command. The second Sikh who offered himself was Dharam Das. Thereafter, three more, Mohkam Chand, Sahib Chand and Himmat Rai, offered their lives to the Guru.

Later, these five Sikhs were given new robes and presented to the congregation. They constituted the *panj pyare*, the Five Beloved Ones, who were baptised as the *Khalsa* or the Pure Ones with the administration of *amrit*. The Guru declared:

> Since Guru Nanak, it is the *charanamrit* (water used for washing the Guru's feet) which has been administered to the devotees. But from now on, I shall baptise them with water stirred with a double-edged sword - *khanda*.

Upon administering *amrit* to the Five Beloved Ones, the Guru asked them to baptise him in the same manner, thus emphasising equality between the Guru and his disciples.

Guru Gobind Singh named the new ceremony *Khanday-da-Amrit*, namely the baptism of the double-edged sword. He stirred water in an iron bowl with the sword, reciting the five major compositions, *Japji*, *Jaap*, *Anand Sahib*, *Ten Sawaiyas* and *Chaupai*, while the five Sikhs stood facing him. The Guru's wife put some sugar-puffs into the water. The nectar thus obtained was called *Khanday-da-Amrit*. This implied that the new *Khalsa* Brotherhood would not only be full of courage and heroism, but also filled with humility.

Briefly, the *Khalsa* concept has been captured by G. C. Narang in *Transformation of Sikhism* as:

> Abolition of prejudice, equality of privilege among one another and with the Guru, common worship, common place of pilgrimage, common baptism for all classes and lastly, common external appearance - these were the means besides common leadership and the community of aspiration which Gobind Singh employed to bring unity among his followers and by which he bound them together into a compact mass.[6]

The creation of the *Khalsa* marked the culmination of about 240 years of training given by the ten Gurus to their Sikhs. The Guru wanted to create ideal people who should be perfect in all respects, that is a combination of devotion (*bhakti*) and strength (*shakti*). He combined charity (*deg*) with the sword (*teg*) in the image of his Sikh.

The *Khalsa* was to be a saint, a soldier and a scholar who would be highly moral and excellent in character. He would be strong, courageous, learned and wise. In order to mould his personality the Guru inculcated in him the five virtues: sacrifice, cleanliness, honesty, charity and courage, and prescribed a *Rehat*, the Sikh code of discipline. His character would be strengthened by the spirit of God revealed in the Guru's hymns. For this purpose he was asked to recite the five sacred compositions or *banis* daily.

The combination of virtue and courage is the strength of the *Khalsa*. This is an assurance against the ruthless exploitation of the masses by their masters, and an instrument of overcoming hurdles that lie in the practice of holiness and spiritualism in daily life. Guru Gobind Singh commanded the *Khalsa* to use the sword only in times of emergency, that is, when peaceful methods failed and only for self-defence and the protection of the oppressed. His spirit will continue to inspire them for the preservation of peace, order and dignity of man for all time to come.

The five Ks

The five sacred Sikh symbols prescribed by Guru Gobind Singh are commonly known as *panj kakars* or the 'Five Ks' because they start with letter K representing *kakka* in the Punjabi language. They are:

1. *Kes* or unshorn hair, regarded as a symbol of saintliness. Guru Nanak started the practice of keeping the hair unshorn. The keeping of hair in its natural state is regarded as living in harmony with the will of God, and is a symbol of the *Khalsa* brotherhood and the Sikh faith. Hair is an integral part of the human body created by God and Sikhism calls for its preservation. The shaving or cutting of hair is one of the four taboos or *kurehats*.
2. *Kangha* or the comb is necessary to keep the hair clean and tidy. A Sikh must comb his hair twice a day and tie his turban neatly. The Gurus wore turbans and commanded the Sikhs to wear turbans for the protection of the hair, and promotion of social identity and cohesion. It has thus become an essential part of the Sikh dress.
3. *Kara* or the steel wristlet symbolises restraint from evil deeds. It is worn on the right wrist and reminds the Sikh of the vows taken by him, that is, he is a servant of the Guru and should not do anything which may bring shame or disgrace. When he looks at the *Kara*, he is made to think twice before doing anything evil with his hands.
4. *Kacch* or the soldier's shorts must be worn at all times. It reminds the Sikh of the need for self-

restraint over passions and desires. Apart from its moral significance, it ensures briskness during action and freedom of movement at all times. It is a smart dress as compared to the loose dhoti which most Indians wore at that time.

5. *Kirpan* or the sword is the emblem of courage and self-defence. It symbolises dignity and self-reliance, the capacity and readiness to always defend the weak and the oppressed. It helps sustain one's martial spirit and the determination to sacrifice oneself in order to defend truth and Sikh moral values.

The Five Ks, along with the turban, constitute the *Khalsa* uniform, which distinguishes a Sikh from any other person in the world, and is essential for preserving the life of the community and fostering the *Khalsa* brotherhood.

The Five Ks are not supposed to foster exclusiveness or superiority. They are meant to keep the Sikhs united in the pursuit of the aims and ideals of the Gurus. They enable them to keep their vows made at the time of baptism. The Sikhs have been known to face torture and death rather than cut their hair or remove any of the sacred symbols.

The *Khalsa* cannot be anonymous. His religion is known to all. He stands out among people, and any unseemly behaviour or action on his part would be noted as unbecoming of a follower of the Gurus. People would easily blame him if he deviated from the disciplinary code of Guru Gobind Singh.

The Sikh code of discipline

Along with observing the Five Ks, the *Khalsa* is required to refrain from committing the four taboos or *kurehats*. These are:

1. Trimming, shaving or removing hair from the body.
2. Using tobacco or intoxicants in any form.
3. Eating of *kosher* or *halal* meat.
4. Committing adultery.

A Sikh guilty of committing any of these serious breaches is regarded as a fallen one *(patit* or *tankhahya)*. Guru Gobind Singh declared that as long as the *Khalsa* followed the Five Ks and Sikh code of discipline, he would win glory, but if he showed indifference, his progress would be hampered.

The Sikh insignia - Khanda

The *khanda* constitutes three symbols in one. However, the name is derived from the central symbol, *khanda*, a special type of double-edged sword which confirms the Sikhs' belief in One God.

*   The double-edged sword is the creative power of God which controls the destiny of the whole creation. It is sovereign power over life and death.

228

* The right edge of the double-edged sword symbolises freedom and authority governed by moral and spiritual values.
* The left edge of the double-edged sword symbolises divine justice which chastises and punishes the wicked oppressors.
* On the left side is the sword of spiritual sovereignty, *Piri*; on the right side the sword of political sovereignty, *Miri*.

There must always be a balance between the two and this balance is emphasised by an inside circle. The circle is what is called the *chakra*. This is a symbol of all-embracing divine manifestation including everything and wanting nothing, without beginning or end, neither first nor last, timeless and absolute. It is the symbol of oneness of the unity of justice, humanity and morality. The *chakra* was also used by the Sikhs as one of the war weapons against injustice and oppression. Almost all Sikh warriors used to carry it in the eighteenth century.

The Sikh flag - Nishan Sahib

The Sikh flag is a saffron-coloured triangular-shaped cloth, usually reinforced in the middle with the Sikh insignia in blue. It is usually mounted on a long steel pole (which is also covered with saffron-coloured cloth) headed with a *khanda*. The Sikh flag is often seen near the entrance to the *gurdwara*, standing firmly on the platform, overlooking the whole building. Sikhs show great respect to their flag as it is, indeed, the symbol of the freedom of the *Khalsa*.

The Sikh ceremonies

All the Sikh ceremonies like birth, baptism, marriage and death, are simple, inexpensive, and have a religious tone. They are held in the presence of the *Guru Granth Sahib* and include *kirtan*, the singing of appropriate hymns for the occasion, saying of *ardas*, formal prayer, and the distribution of *karah prasad*,[7] sacred food, to the congregation. The baptism ceremony called *amrit*, described earlier, is the most important of all Sikh ceremonies.

The naming ceremony

The Sikh naming or christening ceremony takes place in a *gurdwara*,[8] in the presence of relatives and friends. The family offers donations, *karah prasad* and a *rumala* which is a covering for the *Guru Granth Sahib*, made of high-quality silk, cotton or embroidered cloth. Prayers are offered, asking for a special blessing of good health, long life and the Sikh way of life, *gursikhi*, for the child.

After reciting *ardas*, the *Guru Granth Sahib* is opened at random. The first letter of the first word of the hymn on the page is selected as the first letter of the child's name. The given name is common for either sex. The word *Kaur* meaning 'princess' is added after a girl's name, and the name *Singh* meaning 'lion' after a boy's. For example, if the first letter is 'P', the male child may be given a name like Partap Singh, Pritam Singh or Puran Singh. If the newly-born is a girl the name would likewise be, Partap Kaur, Pritam Kaur or Puran Kaur.

When the name is selected by the family, the congregation gives approval by a holy cheer or *jaikara*: '*Bolay so nihal! Sat Sri Akal!*' The ceremony ends with the distribution of *karah prasad*, and the placing of the *rumala* over the *Guru Granth Sahib*. Sometimes, sweets or *langar*, free food from the Guru's kitchen, are served but this is not a part of the ceremony.

The Sikh marriage

Sikh marriages are usually arranged. However, the word 'arranged' is not always properly interpreted by people in Western societies. An arranged marriage does not mean forcing a boy or a girl into a wedlock of parents' choice only. It is agreeing to marriage proposed by mutual discussion between the boy or the girl on one side and his or her parents and relatives on the other. This is in fact selecting the right partner from a number of choices or proposals.

Several criteria are usually adopted before making a marriage proposal. Most important are the boy and girl themselves who show their willingness only after taking into account personality, family background, the educational standing and physical appearance of the proposed partner. Generally, relatives or close family friends suggest a suitable match to the family. The boy and girl then meet each other a few times, to convey their consent to their parents.

The Sikh marriage is monogamous. In the case of broken marriage, divorce is not possible according to the Sikh religious tradition. The couple can, however, obtain a divorce under the civil law of the land. Marriage in Sikhism is regarded as a sacred bond in attaining worldly and spiritual joy. Telling about the ideal marriage the Guru says: 'They are not husband and wife who only have physical contact; rather they are wife and husband who have one spirit in two bodies.'

The Sikh marriage ceremony is called *anand karaj*, meaning 'ceremony of bliss'. The fourth Guru, Guru Ram Das originally composed the *lavan*, the wedding song, to celebrate a holy union between the human soul *(atma)* and God *(Paramatma)*. The Guru wishes that our married life should also be moulded on the ideal laid down for our union with the *Paramatma*. The four verses of the *lavan* explain the four stages of love and married life. The first verse emphasises the performance of duty to the family and the community. The second refers to the stage of yearning and love for each other. The third refers to the stage of detachment or *virag*. The fourth verse refers to the final stage of harmony and union in married life during which human love blends into the love for God.

Lavan is a Sanskrit word literally meaning 'break away', i.e. the bride breaking away from her parents' home. Based on a concept depicted in the *lavan*, the Sikh marriage is not merely a physical and legal contract but a sacrament, a holy union between two souls, where physically they appear as two individual bodies but in fact are united as one. The bride's past and present becomes the bridegroom's past and present. Her present becomes his and his hers. They feel and think alike and both are completely identified with each other. They become '*ek jot doe murti*', meaning one spirit in two bodies.

Sometimes before the wedding day another important ceremony called *kurmaayaee* or *shagan* takes place usually at the bridegroom's house or the *gurdwara*. It is a formal engagement ceremony involving a promise to marry and an exchange of rings and other presents. But the word *kurmaayaee* literally means the coming or the meeting of the parents of both the boy and the girl, and this shows the importance attached to the union of the two families. As soon as the bridegroom and the two families are assembled the *milnee* is performed, a meeting of parents and close relatives of the bride and groom including an exchange of presents. The bride herself does not normally participate.

The marriage ceremony is conducted in a *gurdwara* or at the bride's home or any other suitable place where the *Guru Granth Sahib* is duly installed. A priest or any Sikh (man or woman) may conduct the ceremony, and usually a respected and learned person is chosen.

First *Asa-di-var* (morning hymns) and then hymns appropriate for the occasion are sung, while family, friends, guests and groom arrive. The groom is first seated before the *Guru Granth Sahib* and when the bride comes she takes her place on his left. The couple and their parents are asked to stand while the rest of the congregation remain seated. A prayer is then said, invoking His blessings for the proposed marriage and asking His grace on the union of the couple. This connotes the consent of the bride and the bridegroom and their parents. The parties then resume their seats and a short hymn is sung.

This is followed by a brief speech addressed particularly to the couple, explaining the significance and obligation of the marriage. The couple are then asked to honour their vows by bowing together before the *Guru Granth Sahib*. Then the bride's father places one end of a pink- or saffron-coloured scarf in the groom's hand, passing it over the shoulder and placing the other end in the bride's hand. Thus joined, the two will take the vow.

This is followed by a short hymn. The *Guru Granth Sahib* is now opened and the first verse of the *lavan* is read from it. The same verse is then sung by the musicians while the couple slowly encircle the *Guru Granth Sahib*. The groom leads in a clock-wise direction and the bride, holding the scarf, follows as nearly as possible in step. When the couple reach the front of the *Guru Granth Sahib*, they both bow together and take their respective seats. The same protocol is repeated for the remaining three verses. The ceremony is concluded with the customary singing of the six stanzas of the *Anand Sahib*, Song of Bliss, followed by *ardas*, prayer, and *vak*, a random reading of a verse from the *Guru Granth Sahib*. The ceremony, which takes about an hour, ends with the serving of *karah prasad* to the congregation. Relatives and friends then exchange greetings and congratulations. A few hours after the marriage the bridal party leaves and the bride departs from her parental home with her husband.

The death ceremony

To a Sikh, birth and death are closely associated, because they are both part of the cycle of human life, *ava guvan*, which is seen as a transient stage towards *nirvana*, complete unity with God. Sikhs thus believe in reincarnation. Mourning is therefore discouraged, especially in the case of those who have lived a long and full life. The death ceremony may be split into two parts: *saskar*, the cremation, and the *antam ardas*, the final prayer during the *bhog* ceremony.

At a Sikh's death-bed, relatives and friends read *Sukhmani Sahib*, the Psalm of Peace, composed by the fifth Guru Arjan Dev Ji, to console themselves and the dying person. When a death occurs, they exclaim '*Waheguru*', the Wonderful Lord. Wailing or lamentation is discouraged. For cremation, the body is first washed and dressed with clean clothes complete with the Five Ks (in the case of baptised Sikhs). If the death occurs in the hospital, the body is taken home for viewing before the funeral. In the Punjab, the body will be burnt on the funeral pyre, but in New Zealand and other Western countries a crematorium is used. A prayer is said before the start of the funeral to seek salvation for the departed soul. On arrival at the crematorium, a brief speech about the deceased is generally given, the *sohila*, bed-time prayer is recited and the *ardas*, formal prayer is offered. The cremation is generally done by the eldest son or a close relative. Where cremation is not possible, disposal of the dead body by placing it in the sea or river is permitted. At the end of the cremation the members of the funeral party return to their homes. The ashes are collected after the cremation and later disposed of by immersion in the nearest river or sea. Some families in New Zealand prefer to take the ashes to the Punjab. Sikhs do not erect monuments over the remains of the dead.

The second part of the ceremony is called *antam ardas*, the final prayer during the *bhog* ceremony which includes a complete reading of the *Guru Granth Sahib* either at home or in a gurdwara. This is called a *sahaj path*, and is usually completed in ten days. If the family can read, they must take part in the reading; if they cannot, they must sit and listen to it. The reading is meant to provide spiritual support and consolation to the bereaved family and friends. During *ardas*, the blessing of God for the departed soul is sought. The Gurus emphasised the remembrance of God's Name as the best means of consolation for the bereaved family. Sikhs are always exhorted to submit to and have complete faith in the will of God, *bhana man na*.

Generally, all the relatives and friends of the family gather together for the *bhog* ceremony on the completion of the reading of the *Guru Granth Sahib*. Musicians sing appropriate hymns, *salokas* of the ninth Guru Teg Bahadur are read, and *Ramkali Saad*, the Call of God, is recited. After the final prayer, a random reading or *hukam* is taken, and *karah prasad* is distributed to the congregation.

If the deceased person is elderly, food from Guru's kitchen, *langar*, is served. Presents are distributed to grandchildren. Donations are often announced for charities and religious organisations. Sometimes, at the end of the *bhog*, the eldest member is presented with a turban and declared the new head of the family.

Sikh festivals

A Sikh festival or holy day is called a *gurpurb*, meaning Guru's remembrance day. The celebration is generally similar for all festivals; only the hymns and history of a particular occasion are different. The ceremony for Guru Nanak's birthday is described in detail.

The birthday of Guru Nanak, founder of the Sikh religion, usually comes in the month of November, but the day varies from year to year following the traditional dates of the Indian calendar. The birthday celebration usually lasts for three days. Generally two days before the birthday, *akhand path* (forty-eight-hour non-stop reading of the *Guru Granth Sahib*) is held in the *gurdwara*. One day before the birthday, a procession is organised which is led by the *panj piyaras* (Five Beloved Ones) and the *palki* (palanquin) of Siri Guru Granth Sahib and followed by teams of singers singing hymns, brass bands playing different tunes, and devotees singing the chorus. The procession passes through the main roads and streets of the town which are covered with buntings and decorated gates and the leaders inform the people of the message of Guru Nanak. On the birth anniversary day, the programme begins early in the morning at about 4 or 5 am with the singing of *Asa-di-var* (morning hymns) and hymns from the Sikh scriptures followed by *katha* (exposition of the scripture) and lectures and recitation of poems in the praise of the Guru. The celebration goes on until 1 or 2 pm.

After *ardas* and distribution of *karah prasad*, the *langar* is served. Some *gurdwaras* also hold a night session. This begins around sunset when *Rehras* (evening prayer) is recited. This is followed by *kirtan* till late in the night. Sometimes a *kavi-darbar* (poetic symposium) is also held to enable the poets to pay their tributes to the Guru in their own verses. At about 1.20 am, the actual time of the birth, the congregation sings praises of the Guru and recites the Holy Word. The function ends about 2 am.

The Sikhs who cannot join the celebrations for some reason, or in places where there are no Sikh temples, hold the ceremony in their own homes by performing *kirtan, path, ardas, karah prasad* and *langar*.

Guru Gobind Singh the tenth Guru's birthday generally falls in December or in January. The celebrations are similar to those of Guru Nanak's birthday, namely *akhand path*, procession, and *kirtan, katha*, and *langar*.

The anniversary of Guru Arjan the fifth Guru's martyrdom falls in May-June, the hottest months in India. He was tortured to death under the orders of Mogul Emperor Jahangir on 25 May

1606. Celebrations consist of *kirtan*, *katha*, lectures, *karah prasad*, and *langar* in the *gurdwara*. Because of summer, chilled sweetened drink made from milk, sugar, essence and water is freely distributed in *gurdwaras* and in neighbourhoods to everybody irrespective of their religious belief.

Guru Tegh Bahadur, the ninth Guru, was arrested under orders of Mogul Emperor Aurangzeb. As he refused to change his religion and accept Islam, he was beheaded on 11 November 1675 at Chandi Chowk, Delhi. Usually one-day celebrations of his martyrdom are held in the *gurdwaras*.

Three days before his passing away, Guru Gobind Singh on 3 October 1708, conferred the perpetual Gurudom on *Siri Guru Granth Sahib*. On this day, a special one-day celebration is held with *kirtan*, *katha*, lectures, *ardas*, *karah prasad* and *langar*. Sikhs rededicate themselves to follow the teachings of the Gurus contained in the scriptures.

Baisakhi, also called *Vaisakhi*, is the birthday of the *Khalsa* (the Pure Ones). Guru Gobind Singh, the tenth Guru, founded the *Khalsa* Brotherhood with the 'baptism of steel' on 30 March 1699. On this day, a one-day celebration is held in *gurdwaras* with *kirtan*, *katha*, lectures, *karah prasad* and *langar*. In addition, the *amrit* ceremony is held and is given to those who offer themselves for Sikh initiation. The Sikhs after taking *amrit* are called *Khalsa*. The *Amrit* ceremony can be held at any other time as well. *Baisakhi* is generally celebrated on the 13th of April every year.

The Sikhs celebrate *Diwali* to express the joy at the return of the sixth Guru to Amritsar in 1620, after his release from Gwalior Jail. (Emperor Jahangir had imprisoned him because he was afraid of the Guru's growing power and popularity with the masses.) The Sikhs on this day, which generally falls in November, hold a one-day celebration in the *gurdwaras*. *Diwali* means festival of lights. So in the evening, illuminations are done with *diwas* (oil lamps made of clay) or candles and fireworks, held both in the *gurdwaras* and in the homes and businesses of the Sikhs.

Role and status of Sikh women

In Indian society, women were usually subject to various caste-rules and severe restrictions. They remained illiterate and were ill-treated. Female infanticide was often practised.

Guru Nanak challenged the idea of inferiority and evil associated with women and freed them from slavery and taboos of the society. In one of his hymns, he said:

> We are conceived from woman,
> We are born from woman,
> It is to woman that we get engaged
> And then get married,
> Woman is our lifelong companion
> And support of our survival.
> It is through woman
> That we establish social relationships.
> Why should we denounce her
> When even kings and great men are born from her?

Guru Nanak and his successors gave woman a status equal to that of man. They regarded woman as man's companion in every walk of life. The Gurus thought this equality worked to their mutual benefit. For example, woman is the first teacher of man as his mother. Her function is to mould children and discipline them. She has to be educated so that her children may develop their potential to the fullest. She was allowed to join holy congregations, participate in and conduct them. Women were appointed missionaries. They were called 'the conscience of man'. The practice of *sati* was prohibited and widow-remarriage was encouraged. Women soldiers fought side by side with male soldiers in one of the battles which the tenth Guru fought.

In the Sikh way of life, women have equal rights with men. There is absolutely no discrimination against women. Women are entitled to the *Khalsa* baptism. They have equal rights to participate in social, political and religious activities. Women are allowed to lead religious congregations, to take part in recitation of the holy scriptures, to fight as soldiers in the war, to elect representatives to the *gurdwara* committees and Indian Parliament and Provincial Assembly.

Sikh women have played a glorious part in their history, and examples of their moral dignity, service and upholding of Sikh values are a great source of inspiration. Sikh women have never flinched from their duty, nor allowed their faith and ardour to be dampened, and have always upheld the honour and glory of the *Khalsa*. (One famous example is that of Mai Bhago who bravely fought war for Guru Gobind Singh, when some Sikh soldiers deserted him and returned home.)

Gurdwara - the Sikh temple

Gurdwara (the door or gateway to the Guru) is the name given to the Sikh's place of worship, commonly called a Sikh temple in the western world. There Sikh scriptures are recited or sung and sermons are delivered. The *Guru Granth Sahib* is placed on a high palanquin under a canopy in the middle of one end of the hall. As well as sermons and the singing of the scriptures, the congregation is expected to participate in the ceremonies of birth, baptism, marriage, death and celebration of festivals.

The *gurdwara* is a place for acquiring spiritual knowledge and wisdom. It is open to every one regardless of age, sex, caste, or creed. Here all men, women and children are treated as equal. It offers shelter and food to anyone in need. It provides care for the sick, elderly and handicapped. It is also a centre for promoting culture and health. Moral education as well as knowledge of the religion and history is often taught to children in the Sikh temple. The *gurdwara* is also a place for discussing problems facing the Sikh community. Infringement of the Sikh code of discipline may also be considered and suitable punishment decided. The *gurdwara* plays a socio-cultural role in the Sikh community and is expected to be free from any sectional interests or party politics.

The pattern of congregational worship can be divided into two categories, *katha*, the reading of the holy hymns followed by their explanation, and *kirtan*, the singing of the hymns. Attached to every *gurdwara* is a free kitchen where the food, *langar*, is prepared and served.

The community attempts to establish better relations and understanding between the Sikhs and other communities through occasional visits by them to a *gurdwara*. Such visits are necessary not only to satisfy the curiosity of others but also to help them understand better the Sikh religion, customs and culture.

A *gurdwara* can be identified from a distance by observing the *nishan sahib*, the Sikh flag. The four doors of the temple represent the Door of Peace, the Door of Livelihood, the Door of Learning and the Door of Grace. These doors must always remain open to all. The Sikh temple is a place for training the devotees in the company of pious people. The Gurus wanted to build a model human society through an ideal and benevolent world organisation.

There are two gurdwaras in New Zealand. The first was officially opened at Te Rapa on the northern outskirts of Hamilton on 28 May 1977. The second was opened in the Auckland suburb of Otahuhu at the corner of Princess and Albert Street on 3 August 1986. These are open daily; services are held on Sundays.

Gurdwara protocol

If one wishes to visit a *gurdwara* some protocol must be observed. Consumption of tobacco, alcohol or narcotics is strictly forbidden to Sikhs and definitely not allowed on the *gurdwara* premises. Before entering the hall, people take off their shoes, wash their hands, cover their heads and think of the Guru. Non-Sikhs, too, must cover their heads with a handkerchief or scarf. Upon entering the hall where the *Guru Granth Sahib* is kept, they walk slowly, bow humbly and touch their forehead to the ground out of respect and love for the Guru. As people bow, and place their offering respectfully before the Guru, it may be money, a flower, or a word of thanks. Any sincere expression of gratitude is equally acceptable to the Guru. After bowing and offering, one should sit down in the *sangat*, the congregation, quietly without disturbing others. Usually men sit on one side and the women on the other side in a cross-legged position. Talking is not permitted.

Pritam Singh

Members of the New Zealand Sikh Society hoisting the Sikh flag during annual Baisakhi celebrations at Te Rapa Sikh Temple

The usual service in the *gurdwara* consists of *kirtan*, the singing of the holy hymns; *katha*, the reading of the hymns followed by their explanation; singing of six verses of *Anand Sahib*; *ardas*, prayer; and *vak* or *hukam*, random reading of one hymn from the *Guru Granth Sahib*. This is the Guru's message or 'Order' of the day to the *sangat*. Upon completion of the *hukam*, *karah prasad* is distributed. Then *langar*, food from the Guru's kitchen, is served.

The New Zealand connection

There are seventeen million Sikhs, of whom approximately one million live outside India. They migrated in the beginning of this century to almost every part of the world but the majority are settled in the United Kingdom, Canada, the United States, Malaysia, Singapore, Thailand, and Kenya. Sikh migration to New Zealand is 100 years old this year (1990). The first Sikhs to arrive in New Zealand were two brothers, Bir Singh Gill and Phuman Singh Gill. They landed here about 1890 coming from Australia, to where Bir Singh, the elder brother, had travelled from Hong Kong in search of work. When he failed to communicate with his family back in Punjab the younger brother, Phuman Singh, was sent to search for him and take him back home. Instead, the two brothers crossed the Tasman Sea and made New Zealand their home. Both the brothers died in Palmerston North, Bir Singh in 1921 and Phuman Singh in 1934. Their life in New Zealand makes a fascinating story for early Sikh settlers.

Bir Singh, formerly a policeman in Hong Kong, worked as a herbalist in the King Country and later during World War I cooked for troops stationed at Trentham camp. Phuman Singh's career proved to be a notable success. He first worked as a hawker in the North Island and finally acquired sole ownership of a confectionery business in Wanganui and later moved to Palmerston North. He married an English nurse, Margaret, in 1897 and had four children.

A majority of early Sikh settlers lived in Taumarunui and around Wanganui and worked as hawkers, drain diggers, flax workers and scrub cutters. Later, they moved to the Waikato and Pukekohe where they bought dairy farms and market gardens. G.H. Roche, curator of the Waikato Historical Society, compiled a report on early Sikh settlers at the turn of the century. His description of Indra Singh (correct Punjabi spelling, Inder), an ex-soldier in the British army, as published in the *Waikato Times* on 5 February 1960 is fascinating reading. The 1971 census reported 382 Sikhs. In 1976, there were 543 Sikhs, 597 by 1981 and 768 by 1986. It is estimated that at present there are about 3000 Sikhs in New Zealand.

The Sikh history of migration in New Zealand can be divided into four distinct phases. The first phase, 1890-1912, consisted mainly of men who had been employed in the army or police force in either Hong Kong or Malaysia, who found their way here via Australia. In the early 1900s, many Sikhs also came en route to Fiji or via Fiji and stayed here. The second phase, 1912-1921, was direct migration from the Punjab. Before substantial numbers could arrive, the influx was stopped by the Government in 1920 by passing laws to halt Asian entry into the country. During the third phase, 1921-1940, not much migration took place until after World War II, when immediate families and relatives arrived. From 1941-1970 some small addition to the migration by marriage from the Punjab occurred. The fourth phase includes the arrival in the last two decades of many unskilled workers and some professionals, including accountants, doctors, lawyers, computer experts, engineers, and scientists.

The Sikh community in New Zealand represents 100 years of rich history of immigration, settlement, and growth. It is not uncommon to meet a third generation of New Zealand-born Sikhs.

The New Zealand Sikh Society

The New Zealand Sikh Society was founded on October 3, 1964. Its main objectives are to preach and render instruction in Sikhism, to conduct religious ceremonies and provide religious services, to promote and foster a better understanding amongst the people of New Zealand about the Sikh religion, to promote harmony amongst the followers of the various religious creeds in New Zealand, to give assistance to the poor and needy, and to promote the Punjabi language. The Society has no political affiliation in New Zealand or in India. The greatest achievement of the Society is the building of the two *gurdwaras* in Hamilton and Auckland.

Summary and conclusion

Sikhism is a practical religion - a faith of hope and optimism. Its ideals form a large part of the more progressive elements in humanity today. It shows mankind how to lead a worthy and useful life in the world, which elevates it into the status of a universal world faith.

Sikhs practise *simran* (meditation), *seva* (service) and *sangat* (congregation) and lead a happy, healthy, holy, honest and humble life, leading ultimately to the spiritual union of their *atma* (soul) and *Paramatma* (God).

Sikhism teaches respect for individuals and love for one's neighbours. It tells how to be useful in society, to care for the interests and concerns of others and cherish the values taught by the Gurus. Social commitment and goodwill amongst Sikhs have inspired them to finance and undertake projects of social benefit because of their belief that human beings all over the world form just one family, the family of the human race, namely *manas-ki-jaat*. This concept is reflected in *ardas*, the daily prayer, which ends:

Nanak nam charhdi kala tere bhane sarbat ka bhalla.

O Almighty God kindly shower your blessing on the whole humanity.

Notes

1. Scripture of the Sikhs compiled originally by the fifth Guru Arjan Dev Ji as the *Adi Granth*. It was finally completed and edited by Guru Gobind Singh Ji, who shortly before his death in 1708 invested the holy Granth as Guru; frequently referred to thereafter as the *Guru Granth Sahib*, 'the living voice of the Gurus'. The Sikh Holy Scriptures are treated with the same respect as is given to one of the human Gurus.
2. Literally nectar; used in the Sikh baptism ceremony, a drink made from sugar crystals dissolved in water and stirred with the double-edged sword *khanda* by the *panj pyaras* (Five Beloved Ones) in the presence of *Guru Granth Sahib Ji*.
3. A spiritual guide or teacher; the title given to the ten great human teachers of Sikhism, and to the Holy Scriptures.
4. Literally 'first book'; the name given to the collection of hymns compiled by Guru Arjan Dev Ji, the fifth Guru, in 1604, which formed the basis of the Sikh Holy Scriptures.
5. The *Guru Granth Sahib* was first translated into English by Max Arthur Macauliffe and was published by Oxford University Press in 1909. Gopal Singh and Manmohan Singh have produced excellent translations in free verse.
6. G.C. Narang, *Transformation of Sikhism*, 5th edn., New Delhi: New Book Society, 1960.
7. A sweet pudding made of flour, sugar and ghee (clarified butter) which is shared at the end of the service.
8. Literally 'the door of the Guru', the Sikh temple or place of worship.

Further reading

Cole, W.O. and Sambhi, P.S., *The Sikhs: their religious beliefs and practices*, New Delhi: Vikas Publishing House, 1978.

McLeod, W.H., *Guru Nanak and the Sikh Religion*, London: Oxford University Press, 1968.

McLeod, W.H., *Punjabis in New Zealand*, Amritsar: Guru Nanak Dev University Press, 1986.

Sacha, G.S., *Sikhs and Their Way of Life*, Southall, Middlesex: The Sikh Missionary Society U.K., 1987.

Sikh Studies, parts I and II, Singapore: Sikh Advisory Board, 1985-86.

Singh, Khushwant, *History of the Sikhs*, 2 vols., Princeton, N.J.: Princeton University Press, 1966.

Tiwari, Kapil, (ed.), *Indians in New Zealand*, Wellington: Price Milburn and Co., 1980; chapters by J.A. Veitch 'The religion of the Sikhs', and W.H. McLeod, 'The Punjabi Community in New Zealand'.

Women's Spirituality Movement

Catherine Benland

There is a myth abroad that religion - any religion - is for both men and women (and girls and boys). This is not so. The discovery by women in recent decades (building on pioneer thought by isolated foremothers) that it is not so is a potentially reality-shattering development somewhat akin to the fairytale child crying out, 'But the Emperor has no clothes!'.

The truth is that almost all religion in the world should be seen as male spirituality, not only ill-suited and irrelevant to women, but counter-productive, erasing, damaging, and even life-destroying to women. The alternatives being uncovered and developed by women could be a prelude to the creation of viable practical spirituality for all kinds of human beings and their world. This process of discovery and exploration of alternatives which is going on in many countries is being referred to as the Women's Spirituality Movement.

Women's means initiated and propelled by feminist women, but the movement's aspirations concern all men and children as much as all women. *Movement* indicates enthusiasm and commitment, growth, shared but diffuse direction, and no central leadership or organisation. *Spirituality* is used - rather than 'religious' which means 'binding' or 'bound' (to a particular institution or tradition) - because the movement is so broad that it spans all major religions and many of the world's primal religions. It also includes all sorts of personal non-institutional non-theistic spiritual orientations, the creation of new theology and new religion, and the political activism that all this is legitimating and empowering.

Men's religion

Before we take a look at the women's spirituality movement in Aotearoa let us look at the status quo worldwide that has for millennia preceded this movement's advent and that coexists with it.

Every organised religion or sect of considerable size and duration throughout the world and throughout the centuries has been run solely by males or largely by males. Their founders (where history records these) were males, e.g. Buddha, Moses, Jesus, Muhammad, Baha'u'llah. Doctrinal development and purity have been controlled by males. Liturgies and rituals have been created and performed by males. Money, building, resources, labour force and decision making have been administered by males. Discipline of members, morality, and all authority have been in the hands of males.

In addition to invented or 'revealed' world religions, there have been many primal religions native to a particular place which have existed from prehistoric times, e.g. Hinduism, pre-European Polynesian religions. Although many of these have had powerful female divinities and heroines as well as male divinities and heroes, and although some have allowed a few woman to be mediums or shamans, for the most part the men of the tribe have excluded women from the most sacred rites, places, buildings, objects, dances and lore. Contact with any female aspect has often been considered to break 'tapu' (to taint, damage, dangerously activate, or intrude upon the sacred force-field).

Why has this been so? Feminist theologians posit many reasons, none immutable, most originating in males exploiting superior muscular strength in order to gain advantage (more wealth, more land, more leisure, more power, more status, more sexual opportunity and gratification, more security, and more immortality in the sense of leaving their mark on future generations and on the land). Undergirding and legitimating this physical advantage (which includes not being vulnerable because of gestation, birthing, lactating, menstruating), has been patriarchal religion.

Validating males has meant invalidating females. The religions of 'man' have told women they were unclean, guilty, punished by childbirth, mentally inferior, physically deformed or abnormal, ineligible as images of divinity or eligible only to be consorts or mothers of deities, and fit only to follow or serve masters. They advocated as virtues in women: unquestioning obedience, self-sacrifice, patience, humility, and acceptance of male authority in the home (and everywhere else). The qualities of assertiveness, courage, original thought, self-determination, and self-definition that are promoted in women's spirituality would be seen as sinful by patriarchal religion.

This has been our heritage in Aotearoa, as elsewhere. We may think we have a secular society but patriarchal religion has gone underground and is all the more powerful, influential, and unchallengeable for having done so. To change the roots of sexism we have to dig up and understand the roots of male religion. This is being done by the women's spirituality movement which began in the USA in the sixties and has spread throughout the world.

The movement's beginnings in Aotearoa

The movement had a slow start in Aotearoa. While many Aotearoa women were both spiritual and feminist, I was the only person in the '70s and the early '80s writing and speaking publicly about it at national women's conferences and workshops. Although these audiences were intrigued, most leading feminists in the country regarded anything to do with religion as suspect and irrelevant, and any activism, research, or scholarship regarding spirituality as illegitimate priorities for feminists.

For example, the women running the women's studies courses in the universities either ignored its existence or were actively hostile to it. As late as 1985 when a NZ Women's Studies handbook was published, there was no curriculum heading for Women and Religion (or Spirituality), no resources suggested, and in all the chapter bibliographies only two (old) books on the subject were listed. Similarly, the NZ feminist magazine *Broadsheet* ignored the movement for years (or occasionally published ill-informed pejorative material).

The reason may well have been that they were avoiding the pain of exorcising the residue of patriarchal religion within themselves. Yet feminists who trivialise religion and discount its connections with sexism, blind themselves to the threat to feminism generally that may still be posed by religious resurgence here and elsewhere. Their analyses of problems and solutions are thereby impaired and superficial. They also lose out spiritually, both personally and collectively.

Added to the negativity of many Aotearoa feminists in the decade 1975-85 towards new spirituality was the unreceptiveness of the many non-feminist women whom one would expect to feel threatened. Women in patriarchal religion may feel they have a safe deal. They have traded autonomy and personal responsibility for the security of having male protectors do all the work of leading and deciding what is right and wrong, what is good and bad. They think they are honorary men, honorary 'sons of the Father'. And they fear the wrath of their men, the loss of male approval, affirmation, company, and economic support, should they dip so much as a toe in the swirling, racing currents of this challenging spiritual movement. Such women (and their men) see the present order as 'natural' and sanctified, and what the feminist thinkers propose as 'unnatural' and unholy. At stake is their very sense of identity.

Despite this climate of conservatism and timidity, the seeds of the women's spirituality movement were sown here in that decade and have been flowering over the past five years. More and more Aotearoa women have been discovering and interacting with the deluge of intriguing original books on feminist theology, women in religion, and neopagan feminist spirituality over the past two decades.

Although the movement is fuelled by scholarship and spread primarily by books, it is not confined to academics and intellectuals. Every woman's life experience is seen as a theological resource of unique value. Here, as overseas, women are creating practical alternatives to men's religions, which all sorts of women can share in as equals.

Alternative patterns

The old way of creating a religious alternative was for a single person to attract followers to his (or rarely, her) teachings. The older religion would refer to the new alternative as a cult or a heresy and either persecute or ignore it. If it survived the death of the founder and prospered, it eventually became a respectable sect or religion. Often writings of the founder or of disciples were needed to ensure continuing orthodoxy and to prevent further splits, and often over time these became revered as sacred or as revealed by God. As well as scriptures, ecclesiastic structures were needed for discipline. And missionaries were needed to help the new cult, sect, religion, to spread. Sometimes armies were needed to hasten growth by *jihads* or crusades.

None of that pattern is true of the alternatives that women are creating as prototypes of communal spiritual experience which feels empowering and good for women. They are founding small, ad hoc groups of peers or equals. The initiating woman is not revered as different or special or privileged. A group is local and does not aspire to spread nationally or internationally, to confederate with other groups, or to survive into new generations.

Once a group has grown to an ideal size (e.g. the number that fits into a private living room), it doesn't seek new members, own buildings or other property, or hold or administer funds. It contains many viewpoints and doesn't seek to make these uniform. Rituals, if used, are created by the whole group more often than by the same person. Often a new ritual is created for each occasion and never recorded.

What occasions or needs are celebrated or marked particularly? The need for empowerment for political activism and courage. Life stages such as childbirth, menopause, first menstruation. Crossroads such as divorce, a new partner, a new house, a new job. Taking a new name (which many feminists do at some stage to break patriarchal bloodlines, to announce a new direction to their lives). Birthdays. Sickness and death, anger and loss (not exactly celebrated, but healing, consolation, and solutions are sought communally). The seasons of the year. Solstices, equinoxes and the quarter days between. The gift and glory of other living species and of Earth herself. The awareness of Divine Spirit in each other and in everything and our need for alignment with this Spirit.

Who or what is being worshipped? A lot of the group activity is not worship in the sense of directing adoration, petition, repentance or gratitude to divinity. It may not be consciously theistic. But where there is theistic ritual the deity is personified ultimate Goodness, the names of which are multitudinous. Still God for some, or Godde, more often Goddess. Or Yahweh, Sophia, Jesus, Mary, Christ, Christa. Or any of the powerful ancient female divinities research has unearthed. Or here in Aotearoa, there is new reverence being accorded ancient Maori goddesses such as Te Po, Papatuanuku, Hineahuone, Hinetitama, and Hinenuitepo. For many, all of these together, plus old feelings of childhood reverence for a loving parent God, are amalgamated into the concept Goddess. Goddess can be fully Christian, or fully pagan or fully both, paradoxical as this may seem to those used to a circumscribed God.

Similarly, women are managing to be monotheist, polytheist, and pantheist simultaneously (a faith that is more readily comprehensible to the Indian tradition than to the Judaeo-Christian tradition).

Feminist theology

Feminist theology is so vast, profound, and utterly new, there is no quick way of summarising it. It affects every traditional Christian doctrine: sin, guilt, fall, atonement, soteriology, christology, mariology, eschatology and all previous understanding of divinity. It is holistic; there is no body and soul dualism; sexuality is not excluded from spirituality. Absolutes are shunned, a plurality of beliefs encouraged. Nature is sacred; all forms of life are equally worthy. Personal autonomy and integrity are willed. Discipline and morality have been rethought. Decay and death are accepted. Time is more spiral and cyclic than linear. No political issue is excluded from theological scrutiny.

When these new alternatives started emerging, women felt they had to leave the religion they were brought up in, in order to participate. This was old patriarchal duality; you could not move freely between both or even combine both. More recently, women are continuing to belong to and struggle within the respectable traditional patriarchal religion they were born into, while at the same time they are feeling free to belong to the sort of alternative groups described above.

The women exploring these new alternatives are eclectic, that is, they feel able and willing to choose appropriate elements wherever they may be found and to combine them creatively with totally new insights and concepts. They recognise no barriers, be they erected by the Curia, by synods, by rabbi, by academics - or by racists and nationalists. The movement encourages the formation of a unique personal set of beliefs and practices by each woman: since she does not then proclaim them as the only right-thinking path, why should she not have total freedom of conscience, thought, and religious practice?

The women keep seeing connections and keep realising that there is nothing new under the sun. What is the difference between aroha and charity and agape? What is the difference between Tiamut and Papatuanuku, between Tane and the European gods of the forest? There is no copyright in the area of religion - no-one can claim to own goodness or virtue, hospitality or generosity or family loyalty, courage, or a sense of God within every aspect of life and environment. These qualities and concepts are human, not local. Nor are they more proper to one race or another, to one sex or another. Nor are they the property of the women's spirituality movement.

So women feel free to adopt the religious treasures of every age, country and race, including the treasures of male spirituality. They feel free to add material from the human potential movement, New Age consciousness, psychology and other sciences, the arts, the environmental movement, political theories and goals. Above all, they add their own life experiences and their own original thought and creativity. It's a heady mix. It's fun - it includes a sense of play. It's serious; it is dedicated to liberating all people, all species, the planet, from oppression and violence.

Here in Aotearoa, as overseas, the two main manifestations of the women's spirituality movement are neopagan and Christian, though increasingly the borderline between the two is blurring and there is much traffic of both people and thought to and fro across the boundary. By neopagan, I mean non-Christian and drawing on religious and spiritual traditions other than those of the large world religions.

There are also minority groups of Aotearoa women (e.g. Indian) who have religious and spiritual commitments which are neither Christian nor pagan. They are not networking with Christian and pagan women in the movement here and I do not know to what extent feminism has affected their faith.

I do know within Judaism here that there have been women rabbis and mixed congregations in liberal synagogues, but in conservative synagogues there is still a rigid separation of men and women with no real change in synagogue-based male-dominated liturgies. Women retain high status in the Jewish home and are encouraged to seek higher education and career achievement as well as marriage. Some Jewish women are creating new non-sexist *Hallels* (psalms of praise) for *Rosh Chodesh* (New Moon) celebrations and *Bas Mitzvehs* for their daughters.

The movement in Aotearoa: 1. Neopagans

Neopagan women in Aotearoa tend to keep quiet about their faiths because the main religions traditionally view all paganism as witchcraft. Some of them proudly name themselves 'witches' in 'covens' but most don't because they feel the centuries of Christian propaganda have tainted these terms beyond redemption. (The label 'witch' is discussed later.)

Because of the need to avoid media sensationalism and social attack (and because feminist witches may choose to be 'solitaries' and work alone) it is difficult to assess how many practising pagans there are in the movement here. There are certainly covens of the new witches, with names like Aurora, Hags, Cone, Serendipity, in the main cities. Sometimes these are lesbian or have a high proportion of lesbian members (lesbians are usually unwelcome in patriarchal religions). However, the first coven I came across (about ten years ago) included a white-haired happily-married minister's wife with many children and grandchildren!

There are also feminist ritual groups which sometimes mix pagan and traditional religious elements (the latter mostly Christian). For example, in the early 1980s for several years I facilitated (with others) a group called 'Womanspirit' which created rituals and held discussion-evenings fortnightly. The rituals were basically pagan (though many of the participants, including me, were Christians!).

In 1984, with some trepidation, I went one step further and offered a pagan ritual experience at a national Women's Studies Conference in Hamilton, following a paper I gave on the history of feminist witchcraft (the first public exposure of the concept nationally in this country). I invited those uncomfortable with the idea to leave after the paper - none of the dozens of women present left. After the ritual, they all sat down again. There was a long pause and I held my breath. Then an old woman said emphatically, 'Well! that felt good!' and everybody laughed in relief!

At a later Women's Studies Conference in Christchurch, another pagan ritual was devised by a local coven, but this time it was imposed on the whole conference without warning. This was a mistake: there was a lot of muttering and resentment during it, and afterwards ridicule and complaint. Humanity has had its fill of imposed rituals. Essential to the women's spirituality movement is its emphasis on voluntary participation, spontaneity, personal integrity, and freedom of thought and belief.

Juliet Batten has also used national Women's Studies Conferences as venues to present rituals, at first in the context of the women's art movement in the early '80s. In recent years, however, she has been teaching ritual-making clearly in the context of feminist spirituality. Her most important contribution has been a feminist guide to ritual-making, *Power from Within*. This is an eclectic amalgam drawing on European and North American pagan and feminist sources as well as Aotearoa inspiration.

Gill Matthewson, courtesy of Juliet Batten

'100 Women Project', Te Henga Beach, May 1985, from Juliet Batten's Power from Within *(1988)*

There have also been courses on feminist paganism and rituals offered as part of tertiary education. In Wellington in 1984 I gave a course entitled 'New Pagans of the West' at Victoria University's Centre of Continuing Education, and Lea Holford has held well-attended classes on Women's Spirituality at the Auckland University Centre of Continuing Education since 1984. Also in Auckland, a *Women's Spirituality Newsletter* is published - this has a feminist pagan orientation. In Christchurch a new magazine with a similar orientation has just begun: *Woman-Script*.

Then there are the woman neopagans whose entry into the movement has been neither via the churches nor via feminist activism. These are the women who have been involved in the New Age movement and the human potential movement. Often they are committed to alternative life-styles or to following particular gurus. Their orientation is focused on maximising personal potential for health and wisdom. They tend to be apolitical, except on environmental issues.

The first national woman-focused gathering of these people (men were invited though outnumbered) was the 'Wise Woman Within' festival at Tauhara, Taupo, in 1988. Well over a

243

hundred attended including some workshop leaders from overseas. The festival was 'to explore, nurture and celebrate the many aspects of our "wise woman" sharing through circles, sacred dance, song, play, workshops, good food, magic, miracles, and celebration; to explore together our journeys, the Goddess within, herstories and histories, spirituality, feminine (sic) theology, Papatuanuku Earth Mother links and nature knowledge, mysticism and witchcraft, creativity and expression, abundance, wisdom, visions, dreams and challenges'.

Workshops included 'Cosmic Birth', 'Croneologies', 'Expressing Feminine Energy - A Man in the Aquarian Age', 'Goddess Archetypes', 'Creating Personal Ritual', 'Creating Men's Ritual', 'Knowing the Wise Women', 'The Gaia Perspective' and many more. The word 'feminine' (never 'feminist') was often used throughout the festival and much use was made of Jung's concepts of feminine and masculine archetypes (stereotypes?), of 'anima' and 'animus'.

One popular workshop was that of a young American man who claimed a direct line to the goddess. He sat crosslegged under a tree and went round the group of about thirty, gazing soulfully at each in turn and then shuddering (the descent of the Goddess on him) and giving a 'message' from the Goddess to that person. As with horoscopes, many in the group were amazed at how spot-on their 'message' was. I went up to him afterwards and congratulated him on his 'performance' with a cheerful grin: he looked distinctly cross!

Amongst Aotearoa women neopagans and pagans must be included Maori women who are embracing or who have never lost pre-European Maori religion, but I may not speak for these. However, an interesting recent development in Aotearoa paganism has been the 'Ma-uri shaman' training offered (to Pakeha as well as Maori) by Hemi Fox at a Taupo marae: this too is more a blend of (Maori) primal religion and New Age concepts than feminist, although it offers women equal training and status, and abandons the tapu/noa (i.e., sacred/profane) tradition in which a female is an agent to make 'noa'.[1]

To date, feminist pagans in Aotearoa have had little coverage in the mass media - probably because they have not sought it, since few women could face the social risks of publicity with equanimity. It's a pity in a way because it means most people in Aotearoa are missing out on the opportunity to try something very enriching. It means that, ironic as it may seem, neopagan concepts and ritual-making are currently being spread in Aotearoa more by Christian women than by pagan women.

The movement in Aotearoa: 2. Christians

There have always been outstanding Christian women in Aotearoa: Mother Aubert, the women who led the temperance and suffragette movements, YWCA women, and many more. And the movement to admit women to the diaconate, ministry, priesthood, lay administration, seminaries, and theological colleges preceded the new wave of feminism which reached Aotearoa in the 1970s - as did the non-discrimination of a few smaller Aotearoa churches such as the Religious Society of Friends, known also as Quakers (my own church).

Feminism is affecting the mainstream churches much more than fringe churches or fundamentalist, charismatic, evangelical churches. (These latter tend to be reactionary, i.e. they are reacting to feminism by condemning it out of hand. Their view is well documented in the 'women's' magazine, *Above Rubies*.)

The first national liturgical expression of Christian women's involvement in feminism here was in 1975. I was one of three women who created a non-sexist ecumenical service for the huge United Women's Convention in Wellington. Hundreds of women - including nuns (still in habits),

Salvation Army women (in uniform), and nursing mothers - gave each other Communion (consecrated by a woman priest). This was very advanced for the times!

The second major contribution to the movement was *Enquiry into the Status of Women in the Church*, published by the Women's Committee of the National Council of Churches New Zealand in 1976. This valuable document is still likely to hold true and it could be timely to repeat the exercise.

The next landmark was in the mid-eighties when Television New Zealand showed a sensational BBC documentary on the treatment of women by religions throughout history - it took its name from Tertullian who told women 'You are the devil's gateway'. I took part in the panel discussion which followed and which produced widespread comment.

Currently, the mainstream Aotearoa churches are participating in a worldwide WCC Ecumenical Decade of the Churches in Solidarity with Women (1988-1998). Unfortunately the way this decade has been introduced by the WCC (through its Women's Desk) and by the Conference of Churches in Aotearoa New Zealand (through its Women's Desk) may have given the impression that the decade is for women to be involved in, not for men. That was not the intention.

Study groups are under way in most mainstream churches, and research such as the 'Made in God's Image' project, examining the nature and extent of sexism in the New Zealand Catholic Church. An excellent lectionary, *Birthed from the Womb of God*, compiled by the Rev. Dorothy Harvey, was published by the Presbyterian Church's Committee on Women in Church and Society in 1987. The Methodist Women of Aotearoa have published *Out of the Silence* by Ruth Fry.

Protestant churches are admitting women as ministers, priests (and even bishop(s)!) in increasing numbers. While the Catholic Church is not ordaining, the shortage of vocations to the priesthood has meant that more and more tasks once reserved for men are now being entrusted to women. Catholic women are dispensing (though not consecrating) the Eucharist and also occasionally preaching within Mass. Inclusive-language eucharistic celebrations (ecumenical) are now being held regularly in the main cities.

Early attempts at inclusive language in liturgy and hymns were ridiculed by both conservatives (as unnecessary) and by radical feminists (as cosmetic). Yet women have persevered and the major triumph in this area has been the new Anglican *New Zealand Prayerbook - He Karakia Mihinare o Aotearoa*. It is significant that the Catholic priest/observer on the committee that produced it, Charles Cooper, has commented, 'I find it fascinating that there is no part of (it) which would not be acceptable in Roman Catholic worship.'[2]

Probably the most difficult English word for the churches to come to terms with has been 'God'. Theologically it has long been gender-neutral, but in practice Christians have for centuries invested it with maleness. The same word is also part of the pagan duality: god and goddess - in which god means a male deity.

But the word 'Goddess' has such totally pagan connections that it is not acceptable to many Christians (though some Christian women are cheerfully using it, on the simple grounds that it is their turn to have the deity invested with female personality!). A compromise has been the newly coined word, 'Godde', but this is only a written solution since when spoken it still sounds male. So, many Christians trying to use inclusive language simply avoid the words God and Godde and Goddess altogether, opting for 'Spirit', 'Parent', 'Source', etc.; a solution which happily is proving very subversive theologically.

An unsolved problem in the churches is the different stages women are at. I was a founding member of an ecumenical Christian Feminist group in Wellington in the 1970s. Such women have been reading feminist theology and working within the movement for one or two decades. Yet many other women, particularly those outside Auckland, Wellington and Christchurch, have still never heard of the women's spirituality movement and their faith has yet to be challenged by feminism. These latter women are starting to come forward now in greater numbers, with different needs from the former women.

It is difficult to cater for both when resources of funds and energy are still so limited, and when experienced Christian feminists are also involved in other issues such as Treaty activism; overseas aid/development/justice; the environment; women and child health issues, etc., thus risking exhaustion and burnout.

Christian feminists who are ecclesiastical professionals, such as ordained women, nuns, and paid lay-women working in ministry, make a big contribution to tackling this problem and to challenging sexism generally within the churches. They are the majority of the stirrers among the Christian movement, though groups like the Anglican WOMB (Women Monitoring the Bishops) are also important. Women lecturers in university religion departments and theological colleges (e.g. Rev. Enid Bennett) have also helped with introducing both women and men to the scholarship of feminist theology.

Meanwhile, the traditional women's fellowship groups within denominations, such as the Association of Anglican Women and the Catholic Women's League, are still only on the fringe of the movement. For the most part, they are continuing doing and being what they have always done and been. They provide a respectable social life of friendship and service for the wives, mothers and daughters of Christian men. They encourage personal piety, and traditional feminine virtues. They do not explore or question theology or create original liturgy or rituals. They do not struggle for change, and are largely apolitical (unless actively combating feminists, e.g. the Catholic women's group Magnificat). They still provide workers for such tasks as flower arrangement, embroidery, catering, and childcare.

Yet the women in these fellowships are not unmoved. There have been steps taken. For example, the Auckland Association of Anglican Women refused to pour tea for Synod one year; the next year they were allowed a representative on the Synod arrangements committee. And now they are actually able to participate in the business level of Synod. Such patience may well prove in the end to have been as effective in nurturing change as the activism of the movers and shakers.

It is still true to say that the structures and patterns developed by the Christian patriarchy remain intact: the pie has been made to a male recipe even though women get a bigger slice now. Yet I believe that the presence of women in places they have not been before is itself transformative. Women bring their different life-experiences with them - Penny Jamieson will be a different sort of bishop because she has been a daughter, a mother, a wife, a woman academic, a feminist activist.

The women committed to the movement tend to work at the regional or national or interchurch level rather than at the parish level. The only national denominational feminist Christian network of groups is the Catholic Sophia (I am a member) although there are local ecumenical groups such as the Theological Resource Group in Hamilton.

The only nationwide Christian feminist periodical is the valuable quarterly, *Vashti's Voice*.[3] Useful newsletters are put out in Auckland by the Anglican Auckland Diocese's Women Resource Centre and the Wellington Urban Training Centre for Christian Ministry's Women's Desk.

Many of these Christian feminists are finding they have more in common with each other than they do with other members of their local denomination. They are also finding common ground with feminists who have despaired of their churches and walked out of Christianity, and with feminists who are pagan. Their meetings are ad hoc but nevertheless are resulting in different streams of thought mingling both within each individual and collectively.

A milestone conference

Possibly the first national ecumenical Christian conference in world history to include anything pagan deliberately, was the third National Ecumenical Feminist Women's Conference. It was held in Christchurch in 1988 and attended by a couple of hundred women. The previous two conferences in Wellington and Auckland had been intentionally Christian and had been named 'women and ministry conferences'. Organised by the National Council of Churches, a primary concern had been over the exclusion of women from ordained or official ministry within Christian churches. At the second conference I had facilitated a group ritual which combined pagan and Christian spirituality. (This was a departure from the norm which upset some of the funda-mentalist Christian women, who did not attend but objected to it being held at all.)

Mandala from 3rd National Ecumenical Feminist Women's Conference, 1988

The Christchurch conference, though subsidised by the Christian churches and organised by Christian women, was from the outset inclusive of pagan spirituality. It was labelled a 'women's ministries and spirituality conference', which shifted the focus from the negative (exclusion from men's concept of ministry) to the positive (what women were already doing, being, and becoming within a broader concept of ministry).

It was advertised as being for 'feminist women who are actively involved in the churches but whose needs are not fully met there, women in spirituality and Christian Feminist groups, and women outside the church who are exploring the feminist perspective in theology and spirituality'. The women who came ranged across many spectrums: lay to full-time churchwomen, traditional to radical, orthodox to protestant, old to young, pagan to ordained Christian. But all came in a spirit of sharing, learning, and unity of sisterhood.

Over the five days there was a rich feast of over twenty half-day workshops offered. Some were clearly Christian or biblical in focus, e.g. 'Help! The Church Doesn't Make Sense Any More And I Don't Fit In!' Some were concerned with social issues such as racism or economic injustice. Some were creative or physical, e.g., massage, movement, face painting, clowning, music, weaving, poetry, banner making. And some were pagan, e.g. 'Devas, Dowsing, and the Cosmic Dance', 'Exploring the Goddess'.

Instead of traditional worship services, small or plenary group rituals or worship experiences were created by the participants every day. I offered one called 'Maidens, Matrons, Crones'. Perhaps the most memorable was a gathering of many women which started inside the hall round a great bowl of red wine symbolising women's blood, and also, for Christian women, Communion blood consecrated by the presence of women. (Blood is a very important concept for women because patriarchy has always glorified the shedding of it when this signifies war and the possibility of death, and vilified the shedding of women's menstrual blood which signifies health and the possibility of birth.)[4]

Our oldest women (a 'crone' in her eighties) and our youngest woman (a 'maiden' of nineteen) carried it outside to a large lawn. We formed a big circle, then moved up one at a time to dip a tiny rag in the 'blood' - each then wore the red rag pinned to her breast. Those who had done this filled in the waiting time with an impromptu spiral dance singing, 'We are the weavers. We are the web of life! We are the flow, we are the ebb.'

The conference certainly achieved its two declared aims - one inward-looking, one outward-looking - to provide opportunities for 'personal growth and change' and 'to come to a better understanding of the oppressive and destructive forces in society and ways in which we can work together to transform them'.

The only disappointment was that, as with the previous conferences, Maori women did not accept the invitation to participate - not for any sinister reason, but because they currently need their own space and need to use up all their own limited time.

It may seem that out of the three-and-a-half million people in Aotearoa, a couple of hundred women are of no especial significance. However, for a year before this conference, women in the Christian churches all over Aotearoa formed small groups to prepare for the conference. And for a year after, participants held regional mini-conferences re-offering some of the workshops. These were especially for the hundreds of women who applied to come to the main conference too late. (Places were filled months in advance. The demand was enormous, despite no advertising but word of mouth and women's informal networking.) Planning is already underway for the next.

Another reason this Conference was important was the number of influential women who were included among the participants: priests, ministers, nuns, national office-holders from different churches, lecturers and teachers, journalists and media-women, artists of various sorts and writers, prophets and pioneers. All the women, but these in particular, return to their communities to be leaven in the bread, hopefully for the rest of their lives.

What the movement risks

Two of the women at that milestone conference, both with ecclesiastical office, have been the victims of witchhunting, smearing them with the label 'witch' and lobbying their bishops to disown them. I have been careful in this chapter not to name them, because the destructive power of that label should not be underestimated. Few propaganda campaigns in history have been as virulent and longlasting as the European witchcraft campaign. At its height, over several centuries and many countries millions of people, mostly women and girl-children, were horrifically tortured and slaughtered, a holocaust largely erased from record by male historians, especially churchmen.

The association between the women's spirituality movement and witchcraft has arisen because women researching primal religions began to revalue ancestors, especially foremothers. Here in Aotearoa with our new bicultural consciousness, ancestors (tipuna) are fairly respectable. But what about the Celtic ancestors of the many women in the movement of British/European ancestry?

What survived of Celtic religion following Christian conquest became known as witchcraft. Women with a Christian, Jewish (or Muslim) background have been indoctrinated to see witchcraft as evil. After all, it said in the Hebrew Bible: 'Thou shalt not suffer a witch to live' (Exodus 22.18). While the Goddesses of their ancestors appeal to their yearning to see femaleness as part of the divine forcefield, they are naturally terrified of evil.

Women scholars have helped them re-evaluate this fear by researching the European witch holocaust. Although most of these 'witches' had nothing to do with remnants of ancestral pagan religions, some women creating new myth are redefining the victims as martyrs - taking on the name 'witch' as a badge of pride, remembrance, and protest. This has nothing to do with Satanism or evil. Since they might as well be hung for a sheep as a lamb, they have also helped themselves to some of the ritual elements in the romantic occult witchcraft movement (of nineteenth and twentieth century origin) because this accorded women and the Goddess high status. (However they have rejected the sex stereotyping, the apolitical escapism, and the bizarre elements.)

Most of the women in the movement, however, do not use the terms 'witch' or 'feminist witchcraft' for themselves or for what they are practising. Whether they do, or whether they don't, all the alternatives the movement is exploring are sane, good, and healthy. I believe this is true worldwide and it is certainly my experience in Aotearoa. But the old concepts of the European witch are still widespread (one need only watch children's television to see this!). And the lynching and pillory mentality still bubbles away beneath the surface of our so-called 'permissive' society. Thus women in the movement shun publicity for the sake of their children, parents, and spouses, as well as their own safety and livelihoods.

They say those who ignore history are doomed to repeat it. What caused the fanaticism of the witch holocaust was the persecutors' belief in Satanism. Satanism is not witchcraft but a perversion of Christianity. While now regarded as heresy, it was in times past required doctrine, insisted upon by popes, kings, bishops, priests, Protestant ministers and pastors, and inquisitors (all men, the majority celibate).

Such beliefs persist today, incredible though it may seem. In New Zealand fundamentalist churches, belief in Satanism and demonology is prevalent and warnings against Satan are given from the pulpit. In such churches, the status of women is low: they are expected to submit to the authority of their husbands and the mind-control of their male pastors. (Often newspapers, television, radio, and non-prescribed books/magazines are banned). Language and doctrine are sexist, as are views on social, moral and political issues.

A recent example of preaching about Satanism was published by the *New Zealandia*. An American charismatic, Ralph Martin, spoke at a FIRE rally (rallies held with the blessing of the Catholic bishops - who would not necessarily endorse what was said):

> the ruler of this world has deceived and blinded huge masses of people.... Lucifer and the other rebellious angels ... roam the world seeking the destruction of souls.... Promoting a pagan, secularist world view ... we're turning back into the barbarian pagan tribes out of which we came ... all the pagan practices are reappearing .... One of the things Scripture says is that 'the doctrines of demons will be infiltrated into God's people through plausible liars'.... One of the great doctrines of demons that has been successfully transmitted to our culture is the lies of the sexual revolution and the lie that says 'liberate yourself' from narrow restrictive Christian teaching in the area of sex....
> Satan is today going about the whole world seeking to invite human beings to the same rebellion.... There's no happiness for New Zealand and for kiwis apart from Jesus Christ.... We're seeing blasphemy ... infanticide ... witchcraft ... flood into our cities; flood into our homes ... often these people fall prey to the deception of the devil .... The time has come to recognise we're in a war and there's powers and principalities that are trying to squeeze the life out of human beings and send them to hell. There are powers and principalities in dark twisted beings, brooding over this nation....[5]

I've quoted enough to show Satan and demons are real to this man whom hundreds in Auckland turned out to hear early in 1990. He claims there are over three hundred million charismatic Christians around the world - if they share his mindset they constitute a real danger for the women's spirituality movement since such obsession is identical with that of those responsible for the diabolical European witch-craze.

Nobody in the women's spirituality movement anywhere in the world believes in any god of evil. To believe in an evil god or demon gives reality to the concept and gives the concept power over you. The God(s) and Goddess(es) women are conceptualising, evoking, aligning themselves with and being empowered by, are wholly good and wholly loving. What these women are doing is what the New Testament advocates and what the FIRE rallies might do, instead of conjuring up 'Satan':

> Whatsoever things are true, whatsoever things are honest, whatsoever things are just, whatsoever things are pure, whatsoever things are lovely, whatsoever things are of good report ... think on these things.[6]

Who is in the movement

Just as Christians have often excluded the atypical and the nonconformist (e.g. women, Jews, homosexuals, blacks) from the elite, so the women's spirituality movement could be accused of apartheid since its membership rarely includes ethnic minorities, nonwhites, or males.

Both those who are combating racism and those who are combating sexism, face this problem of inclusion. In both these areas, we are people in transition. There are times when we need temporarily to exclude people of the other sex or other races in order to come to terms with our own identity and experience and goals, without the distractions of having to explain, share, teach, challenge, debate. Maori can need Maori space. Women can need woman space. Concurrently, woman and men need times together for sharing or confrontation, as do Maori and Pakeha.

Within the world of religion, many women have been profoundly shaped - and scarred - by the patriarchal religion of their youth, or their present. They have a lot of sifting and re-evaluating to do, and it is natural to seek the company of others engaged in the same task. Healing is best sought by those who have suffered the same way. And in exploring and creating new forms of spirituality, women are enjoying celebrating or expressing the life-experiences unique to those who are conditioned as females, oppressed and restricted as females, who live inside female bodies. Men also may need to continue with manspace (though since they have always had it they are not so hungry for it!)

Men must not demand togetherness too soon: this transition process must be worked through, not cut short because separation is painful or threatening. (Similarly, Pakeha must not demand togetherness with Maori prematurely). Men can be blind to their own extensive tradition of male-only gatherings and experiences. Also, men must be careful not to demand scarce women-energy to guide them from patriarchy to liberation. (Similarly, Maori elders have too many demands on their energy to spare much time for healing or affirming or sharing with Pakeha anxious to display their non-racism.)

Liberation theology has established the principle that while one party remains in possession of privilege, power, and wealth it cannot expect true dialogue with those it has dispossessed, oppressed and excluded. Dialogue and sharing are best achieved by equals: yet we need not wait for perfection. They can still be trialled and practised partially by people in transition.

The women's spirituality movement in Aotearoa is a microcosm of the same movement throughout the world. It will continue to parallel and reflect much of what is happening elsewhere - because of the rapid transfer of ideas through books, the mass media, and the rapid transportation of people from place to place. At the same time, particularly at the small group level, it will manifest the uniqueness of individual Aotearoa women, of the Maori/Pakeha encounter, and of the multicultural heritage of our many kinds of immigrants. Yet here as overseas, those participating in the movement will probably continue to be mostly white, middle-class, and well-educated. Is this culpable elitism?

It is facile to criticise the movement because many of its members are privileged and not representative. The fact is that because of patriarchy, most other women simply do not have the time, energy, or freedom to participate. Many poor women have had little education and cannot afford the time or money for networking via seditious literature. In a city, a woman often needs a car, babysitting, and evening energy to attend meetings.

And racism coupled with sexism ensures that few non-white women can participate in the movement, welcome though they are - either they don't have the time or energy because of the work they do; or relatives prevent them; or they have chosen racism or democracy as their arena for activism. (There's only so much one woman can do!) The few in New Zealand who do participate are achieving much, e.g. the resurrection of the magnificent Maori goddesses so beautifully pictured and described in *Wahine Toa* by Robyn Kahukiwa and Patricia Grace.[7]

It is a sorrow to the women's spirituality movement in Aotearoa that its members include few Maori and non-white women so far, and that most are privileged educationally and economically compared to many other Aotearoa women. Yet this does not invalidate the work of any woman in it, or of her new insights, beliefs, discoveries, learning, experience, or actions. Those in the movement hold the new knowledge and power in trust for their more oppressed sisters to claim, extend or alter as they will, when they can. And meanwhile they work to eliminate the oppression, for the movement is not escapist or introverted but highly political.

The future

What must not be lost sight of is that although the movement was begun by women and still consists mostly of women, it is just as relevant to all other people. After all, patriarchal religion is seen by its adherents as relevant to all human beings (or at least to those of a particular race, tribe, or place). How-

Courtesy of the artist Robyn Kahukiwa and the Manawatu Art Gallery

Hine-titama, oil on hardboard 118 x 118cm

'Myths provide answers in human terms to the way things are in our world. The characters act as we do but on a grand scale. They can be an important guide to philosophy, values and social behaviour; to correct procedures for certain acts, and provide pointers towards social order....

These wahine all have a great strength and it is fitting that they be accorded the awe and respect which is theirs....

Hine-titama is known as the mother of mankind. She was the daughter of Tane and Hine-ahu-one and was the first true human, being a fusion of the godly and earthly elements and born of woman.'

Robyn Kahukiwa

ever patriarchal religion has viewed its male members as the norm and its female members as 'other' (not the norm, invisible, alien, worthless). It has been blind to women's experience, lives, and achievements. Women's spirituality does not reverse this, so as to exclude or ignore men, or elevate women as superior. It is resurrecting what has been lost, offsetting male violence and hierarchical models with female nurturing and cooperative models, and releasing women's creativity in spheres other than the physical.

But the future is not assured for the movement here or anywhere. It may be difficult to close Pandora's box now, but it could be done. For the movement to thrive it will require the just and democratic structures that produce peace and social harmony - it will also require sufficient shared economic wealth to create the time for assembly, scholarship, and creativity.

If these conditions do not prevail, the old regime could easily be reasserted. The way it was for most of our Western history is the way it still is for women in unjust, undemocratic countries; countries at war, in the grip of sexist religion, and excluded from sharing economic wealth. This is the way it could easily be again - science-fiction writers warn of many sexist-religion future scenarios.

While there is still time, however, the women's spirituality movement is developing prototypes of a new spirituality for all humankind, on which can be based new, just social orders, full realisation of human potential, a healing of the male/female divide, and the viability of the biosphere. In this movement I recognise the fullest expression yet seen on this planet of the politics of faith, hope, and charity.

Notes

1. Manuka Henare, 'Standards and Foundations of Maori Society', in *Report of the Royal Commission on Social Policy,* Wellington: The Royal Commission on Social Policy, 1988, vol.III, p. 19.
2. *Zealandia,* October 1989.
3. Now up to No. 45, and edited since its inception by Mitzi Nairn.
4. See my article on Blood Taboo in the *Listener,* 10 December 1983, p. 35.
5. *New Zealandia,* March 1990.
6. Philippians 4:8
7. Robyn Kahukiwa and Patricia Grace, *Wahine Toa - Women of Maori Myth,* Auckland: Collins, 1984.

Further reading

All books by Mary Daly, Rosemary Radford Ruether, Starhawk (pagan), Merlin Stone (pagan), Phyllis Trible, and Elizabeth Dodson Grey.

Benland, Catherine, 'Doctrine, Language and Imagery', in *Religion in New Zealand: Women and the Church,* edited by Christopher Nichol, Wellington: Chaplaincies and Religious Studies Department, Victoria University, 1984.

Benland, Catherine, 'Womb Makers and Womb Breakers: Women and Religion in New Zealand', chapter 9 in *Public and Private Worlds,* edited by Shelagh Cox, Wellington: Allen & Unwin, 1987.

Goldenberg, Naomi, *Changing of the Gods - Feminism and the End of Traditional Religions,* Boston: Beacon Press, 1979.

Griffin, Susan, *Women and Nature,* New York: Harper & Row, 1978.

Spretnak, Charlene, (ed.), *The Politics of Women's Spirituality - Essays on the Rise of Spiritual Power within the Feminist Movement,* an anthology, Garden City, N.Y.: Anchor Books, 1982.

Zeal and Apathy: The Future

Peter Donovan

If this had been a book not about the religions of New Zealanders but about their sports, obvious chapter-topics would have been rugby, cricket, netball, hockey, athletics.... Yet most New Zealanders cease to take part regularly in those traditional sports once they leave school. Only a small proportion continue as committed players, or as supporters, coaches and umpires. For the rest, television and the sports pages of the newspaper take over, except perhaps for an occasional outing to a major fixture. Some become involved in less traditional sports: motor-racing, yachting, cycling, squash ... the list is long and varied. The more spectacular of these sometimes attract brief public attention, but very few actually participate in them. For the great majority, nowadays, the nearest approach to playing sport themselves is a solitary fitness routine, a turn with bat and ball at a family picnic, or a day's walking in the hills from time to time.

The similarities with religion are obvious. As with this country's sporting mentality, so even more its religious mentality is shaped by memory and habit as much as by first-hand, up-to-the-moment involvement. Most follow their various paths of morality and spirituality in a haphazard way, influenced more by upbringing and schooling than by the lively effects of a current religious affiliation.

Official and unofficial religion

Until well into this century, religious scholarship in the West has been dominated by men who were confessionally and professionally committed to mainstream Christianity and to its official institutions. The rise of the modern study of religion has provided a fresh vantage-point. No longer obliged to serve any particular orthodoxy, students of religion today are able to encompass far more within the scope of their studies. They are free, for instance, to pay sympathetic attention to all the world's faiths. They are able to explore the religious life of individuals and groups previously dismissed as 'heretical', 'sectarian', 'pagan', or 'unchurched'. And they are able to take account of the unofficial realm of lay, informal and popular belief and practice, largely ignored in the past by established religious organisations.

To help identify the on-going religious experience of the wider community beyond formal organisations, writers have devised a number of terms and distinctions. 'Civil religion' or 'civic religion', for instance, are used to refer to those symbols, rites and ceremonies of a nation or state which express emotions and commitments on the part of its citizens that closely resemble religious attitudes and behaviour.

In the case of civil or civic religion in New Zealand, examples are the use of national anthems, flags, oaths of allegiance to Queen and Country, prayers opening parliament, official services such as those on Waitangi Day, and Anzac Day commemorations at war memorials. By these and other ceremonial practices, citizens express their patriotism and show they have aspirations for their country which transcend the daily routines of politics, business or popular entertainment.[1]

Other concepts include 'implicit' or 'diffused' religion, 'folk religion', 'common religion', and 'popular' or 'ordinary' religion. Each of these is an attempt to indicate dimensions of human life with apparently religious overtones, yet which are not a part of the concerns and activities of the recognised religious bodies. A thorough study of folk religion in New Zealand, it has been suggested, would have to include:

> the cultic aspects of certain sports and recreations, school traditions, nature-protection movements, popular opinions about the supernatural or occult, alternative ways of coping with illness and despair (chiropractic, yoga for health, horoscopes, weight-watchers, Alcoholics Anonymous, and so on), the kinds of wisdom expressed on talkback sessions or in advice columns, and the annual Telethon appeal....[2]

There are, then, many goings-on beyond the bounds of organised religion which carry overtones of spiritual belief, piety, or superstition. (One figure who, in his tongue-in-cheek way, mixes this 'folk' dimension of religion with a blend of patriotism and fantasy, is the country's 'Wizard'. At the Bastion Point concert inaugurating the 1990 commemorations, he cast spells and called on the spirits of fire, earth, air and water, to ensure a good year for New Zealand.)

Manifestations of 'folk religion', it must be added, are by no means always benign or socially approved. They may embrace such things as counter-cultural lifestyles centred on rock music, commercialised youth fashions and pop culture, gang rituals, occultist crazes, the drug underworld, and the mob mentality of race rioting and football hooliganism.

Otago Daily Times

Tongue-in-cheek folk religion? The Wizard, at the Wanaka Snowfest in September 1989

Even within the life of religious organisations there are subtle and implicit 'folk' dimensions of great importance to the members: unspoken opinions and expectations, internalised role models, private satisfactions and benefits, hushed-up scandals and embarrassments. Every group and institution has its own peculiar history, its distinctive ethos. The question 'What is it like to be a so-and-so ...? to belong to such-

and-such a faith ...?' is not answered simply by referring to a list of beliefs and practices and organisational structures. It requires an introduction to a whole world of social and personal details, mostly discovered only through lengthy participation and experience. As with the questions 'What's it like to be a golfer ... an orienteer ... a show-jumper ...?' rule-books or statistics can tell only a fraction of the full story.

It is clear, then, that the formal and the informal, the official and the popular, are interrelated in religion, and each depends upon the other. Without permanent, recognisable institutions of some kind, society's religious impulses would lack coherence and continuity, and could not be channeled into effective activity. At the same time, religious organisations organise something other than themselves, namely, the spontaneous, unstructured inclinations people have to pursue non-material goals and cultivate their own private spiritualities. Like the cosmic dust and gas clouds not visible in the night sky to the naked eye, such diffuse, unstructured raw material may be far more fundamental in understanding the universe of religions than the traditional approach to the subject has recognised. Interest in the future of religion in New Zealand, then, will need to focus at least as much on what is happening outside the familiar, named denominations and religions as on what is taking place within them.

Diversity and interaction

The predominantly Christian viewpoint presupposed in Western culture has been reinforced by this country's past 150 or so years of history. Thus most New Zealanders can hear the phrase 'non-Christian religions' without any recognition of its oddness, let alone the arrogance and insularity it could be taken to reveal. (Consider classifying all sports besides football as 'non-football sports'!)

Followers of world faiths other than Christianity (and some branches of that faith too) do face a particular difficulty in Aotearoa, however. Their religions are all too easily looked on as the incidental by-products of immigration: as evidence of foreigners failing to 'fit in' completely with the predominantly Anglo-Saxon, and Christianised Maori, environment.

Those 'ethnic minority' associations which the other major world religions have in New Zealand's thinking can nowadays, however, be turned to their advantage. As our global awareness grows, local representatives of other great civilisations are gradually coming to be appreciated in their own right (at the very least because it is to our economic and political advantage to know and understand more about their homelands and cultures).

Official religious pluralism is something which our laws themselves, for over a decade, have recognised. The Human Rights Commission Act 1977, in particular, imposes strict duties of religious tolerance and non-discrimination in areas such as access to employment, housing, and education. While these duties may be only reluctantly acknowledged by some New Zealanders, they are here to stay, having the backing of United Nations conventions and broad international opinion.

In modern societies throughout the world, followers of faiths even with long-standing traditions of enmity and suspicion towards one another increasingly find themselves working together. They share common concerns for peace, improved community relations, refugee re-settlement, disaster relief, employment, housing and education, political freedom, national independence, and so on. Experiencing the benefits of cooperation and the satisfaction gained through mutual respect, those involved in such common endeavours are inevitably under pressure to reassess some of their historical and ideological differences.

In Aotearoa/New Zealand the formation in 1989 of a branch of the World Conference on

Religion and Peace marks a major development in inter-faith activity at the organisational level. A Council of Christians and Jews, likewise, has been holding regular meetings in Auckland and elsewhere since its inauguration in October 1986. As similar countries abroad show, we can expect multi-faith community relations groups, inter-religious study circles, and combined meetings for dialogue, prayer and worship all to be a part of New Zealand life as our society becomes increasingly cosmopolitan.[3]

As was noted in previous chapters, some faiths and churches (Sikhs and Baha'is, for instance, and Quakers, Unitarians and Theosophists) have long taught ideals of religious tolerance and universalism; co-operation with other faiths poses few problems for them. For most of the Christian churches, however, and particularly some of the alternative ones, anything other than strict exclusivism towards other religions will involve considerable rethinking of their traditional views.[4]

Quantitative or qualitative significance?

Successive scholarly writers on religion in New Zealand society have focused attention on the Religious Profession figures in the five-yearly official population census. It is understandable that numerical statistics, which look like hard data in an otherwise vague and subjective field, should carry weight in the minds of scholars and the public. The qualitative study of religious affiliation in New Zealand has, however, received far less serious attention.

Preoccupation with numerical size, growth and decline often stems from the assumption that religion in modern societies is a spent force. Its overall 'shrinkage' being assumed to be the most noteworthy thing about it, little time or effort has been put into taking a closer look at its other features.

The questionable nature of that assumption will be discussed in the next section. In the meantime, the most recent census figures must themselves be briefly considered. Table 1 gives figures for the religions New Zealanders recorded themselves as belonging to on the census day in March 1986, for all categories or denominations recording 1000 or more adherents. Comparisons with the 1976 and 1981 census results are included, showing growth or decline in numbers, and percentages of total population.[5]

Interpreting such results is notoriously difficult and prone to wild oversimplifications. Here, for example, are comments from a fairly typical news-media report when the figures were first released.

> Fundamentalist and fringe religions have enjoyed a big jump in popularity during the past 12 years.... Interest in traditional eastern religions has also increased markedly ... with steady rises in the number of adherents of Buddhism, Islam and Baha'i.... While many New Zealanders embrace beliefs far removed from traditional Western religions, even more are saying they have no religious beliefs.[6]

No doubt this was an attempt to make news out of otherwise dry statistics. But phrases like 'a big jump', 'increased markedly', and 'many New Zealanders' are practically meaningless when no comparisons are given. Relative to what, we may ask, is a rise or fall in membership to be called 'big' or 'marked'? Misleading inferences are drawn, too, through other relevant factors being left out of consideration. Is it really 'increased interest in eastern religions', for instance, that explains the steady rise in Buddhist numbers between 1981 and 1986? What about the arrival, during that period, of several thousand refugees from Cambodia, Vietnam and Laos?

Table 1

	1976		1981		1986	
	Number	%	Number	%	Number	%
Anglican (Ch.of Eng.)	908,415	29.3	807,135	25.7	791,847	24.3
Presbyterian	564,735	18.2	521,040	16.6	587,517	18.0
Roman Catholic	475,452	15.3	452,871	14.4	496,158	15.2
Methodist	171,816	5.5	147,192	4.7	153,243	4.7
Baptist	49,059	1.6	49,536	1.6	67,935	2.1
Christian (not otherwise designated)	51,963	1.7	100,815	3.2	42,351	1.3
Ratana	35,079	1.1	35,763	1.1	39,729	1.2
Mormon (Latter-day Saint)	35,958	1.2	37,431	1.2	37,146	1.1
Brethren	24,351	0.8	24,213	0.8	19,710	0.6
Salvation Army	21,951	0.7	20,406	0.6	16,821	0.5
Jehovah's Witness	13,338	0.4	13,689	0.4	16,377	0.5
Pentecostal (not otherwise designated)	4,830	0.2	6,369	0.2	15,717	0.5
Assemblies of God	5,547	0.2	12,465	0.4	14,352	0.4
Seventh-day Adventist	11,877	0.4	11,427	0.4	12,015	0.4
Hindu	5,073	0.2	5,940	0.2	8,148	0.2
Ringatu	6,228	0.2	6,114	0.2	7,332	0.2
Buddhist	2,142	0.1	3,330	0.1	6,255	0.2
Lutheran	6,057	0.2	5,313	0.2	5,106	0.2
Associated Churches of Christ	7,983	0.3	6,291	0.2	4,770	0.1
Apostolic	2,682	0.1	4,497	0.1	4,194	0.1
Samoan Congregational			2,277	0.1	4,017	0.1
Eastern/Greek Orthodox	4,110	0.1	3,762	0.1	2,940	0.1
Undenom./Christian	6,738	0.2	4,830	0.2	4,881	0.1
Hebrew Congregations	3,783	0.1	3,186	0.1	3,048	0.1
Born Again Christian					2,988	0.1
Indigenous Pentecostal			5,280	0.2	2,796	0.1
Exclusive Brethren					2,697	0.1
Spiritualist Church	1,725	0.1	2,403	0.1	2,679	0.1
Islam	1,341		1,701	0.1	2,544	0.1
Congregational	6,492	0.2	3,702	0.1	2,292	0.1
Elim Church	258		1,257		2,157	0.1
Baha'i	972		1,440		2,079	0.1
Protestant (not otherwise designated)	32,232	1.0	15,849	0.5	1,839	0.1
Christadelphian	1,662	0.1	1,683	0.1	1,785	0.1
Agnostic	14,016	0.5	23,991	0.8	1,692	0.1
Atheist	14,178	0.5	21,342	0.7	1,248	
Society of Friends	1,056		1,056		1,206	
Christian Fellowship	87		240		1,074	
Reformed	537		249		1,053	
Orthodox (not otherwise designated)	1,038		444		1,023	
No Religion	100,398	3.2	166,014	5.3	533,766	16.4
Object (to stating a religion)	434,898	14.0	468,573	14.9	244,731	7.5
Not specified	35,460	1.1	104,310	3.3	58,686	1.8
All other religions or denominations	37,761	1.2	37,875	1.2	33,348	1.0
Total	3,103,263	100.0	3,143,307	100.0	3,263,283	100.0

The report notes: 'by 1981, all the established churches faced the problem of dwindling numbers and an even faster slide in the proportion of the population belonging to those churches.' However in the light of the 1986 figures, it announces, 'some of the established churches have now arrested this trend.'

But have they? What is not mentioned is a significant change in the format of the census return itself. In 1986, for the first time, there were boxes to be ticked for the five largest denominations, while names still had to be written in for the others. The apparent reversal of downward trends by those major churches may have come about largely because some people found it easier, while completing the form, to tick a roughly correct ready-made option rather than having to write in a more precise one. A similar factor also helps explain the more than 300 per cent rise since the previous census in the figure for 'no religion' (which had a box provided), and a startling drop in 'agnostic' and 'atheist' which, if written in, had to go in a box indicating 'other religion'(!)[7]

Other features of numerical statistics for religious groups over the years which can mislead the ordinary reader are: the inclusion or non-inclusion of Maori figures in the overall population; the merging and splitting of denominations; differences in the size of groups considered worth listing separately; whether or not children as well as adults are included; and the variations, as between different groups, in relative numbers of 'nominal' and 'committed' members.

There is a further obvious factor to which purely quantitative readings of religious statistics are often blind. The overall profile of religious options has far more to do with early settlement and subsequent immigration and birth-rate patterns than with competitive success or failure in the market for converts. Our history, in other words, offers nothing like a 'level playing-field' for religions.

The limitations of numerical statistics, when assessing religious significance, are well illustrated by looking at the major research project published recently as *The Religious Factor in New Zealand Society*.[8] That work is based on the New Zealand Study of Values, a questionnaire/ interview survey of 2009 individuals drawn from approximately 1000 households, conducted in March 1985. Using sophisticated social-scientific analytical methods, the report demonstrates the cross-correlations between degrees of religiousness in belief and practice, and the holding of a wide range of value-positions on ethical and political issues.

While the report amasses more statistical data than has ever before existed on the subject of religion and values in New Zealand society at large, it proves to be largely uninformative about the significance of minor religious groupings, including all the world religions other than Christianity.

There are, it turns out, a total of only thirty-seven out of the 2009-strong sample who indicate a religious affiliation other than Christian or 'no religion'. (How few households those thirty-seven belonged to is not stated.) Furthermore, the authors admit that their total sample under-represents both the Maori population (by 7 per cent in relation to census figures) and people born other than in New Zealand, Australia, and the United Kingdom (by about 2 per cent).[9]

The thirty-seven 'other religions' respondents are in fact pooled, with no indication given of the actual composition of the group (how many Hindus, Sikhs, Rastafarians, etc). The results from that composite group, we are told, suggest 'a fairly consistent pattern'. But all this seems to mean is that, on average, they register a rather higher level of religiosity than some of the larger groupings of Christians. That tells us very little indeed, even if the sample does accurately reflect the relative proportions of 'other religions' in the population at large (which with such small numbers seems improbable).

When the minority-religion respondents are simply taken together as an 'other religions' group, any unique or distinctive characteristics they may have simply disappear. The averaged figures obtained for the combined group's religiosity scores and value-opinions have thus only the remotest connection with the things that make each of the component minorities interesting from a religious point of view.

Quantification inevitably standardises its subject-matter, treating it as consisting of more-or-less uniform items able to be counted and measured. Differences amongst minorities are simply smoothed over, as 'statistically insignificant'. But minority groups in society are what they are not because of their being small, but because of their being different. Therein lies their true significance.

Minority power

In evaluating minority groups in our society, most attention must be paid to their qualitative features: those features by virtue of which they are minorities. These include the different ways they view the world, the unfamiliar values they promote, the distinctive strategies they employ, what special contributions they have to make, what unexpected demands they may impose, what problems their presence may give rise to. It is from details of this kind that judgements must be made about their actual or potential significance. Statistics showing growth, decline or relative size, on their own, tell us very little.[10]

Though all but a few religious groups and organisations nowadays appear to attract the active support of only a small proportion of the population, there are compelling reasons why they should not be dismissed as insignificant or irrelevant to this country's future.

First, minorities in New Zealand may be majorities elsewhere. Like embassies and their staffs in foreign lands, the presence of even a few local representatives of faiths which are powerful and influential on the world scene can have enormous implications. Given modern communications the slightest incident occurring in almost any country can, virtually overnight, come to assume major proportions: sanctuary granted to a wanted person, perceived insult to a leader or holy personage, unthinking desecration of a grave or shrine, incautious expression of political opinion ... examples come readily to mind. (And perhaps the more secular in their thinking a country's leaders, media and general public are, the more likely it is that such incidents will catch them unawares.)

Second, given the availability of mass media, numerical size may be largely irrelevant in the case of zealous minorities with clear aims and objectives. Whether we choose terrorists and hijackers on the one hand, or tiny but committed activist groups (HART, Greenpeace, ASH and the like) on the other, it is obvious that ideological impact and practical effectiveness may have very little to do with numbers, growth-rate, or overall 'market share'. Such examples make a mockery of merely quantitative estimates of significance.

Third, readers of quantitative studies too readily assume growth to be the 'performance indicator' that matters most to everybody. But in fact religions themselves commonly discourage popularity, and even make a virtue of minority status: believers are the elect, the enlightened ones, the chosen few, the salt of the earth, and so on. Loyalty to traditions or to their distinctive missions may be every bit as important to them as gaining large numbers of adherents. And as religious history shows, faiths which hold such views - Judaism, for instance, or Zoroastrianism - have continued to be remarkably durable and influential. Again, a preoccupation with quantity as the criterion of significance misses the point entirely.

Fourth, since minorities cannot wield influence simply by weight of numbers, their strategies are likely to be more subtle or more daring. They understand the power of selective activity, skilful means, symbolic gesture, or of simply 'being there'. Religious majorities, used to having things their own way, tend to become flabby and lax, and may go to pieces when hardship comes. Minorities, on the other hand, have usually learned from their marginality, and developed their own means of adapting to adversity (whether through intensity of group loyalty, other-worldliness, mystical experience, or alternative ways of valuing the here-and-now). All these features make religious minorities worth studying, not only for their intrinsic interest, but also for the valuable, distinctive, and even alarming contributions they are in a position to make to our society's future.

There are implications here too, of course, for the religious majority. With even 'mainstream' church denominations becoming numerically marginal, we can expect to see organised Christianity more and more learning to utilise the resources of minority power.[11]

A secular future?

For more than a century, prominent thinkers in the West have proclaimed that a secular future is on the way. Levels of active public participation in religion are declining. State institutions and voluntary agencies have taken over more and more of the traditional roles of churches, while science and education have undermined the authority of their teachings. Rational, technological, this-worldly solutions to human needs and problems have increasingly been found. All this evidence has been drawn on to support the prediction that civilisation will become less and less religious in anything like the traditional sense.

Major world faiths, we are told, may survive in a supporting role, reinterpreting themselves as promoters of humanitarian goals and ideals. But a God or gods beyond space and time, spiritual realities, supernatural sources of help, or a life to come, will drop out of the picture. Religion will have come down to earth. At most, a fringe of minor sects and cults will persist in clinging to the ways of the past.

Among the best-known proponents of such a 'secular future' theory in this country is eminent scholar and communicator Lloyd Geering. About the religious future for New Zealand, as for the world, Professor Geering has written:

> Religious man of the Secular Age must now assume the responsibility to explore, and enunciate for himself, the answers to the ultimate questions of life. Some will do this in a very superficial way: others will do it at greater depth; but all must do it. The only other alternative is to surrender both the freedom and the responsibility which have come with the secular age and return to, or cling even more tightly to, one of the fragments of the pre-secular authoritative structures which have survived into the secular age. There is a mild resurgence of this in the western world. This is very understandable. Such structures appear to offer security, and hence a welcome relief, from the uncertainty and responsibility which the Secular Age has brought to the religious quest of the New Zealander today. As the full force of what it means to live in the Secular Age comes home to people, even more may they be tempted to turn back to one or other forms of the 'old-time religion'. But it cannot offer any long term solution. The transition is ultimately irreversible.[12]

The prospect of a growing secularity in this country is reaffirmed by Webster and Perry on the strength of their Values Survey findings.

The vast majority of New Zealanders are not really religious - only about 12-15% would meet the more truly religious criteria.... Nearly one in three New Zealanders believe in a personal God, but only about a half of these are personally religious. The young and the well educated are less likely to be religious. The future appears therefore to be likely to be more secular.[13]

Yet there are other scholars who view widespread secularity as far more likely to be a temporary state of affairs than a permanent, increasingly global phenomenon. Rather than a secular future scenario, they predict a future of probable religious revival and innovation. American sociologists Rodney Stark and William Bainbridge, for instance, have written:

To focus only on secularisation is to fail to see how this process is part of a much larger and reciprocal structure. Having erroneously equated religion with a particular set of religious organisations, Western intellectuals have misread the secularisation of these groups as the doom of religion in general....We argue that the sources of religion are shifting constantly in societies but that the amount of religion remains relatively constant.[14]

The reasons such theorists give for their expectation of religious persistence and revival are quite simple. Secularity has limited resources; religions offer unlimited ones. Supernatural belief systems have 'the unique capacity ... to provide people with compensators for scarce or wholly unavailable rewards'.[15] Even though science has challenged some of the claims made by historic religions, 'it cannot provide the primary satisfactions that have long been the raison d'etre of religions.'[16]

Stark and Bainbridge further observe that 'those who have abandoned a specific religious affiliation and who report their religion as "none" are hardly the scientific, secular humanists they are often thought to be.' They produce figures from their America-wide surveys showing that these 'nones' often accept supernaturalism in the form of astrology, and are commonly attracted to yoga, Zen, and transcendental meditation.[17]

In the Roman Empire of the first century CE, Stark and Bainbridge remind us, majority disillusionment and scepticism concerning traditional religions, along with a volatile fringe of counter-cultural groups, turned out to be just the seedbed in which an obscure Jewish reform movement from Galilee was able to take root. Within only a couple of centuries it was dominating the known world. (Similar comparisons have been made with the spread of Buddhism in post-Confucian China, and with the rise of Islam in seventh-century Arabia.) Thus they write:

it takes only a few effective cults to serve as the vehicle for a massive religious renewal. Indeed, it might take only one.[18]

Given their line of analysis, they conclude:

the weaker the established religions become, the more religious innovation ought to occur and the more such innovation will be sustained by a growing population in search of new religious alternatives.[19]

Stark and Bainbridge's methods and findings have not gone unchallenged.[20] However, their general warning about not taking continued secularisation for granted is echoed by other scholars. A symposium on 'The Changing Face of Religion' which formed part of the World Congress of Sociology in New Delhi in 1986 brought together a number of research projects on modern societies throughout the world, including Italy and France, Brazil, Iran, Malaysia, Africa, India and New Zealand. Almost all of these (New Zealand being the nearest to an exception!) called in question the assumption about the world's future inevitably being a secular one. As the editors of the symposium's published findings put it:

> No support is given to the triumphalist scenario of secularisation, according to which the declining significance of religion is a necessary feature of modernising and modern societies.[21]

One aspect of the 'secular future' theory, which is especially challenged by the scholars mentioned, is the assumption that religion is becoming increasingly private and subjective (and thus socially and politically less relevant). On the contrary, writes Roland Robertson:

> religion has been politicised quite drastically during the past fifteen years or so, following a period of diffusion of the idea of the separatedness of the spheres of religion and politics.[22]

From Poland and the Soviet Union to Japan and Korea, from the Muslim world to Central and South America, from India and Sri Lanka to Southern Africa, and even in the United States and western Europe, religiosity, rather than being less and less a public phenomenon, is increasingly manifesting itself in political involvement.

Even if New Zealand society has become predominantly secular, then, it will not necessarily stay that way. Supernatural belief-systems, far from slipping further and further out of sight, may yet come into greater prominence. And those organisations dedicated to pursuing them, representing minority groups of zealous people with ideals and life-styles markedly different from a religiously apathetic majority, may be in a position to exercise social and political influence well in excess of their numbers.

A recent Department of Statistics report predicts that this country's population next century will be very different from that which is present in the late 1980s. 'Even without significant changes in immigration,' it observes, 'there will be more ethnic diversity.'[23] And while precise ethnic migration statistics are difficult to obtain (following the removal, in 1986, of a question about ethnic origins in international arrival cards), one pointer, at least, can be found in recent figures for arrivals from Fiji as 'country of last permanent residence':[24]

1984	5467
1985	6355
1986	6582
1987	9202
1988	10923
1989	9508

The increased numbers of those immigrants in the years since the 1987 military coups include a high proportion of Hindus, Sikhs and Muslims, as the 1991 census will no doubt confirm. Present policies of openness towards Asian immigration, also, will inevitably add to the growing ethnic diversity. (A future edition of this book may well have to include chapters on Chinese and Japanese religions to be found in Aotearoa.)

A tolerant future?

What levels of tolerance can be expected in a future New Zealand society in which the faiths of the world are represented by zealous minorities, against a background of general religious apathy? A fairly easy-going climate of liberalism may have been congenial while it lasted, but it cannot be relied on as a permanent feature of our society. As the range of diversity in belief and practice diverges more and more from the homogeneity of the past, public sympathy towards and patience with at least some aspects of religion is likely to decline. Majority apathy might well become majority antipathy.

No longer will there be only the familiar and relatively minor quirks of the churches to contend with (Catholics against contraception, Baptists against drink and gambling, Jehovah's Witnesses against blood transfusions, and so on), but fresh Christian groupings, challenging what they see as a society sold out to secularism, may seek for themselves a far higher profile. (As the charismatic and fundamentalist Rise Up campaign's glossy magazine puts it, 'God wants His people to be a warring people, a strong, bold, militant church in the 90s.')[25]

And from other faiths, strengthened by immigration and increasing ethnic diversity, a whole new rash of demands or scruples may have to be taken into account: observance of different 'holy days'; provision of separate forms of education; requirements about dress, behaviour, activities in schools; facilities for alternative burial rites; requests for vegetarian or kosher meals; new ideas about child-rearing, marriage, sex; unusual types of building; different standards in manners and tastes in music and art; fresh attitudes to old age, wealth, possessions ... a very mixed bag of new values, many exemplary and inspiring, some exotic, some ominous and off-putting. Given these potential sources of disagreement or conflict between religious minorities and a majority secular culture, an increasing strain on public tolerance seems inevitable.

In the past, religion has notoriously been a breeding-ground for intolerance, and there are many indications that it may continue to be so. But tolerance, too, can be bred in the right surroundings. Those surroundings may be the calm, congenial ones of inter-religious dialogue and scholarly debate, to which books like this, it is hoped, may contribute. Tolerance may also be forced on people in crisis situations, whether they be devastating earthquake or famine, unstoppable epidemic, or threat of global climatic catastrophe.

During September 1986, thousands of followers of different faiths made pilgrimages to Assisi in Italy, birthplace of St Francis. There the World Wildlife Fund (now called the World Wide Fund for Nature) held its twenty-fifth anniversary celebrations. From that encounter was formed an international network on conservation and religion, including representatives of the Baha'i faith, Christianity, Hinduism, Islam, Judaism, Sikhism and others, all of which have subsequently initiated projects for reflection and action on ecological concerns.[26]

Aotearoa/New Zealand is becoming more and more ecologically conscious, helped especially by the examples of its tangata whenua, its women and young people who care about the natural heritage, and its scientists faced with abundant evidence of an endangered environment. Perhaps people here, of all races and all faiths, will find themselves compelled to work together in seeking solutions to our common predicament. Perhaps the lessons of ecology itself - wonder, humility, respect for diversity, non-violence, and co-operation - will be the very means by which religious tolerance amongst all peoples may at last be learned.

Notes

1. On ways in which these common symbols and sympathies may be manipulated for political or other ends see Michael Hill and Wiebe Zwaga, 'Civil and Civic: Engineering a National Religious Consensus', *New Zealand Sociology,* vol. 2, no. 1, May, 1987, pp. 25-35.
2. *Religion in New Zealand Society,* edited by Brian Colless and Peter Donovan, 2nd edn., Palmerston North: Dunmore Press, 1985, p. 11f. On New Zealand's 'cultic milieu' see Michael Hill, 'The Cult of Humanity and the Secret Religion of the Educated Classes', *New Zealand Sociology,* vol. 2, no. 2, November, 1987, pp. 112-127.
3. In the United Kingdom an Inter Faith Network formed in March 1987 links more than sixty groups and organisations concerned with co-operation between religions.
4. See my 'Theologizing about Religious Plurality', in *Science and Theology in Action,* edited by Chris Bloore and Peter Donovan, Palmerston North: Dunmore Press, 1987, pp. 161-166.
5. From *New Zealand Census of Populations and Dwellings,* 1986, Religious Professions, Series C, Report 14, Table 1.
6. *Dominion Sunday Times,* 17 January 1988, p. 8.
7. See p. 184 (above), note 9.
8. Alan C. Webster and Paul E. Perry, *The Religious Factor in New Zealand Society,* Palmerston North: Alpha Publications, 1989.
9. Ibid., p. 156.
10. For a much-acclaimed example of how qualitative and quantitative approaches together can be brought to bear on a minority religious movement, see Eileen Barker, *The Making of a Moonie,* Oxford: Blackwell, 1984.
11. On how the main churches become more sect-like in a secular society see Michael Hill, 'Religion and Society: Cement or Ferment?' in *Religion in New Zealand,* edited by Christopher Nichol and James Veitch, 2nd edn., Wellington: Tertiary Christian Studies Programme, Victoria University, 1983, pp. 253-286. See also the recent Australian study by Michael Hogan, *The Sectarian Strand: Religion in Australian History,* Ringwood, Victoria: Penguin Books, 1987.
12. 'New Zealand Enters the Secular Age', in Nichol and Veitch, pp. 161-186, p.181f.
13. Webster and Perry, p. 142.
14. Rodney Stark and William Sims Bainbridge, *The Future of Religion,* Berkeley: University of California Press, 1985, p. 3.
15. Ibid., p. 9.
16. Ibid., p. 431.
17. Ibid.
18. Ibid., p. 437.
19. Ibid., p. 438.
20. see Hill, 'The Cult of Humanity', (note 2 above).
21. James A. Beckford and Thomas Luckmann, *The Changing Face of Religion,* London: Sage Publications, 1989, p.2.
22. Ibid., pp.13-14.
23. *The Human Face of New Zealand,* Wellington: Department of Statistics, 1990, p. 31.

24. Department of Statistics, 'Key Statistics', May 1990.

25. *Rise Up Together,* no. 4, April/June 1990, p. 29.

26. For instance, a 'World Convocation on Justice, Peace and the Integrity of Creation' conducted by the World Council of Churches, with participants from other faiths, was held in Seoul in March, 1990.

Details of Contributors

Catherine Benland has an honours degree in religious studies and is director and co-founder of a Wellington advertising agency. She is 'by birthright Catholic, Quaker by convincement, and neopagan shaman'.

Colin Brown is a Reader in Religious Studies at the University of Canterbury.

Brian Colless is a Senior Lecturer in Religious Studies at Massey University.

Peter Donovan is a Senior Lecturer in Religious Studies at Massey University.

Betty K. Duncan has tutored in religious studies at the University of Otago since 1978 and is doing research with a particular interest in religious symbolism.

Beverley Earles has a PhD in world religions from Victoria University of Wellington, specialising in Humanism, and now lives in the USA where she holds part-time university lecturing positions.

Robert Ellwood is Professor of Religion at the University of Southern California, Los Angeles. He visited New Zealand on a Fulbright Research Grant in 1988 to study the history of alternative spirituality in this country.

Bronwyn Elsmore is a Lecturer in Religious Studies at Massey University.

Manuka Henare is Executive Officer of the Catholic Commission for Justice, Peace and Development, Aotearoa New Zealand; a member of Te Runanga o Te Hahi Katorika ki Aotearoa; a member and former president of Te Runanga Whakawhanaunga i Nga Hahi o Aotearoa.

Elizabeth Isichei is a Reader in World Religions at Victoria University of Wellington.

Raymond Oppenheim is Vicar of St Mark's Anglican Church, Wellington, and an honorary Lecturer in World Religions at Victoria University. In the 1970s he was chaplain to the foreign community in Moscow, and is National Chairman of Keston College New Zealand.

Norman Simms is a Senior Lecturer in English at the University of Waikato.

Pritam Singh, originally from the Punjab, India, is a New Zealand citizen and works as a scientist. He is a member of the New Zealand Sikh Society, and has lectured widely on Sikhism and conducted summer youth camps for New Zealand-born Sikhs.

Te Pakaka Tawhai was a Senior Lecturer in Maori Studies at Massey University. (He died in August 1989.)

Christopher van der Krogt has lectured at Victoria University and is now a PhD student in history and religious studies at Massey University.

James Veitch is a Senior Lecturer in World Religions at Victoria University and a minister in the Presbyterian Church.

Ajahn Viradhammo is Senior Monk at the Bodhinyanarama Buddhist Monastery in Stokes Valley.

Jim Wilson is a former Senior Lecturer in Religious Studies at the University of Canterbury.

Index